LEWIS FUNKE [New York Tim...] wrote the weekly "News of the Rialto" column for the Sunday edition for thirty years. He also served as the paper's Assistant Cultural News Editor from 1970 to 1973. Mr. Funke has written articles on the theatre for various national magazines, including *Esquire, Theatre Arts, Saturday Evening Post,* and *McCalls.* He is the co-author with Helen Hayes of *A Gift of Joy* and with Max Gordon of Gordon's autobiography. He has also written a juvenile biography of Ossie Davis. Mr Funke is currently Adjunct Lecturer at Queens College and Visiting Distinguished Professor at Florida State University.

JOHN ERLANDER BOOTH is currently Associate Director of the Twentieth Century Fund. He is President of Theatre Development and on the Board of the American Place Theatre. Mr. Booth undertook a study for the Rockefeller Brothers Fund on government support of the performing arts in Western Europe. He has written articles for *The New York Times, Harper's* and *The Atlantic Monthly* on theatre and other subjects.

ACTORS TALK ABOUT ACTING

FOURTEEN INTIMATE INTERVIEWS

EDITED BY
LEWIS FUNKE AND
JOHN E. BOOTH

 DISCUS BOOKS/PUBLISHED BY AVON

AVON BOOKS
A division of
The Hearst Corporation
959 Eighth Avenue
New York, New York 10019

First Avon Printing (Vol. I and Vol. II), May 1963
First Discus Printing (Third Printing)

Printed in the U.S.A.

PART I

Introduction

The theatre through the ages has nourished the mind and spirit of man, reflecting the time in which he lives and, at its best, illuminating his endless quest to know himself and his fellow men.

In this quest the actor has played a major role. He has played it as an instrument of the playwright and as an artist—interpretive or creative. How has he done it; what is the essence of his art; what is that quality and power that enables the talented performer to capture this essence, to move us to laughter or to tears, to evoke in us the strongest emotions, the most sensitive yearnings?

Many have sought the key to this essence, the clue to the actor's art. And varying have been the insights, and varied have been the conclusions. Indeed, not in years has the discussion of the actor's part been as lively as it is in our time—in the Sunday drama sections of newspapers, in magazines, from lecture platforms and in the living room.

No doubt the contemporary vogue of the Actors Studio in New York City, dedicated to the Stanislavsky system, or the Method, has had much to do with interest in the subject. To be sure, diverse, imaginative and fantastic have been the tales surrounding the Studio. But, let it be quickly noted, this book is neither pro-Method nor anti-Method; neither pro-Studio nor anti-Studio, although talk of both runs through many of its pages.

Recognizing that each generation has its own fashions in acting and its own rallying cries, this book has had as its aim the probing of the actor's art in its timelessness, the exploration of questions that are of as vital concern to the actor today as they were to the actor of yesterday and will be to the actor of tomorrow. We have done this through conversations with actors (recorded on tape and transcribed verbatim), conversations not designed to reflect the theory of acting but, instead, to distill the wisdom the actor has acquired in the crucible of experience. We believe the answers here provide light on an always fascinating art, not only for the practicing professional, but also for those who enjoy acting as an avocation and those who love the theatre as devoted laymen.

For our part, we made discoveries along the way—discoveries about the practice of acting as differentiated from theory: of how roles are created, perfected and sustained. But among the most illuminating of these discoveries was the intensely individualistic approach of the various actors, not only to their art but also to life, and of the interrelationship of their experience in their art with their experience in life.

It should also be said that we started with the conviction— a conviction steadily bolstered by those we interviewed—that first of all the actor who achieves success of the highest order must have that indefinable something called "talent." With this in mind we interviewed fourteen actors representing a broad cross section of the actors at work today. All have achieved a considerable measure of artistic and popular success; all have talent.

Finally, we are grateful to those we interviewed for their generosity in the time they gave us—on occasion, during rehearsal or during periods when they were engaged in production. But going beyond even their generosity with their all-too-scarce time, was the full measure of their cooperation in exploring with us—with remarkable perceptivity and without holding back—the very wellsprings of their art.

LEWIS FUNKE

JOHN E. BOOTH

ACTORS TALK
ABOUT ACTING

Sir John Gielgud

BIOGRAPHY

John Gielgud had what he acknowledges to be the advantages of coming into a well-known theatrical family when he was born in London in April, 1904. His grandmother was Kate Terry, his great-aunt the famous Ellen Terry. By the age of sixteen he had set his heart on the theatre, and went about preparing himself with drama schools, spear-carrying parts during vacations and early roles gotten with family help. By the time he was twenty-five, however, he had already made his mark very much on his own. He had played Romeo in a London production at age twenty, gone on later to replace Noel Coward in *The Vortex,* subsequently succeeded Mr. Coward again in *The Constant Nymph* and appeared briefly in New York City in *The Patriot.* In 1929 he joined England's Old Vic, ending his first season there playing both Macbeth and Hamlet!

His most spectacular personal success as an actor in England was in *Richard of Bordeaux,* by Gordon Daviot, and it was *Hamlet* which brought him his first great American success in 1936. From that time on, he took his place among leading theatre personalities on both sides of the Atlantic, as

11

actor, director and producer. His position was recognized further when he was knighted by Queen Elizabeth in 1953.

Among the multitude of Sir John's productions—some of which he has directed and produced as well as acted in—the best remembered might well include *The Importance of Being Earnest, Love for Love, Much Ado About Nothing* and *The Lady's Not for Burning*. Recently Sir John took on tour, in England, Canada and the United States, his *Ages of Man*, creating new audiences for Shakespeare in a highly successful one-man show of readings from various of the Bard's plays and sonnets.

Sir John has appeared in a number of movies, as well as on television, but he acknowledges that his preferred world is the stage.

SETTING

For a man whose chief ambition is to be wholly immersed in the theatre, Sir John gives an unstudied impression of being not at all theatrical, although the voice serves Sir John on or off stage with unerring effectiveness. His manner is genial, if a touch formal; his appearance undramatic but not unimpressive.

Dressed in a blue shirt, blue blazer with a neatly folded blue handkerchief in the breast pocket, a quiet necktie and gray slacks, Sir John received his guests at his temporary home in New York—an apartment of two floors he had rented from actress Edith Meiser in a one-time private house between Lexington and Third Avenues in the lower Sixties. The living room is light blue, its furnishings and decor largely Victorian and Chinese, with a big glass chandelier and a good many lamps and vases about, but not too busy. There is a phonograph in one corner. A Chinese ancestor portrait stares down with authoritative dignity. There is nothing of the theatre in the room, perhaps the only hint being some issues of *Theatre Arts* in the foyer.

Sir John speaks rapidly, but not a word is lost. He is extremely articulate and gets the point of a question almost before the question is asked. He is obviously fascinated with every facet of the theatre and the people of the theatre. He obviously, too, has thought deeply about it. Over two hours of continuous conversation about the theatre and about his acting

was broken but once, briefly, for refreshments—with Sir John
taking milk.

Sir John may gesture occasionally, such as when tracing in
the air an accompaniment to a phrase like "the embroidery of
language." But the gestures are few and his hands are more
likely to be busied with a cigarette or his key chain. His expression is intensely alive; frequently a rather quiet smile
lights his strong but gentle face.

Interview

INTERVIEWER   May we begin with some elementary
questions—a sort of warm-up?

GIELGUD   Yes, of course.

INTERVIEWER   Well, then, the most elementary would
be, when did you start acting?

GIELGUD   I went on the stage in 1921. But I did not
start acting until 1923, because until then I only held spears
and walked on, and went to dramatic school.

INTERVIEWER   What, mainly, did you get out of dramatic school?

GIELGUD   Schools do give you some preliminary training
in discipline and orderliness. They may help to lessen your
self-consciousness, especially in working with others, which
one is apt to find very embarrassing at first. Above all, the
influence of one really sympathetic teacher may be invaluable,
as you may receive personal and skilled criticism from him
which you can hardly hope to experience in your first professional engagements in small parts, where the professional
director is harassed—probably terrifying—and is a very busy
man.

INTERVIEWER   We understand that your parents wished
you to become an architect and that you made a deal with
them to avoid that.

GIELGUD   Yes, I did. They wanted me very much to go
to Oxford University first and then become an architect. But
I said, "Oh, I am so bad at mathematics that I'll never be
any good as an architect." We agreed that I could try the
theatre until I was twenty-five and that if I did not make a
success by then, I would try architecture. Actually I wanted
to be a stage designer. That's really what I wanted to be. I
was mad on the theatre, mad about scenery. I wanted to do

scenery, to follow in the footsteps of my cousin Gordon Craig (Ellen Terry's son), and create ideal physical settings for an ideal theatre. I loved the pictorial magic of the stage, the wonderful magic of scenery, costumes, lights, groupings—the pictorial and dramatic value of the theatre as something that took me from myself. I didn't really want to act at all. But I was too lazy to learn the technical requirements of the stage designer—arithmetic, blueprints, accuracy of drawings and so forth.

INTERVIEWER   Did you at the outset try to imitate other actors?

GIELGUD   I imitated all the actors I admired when I was young, particularly Claude Rains, who was my teacher at dramatic school. I admired him very much. I remember seeing him play Dubedat in *The Doctor's Dilemma,* especially his death scene, in which he wore a rich dressing gown and hung his hands—made up very white—over the arms of his wheelchair. And then I understudied him. I also understudied Noel Coward, whom I felt I had to imitate because he was so individual in his style. I followed him in *The Vortex* and, naturally, the only way to say the lines was to say them as near to the way he said them as possible because they suited his style. It was, after all, written by him for him. Of course, it got me into some rather mannered habits. He has a very individual and particular style, which isn't quite mine, although my sort of clipped vowels and rather staccato manner were not altogether unlike his. Perhaps all we young men in the twenties talked a bit like that.

INTERVIEWER   Who would you say were among the strongest influences in the development of your own style?

GIELGUD   I don't know really. Certainly I think Shakespeare has eventually been the most important. Above all, Harley Granville-Barker, who wrote me letters over several years, though I only was actually directed by him for ten days in *King Lear* in 1940. And Komisarjevsky, the Russian director. I played in some Chekhov plays under Komisarjevsky in 1924. He was an enormous influence in teaching me not to act from outside, not to seize on obvious, showy effects and histrionics, not so much to exhibit myself as to be within myself trying to impersonate a character who is not aware of the audience, to try to absorb the atmosphere of the play and the background of the character, to build it outward so that it came to life naturally. This was something I had never thought of and it seemed to me a great relaxing exercise. I recall how the force of this struck me for the first time. It was when I played Trofimov, the student in *The Cherry Orchard,* with only a week's rehearsal—not with Komisarjevsky but with another director—and I did not understand the play at all and there was no time for the director to explain it—hardly any Chekhov had been done in those days. I played this with a repertory company at Oxford when I was about twenty, and suddenly having to put on a bald wig and glasses and a shambling walk, I found a kind of impersonating release from my own personality that seemed to give me a freedom of expression which I had never found before. I had looked into a glass, as it were, and suddenly seen and understood how this man would speak and move and behave. I found that this picture remained in my mind and I was able to lose myself completely in the role. I was relaxed for the first time. This relaxation is the secret of good acting. Young actors when they are nervous tighten up as soon as they try to act. This tension sometimes is effective. But it is terribly exhausting and is only briefly effective. Until I played Trofimov I had been determined to be as much myself as I could be—either romantic or rather hysterical, which were my two strong suits I thought in those days. And indeed they stood me in very good stead, because I played a number of those very highly strung young men who were fashionable in the plays of that time. I played Dion Anthony in *The Great God Brown.* I played Nicky, the son, in *The Vortex* and I played a very good part, a modern part, in a play called *Musical Chairs,* by an author who died in 1931, which was really my first modern success. And these were all fairly related to myself. Then in 1929 I went to the Old Vic and played a whole gallery of Shakespeare leading parts and one or two supporting ones, and this, of course, was a great excitement to me. I'd always loved the costume play, the feeling of fustian which I saw in the plays of the actor-managers who were then rather at the end of their time. My great-uncle Fred Terry, Sir John Martin Harvey, Matheson Lang, Robert Loraine in *Cyrano* and Strindberg's *The Father*—these were all bravura actors. All these were in plays I saw as a boy and they made an enormous impression on me. I was very anxious to get into velvet and silk, wave a hat about and fight duels and make love to ladies on balconies—and this was kind of contrasted with the very modern work in which I was representing my own period of the twenties which, as you know, was very neurotic and very party-conscious—I mean party in the social sense—and so very highly strung and rather mad.

INTERVIEWER You wrote a preface to *An Actor Pre-*

pares. You are, therefore, we assume, in favor of the Stanislavsky Method.

GIELGUD   I don't know what the Stanislavsky Method
really is. I keep on reading those books and trying to decide
for myself. I think that it's really only to make the actor feel
that the work is difficult and that he must be humble towards
it, and not imagine that by getting up and spouting or being
an exhibitionist he will really do anything very exciting.

INTERVIEWER   You refer to spouting—what of the com-
plaint about Method actors being frequently inaudible?

GIELGUD   Yes, I know. And yet I think that Stanislavsky
was probably the first to admit that this was also necessary
—the projection. I find it so hard to convince modern actors—
I've been working with a modern play just recently*—to convince them that they must be heard, seen and understood.
They seem to think—and I suppose the microphone is very
largely responsible—that to play with their backs to the audience, which a few years ago was only allowed to Alfred Lunt,
who probably does it better than any other actor—he and the
late Louis Jouvet—is a kind of glory in itself. But nothing is
more maddening to the public than to pay to see an actor and
not hear him or see him properly all the evening, however
much he may have integrity in his performance and however
much his shoulder blades may express his feelings.

INTERVIEWER   Quite true, Stanislavsky was most in-
sistent upon the voice projection.

GIELGUD   Yes. And I think that most young actors don't
understand what Shakespeare gives you—the idea that even in
the most colloquial modern speech there is a pattern which
must be found by the actor and which, if he will find his individual approach, will have much more significance than if he
allows monotony to take over. In a way I have the feeling that
modern dialogue requires color and tone, more variety even
than verse. In Shakespeare the verse sustains you. You get a
fine speech in Shakespeare, you mustn't put in too much expression. But if you get a play like *The Bells,* or some old
melodrama, you can put in as much expression as you like.
I always imagine that Henry Irving, when he put his performances in between the lines of Shakespeare, as Shaw did, did a
great disservice to the text, but where the text was only a
second-rate framework of action and situation, that was not a
bad thing. His greatest performances were those that he im-
provised out of very clumsy old texts, a lot of which I suspect

* *Five Finger Exercise.*

he rewrote during rehearsals or during performances. The actors of those days—those that I admire, the actor-managers —could invent a kind of pantomime on the scenario of a very sensational story which wasn't well written at all. And that's one kind of acting. If you are clever enough to do that, it's fine. But when you get a classical text, it's very important that you should keep to the text and allow it to be the most important thing. You are only the instrument executing it as correctly as possible. The more correctly you execute it the better it will be. Bernhardt's greatness in *Phèdre* is said to have been as undisputed as her acting in *Camille* and the melodramas of Sardou.

INTERVIEWER   Yes. You said in an interview, in *The New York Times* before the opening of *Ages of Man,* that there is an athletic quality in the verse that carries you along, if you give it a chance.

GIELGUD   It's like swimming, you know. If you surrender to the water you keep up, but if you fight it you drown. Actors are so often unmusical, and often, too, the rhythm of the verse turns into singsong and the meaning is obscured. Or they break up every speech with realistic pauses and breaks to give the illusion of spontaneous thought. This is equally fatal. The phrasing and rhythm and pace should support one, as water does a swimmer, and should be handled with the same skill and pace.

INTERVIEWER   What is it that misleads these actors?

GIELGUD   Modern actors, I believe, are inclined to think that Shakespeare must be made naturalistic instead of being selective in what they choose to make naturalistic. When Shakespeare wants to be naturalistic he is naturalistic. When he says, "Pray you undo this button," or, "Do you not see the baby at my breast that sucks the nurse asleep," or when he says, "All the perfumes of Arabia will not sweeten this little hand," he's extraordinarily simple and modern, and every audience finds these moments moving. But those are moments given you by the author, and they are even more beautiful if they are combined with the rich scaffolding round these simple lines which Shakespeare already has erected: a fine verse, rhythmic speaking, which will allow these moments to have an extraordinary significance just like music.

INTERVIEWER   What did you do to cultivate your voice so that it is the instrument it is?

GIELGUD   I study the sound, shape and length of the words themselves, and try to reproduce them exactly as they are written. In a verse speech—and often in a long prose too—I am constantly aware of the arc: the beginning, middle and end of the speech. I try to phrase this correctly, for breathing, punctuation and emphasis, and then, conforming to this main line, I experiment *within* it for modulation, tone and pace. I try to be very careful of the final consonants D, T, P, and so forth, so that the ends of my words may be clearly heard and understood.

INTERVIEWER   Aside from the matter of speaking the verse, what is the trouble with most Shakespearean acting?

GIELGUD   Well, there usually seems to be a clash of ill-assorted styles of acting, caused largely by the haste and cursoriness with which a Shakespearean company is collected and the short time allowed for rehearsal. The older members are apt to be as old-fashioned and inflexible as the young ones are raw and clumsy; both may be poor speakers, who mouth, rant or are inaudible. The leading Shakespearean exponents of every decade are an influence on their contemporaries, but their success may also encourage young actors to turn out indifferent imitations of their more successful fellows, and the essential secret is not to be so easily achieved.

INTERVIEWER   Would you say that the Method is or is not conducive to classical acting?

GIELGUD   I don't think that it is unconducive. I don't understand people who work by a method, really. I don't think you really know how you work. I think you have to find the way you work and then it's a kind of secret of your own. All I think you have to do is to find the way of selecting your effects from what you seem to have found in all kinds of different experiments at rehearsals: experiments of movement; experiments of give and take with the other players; experiments with the flexibility which the director is trying to achieve in the whole scene or the whole play which you must not be unaware of, and mustn't fight because otherwise you are at odds with him. If you are playing the leading part, it can be a terrible difficulty. Of course, if I direct a play with wonderful actors, I know that my work will not be as difficult or will not be the same as when I get an ordinary cast of fairly good actors. I mean, if you get Peggy Ashcroft and Edith Evans, as I had in *The Chalk Garden,* I say that I just put up the tennis net and clear the court and act as referee, because they know much more about what they want to do than I do. I'm only there as a kind of audience to check the spacing, the movement, the pace of the play. You can't really direct people who are enormously talented, I don't think. At least, I can't.

INTERVIEWER This suggests a question that I have been wondering about. When you are being directed by someone else, are you permitted to work out your roles on your own?

GIELGUD I hope I am a fairly obedient pupil. If I agree to work under a director, I always try to do what he tells me, unless I feel strongly that he is not helping me, in which case I would probably get out myself rather than go on. But with Peter Brook and with Michel Saint-Denis and Komisarjevsky, I was always pretty happy. With Saint-Denis, I must say I found it difficult, because in both cases— one was with *The Three Sisters,* and the other was with *Noah,* Obey's play—he had very strong ideas of how he wanted the parts played. And I never felt that I contributed very much. I only felt I was a good working instrument on whom he could work to get what he wanted. I carried his ideas out as best I could. I didn't contribute many ideas, because he was too strong and his ideas were hard for me to carry out. I carried them out more like a good cook trying to cook a dinner that's been ordered but which he has not quite created himself, if you know what I mean.

INTERVIEWER What, Sir John, influences you in the choice of a role?

GIELGUD I suppose the sympathy I feel towards the character as I read the play—and the hope that I can interpret it better than anyone else could. The feeling, I would say also, that my own limitations, physically and spiritually, might, in this particular role, find adequate means of expression; if possible, that the part might stretch me even beyond my own expectations, through the desire I feel to undertake it and give my imagination scope to encompass it.

INTERVIEWER It has been said that occasionally you have chosen to act the more difficult roles, the less appealing ones, in plays where the 'fatter parts would have suited you. What is behind such reasoning?

GIELGUD That is not entirely true. For instance, Joseph Surface was the only part possible for me in *School for Scandal*—though, yes, I might one day wish to play Sir Peter. In *The Sea Gull* I had already, as a young man, played Treplev, and I was anxious to try Trigorin. Cassius is, I think, the best acting part in *Julius Caesar*. I did play Mark Antony once and did not think myself good in it. And Brutus is very difficult and ungrateful, but one day I think I should like to have a shot at it.

INTERVIEWER   Has acting been easy for you, or has each role been a struggle?

GIELGUD   Acting is never really easy. Sometimes, you know, it is an escape, occasionally a pleasure, often a responsibility. I enjoy it most when I am acting with other players whom I admire and respect, and, of course, when the audience is particularly responsive.

INTERVIEWER   Do you constantly seek to improve an interpretation of a role even after you have opened in a play?

GIELGUD   Yes. I never feel I have a part under control until I have played it in public for at least six weeks. After that I try to set it, and to simplify rather than elaborate in executing it.

INTERVIEWER   How about those technical problems in acting? For instance, memorization. How do you memorize your lines?

GIELGUD   Well, the truth is I do *not* learn the lines by rote, at any rate, until I have read my part with the company several times. I used to be able to learn very quickly, but nowadays I write out the whole of my part in longhand in order to learn it—sometimes more than once—as I have a bad tendency to learn sense and rhythm, with inaccurate detail as regards actual words. I am quick to feel when cuts would improve my speeches, and occasionally I beg leave of a modern author to change the shape of a sentence if I feel the rhythm is better to speak another way. When one is studying, one is subconsciously affected—like a woman with child, I imagine—by everything one sees and hears going on about one. One's imagination is already geared to the implications of the character one is trying to bring to life.

INTERVIEWER   How important is technique to an actor?

GIELGUD   It is essential, except possibly when he may be cast, very early in his career, for a role to which his physical and other qualities are ideally suitable. He may then be lucky enough to succeed, with a good director's help, knowing nothing of technical deficiencies in his performance. The lack of technique may even, in this case, be of advantage to him. But he will not be able to make a career without learning it eventually.

INTERVIEWER   What would you say are the risks of too much technique in performing a role?

GIELGUD   I would say that timing and emphasis can easily become false and exaggerated. For example, I think there is a temptation to play for laughs. I think it is often better to smother three or four small laughs in a fine comedy scene—by speaking so firmly, and sustaining the pitch, that the audience is prevented from laughing by not wishing to miss the next words—in order to gain the important big laugh, later on, which is the culminating point of the author's wit. I wish I could play for you as a perfect sample a recording of the "Bag" scene in *The Importance of Being Earnest*. I would love for you to hear Edith Evans do the "Bag" scene and hear her slow crescendo. Technique is necessary to execution and to the discipline of playing a part over many consecutive performances. But it can be very dull and empty if there is no spark behind it, like boring academic paintings, or cold virtuoso playing of an instrument.

INTERVIEWER What is your procedure, Sir John, in developing a role when you also are the play's director?

GIELGUD Very often I go on the road with only a very vague idea of what I am doing. I am terribly interested in everything in the play except my own role. That's my great difficulty, that as a director I take too much interest in what's going on around me: with the scenery and the dresses, with the groupings and with the positions. What I like best first of all is to work very hard with everybody, leaving my own part aside a little bit, just fitting in as best I can, trying to see where I seem to have to take the stage and dominate certain scenes. Then after we have been on the road for about eight weeks, I have a rehearsal of the play with my understudy walking my part in my costumes, if possible, and then I suddenly am able quite easily to see, when everything else is set, where I ought to be more prominent myself, or more retiring, or should take a certain part of the scene that I have not been able to up until then. It's rather hard on the first audiences who see the play. But this is the method I have always used over the last fifteen years, when I have been very largely directing my own plays. When somebody else is directing, then I do concentrate enormously on my own part and try and work a bit with the director, so that his ideas and mine seem to create something always together. I think probably I interfere dreadfully with other directors, but Brook, particularly, I find extraordinarily easy to get on with even though we usually have certain disagreements. We have done some good work together.

INTERVIEWER To get back to how you prepare for your part. Stanislavsky describes the intense preparation that should be made . . .

GIELGUD That again was the director's interest. Actors

are so different. An actor can giggle and play the fool at the side of the stage and go right on and be wonderfully dramatic, break into tears or shriek with laughter or fall dead. Some actors can do that. Other actors must not be spoken to during a performance. They go into a great huddle with themselves, and concentrate, and go through their lines in the dressing room, before they go on. And these two types can be equally fine actors, in my opinion. I don't think it's a thing you can lay down rules about. Naturally, with young people you try and encourage them to take their work very seriously. But I think an actor who is too solemn about his work is really rather a bore. Unless he is a very fine actor. I don't know any great actors who are too solemn about their work. It becomes tedious.

INTERVIEWER I still would like to know about how much preparation you do for a role. For instance, in *The Importance of Being Earnest*, would you have been inclined to read up about the times?

GIELGUD Not really. I have always had a great feeling for that period. After all, it wasn't so very long ago for me, and my parents belonged to it. But what I would like to say is that what I have found interesting about *The Importance of Being Earnest* was that when we played it too long and lost the inner feeling of fun, it wasn't funny any more. This was interesting, because it has to be played with the most enormous solemnity. But inside you must play the whole play as if you were doing a practical joke—with immense seriousness, knowing yourself that you are being killingly funny. And yet if you were to betray with the slightest flicker of an eyelash that you know you're funny, you are not funny either. When we lost the inner fun after six or eight months—when we got sick of the play—it immediately told and the play became a sort of affected exercise.

INTERVIEWER That's interesting. I recall that when you came over with your troupe to New York you scored a sensational success with *The Importance of Being Earnest*. Mr. Atkinson said in the *Times* exactly what you said, that you played it with solemnity but you knew all the time right to the finger tips that you weren't taking this thing seriously. Yet the following week or the following night, I don't remember which, in *Love for Love*, he said the fun had gone out of it. What happened?

GIELGUD Well, that's it. We had played it much longer than *The Importance* in England, and it is a much more remote and difficult play. I think also that we hadn't such fine actors as we had in London. And you must remember that this play of Congreve's is, I believe, much less agreeable to modern audiences than Wilde's. It's much more heavy going, and I think in some curious ways the coarseness of Congreve rather shocked Americans. It seemed to be coarseness for coarseness' sake, whereas in England it seemed more to belong. And it is a very hard play to take in some ways, unless superbly executed. It's a very long, heavy play. I mean, it's like Mozart. It needs to be played as brilliantly as Mozart, and probably we weren't very good in it. Well, that's candid.

INTERVIEWER If you were asked what the basic requirements are for an actor, what would you say?

GIELGUD Imagination, self-discipline, industry, a sense of humor if possible. And certain basic qualities either of appearance, of authority, of originality. Sort of commonplace prettiness is not very interesting, you know. Just good looks aren't interesting; but interesting looks which can be used—a malleable, flexible body and face, and voice. Voice, of course, I think is wildly important. And to have a good ear, which I find so many of them haven't got.

INTERVIEWER When you say a good ear, what do you mean?

GIELGUD I mean an ear for tempo, for rhythm, for musical quality, and for being able to hear when they've done one thing and to be able to change it and go on to another, you know—variety. I saw *The Connection* the other night. It's marvelous realistic acting. But the actors didn't seem to have any idea that any one line must be tipped to make it more interesting. With modern works I think you need *more* tipping, *more* variety, *more* tone interest. You cannot sit the whole evening listening to someone speaking in monosyllables in the same tone of voice. It may be as realistic as you like, and in a small theatre it's very effective and sometimes on the microphone it's very effective. But you feel the actor is so limited. You feel he's just coming on and doing what he is, which is not very interesting. He doesn't create anything.

INTERVIEWER About imagination. How does it work for an actor?

GIELGUD I think that when you read a play—that when you're offered this part—you suddenly imagine, "Oh, I could do something wonderful with this part." You sort of smell it. And it has nothing to do with the understanding of the details. You suddenly see the way you're going to look, the way you're going to speak, the way you're going to move. And you kind of imagine you can do it. And if you didn't imagine, you wouldn't dare to do it. I did this with all the great parts which I played when I was young, Lear, Macbeth, Hamlet. When I read the parts I thought, "Oh, I think I can take a crack at those parts." I imagined them, and in some cases, particularly in Macbeth, I had more success the first time than ever afterwards, because I had imagined it—like telling a story to a child—and I just played it for the main kind of masses of the character without worrying about the technical difficulties and the intellectual difficulties and the psychological difficulties. I just played it from scene to scene as it seemed to come to me as we rehearsed the play. With three weeks' rehearsals there wasn't time to do more than that. Yet in a funny way I got an all-over effect out of this—it may have been very shallow but it was sort of exciting, I think.

INTERVIEWER   Then an actor with a small imagination limits the range of his capacities.

GIELGUD   I think so. I think if you fly high you probably may reach heights.

INTERVIEWER   But can this be done without a very finely attuned understanding of life?

GIELGUD   Well, I think so; I think so many actors are such babies. I am a terribly immature character myself. I've never understood so many, many things. I'm appalled now to think of the time that I've wasted when I could have learned things, but it hasn't really affected my work very much, because the joke is that people think of me as an intellectual, a cerebral actor, which I'm not in the very least. I've always done everything on my emotion and instinct.

INTERVIEWER   What do you mean specifically?

GIELGUD   Oh, because I'm very emotional. In real life I cut all that out. I'm not at all emotional in real life. I restrain everything to a degree that I'm rather frustrated and just kind of cold and hard in real life. But the moment I get into a theatre either to watch or to act, I can pour out emotion fit to beat the band. But I have then to select from those emotional outbursts what will be effective on the stage, and this is what is so difficult and what one only learns much later on—how you then choose out of three or four big powerful feelings the one that is going to be right for the scene and right for the situation and which the audience will immediately recognize as *your* most personal reaction to this particular episode in the play. Edith Evans once said to me, "I will never play a part, say, of a mother losing her child, unless when I play that scene, I feel that the audience will say—the women in the audience will say—this woman on the stage knows more about a mother losing a child than I do."

INTERVIEWER   In other words, the larger-than-life idea.

GIELGUD   Yes.

INTERVIEWER   But she doesn't really need to know it.

GIELGUD   No.

INTERVIEWER   This seems to suggest something about intuition in acting.

GIELGUD   Yes. Some actors are not intuitive at all. But I think the best ones always are. If one acts really well, one conveys an all-over conviction to the whole audience at the same time, as one may prove by their silence and attentiveness; but also one may convey to individual members of that audience implications of which one was not even oneself aware. This, I imagine, is intuition: an intuitive, spontaneous association of oneself with the character which transcends, at its best, one's own deliberate planning and intention.

INTERVIEWER   Which raises another matter. What is truth in acting?

GIELGUD   Acting is pretense, but it is also an art. It may convey poetry, realism or abstraction, or all these—as a picture, music or sculpture may—but acting must always be interpretative except in the case of clowns and improvisators. Therefore, the dramatic truth is the most important thing for the actor to find in a first-class text. With poor material he may sometimes find a different kind of truth—in melodrama or farce, for instance—and he has to find the right kind of truth, and style for that particular kind of play: a broad, larger than life, kind of melodrama; a solemn, yet light, kind of farce—and sometimes, too, insert his own actor's truth in between the lines and situations given him by the author. But this does not ever apply in Shakespeare. As Shaw says of acting Shakespeare, "Play on the lines, and within the lines. Never in between the lines."

INTERVIEWER   What of images, of memories of events, of happenings? How do these serve an actor?

GIELGUD   Oh yes. I think you always do find images. Stanislavsky talks a lot about the image method. And I must say that in plays like *Richard II,* which have immense graphic descriptions of things and places, I always used to have the same color image, the same thing I thought of at the same moment in my part every night when I knew those words were coming. When my mother died two years ago— I had never seen anyone dead before—it naturally made a tremendous impression upon me, and at a certain moment when I was doing the recital* which came soon afterwards, in the "To be or not to be" speech, on a certain line, I always thought of her, of exactly how she looked when she was dead. It came into my mind, it didn't hold me up, but it gave me exactly the right feeling of the voice for the line. It came to me naturally, you know, without knowing it the first time, and it was so vivid that I thought I could never speak the speech again without thinking of it, because it would help me to make the line right, and it always did. It has never failed.

INTERVIEWER   But this suggests that in addition to imagination, experience will react together with the imagination.

GIELGUD   Yes, one's danger is that in real life when one studies so much, one is so much apt to put everything into theatrical form; every experience, like seeing your mother dead, is something that you remember for the theatre, which is an extraordinary thing, which is rather obscene really.

INTERVIEWER   The same thing happens in Chekhov's *The Sea Gull,* where the writer is constantly entering notes in his book.

GIELGUD   Certainly, but I suppose we all do it to some extent. And then this selective thing, I think, is so frightfully important. I've always said that when you see the picture of the Van Gogh chair you suddenly think what an extraordinary way to paint a chair—at an angle—and it's yellow—and a funny color. But after you've seen that picture you can never again see a kitchen chair without thinking of Van Gogh. This is because his own particular view of it was so strikingly original and so strikingly personally felt that it affects one always afterwards in seeing chairs. In the same way I think any great actor's moment in a play— one has seen this many times—is brought about by the fact that he has felt this moment so individually. But not only has he felt it, he has observed it and registered it in his memory book, and he can then repeat it technically over and over again, possibly with the help of a visual image which may be his own private affair. Or possibly through a sheer technical effect of pausing, or emphasis, or some-

* *Ages of Man.*

thing which will make this particular line or word or emotion or situation particularly poignant and particularly well placed. But then you have to learn through long technical experience exactly how to time and how you would do a thing by accident in a performance which is suddenly rather effective; how you can make it perhaps a little more—a few in the house will see that you have made a certain effect, but you are quite aware from the lack of complete stillness that the whole audience isn't getting it. Then you have to spread it a little more so that the whole house will get it, or you must close it up if it is too broad. And that is the excitement of long runs and the discipline of playing parts again and again: you know certain effects you get and you must relate them to the production and the other players. You may be able to do something in *Much Ado* or *Lear* with one set of actors, but when you do it with another set of actors it won't be right because they will react differently. Therefore your timing and pace will be different. Naturally you don't want to abandon something that you have found very effective every time you have played the part. But you may have to, or you may have to do it differently because the actors around you are different, or the audiences are different, and it is a continual adjustment, like putting the screws in a wireless. You know that you never are quite sure that you've struck twelve and that you can really leave it at that. But I do find that as one gets older and more experienced one is inclined to leave things alone when they are good, whereas when I was young I was always elaborating and piling on things; and I find with other actors I direct that they've spoiled performances by elaborating their effects and giving much too much, and trying to put in pauses and expressions and all sorts of by-play. For about eight weeks I think actors go on improving in a play. Then the really fine actors begin to cut away, and they keep it down, simplify. If you see them a year later they are doing less rather than more. But the bad actors begin to elaborate and drag and become out of key, and out of harmony with one another, and lose their pitch, and then you have—it's like an orchestra—you've got to redirect the whole thing again.

INTERVIEWER I was wondering about the discipline you mentioned. What is meant by discipline in an actor?

GIELGUD Well, the discipline of an actor is getting there every day a good hour before you go on, which I usen't to do when I was young, but which I would not dream

of not doing now—being ready. And I think that in a way
—Martha Graham said this in a film I saw the other day—
there is the actual relaxation of making up for the theatre—
make-up isn't very fashionable any more, a lot of people
go on without any, and it's very nice if you can, like I did
in *Ages of Man*, because it saves a lot of time—and it is
a wonderful thing, in a way, to get to your dressing room,
especially if you're worried outside the theatre, and sit down
at your table with all your things, and to make up—exactly
as one shaves, as a daily routine, which becomes more and
more mechanical as the play runs—and to find yourself kind
of going into the part. Putting on your costume, going down
on the stage and hearing the beginning of the play, and
knowing that it will be that time particularly, and not earlier
and not later, and not that awful uncertainty of the movies
when you sit all day long and suddenly you have to do a
bit and then suddenly you sit again. There's a great joy to
me in the routine of the theatre, though in a very long run,
of which I've had many, it is appallingly arduous to repeat
a thing for perhaps a year and a half, however well it goes,
because the audience deteriorates and the actors deteriorate
and you dread being asked to rehearse and yet you know
it's what you really need.

INTERVIEWER   When you are working, do you have
any set routine? I mean, do you have any system for keeping
in condition?

GIELGUD   Well, no, not really. Nothing too rigid. But
I do always like to sleep for at least one hour, sometimes
more, every afternoon. And I eat very sparingly before going
to the theatre, where I arrive an hour before the play begins.
After the play I can eat quite heavily without its preventing
me falling asleep as soon as I go to bed.

INTERVIEWER   What discipline does one require in
one's life outside the theatre? Is there anything—like singers
or violinists . . . ?

GIELGUD   Well, I don't know. Of course, I always
think that we ought to do exercises, and we ought to do
improvisations and go through our things at home like
dancers do, because there's no doubt that dancers who limber
up for half an hour before the performance—there's a play
now in London called *The Hostage*, in which the cast is
required by Joan Littlewood to come in an hour before the
play begins, meet on the stage and have a kind of singsong
and improvise. This is a rather Brechtian device to get them
really in the sort of spirit of their work, and there's some-

thing in it, even though to me it sounds a bit affected. I think it would embarrass me very much. I try not to be theatrical out of the theatre. Yet I am sure that one does, without knowing it, save one's self all day for one's performance if one is playing an important part. You find you can't tear around, although when you are young you always do, and I think that you find all the more that everything you look at and watch and hear and see does affect your work in some ways. I used to cough in private life when I was acting a consumptive part in a play, and one or two actresses I know have seemed to be happier and sweeter, or more ill-tempered and difficult, according to the kind of role they were acting at the time.

INTERVIEWER What would you say you conceive to be the function of an actor as an artist? Stanislavsky makes a great point out of this, the dedication that is required.

GIELGUD Ah, yes. Great artists are very dedicated. Dame Edith Evans and Martha Graham are two of the most dedicated people I know. Now, Sybil Thorndike is also a dedicated woman. But she is an enormous humanitarian, she is at every committee meeting, she'll go anywhere to appear for charity, she will got to miners' homes and recite *Medea*. She'll do anything in the world. She's a woman of extraordinary character, but I would not say that she is quite as great an artist as Edith Evans, who is much more difficult to pin down. She is not a sociable person, and she is a woman of great selectivity in her life as well as in her work. Sybil Thorndike is a great, generous, giving woman who sometimes can act less well, whereas Edith Evans can never act badly because she would never allow herself to act badly, and whether the one is more great than the other is very hard for me to say. They're both tremendous people. I think that one is probably happier than the other. It's like Bernhardt and Duse, it's hard to compare.

INTERVIEWER Is discipline a part of this?

GIELGUD Yes, I think it is. I would say that Edith Evans is more disciplined than Dame Sybil.

INTERVIEWER When you say discipline, does that mean an attitude toward life?

GIELGUD I think it's a personal taste and a personal feeling of what they need to preserve in order to do their best before the public. I don't think that Sybil Thorndike ever considers her own health or her own comforts for a single moment, or that she will not be ready to play in the evening. She loves extracurricular affairs. She has an enormous zest for them, whereas Edith Evans only acts with difficulty. It is like something torn from her innermost, secret self and she could never . . . I always feel that she's almost afraid of dispelling her genius by any promiscuous kind of wasting her time in any way, you know.

INTERVIEWER I would like to take the idea of the function of an artist in another direction—what does he owe the audience?

GIELGUD Well, that's also very difficult, because I think that—I always feel that—I'm a bit too fond of pleasing the audience, and yet they are there to be pleased, to be entertained. How much are you to deliberately entertain? I think the important thing is that they shouldn't be bored, or go to sleep, or walk out. But I think that if you once allowed them to order you about, if you are too responsive to popularity and you covet success—audiences can make you rather vulgar as an actor. They are sometimes inclined to like very often the things that are not the best about you, and not to know the very best things that you do.

INTERVIEWER Where do you see evidence of this in our theatre, where we may be debasing . . . ?

GIELGUD I think the films do it so much, you know— I mean a man like Brando, who is a thrilling artist. But I would think that he has been forced by the public to acquire this kind of mannered technique, which is apt to lead him into not making the experiments that his talents might allow him to develop tremendously more. I once asked him why he didn't play Hamlet; but he never would be allowed to play Hamlet, probably his agents wouldn't allow him to play it, or his film company. You know your actors get caught here, and yet they envy us in England for doing all the classics. But it's their own fault, because they should. It is an awful temptation to make more money and keep in the particular vein which is most popular with the public, and which you obviously do the best, but although it is always good to do what you do best, if you can, you must also try things which you are not going to be quite so successful in, or in which you may surprise yourself by finding that you are more successful in than you thought you would. You mustn't have too much at stake in every play. That's the danger of being a great success and a great box-office person. You dare not take a risk.

INTERVIEWER That's particularly true here, isn't it?

GIELGUD I think so. I would never dare to come here in a play that I had not made a success in, if I could help it.

INTERVIEWER You worried a lot of people not too long ago by saying that you didn't like acting, that you thought you might like to give it up.

GIELGUD Yes, I know I said that, and I do say it every now and again. I think all actors do, who work very hard. I mean, I've had a most wonderful career, really. To have been a leading man for so long doesn't happen to many people. But every so often one suddenly feels that one has reached the end of the things one had ambitions to do, and one doesn't know where one's going. Besides, now that one is the important character in a venture, there is all this commercial thing that if you agree to play a play you must then agree to play it for nine months because of the author, the management getting its money back and, of course, the rest of the actors. If you happen to say, "Yes, I'll do a certain play, it's rather interesting," and then in three weeks' time you read it again and don't like it so much, the entire project has either to be shelved or you've got to honor your promise. This is a terrible responsibilty because it means that one can't be in the least casual. In the old days you could say, "Well, I'll do that play for a few nights, for a Sunday night's show, or something." It would be fun to try and, perhaps, you'd make a great success in it. Then it would run for a year. But this great responsibility towards your fellow artists, towards the authors and towards the managers is a terrible thing for anybody in a big position to live up to. You don't want to disappoint people and you don't want to do what is too easy. And your plans are of too much interest to everybody. The moment you are connected with a play, then the play must be important, you must be important in it and you must make a success. There's no creeping in and doing something just for fun to see if it will go.

INTERVIEWER It must be terrifying.

GIELGUD It is. There's too much responsibility laid upon you quite apart from your performance.

INTERVIEWER But you still get that joy of creating something when you are involved in a production.

GIELGUD I've done an awful lot of revivals and I'm rather tired of that. And besides, I am not always happy in those parts, however much I loved them once. For instance, I always wanted to play *Richard II* again, very badly, and a lot of people encouraged me, especially when I did the recital. But those who know me well and are my best critics told me, "Don't play it, you are too old, you have too much authority now for the early scenes." Then a few years ago I did play it in Bulawayo, Southern Rhodesia—I thought nobody would notice it there and it would be fun to play it again. So I went out to the Rhodes Centenary and played it there for a week or two. I was terribly disappointed to find that contrary to my expectations it gave me no joy at all. I could only imitate the performance I saw when I was a young man. And I thought, "No, I must leave this part alone because the fact that I am older and wiser doesn't make me better in the part. I just give an imitation of what I used to do and I did it better then because I was young." You can't imitate a young part with any pleasure. Perhaps I could play a young role—as Olivier does so wonderfully in the film, *The Moon and Sixpence*—if it happened to be a new part in which I had to impersonate a young man for one scene. I probably could do it, but I don't think to go back to the parts you played when you were young is any good. That's why I won't play Hamlet any more though I, perhaps, could get away with it. I know a lot of people would like to see it, but I would make myself mad. When I played it the last time, in 1944—I had played it for fifteen years on and off in five different productions—I found that not only was I muddled in my interpretation because I had had too many directors and I was a bit between a lot of them, but also I knew that in the early scenes I was giving an imitation of my performance when I was a young man. This gave me no pleasure; it was a sort of pallid looking back, and one knew one was better then because one wasn't so conscious of putting it on. It was natural to me then, and now I was having to act.

INTERVIEWER   This seems to indicate something about the whole current of a career. It would seem that one has to move forward continuously. How does one do that?

GIELGUD   Yes. That's why I like directing. I've had the Fry play, *The Lady's Not for Burning*, and this play of Shaffer's, *Five Finger Exercise*, which are modern plays. I mean that I think Olivier had the most wonderful break in *The Entertainer*. He had a very interesting and a sort of controversial modern play by a very interesting writer, in which he had the most wonderful part, in which he could be really much more important than the play. He made the play a success for the author and had the most wonderful personal success and was somehow very much in the avant-garde, suddenly, which, is, you know, what we all long to be once we get into our middle years, because one doesn't want to

be left behind, stuffed and put in a museum. You want to
be in touch. But when they wanted me to play *Endgame,*
I couldn't find anything that I liked in the play. I thought
it's no good pretending for pretension's sake that I would
play this play, because it nauseates me. I hate it and I won't
play it, and yet I long to be in something as avant-garde as
that, since I'm sure the moment will come, with any luck,
when somebody will send me a play which may be strange
and new, like a MacLeish play or one of Eliot's plays, in
which one could say suddenly, "I could play this part."
I'm so afraid of being pretentiously avant-garde, when I
don't understand it, or being too traditional and therefore
old-fashioned. One is torn between these two desires, and
you try by knowing young people and talking with older
ones to balance the mixture, because I do think a leading
actor has an enormous influence. One thing I'm proud about
in my career is the influence I've had on other actors who
worked in my company, before the war particularly, and
the general influence I've had in the theatre, because I am
a very timid, shy, cowardly man out of it. But once I go
into the theatre I have great authority and I get great respect
and love from all the people working in it—from the stage-
hands, the costumers, the scene designers and the actors—
and this suddenly justifies your entire existence. I think that
it is something that is much more precious to me than any
personal success that I have had as an actor.

INTERVIEWER I get the impression that you want to
leave the classics behind, that you want to do plays by
contemporary playwrights.

GIELGUD I would love to, yes. And, of course, I would
love again to play Lear and Prospero. But I will give them
another five or six years, because when I am between sixty
and seventy I shall be very glad of some fine parts as old
men to play, and I think that I will play them better if I
leave them alone for a while. There are some Shakespeare
plays I've never acted in which will be very interesting to
do. But I think there's been too much Shakespeare played
in the last few years and I've done what I consider my—the
pioneering work. I have done the Old Vic. I've done Strat-
ford-on-Avon in England. And although it would be nice to
work with young actors at Stratford, Connecticut, or Stratford, Ontario—which they've asked me to do—I somehow
feel that it's work I've already done the foundation of, and
I'd be tempted to go back on my tracks, try to teach them
what I taught my actors in 1930, which isn't quite up to

date. I don't think I'm sufficiently up to date as regards Shakespeare.

INTERVIEWER   What does that mean?

GIELGUD   I don't know, I don't know. I think I know about the speeches. But as regards directing the plays, I wouldn't have the modern touch.

INTERVIEWER   Modern touch?

GIELGUD   It is something that a young man finds in the plays. I don't mean in modern dress, or anything stunty, or even gimmicks or costumes. But I think that a man who reads those plays with a fresh young eye, as I did when I was at the Old Vic in 1929, can suddenly come up in them in a way that is new. I think every ten years the actor turns up who can—or the director.

INTERVIEWER   You mean in terms of the social milieu of the times?

GIELGUD   Yes, the smell of the times. There's something about this. They relate it in some curious way—like when *Coriolanus* was done in the French theatre at the time of the most frightful troubles, political troubles, in France. It suddenly jumped with the public, and the time I played Lear under Granville-Barker—at the time of the fall of France in 1941—was the only time that I felt I'd touched King Lear. I think it had something to do with the fact that France was falling outside the theatre, that we thought the raids would come in about four weeks. People used to come around and say, "This play is absolutely extraordinary, it's given us such pride," and I'd say, "But how can you bear it—this tearing out of the eyes, the death of the king, the cruelty . . ." but they would say, "Well, there's a kind of catharsis, and when we come out of the theatre we are uplifted, like after hearing Beethoven. It shows that with all the appalling horror that is going on, there is some glory, and something that's worth everything." This seemed to me extraordinary, and I felt it so deeply; we all did in the company at that time.

INTERVIEWER   Is that something which has interested you—the effect you have had on people, on bringing to light problems, great human problems?

GIELGUD   I'm afraid not. No. I think the exciting thing about the best acting is that you feel everybody gets a different reaction from it, like they do in a concert hall. I've had so many letters when I've had a success in a part like Hamlet. I had so many letters praising me and noticing things that I never intended to convey at all. When you are playing well, you arouse the audience's sensitiveness and they imagine they are seeing things they want to see.

INTERVIEWER It is a sort of illumination then.

GIELGUD Yes, you've, in a way, opened the windows for them. They find one thing and you're acting another, but it all harmonizes together in some extraordinary way.

INTERVIEWER I think that is what I was trying to drive at before in terms of the function of the actor as an artist. I think that Mr. Atkinson in his review of *Ages of Man* said that the office of the actor is an illustrious one, that reading lines, acting parts are only two of the actor's duties and that he can also enrich the lives of the audience.

GIELGUD That's the text to begin with. Anyway, I would like very much to add that I think concentration is another frightfully important asset for an actor. I'm not at all good at concentrating, and I think that until you learn to completely concentrate on the stage every night, and through your whole role, that you don't really play your best, or give the customers their money's worth. I must say that I'm not sure I've mastered it, but I do think that if there is any special secret to give as to concentration I would say that it lies in relaxation rather than pressure of intensity: the mind clearly divided between the imaginative impulse and the deliberate execution of the part, with nothing allowed to distract one from these two processes, which should be complementary—the one feeding and sustaining the other. In *Ages of Man* I really had to concentrate, and the least noise—an airplane going overhead or fire engine sirens—absolutely drove me mad, because I did find in that particular thing that for the first time, almost, I didn't have any difficulty in concentrating. I was alone up there on the stage and had this wonderful text and I just had to keep with it, whereas in a play it is very easy to have your attention distracted—you get a passage where you are not speaking—or the role has become mechanical after many performances and your mind is no longer full of it. That's why I do think that it is a good idea to relate your speeches, as you rehearse them, to certain visual images which come up very naturally. First of all, it helps you remember your moves and your planning of the *plastique* of the part. Through rehearsing you connect the words with certain moves and the moves seem to be dictated in a way by the words. The words may make me feel that I must get up from this chair and walk across the stage and be nearer that person or further from him, or whatever it may be. This is one thing. And then you learn the part, the words of the part, and the words and the movements are connected. Then, if you revive the part some years later, you suddenly feel, "Oh! I used to walk across the stage here, or my actual *plastique* of movement was different." You will find if you change it—the movement—it will very often give you a fresher view of the words. I think that the words and movements are very much allied. Reading your lines again in print freshens your acting sometimes, too. I sometimes read over my Shakespeare parts in different editions, so that while the words are the same, they look different. When Craig talks of Irving's dance in *The Bells,* I sometimes look at the floor of the stage and think what extraordinary patterns my legs have made during the evening in moving and filling the stage. In a leading part I try to people the actual floor of the stage in a curiously patterned way, which seems to relate, without my knowing it, to the emotions of the part. I can't quite explain it, but . . .

INTERVIEWER   Stanislavsky makes this point that you've got to relate the inner feeling to the words. The relationship between the psychological drive is all very definitely related in order to create reality on the stage.

GIELGUD   Certainly, but are you—but is one really trying to create reality? I mean reality on the stage is not the same as reality in real life, although it can seem to be. In the Chekhov plays, of course, the action is very realistic, and I learned from Komisarjevsky to play, as I say, with the fourth wall down instead of the projecting, declamatory method which I would use in Shakespeare. But I think that both methods can marry one another. After all, in Chekhov the audience must still see the actors' faces. They must still sit facing the audience in many scenes. They must trick their faces around so that they can be heard, and there are very long speeches which even in translation have rhythm and pace, and there are even more subtleties of pauses and intervals which have to be defined by the director and the actors and this is a tremendously elaborate technical problem. Just as difficult as reciting a great speech in Shakespeare in which, also, you must face the public, and you must have actors below you and round you to give you the kind of space relationship and to give you the reactions that you need to make a speech seem like a speech spoken to other people but really to the public. This is all a wonderful trick, which is the technical fun of our business. I think that in classical work, as well as in real life, as well as in modern, realistic, colloquial acting, you have to really apply the same rules.

You apply them in a rather more muted way, just as when you get into the movies you suddenly find you have a lot of tags and marks to remember; for instance, not to get out of the camera and keep your face at a certain angle. This is a completely new kind of set of boring rules that you have to learn in the movies, and another one again when you are recording for the gramophone. You know you can do a speech you played on the stage quite differently when you make a record. And in television there is another lot of rules. I think it's harder for young actors today who have so many different media to try and conquer, whereas in the old days there was only the theatre.

INTERVIEWER Would you have said that you could have ever mastered your art to the extent you have if you had had to do all this?

GIELGUD I don't think I would. No, I think I concentrated far more on the theatre because there wasn't anything else in those days.

INTERVIEWER It really is a problem of appalling scope.

GIELGUD That's why they don't get enough experience, you see, because they get a lot of money for working in the other media. But it works the other way around, of course. Movies and TV and recording and radio can't do without the actors, but they're inclined to find that actors who come straight from the theatre, especially if they are not very young, sound mannered and false. They'd rather have a young voice which was sort of impulsive and natural for a few moments—on radio or on TV—because it tells better than an actor of enormous skill who may be showing off the experience of fifty years—which can sound very phony, and that's what they mean by ham, isn't it? If as an old actor you suddenly come on and begin to lay it on, very thick, you seem too solemn, too pompous, too heavy, too unreal—and the audience sits back and doesn't believe a word of it. This is what I mean about modern Shakespeare. You have got to somehow reduce it to a terribly fine point of truth so that it doesn't become just sound for its own sake. And yet you have to know that a great speech like Cleopatra's speech on the death of Antony is written for the sound and not for the sense. Actors are inclined to worry about the sense in Shakespeare, and to worry about the life of the character before the play began, which is one of the things that Stanislavsky talks a lot about. Granville-Barker once told me a wonderful thing—that realistic off-stage time did not begin till Ibsen. Therefore, in Shakespeare, it is no good asking what Portia's father was like, or whether Lear married twice, and things like that, because there is no life except in the play. That's why there is all this argument—about *Othello,* about Desdemona not having time to commit adultery; whether Hamlet is young or old; whether Macbeth is older at the end of the play. It is quite plain to the audience, who have sat there, that a certain time has passed. Shakespeare never bothers to tell us exactly what the period of time was, unless it has something to do with his plot that he wants to put over. When you watch Hamlet you are aware that he is older at the end—and you feel older as an actor when you've played through *Hamlet,* I can tell you, and older still after you've played a performance of *Macbeth!* But I think that it is a very interesting point—that the classics don't demand the same kind of imagination of the character.

INTERVIEWER   It is a fascinating point.

GIELGUD   In Ibsen, you see, it is accounted for. You leave the stage to write a letter, or you leave the stage because something has happened, and when you come back that thing has happened. Galsworthy and Shaw, and all those people, adopted it, and since Ibsen this has been the customary writer's craft. Therefore, actors are inclined to think that in Shakespeare you must do the same—or in Restoration plays—they have no life outside of the plays. In the *Importance of Being Earnest,* when we talked years ago of making a film of it, I said, "Do you mean to say you are going to have Jack coming down from London in the railway carriage in that deep mourning costume? It won't be funny at all. It's only funny when he comes walking into the garden. There's no life before or after. It's like a costume play or a costume ball. He goes and puts on that ridiculous mourning and walks into a sunlit garden with roses. But if you saw him leaving home in this costume, or in the train, or any outside scene, the entire invention of the dramatist would be lost. In the same way even in Barrie's play, *Dear Brutus,* if you tried to make a film of that, and you showed the wood growing outside the house—what is marvelous is that it is a completely theatre effect, that when you are in this country-house drawing room suddenly they draw the curtains and the wood is outside which is a marvelous piece of theatrical effect. All plays that are written with magnificent stagecraft are almost impossible to transcribe into another medium. Thank God! Because otherwise we would have nothing left. There are certain stage plays which will never be so good in any other medium. I think that you may do a very good Shakespeare film—there have been one or two—but, of course, they don't move easily into another medium. He was too great a genius. It's like trying to rewrite the Bible. That's the worst tendency to me of the modern world—that every film must be turned into a radio play and everything must be turned into a digest so you can read it in three easy lessons. This is so disappointing, because it destroys the pauses and the leading up. Audiences are not prepared to sit through a long—not dull—but rather measured passage in Shakespeare, so that they will come to the exciting bit. They want to get on from the "To be or not to be" to "What a rogue and peasant slave" in two easy lessons because they know those bits, and anything that isn't famous is apt to be ignored. This is the only thing I don't like about *Ages of Man*. I feed them too many purple passages. Therefore you have got, as a director, to make it more and more and more exciting, otherwise they won't listen to it. They think it's long and tedious. It's only in music that they will put up with very, very long plays. It's true that O'Neill's plays have been very successful here, even not cut, and Shaw, who would never allow his plays to be cut—and now, of course, they will be. I don't agree in people being bored and things being too long and drawn out, but I think it is a terrible pity when we want to see everything too quickly.

INTERVIEWER   That's right, when *we* won't give anything.

GIELGUD   No, we won't bring anything of ourselves. You know, we can turn it on—the radio—and turn it off with a switch. And, then, half the time, of course, people don't listen, because they put it on while they're cleaning the house or cooking the dinner. They only get it with one ear, and it's going on—Beethoven's best symphony, or something—and it's just background music—and this is terrible. To me that's the great insult of television. Although you may say that there are fourteen million people listening, probably eight million of them are turning off that very minute or some of them will go away.

INTERVIEWER   They're worrying about opening up a bottle of beer.

GIELGUD   I was watching *The Cherry Orchard* one night in the country. I very rarely see television, but this happens to be my favorite play—in England this was—and we saw the first act. Then we changed over to a comedian whom I happened to want to see, and when we saw him for ten minutes we had dinner. Then I went back, and it was the last act of *The Cherry Orchard,* and I thought that I not only had insulted Chekhov but also the actors who had been playing away there all the time for me, and I hadn't even bothered to look.

INTERVIEWER   In preparing for this meeting, Sir John, we came across references to your early shambling gait. In fact, we gathered that one of your early teachers said that you walked like a cat with rickets. How did you set about correcting this?

GIELGUD   As a young actor I pranced and was very self-conscious. Then I became too graceful and posed. Now that I am less shy and able to study myself with more detachment, I have tried to control my physical mannerisms by observing them and asking to have them checked by others, which I was originally too vain and shy to do.

INTERVIEWER   Now then, we also found a note saying that while you were regarded as very able to wear costumes, that is, you wore costumes well, there nevertheless was some question as to whether on-stage you wore modern clothes well. I was wondering—we haven't seen you here in modern outfits—in going into modern plays do you feel that you have . . . ?

GIELGUD   I think audiences do think that I'm a bit drab in modern plays. It's a funny thing, but I have played on the whole very disappointing parts in modern plays. In Noel's play, *Nude with Violin,* which was a kind of fantastic experiment, I wore butler's clothes, which was kind of amusing nonsense and which they liked pretty well, and I've played diplomats in dark suits, you know, and dim, sad fellows in sports coats and slacks. But I think there is something about me that is difficult to cast in the modern play. I don't altogether blame the authors for not providing me with good parts. I've made rather a success as prigs and diplomats. I played the husband in Maugham's *The Circle* well, I think, and a part in *A Day by the Sea,* which was successful, and *The Potting Shed,* which Robert Flemyng played here, I played in London—and those kind of parts which are in a way rather dim men. I think I am quite good at playing a part which could be a bore if it were played by an actor without personality. I try and see the humorous side, and I can make a rather boring man quite amusing to the audience. But, naturally, if one could find something that was powerful and heroic—but also in modern dress—I think it would be better for me. I could never play a tycoon or a truck driver or a

low-life character at all, I don't think. I have no gift for
impersonation, or dialect, or of being a man who works on a
farm or works with his hands. In *Noah* the great difficulty
for me was that I had to measure the boat in the first scene.
I'm very clumsy with anything that has to suggest machinery,
nor I think do I give the impression of a very worldly man.

INTERVIEWER To what extent, then, do you think an actor should stick to his own last?

GIELGUD Well, I think you've got to. After a certain
time you must judge your limitations. I played a lot of parts
that didn't suit me and it was very good for me when I was
young, but I think you can't take that risk once you are the
backbone of a play because, if you play the wrong part, the
play will fail—not only you will fail but the play will fail. And
this, naturally, one wants to avoid at all costs.

INTERVIEWER And yet you don't restrict yourself to a
very narrow road.

GIELGUD I always said that if anybody looked carefully,
it could be said that *Ages of Man* was a bit snobbish because in
it I play nothing but patricians and kings and heroes—and I
never dared to touch the Falstaffs, and the Sir Toby Belches,
and even the parts like Malvolio and Iago, which people
have sometimes thought I could play. But I've always thought
that the point about Malvolio and Iago is that they are coarse-
bred men who must show in their personalities that they are
jealous and demeaned by being in this lower-class bracket.
I can't suggest that on the stage, much as I would love to be
able to. I think it's just something I can't do. And it isn't that
I think I'm grand or aristocratic, but I know that I make that
effect upon an audience, whether it's true or not.

INTERVIEWER Do you have any strategy in controlling
an audience?

GIELGUD Yes, after a fashion, I suppose. Seriously, I
try to listen for the coughs and the silences, but I try not to
force when they are inattentive in front. I try to relax and
concentrate on my role, keep strict tempo, neither gabbling
nor dragging. When you can feel they are moved, to laughter
or tears, you need to do less and less yourself. Your own
emotion had better be squandered and exhausted at rehearsals.
There you must go all out in feeling, and select the simplest
form of your emotion to give clearly to the audience in performance later. To indulge one's capacity for violence and
tears without complete control is bad acting, and physically
exhausting both for the actor and audience, though this in-

dulgence can sometimes fool the audience—and the critics, too.

INTERVIEWER Would you say that your approach changed over the years—that is, we have the impression that you have striven for greater simplicity in your acting. Why?

GIELGUD When I was young I was unduly impressed by effect in the theatre. Melodrama and plays of action, now almost entirely absorbed by the movies, thrilled and delighted me. The show was everything to me—spectacle, broad dramatic acting, scenes of violence, romance, adventure. Everything larger than life. Then I began to see how pictures were selective—in pattern, color, line and so on—how the individual eye could suddenly give new meaning to a common object like Van Gogh's kitchen chair. I began to seek for something that I alone could express in depicting emotion, something resembling life, yet somehow the essence of important moments, avoiding the boredom of everyday life and choosing only the significant ones, as a dramatist as well as the actor has to do.

INTERVIEWER And, finally, would you say that you are still trying to develop as an actor?

GIELGUD I hope so, indeed.

Helen Hayes

BIOGRAPHY

Helen Hayes, born in Washington, D. C., in 1900, was on the stage in her first role in 1905. Four years later she was appearing on Broadway in *Old Dutch*, a musical starring Lew Fields. By the time she was fourteen she had an important assignment with John Drew in *The Prodigal Husband;* and three years later she started out on the first of the many road tours that mark her career—this one in *Pollyanna*. Meanwhile, she managed to complete her courses and graduate in 1917 from the Sacred Heart Academy in Washington.

In 1918, Miss Hayes was a critic's favorite in Sir James M. Barrie's *Dear Brutus*, going on to various roles from there and scoring again, in another Barrie play, *What Every Woman Knows*, in 1926. The next year Miss Hayes starred in *Coquette*, to critical raves and a long run. In 1928 she married playwright Charles MacArthur, who died in 1956. They had one daughter, Mary, who died in 1949 of infantile paralysis when she was nineteen years old. An adopted son, James MacArthur, is today carving his own career in the theatre, films and television.

Among the plays that followed *Coquette* were Ferenc Molnár's *The Good Fairy* and Maxwell Anderson's *Mary of Scotland*. Then in 1935 came the role for which Miss Hayes is, perhaps, best known—Queen Victoria in *Victoria Regina*, by Laurence Housman. Altogether Miss Hayes played the part over 1,000 times, touring with it all over the United States after its Broadway run of 517 performances.

Her most recent appearances have included *Time Remembered*, by Jean Anouilh, and *A Touch of the Poet*, by Eugene O'Neill. She has appeared in a number of films, including *The Sin of Madelon Claudet*, in 1931, for which she won an Oscar. She has made many appearances on television in a wide range of plays and is well known to radio. Miss Hayes is among the few actresses to have a theatre named for her along Broadway.

SETTING

Helen Hayes lives in a gracious old house quite high above the Hudson River in Nyack, not far from New York City. It was here that she was interviewed, in the Victorian living room. It seems to be a congenial setting for Miss Hayes, although Miss Hayes gives every appearance of being very modern, crisp, informal and forthright—not at all Victorian. Miss Hayes lives here alone, save for a small household staff.

The room itself is white with mauve carpeting, its large windows giving onto a porch and providing a lovely vista of the Hudson beyond a swimming pool and terraces leading down from the house. Cream-colored curtains are hung below heavily carved and gilded valances. The accent of the room is on comfort and there is a good deal of furniture. There are such determinedly Victorian notes as a wreath of artificial flowers under a glass bell on the mantelpiece, but there is also a very businesslike brown metal lamp over the card table. Bookshelves cover one side wall, and a number of the books are on Queen Victoria and her time. These books, incidentally, Miss Hayes told us, were *not* used in preparing for the role she made famous, but rather in assuaging her own interest which grew out of playing the role. Separating the books on one shelf is a little shadow box with a stage setting of one of the scenes in *Victoria Regina*. We noticed there was a play script on a coffee table—Miss Hayes told us she keeps reading a good many of these—and another one on a little Victorian chair, under a copy of *Equity*, the magazine of the actors' union in which Miss Hayes maintains an active and lively interest.

There are a number of paintings on the walls; the most impressive is a full-length portrait in oils of Mary MacArthur, Miss Hayes' daughter. Various family photographs, most of them in silver frames, are placed about the room: a thoughtful one of Mary; a smiling threesome of Miss Hayes, Mr. MacArthur and son James; and others of Mr. MacArthur. There is a prominently placed one of Laurette Taylor, with a long inscription to Miss Hayes.

For the interview Miss Hayes sat on a sofa, her back to the window. She was dressed in light blue, and had a matching scarf over her hair, through which could be discerned the outlines of curlers. (Miss Hayes explained that she had just washed her hair.) She had on small earrings, a gold bracelet with a watch and a couple of bangles, a wedding ring. Next to her on the sofa, there reposed with dignity a large black French poodle and a fawn-colored one. Very much members of the household.

Miss Hayes talked with animation and enthusiasm, and with mounting conviction and forcefulness when her feelings became involved. She was relaxed, though, most of the time.

A maid brought in coffee midway in the interview, but Miss Hayes seemed to need no seventh-inning stretch to break the two hours of talk about the more than fifty years she has had in the theatre.

On the way out she talked a bit about the house, explaining how and where she had remodeled. She brought us into a room on the first floor, where a great picture window gave a magnificent view of the Hudson River; she had had it done for Mr. MacArthur, but he had not lived to see it completed.

A mark of her hospitality—and of her devotion to the theatre and to talking about it—was that she kept the appointment with us at all, for she was expecting at any moment a call from the hospital to tell her that her first grandchild, already overdue a few days, was on its way! Several days later her son James and his wife did indeed make Miss Hayes a grandmother.

Interview

INTERVIEWER You were a child actress; you are one of the few in the theatre who went on to success. How do you account for the fact that so many kids who start out at age five, six, seven, eight don't go on in the theatre?

HAYES   Not knowing the personal history of most of them I really don't know. But I would say—I would say as an overall guess that they don't go on because possibly they don't work at learning the job as I did, and, I am sure, as Fred Astaire and Maude Adams and Minnie Maddern Fiske— and a few other of those child actors who went on and became adult stars—worked at learning their jobs. I don't know whether they give up study and just go on for a while on the "charming child personality" bit, and when that is worn out have nothing more to . . .

INTERVIEWER   That sounds like a salient point—that a lot of them get by during their early years on personality and then don't do anything really about developing themselves as performers, as you did. I know the arduous and disciplined career that you followed.

HAYES   Yes, I think that. I don't know. As I say, this is only a guess that those who fall by the wayside, those children —those great child talents that disappear—are probably not developed. It's awfully hard in our theatre of today, of course, to develop. I was lucky. I had a producer who guided my every footstep.

INTERVIEWER   That was George Tyler, wasn't it?

HAYES   Yes. And he had plays written for me that would stretch my ability—you know, my talent—and he was willing to take a chance on my not succeeding in these plays just so long as I was doing something different. Of course, producers can't do this any more; it isn't in the make-up of the theatre today.

INTERVIEWER   This is a great flaw in the theatre in general.

HAYES   Yes, but the young actors seem to have taken it into their own hands and they have their own groups—the Actors Studio and other places—to try to grow and enlarge their talents.

INTERVIEWER   Do you think that, by and large, they are succeeding in doing that—in developing themselves through these various work groups?

HAYES   I hope so—yes, I think they must be, because all of the greats of today have been working in those work groups, haven't they?

INTERVIEWER   Yes. I would say that's true.

HAYES   Look at Anne Bancroft and Julie Harris and Kim

Stanley and Geraldine Page—oh, right down the line, you'll find that they've all been working in these groups.

INTERVIEWER   Do you think that in general it's a good idea for someone to start in the theatre at the age that you did?

HAYES   No, I don't.

INTERVIEWER   Well, why?

HAYES   Because I don't think that my starting so young really was responsible for my learning my job. If anything, it might have delayed me, because I think that everything that happens to you in life . . . You see, I have a theory about higher education. I don't care what you study, if you study mathematics or anything else—I think all of these things eventually apply to the business of acting. I really think that everything that happens to you is applicable to your growth in the theatre. And so, just playing away in children's roles was not particularly—it didn't forward me as an actress at all.

INTERVIEWER   And yet, even though you did not have this broader experience, you did continue to develop, just as if you had had it, in a way. I guess you were particularly fortunate in having someone like Tyler. When did you start working for Tyler? How old were you then?

HAYES   At the age of seventeen, in *Pollyanna*.

INTERVIEWER   Should one start at the age of eight, nine or ten?

HAYES   No. I really don't think that there is any particular value in that. You have the great excitement—and it is good for all children to have a sense of great achievement, and someone, I think, like Patty Duke might really turn it to good account—but I don't think that it is any advantage. I really don't. All children, I believe, are good actors. They're born with a sense of make-believe—all normal children. They are using just what they have, you know, as children.

INTERVIEWER   In other words, you lose nothing by waiting until you're fifteen, let us say?

HAYES   No, or even twenty-one—when you finish college, or have gone through some school of the drama, or worked with a college drama and speech department. I think that all of these things are very good.

INTERVIEWER   That clears up the point as far as I'm concerned, because Lee Strasberg once said that too—that he didn't think it was necessary to start too early; that you picked up a lot of bad habits when you started too early. I imagine you would be in agreement with that, wouldn't you?

HAYES   Yes, I would, because I've had to have some of

those bad habits knocked out of me. They were due mostly to conscientiousness: attempts to keep a performance alive, vital, without the knowledge of how to do so—because you can't learn that by going on the stage and playing the same kind of cute little parts year in year out. This doesn't give you any real understanding of how to keep the freshness and vitality of a performance; that comes with real, solid, technical training, and I had to go out and get that.

INTERVIEWER   You have said in the past that this was a very definite problem for you; that in *Dear Brutus*, for instance, you coasted on your natural exuberance and your natural incandescence, but that when it became a matter of really learning technique you had to go out and work at it. What did you really do?

HAYES   I feel that I began around, just after *Dear Brutus*, when I was faced with carrying big roles—because they naturally followed after a hit like *Dear Brutus*—and realized that I wasn't equipped for them. I didn't know how to carry them and how to get variety into a performance and how to sustain a long role, and I hadn't learned that. Let's see, *Dear Brutus* was when I was nineteen, and around about twenty-one I knew that I was licked unless I did something about learning it.

INTERVIEWER   And what did you do?

HAYES   I went out and studied. I studied everything and anything that I could find. I studied with—well, she was a forerunner let us say of the Method, and her name was Frances Robinson-Duff. She was a teacher of many big actors of that time, and she used the Delsarte chart—which I never hear of any more, but it was like the Method, which derives from Stanislavsky; it was a method which was derived from Delsarte, a French elocutionist.

INTERVIEWER   The Delsarte chart had certain positions for certain emotions.

HAYES   Yes, and it worked with—you know—it worked with the diaphragm, with breathing, with the whole use of the body, and so on. And it was very complicated and some of it seemed a little ridiculous, but it probably all added up to giving one a little more understanding of how to communicate what you wanted to an audience. When Lee Strasberg speaks of bad habits . . . Goodness, I had them—by twenty-one I had learned to overact pretty frightfully and to use all the cute tricks that had stood me in good stead, and I was really just going in for being very cute, and very much with a little bag of tricks.

INTERVIEWER   When you say cute, what do you mean?

HAYES   Oh, you know, the jumping about, and the never-sit-on-a-chair, always-kneel bit—you know, jump on it and kneel—or sit on tables if there's one handy, and all the little things which in that period were supposed to be cute-little-girl things.

INTERVIEWER   Why, during the years from, let us say, eight—when you really began to work in the theatre—up until eighteen or nineteen, had you not been given real professional training or study? Why hadn't you gone to school?

HAYES   Because even the wisest can be misled by success, and I had just been having one role after the other that suited the small capacities that I had developed, that little thing that I had brought originally—that fresh sense of make-believe that children have—and they were using it over and over and over again. I was charming, that's what I was, charming.

INTERVIEWER   Would it be fair to say the difference between an actress who grows and one who doesn't is that the actress who doesn't grow continues with these artificialities that you are talking about?

HAYES   Yes.

INTERVIEWER   And that actually the difference between a grown actor of stature and one not of stature is that the one of no stature is still using these artificialities and meaningless things which you decided you had to overcome—is that a fair statement?

HAYES   Yes, except that I think there are very few actors today who use these artificialities. In that period when I ran into trouble there was an awful lot of—there was a great tendency to play up personality in the theatre, and it was my good fortune that I had a producer who was determined not to just follow along and exploit the things that he knew I could do best, but who put me into things, as I said before, that I might not be able to do well—that I might fail in—but, at least, it would be a change; there would be something new, something different. And this was my good fortune. But there were others in that day and age who were just always put into the same thing. That was in that period of type casting—but I don't think that exists so much today, do you? I think it's just so hard to get from one play to another, even when you have a name, because there is so little continuity of opportunity that everybody just has to be able to fit into any kind of role. I mean, the roles aren't being fitted to the actors any more—the actors are being fitted to the roles. So

I don't think there are too many who just rely on the little tricks any more.

INTERVIEWER   What was the play that made you realize you had to learn more about acting—the play that made you aware that you really had to stretch beyond what you were doing?

HAYES   Well, I first began to suspect it in *Pollyanna,* at seventeen—by the end of a long tour that lasted thirty-odd weeks. I shudder right now to think of what that performance must have been. From ecstatic reviews at the beginning of the tour, by the time we reached New Orleans and the Eastern Seaboard, I was getting some pretty appalling notices. It must have been horrifying to watch me up there, but, of course, there was such devotion to *Pollyanna,* you know, that people continued to swarm in. But I continued to alarm those adults who were watching me; and the people in the company —some of the older actors—were trying to give me a little help but I was too frightened to accept the help then, I just wanted to shut it all out. I went on and got some good help from William Gillette and Ben Iden Payne, the director of *Dear Brutus.* Extra work during rehearsals with Gillette at night, you know, in Charles Frohman's office—he took me up there and worked with me in the evenings, because I was in great danger of losing that job. I must have become a really bad young actress by then, full of mannerisms and tricks and terrible strain. The mannerisms and tricks were the only things I knew to try to cover up the truth that I didn't know how to play parts any more.

INTERVIEWER   Was it because you didn't understand the parts?

HAYES   No, it wasn't that. It was that I didn't know how to communicate my understanding in a simple and straight fashion.

INTERVIEWER   Is this that something at the heart of being a good actress—being able to communicate?

HAYES   With simplicity, and not to overlay that—your method of communication—with any kind of personal mannerisms or persuasions for the audience. You know, it's that thing that they say in the Method: the actor's life is just one long search, a search for truth in his work, for the ability to be absolutely truthful. Just as I learned, when I was studying the Delsarte chart, that every child is born with perfect breathing, every baby knows just exactly how to use the diaphragm. Yet somewhere in the course of early life we begin to breathe in odd ways: we copy, maybe, from other children—I don't know what happens to us—or we copy our parents or something, and we soon lose the ability to actually breathe as animals do. Similarly, we lose that ability of simple honest make-believe which children have. We get complicated and we try to do it in more elaborate ways—I'm speaking, of course, from my troubles and what I ran into—and we have to get right back again and strip ourselves of all that and find the truth again, just as I had to learn to breathe as I breathed when I was a baby. I had to work for three years to get back to honest breathing so that I could carry a role.

INTERVIEWER   During what period was this?

HAYES   It started by the time I was twenty-one and was a star in *Bab*. This put such fear in me—my fear had been growing since seventeen on; but with the help of Gillette and Ben Iden Payne, and the constant supervision of Gillette, I got away with *Dear Brutus*, and my performance must have retained some of the purity and truth that it had at the beginning—throughout the run, which was only five months. But then I got into *Clarence*. I started out well—after I had been well trained by a director—and then I lost it again and, you know, there was consternation with Alfred Lunt and Mary Boland and all of the wonderful cast involved in that play, the consternation about little Helen, who simply couldn't hold onto a performance. This began worrying me frightfully and I was very scared and frightened—I couldn't think very straight—so I never thought of going out and trying to learn. My mother was not familiar enough with the ways of the theatre—she was just following along there really, giving me love and encouragement and help in my roles when I was working on them, but she didn't know about this thing of really having to learn the fundamentals of how to keep acting.

INTERVIEWER   Could you specify a little more closely what happens. I mean, for instance, you think you're doing the same things that you did in the first performance, but by the twentieth performance the same things that were good for the first performance are no longer carrying through to the audience—now what happens?

HAYES   Well, I said earlier that I think it's conscientiousness. I think that we all want to retain what we had in the beginning, and we just want to give the public the best that we have, so we become aware that we have certain scenes that are tremendously moving, and in our attempts to keep them tremendously moving, we become a little more moving all the time, you see. We don't know where to stop the projection of that emotion; it's the difficulty of the long run, and yet it's something that even if you don't have long runs, you must learn to control. If we haven't any control, we do a thing spontaneously, instinctively, and it's fine, it lasts for a little while; but then if we have no fundamental knowledge of how we did that—we don't know how we did it.

INTERVIEWER How do you acquire this fundamental knowledge?

HAYES You acquire it by taking yourself apart in every way: you learn your voice, you learn about every note of your voice and just where to place it for certain things. This sounds so terribly mechanical, and it is. It almost sounds as if you—as if you have to banish all inspiration and all of God's gift to you from your being. And maybe you do, for a while, when you're learning. It's like tennis: you've been playing tennis and you can whack at the ball and get it over the net wonderfully and everything, but if you ever want to get into playing really good tennis, what do you do? You have a teacher come and he just destroys your whole game for a while, and you get very discouraged and you can't do a thing—and yet all the time you are learning exactly the snap of the wrist and the use of the shoulder and the follow-through of the stroke. Well, this is, maybe, a wasteful analogy, but anyway, that is what personally had to happen to me, because I was mostly playing in comedy and that is the most tricky and the most hazardous of all theatre media, isn't it?

INTERVIEWER I was going to ask you that.

HAYES It is the trickiest form in all the theatre, comedy, and it requires the most self-discipline on the stage. And poor old me, you know—there were moments, like in *Clarence* . . . Heywood Broun once listed it as one of the three great moments that he had ever experienced in the theatre—one with Lionel Barrymore in *The Jest,* something that he did in *The Jest;* and I forget what the other one was, but the third was my making an exit saying, "Wash my face, wash my face," in indignation and bravado. I was in the midst of an adolescent tragedy, and my father had turned around and said to go upstairs and wash my face—and I just went upstairs, saying, "Wash my face, wash my face." Well, this was great, and the opening night the applause was so—it lasted so long on my exit that one almost wondered if I had to go back and do it again. And yet after a few weeks there it was—I'd just go off to a kind of embarrassed silence. And I was, poor me, trying to re-create what I had done the opening night, which had been instinctive, right and true—and I didn't know how I did it. And that's the whole thing. Now I've got to some degree of security through study. I studied everything. I studied with about four or five different interpretive dancers, including Charles Weidman, so that I came to know what I looked like when I was moving—so in my mind's eye I know how my body is articulating something that I am feeling. And I knew through my work with voice, with Frances Robinson-Duff and with other voice teachers—I feel that I know in my ear just where I'm overexpressing something; and I see others who don't and they just go crazy.

INTERVIEWER   One of the reasons that you reached the top is because you worked, and worked, and worked. We talked to the Lunts, and Lynn was saying very much the same things—about how she'd stand in a mirror and see how gracefully she could arch her arm and hand. You don't hear young people talking about this quite this way, or am I wrong?

HAYES   You certainly are not. They would scorn this whole thing.

INTERVIEWER   Well, that's what I mean.

HAYES   Why, it frightened the wits out of me, you know, the way I'd feel: "Oh, dear, I'm a mechanical marvel—and not even a mechanical marvel. I'm just a mechanical object up there—and shame on me." And yet I have worked with young actresses quite recently, whom I've seen suffering, going through the same suffering that I went through thirty-odd years ago, because each performance is for them an almost insurmountable hurdle.

INTERVIEWER   Because they don't have the technique?

HAYES   Because they don't know whether God is going to come down that night and touch them on the shoulder. And I think, you know, that you just shouldn't depend on God for that. You have to be able to just call on something within yourself. And I cannot believe that learning a fair knowledge of the use of yourself, which is the actor's only instrument— as Heifetz learned to use that violin and Horowitz learned to use that piano—I just don't think that my learning as much as I could learn to use my instrument for the interpretation of an author's thought—I don't think my learning that took me too far away from understanding the author's thought. You see, that's the trouble—the young people, some of them, sometimes feel that if you get too far away from this inner search for the truth of what you're doing and think only of the outside, of how you communicate it, of how you put it before the world—they seem to be fearful that they will lose touch with that seeking for the inner truth. And this is where I worry sometimes and wonder if they don't misinterpret the

Method, and whether it doesn't fall down there because they miss that step which to me is vital. I think you can seek after the understanding of the author's meaning, and you must seek that; and you must know that character inside out, and you must know how that character operates in life as related to you—how you yourself would react in that same position. All of these things the Method holds with. And I hold with it, too, because this is one of the things that just goes on, that an actor does instinctively—this is the instinct—but then, beyond that, how do you communicate this when you've achieved it?

INTERVIEWER   Willi Schmidt, the German director from the Schiller Theatre in Berlin, said that you must stick to the intent of the author—the intent of the author is in the lines. And Schmidt added that there is too much theorizing among our actors. He cited the fact that when he directs he likes to get the people up on the stage right away—he doesn't want all this theorizing. He wants to work at the scenes and on the lines, over and over again. In a sense, that's what you were saying, if I understood you correctly.

HAYES   Yes. And it's a real, definite cleavage between my generation and the present generation. Eric Portman, at a meeting that was held on the stage of the theatre in which we were playing in *A Touch of the Poet* last year, said this very thing. He said, "I don't understand this. I've been working with one of your best directors"—he was referring to Harold Clurman—"I had the play for a year, the director had the play for more than a year, and we both had a chance to study it and learn what we felt it meant. And then all I wanted at rehearsals was to get on my feet and find the best way of projecting what I had learned in my study of this play. Instead of which," he said, "for five days we sat about while the play was described to us and explained to us, and we discussed what we felt about it." Well, of course, you know, I sympathized with Eric. There was a great deal of groaning from the front, from the young people, when he said this, and I knew that he was saying something extremely unpopular, but I sympathized with him very much, because, curiously enough, this business of opening up these secret places of an actor's heart, of some kind of secret understanding that I have with that author and am going to also have with that audience . . . Now, there are secret places in my heart and I cannot open these up and talk about them with a director and with my fellow players. I expect, and have nearly all my life sensed, that my fellow players have reacted to them, have sensed them, have felt them in performances—and in rehearsal, when we are on our feet and working. I have sensed their secrets, too, but to talk about them is to me embarrassing and destructive.

INTERVIEWER Well, it's the same way with playwrights, isn't it? They don't like, many of them, to talk about what they are writing, because they have the feeling that once they talk about it, they somehow lose a sort of freshness when they get to the typewriter.

HAYES Yes. For instance, Tyrone Guthrie—speaking of playwrights—says he asked James Bridie once what a play was about. "Give me," he said, "the real meaning of this play." Bridie said, "How do I know, I only wrote the thing." Well, Guthrie pressed him, and finally Bridie said, "A play—a masterpiece in the theatre—is something like an iceberg, because nine-tenths of its meaning lies below the surface of the consciousness of the writer."

INTERVIEWER Just to get another viewpoint. Take a play like *The Visit*—I don't know whether you saw *The Visit*.

HAYES You bet.

INTERVIEWER Now, there are people who disagree on the merits of this play. There are people who think it is a fine play, that it is meaningful. There are people who think it's a cynical, a nihilistic play. You can discuss, certainly, that play. The author has his idea, and so on, but it still is open to discussion. And might not a director like Clurman, who approaches directing in this way—might he not think it is a good idea for the actors to discuss it, for the actors to work out what they feel about it? I can imagine two or six people reading that thing and getting quite a different idea. So might there not be some justification for some of this discussion, in order to try to get perhaps a deeper meaning in the play which may escape somebody, or a different meaning which your own mental apparatus may prevent you from seeing?

HAYES This all happens naturally and normally in the course of rehearsals. A director says, "Oh, I think that you must play that scene with more brightness," and another actor stops and says, "What are you talking about, I have a different, a completely different, concept of this scene"—you see? And another says, "Oh, no, no, I don't see it that way." And there are sometimes very heated discussions. This, to me, is exciting and stimulating. But this sitting about and exploring the meaning of the play is nerve-racking to me and it depletes me of my sense of creativity—or something.

INTERVIEWER May I ask you something else attached

to this? You are an actress who has played a great variety of roles. I have often wondered, while watching you in a play, how you, who are not the person you are playing, gets the feel of this person. I have felt that you must know, that you must have lived, this character's life. What can you say about that? What must be in an actress's make-up or in an actress's experience in life to be able to understand this great variety of hearts and minds?

HAYES I don't know. I just . . . Let's put it this way. What is talent? Perhaps it is an instinct for understanding the human heart. I really think that actors—perhaps that is why we're supposed to be so volatile and so emotional. You can't understand with exceptional clarity all the pain, the hidden pain, and some of the almost painful joys of people's hearts without becoming a little overemotional, you know; and I guess we can't ever be cool and collected and detached as most people, because we have either been given this gift or developed the gift of much understanding than is good for us.

INTERVIEWER What you are saying is that artists, writers, painters have an extrasensory reaction to so many things, and that is why they're high-strung.

HAYES And understanding. Yes.

INTERVIEWER That's right. Because they feel more deeply, they reflect the light better than the average person, let us say. I don't think this sounds pretentious. I think it's pretty close to the truth. And this is why you feel that an actor should have more experience—shouldn't be a child actor—because a good actor needs this experience in life.

HAYES Frankly, I do believe that. I never thought of it until you asked the question, but I believe that that was what was in my mind when I thought—I know it was, and you brought it out, thank goodness, at last—that just the experience of traveling around with theatrical troupes and playing one character for weeks on end is not enough, and doesn't give as much material to that actor for the future as being out in school, associating with other people, and others one's own age, and learning—learning people. I think that's what I believe is more helpful to the young—to learn people.

INTERVIEWER You would say, then, that living mostly among actors is living in a world of make-believe.

HAYES Well, they're all people who are interpreters of people—we are all interpreters of people. And I think it is much more important, frankly, to get out and learn people —not only learn just the people that you encounter, but learn all about what people of all ages, of all times have written.

Craftsmanship is not enough. An actor must enrich his life by studying literature, science, philosophy, other countries, other peoples, other times.

INTERVIEWER How have you best learned life? You once said that you had the "subway method." Maybe you could describe the "subway method" for us.

HAYES That acting talent that I just defined as a peculiarly alert awareness of other people and their problems and their lives—maybe that asserted itself at an early age. But, whatever it was, I only know that I wasn't just saying to myself, "Now look, there's a man who holds one shoulder higher than the other and has a funny twist to his head and that'll be a good position to assume on the stage some day for effect." No, not that. I'm like some awful amateur self-taught psychologist, you see. I say, "That man has a shoulder that's higher and a peculiar twist of his head—why does he have that? What ever caused him to have that?" What, I wonder, went on in his youth. I wonder why he seems to be cringing away from something. I wonder where he lives and how he lives and what kind of life he has. And I'd sit there staring at the man with the uplifted shoulder, and figuring, figuring, figuring—this is sitting on the subway—and my mother's elbow would finally come into my ribs and she'd say, "Helen, stop staring." This, over and over again. And I would, you know, jerk out of it, but I'd be back again, I had to solve the mystery of that man who looked like that. I once wrote an article in which I told of all the visions that go across an actor's mind—this actor's mind—in the course of performance. Now, this is all part of the Method, but as Lynn Fontanne once said to me, "What is all this business about this Method that's supposed to relate everything to something that's happened to us? It's what we've been doing for years. You have to go on, be overwrought in a scene, all right, so you stand out in the wings and you think of the worst thing that's ever happened to you, and then you go on, you're overwrought—that's what we've been doing ever since I can remember, isn't it?" Well, anyway, this one, this actor, has been doing, apparently, the Method. When I was preparing for my role of the duchess in Anouilh's *Time Remembered*, I had some difficulty capturing the spirit of the role, until one day in Boston, while listening to the radio, I heard some music written by Giles Farnaby for the virginal —you know, one of those sixteenth-century instruments. I listened for about half an hour, and suddenly the idea came to me. That old duchess, I told myself, is like the music, light, dainty, period, pompous, tinkling. And, poor me, I'd been playing her like a bass drum. I had one scene in *Victoria Regina* that I played like one of my poodles. Believe it or not, it was just extraordinary how that communicated. And this vision came across my eyes once about that scene . . . Now that gets into those secret things I mentioned before: that if you ever said at rehearsal, "Well, I think that this scene is like a poodle dog," that's the end of that—you'd never get it, you'd never capture it. It's your secret with the audience and with the playwright. But, anyway, it was the scene in which Disraeli was buttering up the old queen something shamelessly, and he was just paying her these florid compliments and going on—and it was a long speech, you see, and on and on he went. I sat absolutely immobile. I didn't blink an eye. And there were times when the communication was so great —well, it wasn't very nice of me, in fact, it was naughty of me, but the audience would start to laugh, and finally break into applause in the middle of the actor's speech. But it was only that inside I was just blowing up and I knew just how it felt, because I had a poodle that used to just sit, and he'd almost look intoxicated when I'd say, "Oh, Turvey, you are the most beautiful dog, Turvey, you are so beautiful, what a good animal . . ." And I'd do this just for my own amusement, and watch this poodle become a little, just a little, intoxicated—and believe me every night for the thousand and some performances of that play, I saw that poodle. And I had other things, of course. There was a famous moment in *Coquette*—I didn't know what really true way to accept the news that my lover had been shot and was dead. I just didn't. There are a thousand ways that you could accept a scene like that. And I remembered a picture on the front of one of the tabloids—the *News* or the *Mirror*—of a mother standing over her son's grave. He was a gangster, in Chicago, and this coffin was being lowered, and this woman was standing there and she was holding herself as if she'd had a terrible, terrible pain in her insides. And I knew that this was the complete, complete reaction to something like this. You'll find in the reviews of *Coquette*, they spoke of that scene and the way I played it—this moment.

INTERVIEWER   You have given us a most articulate expression of your creative process. Some actors, I have found, cannot.

HAYES   I think that if you'd caught me some years ago I would have been inarticulate, too. But everybody has been asking me so much for the last ten, twelve, fifteen years, you know, that I just said to myself, "Oh, goodness, I can't keep on saying, 'Well, I don't know,'" so I've had to think this stuff out.

INTERVIEWER Do you think, then, that actors can be made?

HAYES I think that they can be given a good solid set of scales, a good knowledge of the use of their instrument. But I am not so sure that an actor's spirit can be created within him.

INTERVIEWER I suppose that goes for writing, too.

HAYES I think that an awful lot of what's happening—it embarrasses me, it embarrasses me frightfully to hear actors picking themselves apart; it would embarrass me to be saying these things while I was working on a part. I couldn't tell you until after it was all over—and well over—what I did with anything. But I couldn't do it while it was happening.

INTERVIEWER In other words, we would be very unwise, if you were in a play right now, to ask you the secrets of what you were doing in the play?

HAYES I bet I wouldn't be able to put it into words too clearly. I hope I wouldn't.

INTERVIEWER You mean it's only afterward that you can actually clarify what happened?

HAYES And I would like to add this. Laurette Taylor was a genius. And I was so angry—irritated, not angry; but just scoffing, really—when I went to hear Robert Lewis in some of his "Method or Madness" lectures a year ago. I mean, when he reported a whole long discussion with Laurette, and what Laurette said about acting and how she did this and how she did that and the other. I can't imagine Laurette saying that. I knew her very closely and we were together all the time when she was in Chicago doing *The Glass Menagerie*, and I just cannot imagine that she would ever sit down and talk about how she did something. In fact, she really was awful when it came to trying to get her to talk about herself.

INTERVIEWER What is it that you don't think an actress like Laurette Taylor would talk about?

HAYES Well, it was her means of achieving certain things.

INTERVIEWER You are saying, are you not, that she was not an actress who analyzed her performance?

HAYES That's right. She wouldn't really know—Laurette wouldn't know. She would just know what was the one right way to do it out of the many ways that you could do something. Laurette would just do it the right way.

INTERVIEWER Was she more of the instinctive, intuitive actress—more so than most others? More than you, for instance?

HAYES Yes. Oh, yes. I'm anything but that, and I sometimes am so envious of those others who can defy . . . You see, I think that mine is more made talent.

INTERVIEWER I don't go along with that.

HAYES Oh, I had plenty to begin with, but I made a lot of it, and had to.

INTERVIEWER We said that Laurette is the one exception that proves the rule. I mean, she is the maverick . . .

HAYES An exceptional person. And Bea Lillie, also a genius. And there may be others, but they do more harm than good, those people, because then other people think, "Well that's the way you get to be wonderful like Laurette Taylor and Bea Lillie, who just blindly perform."

INTERVIEWER That's a good point, because what you're saying is that people get misled into thinking that this . . .

HAYES Can be the way to do it; that that's a good way to do it. And it isn't, because that way is only for certain ones, especially favored by God. We all don't have that same degree of talent and genius.

INTERVIEWER What do you mean by the process of elimination in acting in rehearsals?

HAYES This process of elimination is one that I just enjoy because it gives me courage to do things. I think you have to take a chance, and I just seem to have to do all the wrong things in any part before I can get to do the right ones. This is apropos of what I said a little while ago. I said it's such hard work for me—acting—and always has been, to get to a good performance, and I look with such envy at those who just walk in and don't do anything wrong. I don't mean that they're rigidly and uninterestingly correct and perfect; I mean they just have a right way of approaching things, while I have to go through all the wrong ways. But that doesn't matter. It's important to go through some way, and not to rehearse in whispers. And this is what I mind you see. It's the people at rehearsals—and I know it's fear, a fear of doing the wrong thing that makes them do nothing, do you see? And then it makes them scared to death when it comes the time to come on, deliver. I watched Kim Stanley do that the day she rehearsed in whispers the whole time in *A Touch of the Poet*—and I knew she was absolutely beside herself. Now I'll tell you a little anecdote about the great Edith Evans. Edith Evans was playing Lady Fidget in *The Country*

Wife, and one day Edith was carrying on like a maniac up there, like one demented—posturing, waving imaginary fans, doing crazy things with them—when, from the back of the auditorium, came the voice of Tony Guthrie, who was rehearsing us. And he said, "Edith, what in God's name are you doing?" And she went down to the footlights and said, "I'm trying things—I'd rather be an ass in front of my fellow actors than do nothing on opening night." Now, see, of this I approve. I approve this with my whole heart. Do anything, do anything that comes to your mind, but don't ever allow yourself to be afraid to try things, because it just might be that something glorious will come out. Of course, nine times out of ten it's terrible. That's what I mean by the process of elimination: I do all the wrong things, and then I finally get down to maybe what's right—I hope.

INTERVIEWER Have you felt the absence of classical training? The French actor, for instance, in the Comédie Française, gets a chance to play in works of Molière, Racine, and to develop a sort of style for these works. Have you felt the absence of such opportunity for yourself and American actors in general?

HAYES You bet I have, and I've minded it very much. Above all things I'd like to have, to feel, the courage—and I do lack the courage—to attack the classics. I would love to play Hecuba in *The Trojan Women.* I just love that lament—Hecuba's lament over her broken grandson, you know, Hector's son. I'll tell you a secret. In the summer of 1959 I went abroad, and when we got to Greece I went to that outdoor theatre in Epidaurus. I just stood in the empty theatre—that extraordinary theatre with its extraordinary accoustics—and there wasn't a soul there. I had Hecuba's speech all marked, and I stood there on the stage, and my two young companions, a lawyer and his wife, went and sat way in the back and I read those lines to them. It was grand. Yes, it is a terrible loss to me that I don't know the classics better than I do, that I just have read the plays, some of the great plays of Greece, and some of, not all of, Shakespeare—and that I don't know it all as well as I wish I knew it. When I did attempt to play in Shakespeare, I felt ill at ease and inadequate.

INTERVIEWER Would this be due to the lack of repertory theatres and classical theatres?

HAYES Well, in my particular case it was that I was that child actress who was just going along, wasting all that time being an actress and not training. If I had been at a good drama school, if I had been sent over to England, or if this lovely school of Shakespeare in Stratford, Connecticut, had existed, I could have . . .

INTERVIEWER   Actually, what can a school do? Once you grant the point that you made so well—that one of an actress's greatest assets is having intuition for the human heart—what beyond this does a school do?

HAYES   It teaches you the best way to interpret what you feel, and what you have understood that the author meant when he wrote that play. And there are certain areas of the theatre in which I don't know the right way or the best way to make that step of interpretation—and that's in the classics —because I didn't have any training. But a school could have taught me that.

INTERVIEWER   To what extent is television valid training for the stage?

HAYES   I used to have high hopes for television as valid training for the stage, and I've been exploring it, working in it, which is the only way I know to explore it—I don't think you can sit and watch it and get anything; I can't. I think, I still think, it is better than no training, but I don't think it's as good—nothing is as good—as working in the living theatre. And I don't mean particularly the commercial theatre. I mean the living theatre, if it's on a university campus or a civic theatre in Peoria, or a little theatre group in Oswego, or wherever there is living theatre and people can go out on the stage. But I think they should have the guidance of trained and professional people. But getting back to television. I thought it was good because in comparison movies didn't allow an actor enough practice in sustaining—it's all done in the movies in little tiny bits.

INTERVIEWER   The short takes.

HAYES   Yes, the short takes; and this is a special, different kind of technique and I admire it. I think it's remarkable, you know, that Garbo could give those sensitive and beautiful performances under those conditions. But, goodness knows, I can't. I don't know how you do it, but they do it, and God bless them for it—those who have the gift for it and the training for it. But for young actors I do think it's sad—unless they're just going to be picture actors always—to be, you know, limited to that.

INTERVIEWER   Confined to the camera range.

HAYES   Yes, limited to that kind of work. Because there's no projection, there's none of that wonderful, exciting problem of trying to project to the last row of the gallery and still keep it within reality. That's a wonderful challenge, you know, arid it's lovely to be able to do it. True, in television, they are never going to learn about projection, and how to fill a theatre and yet never seem to be filling it—never declaim but still project. How do you do that unless you are told, unless you've studied it; and this is all very exciting and part of the things that make us love playing in the theatre. But I thought in television they'd learn to sustain—and that was good. They might not learn projection, they might not learn to move with grace and with authority, because they have no space to move in, but they would learn, at least, to carry on long things, you know, in a sustained role. This is so to some extent. But the thing that worries me now is what happened when I tried to do *The Cherry Orchard* on television. We finally achieved in the rehearsal hall a very good production—we felt, every actor felt, that this play had come to life. Then the director, who was a very fine, sensitive director—Dan Petrie—came around to discuss the play. And he said that it was fine, that it was beautiful; he said, "That was a fine performance of *The Cherry Orchard*, but I have some news for you, we're eight minutes over." So there we were, faced with having created Mr. Chekhov's mood as we felt he'd want it; felt that we had interpreted properly the mood that he had created in his writing—only we had to get eight minutes out of it! So we ended up playing it like one of those old-time George Abbott farces. My goodness, we rattled through that thing! And this was sad to me, and I thought, "Oh, dear! I don't know that I can ever look to this now as a means for people to learn the magic that is the theatre, the magic that is acting. How can you learn it when you are under such strain—and under such handicaps?" The whole cast was so dismayed by what had happened to us that I went down and played it for a week in Palm Beach with nearly the whole cast—a few of them couldn't go, they had other jobs, you see.

INTERVIEWER   Just for the pleasure of doing it?

HAYES   Yes. We played *The Cherry Orchard* in Palm Beach, then went out to Phoenix and played it. We had two weeks to play it and feel our way and achieve a performance of *Cherry Orchard*—which we did, I think. But isn't that sad?

INTERVIEWER   Yes.

HAYES   And now I don't know what to think about television.

INTERVIEWER   But I think it's wonderful that you did that for them—for those others in the cast.

HAYES   And for me! I needed it much more than they

did. I'd have been frustrated the rest of my life, doing it with those eight minutes out!

INTERVIEWER   How have you selected your plays over the years? What made you determine that you would take a role?

HAYES   Because I fell in love with it. And I didn't just fall in love with it because it was a character of nobility and perfection, I'm sure, because I am rather inclined to love the roles that I've played that have had some human, very human, frailities. But I have, for some reason or other, responded in my heart to that role and loved it and wanted to play it because I wanted . . .

INTERVIEWER   Which role are you talking about now?

HAYES   —Any role.

INTERVIEWER   Have you ever violated that precept?

HAYES   Yes, I've played plays for other reasons, and never successfully. I will never forget the time that we all launched ourselves in a play that we thought was going to be good for the public to see. We were going to goad the American people into a true understanding of the peril of the times, in a play called *Candle in the Wind*. Some pretty good talents were mixed up in it—Maxwell Anderson wrote it and Alfred Lunt was the director and I was the star. So we went on there, you know, went marching in there like crusaders and put on a play not because—we all knew that it was a faulty play, and I knew that I wasn't right for the role, but, oh, we had a message to give. And did we fall on our faces! The message went out the window—everything went out the window!

INTERVIEWER   Maxwell Anderson was, perhaps, fulfilling what he felt was his highest function as a writer. He was relating to the pressing problems of humanity at the time and so it was valid for him to try even if he failed. You, as an artist, to be a little hifalutin about this, feel an identity with this. I mean, in this case you did, and you did want to forward human aspirations by bringing it to the stage. Does this enter your considerations at all, this matter of art and human progress?

HAYES   No, and it isn't just because I came a cropper in *Candle in the Wind* that has made me shrink away, cringe away, from any such use of the theatre. I never would use the theatre as a platform again for a sermon, you know, or a pulpit, or whatever you call it.

INTERVIEWER   There has been much feeling this season, and in several seasons past, that Broadway hasn't related to life. The theatre is not grappling with the central problems of today, and perhaps this is a reason why the theatre isn't as powerful a force as it should be. The theatre is one of our most important arts, and if art becomes separated from the great concerns of man at the moment, it loses its place. So, in a certain sense, isn't this a bad thing—for actors, writers, for everyone, not to feel that the theatre should be saying something, should be speaking out?

HAYES   But I believe so firmly that the theatre does have a message and does say something. When people are writing of the heart and spirit of human beings in certain situations, from that there is a message, a definite message, for anyone in any time. But I just don't think if you set out to write a message in the form of a play, that you could possibly succeed as a play with a message.

INTERVIEWER   You would say that there's a message in *A Touch of the Poet,* that there is a message in *Mrs. McThing?*

HAYES   As there is a message in *Fiorello!*

INTERVIEWER   Or *The Miracle Worker.*

HAYES   Or *The Miracle Worker.*

INTERVIEWER   How do you work on a role before going into rehearsal? You read the script, of course, but how do you try to get to the heart of your role?

HAYES   That's an interesting question, and I haven't thought much about it. I just know that I read the play over and over, but in the course of that reading it over and over I do not try to memorize lines, although, believe me, I would be very glad if some of them stuck in my head, so that during that wonderful period of rehearsal, where the thing begins to come to life inside your heart and head, you wouldn't have to be handicapped—you wouldn't have that hurdle of lines in the way. It would be lovely if you could learn that in advance, but I never have. But, really, when I'm reading that play in advance, what I'm doing, I guess, is trying to just improve my acquaintance with the play.

INTERVIEWER   Did you, in preparing for *Victoria Regina,* do a lot of reading about Victoria?

HAYES   No, I didn't. And furthermore, I've never liked to do that. When I played *Mary of Scotland* . . . You'll find a whole row of books over there on the wall about Victoria, and you'll find quite a number of books about Mary Stuart, because by the time I had played those parts for a long while, my interest in those people—I had become so intimate with those two women that I couldn't learn enough about them. But I didn't do that in advance, because I think . . . I don't know whether I thought this out then, or whether I've looked back and said, "Now why was it that I shied away from all research about Victoria before I did it?" And Harriet Beecher Stowe—I didn't do any research about Harriet Beecher Stowe, and the reason is that I think that whoever writes the play, has written it—a character—from their point of view, and you have to interpret that author's idea of the character.

INTERVIEWER That goes back to what Willi Schmidt said. You do what the playwright had in mind, you learn this character, and not what went on twenty years before.

HAYES Yes, that's true. I wouldn't want to muddle my head up with a whole lot of different people's ideas of what Mary Stuart was like. It was what Maxwell Anderson felt she was like that I was concerned with.

INTERVIEWER Now, through the author's lines you get the feeling of the person. But do you get a sufficient feeling of the person to . . . ?

HAYES You jolly well better, or don't play that part. Because if you haven't got his message, then that's the play you turn down. As I said, sometimes I have gone into plays because people advised me to, because people thought it was right for me to be in a particular play—or some reason, you know, such and such a role was a good change in my career. All those phony reasons that you get except the one important one—that you love it, that you understand it, that you know that you get some message from it, and feel that you have something to give to it, and that's the only basis on which I've ever chosen a play successfully.

INTERVIEWER What special problems do you recall that you encountered with *Mary of Scotland*, and how did you solve them?

HAYES You're talking about the business of the height, I suppose.

INTERVIEWER That's one thing. In fact, let's broaden the question. I would like to know what problems you've encountered and solved in plays.

HAYES Well, one of the chief problems that I always had with a play, say, like Mary Stuart, a character like Mary Stuart, and Cathy in *A Farewell to Arms,* when I did it on the screen, and other such characters who are primarily highly romantic figures, was that it's very hard for me, and always was hard for me, to consider myself a romantic figure. I just didn't, you know. I felt I was accepting the role and being cast against my physical type and my very temperamental type. I just don't—and never did, you know, even in my youth—ever think of myself as a very romantic figure. There-

fore, those were the problems that beset me in the playing of
Mary Stuart, who was, after all, a great romantic figure as
written by Maxwell Anderson. And in *A Farewell to Arms*.
How I overcame them, I don't know for sure, but I know for
one thing that I thought of myself in Mary Stuart—I had a
picture of myself as a . . . It was kind of maybe like self-
hypnosis, and maybe I managed to do a little hypnotizing of
the audience to accept this vision that I had created for myself,
of myself in the role. Oh, I believe, you know, firmly in minor
miracles happening in the theatre all the time. I just do believe
it, and I know that that was one of the minor miracles of my
career, in *Mary of Scotland*, because I did think of myself as
a tall woman of queenly bearing. I did think of myself as
wholly romantic and passionate—all the things that she was
supposed to be; and then with great purity of being as well,
as Max had conceived it. And I have some photographs—I
don't have them here—that people took from the audience
during performances, and someone has one of me with my
arm out and a cape around it, and it isn't just a flamboyant
dramatic thing, it *is* Mary Stuart, and I swear to you that that
happens. It's like those spirit photographs of Conan Doyle's.
When I was out there on the stage playing, what they got on
that film—they got Mary Stuart, they didn't get me. There's
a very clear one—my face and my features are there—but
there's something about what I had in my head that is there on
that film. Now, isn't that odd?

INTERVIEWER   No, I wouldn't say it was odd.

HAYES   Well, that's miracles. Magic.

INTERVIEWER   What are your working habits when you
are in a play? I bring this up because Lynn Fontanne was
telling us that when she is in a play she cannot do anything
else except rest, let us say, all day to conserve herself for the
performance. Now, you are a woman who has given a good
deal of herself to public life. How have you reconciled your
activities? Have you given up participating in public when
you've had a role, or have you continued?

HAYES   I'll tell you, it's been very difficult for me in the
last years because once I got into public life, as you call it, it
was very hard to retreat—it's still hard to retreat. There are
things that are very dear to my heart that I couldn't any more
toss aside than I could walk out on my family, you know, or
could have ever just brushed them aside because I was playing
in a theatre and had a problem there. So it's crept up on me. I
used to say, "Why is it that I can do all this—and Lynn and
all the others can't. Just look at me—why did God give me all

this strength?" But I can't do it any more as I used to, and I've tried so hard to balance the two. And I don't think it's just age. I think that the strain has got too much for me, so that, unfortunately, in the last two plays that I was in, I was tired and ailing and strained all the time and a prey to colds and such ailments. I look back on *Time Remembered* and *Touch of the Poet* and shudder a little bit, and I know that it was because I was straining so hard to try to keep up that dual life. I simply can't do it.

INTERVIEWER   In other words, you would say that you tried to be the public citizen as well as the artist, and you have found that it's not easy to mix them.

HAYES   I don't think it is. I don't think it's possible to mix them to any extent, and the rather tragic thing with me right now is that the recollection of the terrible strain, the additional strain, that those two roles put on me has made me flinch away from reading plays and settling on a play. I just know that I have read play after play and have just said oh no, no, no—and I don't know for sure whether it isn't the memory of those last two winters that were so miserable.

INTERVIEWER   So you find it easier to work for television, for instance, where it's a drive for one performance.

HAYES   And it's not such an interruption to this other side of my life, which I would like very much to continue. I keep saying to myself, "What are you doing? You're an actress, that's what you have to give to the world—not going out making speeches for WAIF and National Foundation and traveling around the country." I went on a one-night-stand tour for the National Foundation three years ago when I wasn't working—before *Time Remembered*—and I've been working hard on these things and I love it, and I get great satisfaction out of what I've done for them. But I keep on telling myself I'm an actress and this is my profession.

INTERVIEWER   You feel that the artist should be satisfied that he doesn't have other obligations beyond giving of his art.

HAYES   I believe this, and I think that the other people were much wiser than I—Kit Cornell and Lynn and all of them who have kept themselves fresh for their work. I was . . . I don't know what I'm going to do. I remember once lovely Mildred Dunnock saying something to me—we were doing a radio thing together years ago, and I was fretting because I was down there, and it was something to do with my children. It was a special day, maybe somebody was having a party, a birthday, I don't know, but I was down rehearsing for the radio, and I was the whole day in that rehearsal. I was shaken inside and, of course, I blurted it out at some point, you see, that I felt oh, so awful, that "I just don't know what I'm doing with my life. I'm here doing this and there's, you know, whatever it was at home"—and Mildred's head came around slowly and she said, "Oh, you live in a guilt box, too!"

INTERVIEWER   Which of the roles that you have played have you enjoyed most? From which have you received your greatest satisfaction?

HAYES   Oh, have you got any quick and definite answers from people on that question? It's like asking a mother which of her children is her favorite. I really wonder if anybody else has been able to tell you.

INTERVIEWER   Do you feel you might offend anyone?

HAYES   Oh, gracious no. It's that every role that you play . . . I've told you that I pick roles on the whole because I respond to them, some need in me at that moment is filled by that particular role at that time; and it isn't just the need for success, it's a need for some—I don't know, the role answers something that I want, and then I say, "Oh, I want to do this. Believe me, when I said I wanted to do *Victoria Regina* I was passionately in love with the play and that role, and I didn't have a word of encouragement from anybody about that. My husband thought that I was out of my mind. There was no play there, it didn't have any form, it didn't have any climaxes, it didn't have anything. It was just—what was it?— just a series of little scenes, like a pageant. And they thought that nobody but me . . . I just loved it. I wanted to be that woman.

INTERVIEWER   What do you think it satisfied in you at that particular time?

HAYES   When I said needs at a certain time, you know, I don't mean that you're starving for some kind of . . .

INTERVIEWER   There's nothing Freudian then?

HAYES   Oh, I don't think that. I just think that what happened to me in that play was that I loved seeing somebody who had just gone about doing her job well, being made into someone exciting. I think that's a wonderful thing, to know somebody who's exciting because she did her job well. She didn't have any thing else that was exciting about her, did she? She was little, a kind of dumpling of a woman, and she wasn't a bit amusing. She just didn't have one ingredient of an exciting human being about her but that one thing—that she saw her duty and she did it, and she did it well. She did it untiringly, and she triumphed over everything in herself and in the world in which she lived.

INTERVIEWER   What can actors do to increase their position in the community? Isn't there still some vestige in the public mind of actors as clowns?

HAYES   I don't think it's the actors' fault so much as the public's fault. I think that there is one basic, terrible misunderstanding about actors that I keep reading about in books, you know. I have never in my life known a thoroughly conceited actor. I think that actors are the least conceited people in the world. I have known ever so many conceited writers, and I've known ever so many conceited . . . You just look at Mr. Hemingway—that man thinks he's God. There's no question in his mind that he is a completely perfect artist in what he set out to be in life. And I've known conceited people in all kinds and walks of life, you know, even people working in your kitchen sometimes—they just don't really think that anybody can do it as well as they can. But an actor by the very nature of his profession is never allowed ever to get over an inner terror that this is the time he's not going to do it, and a constant straining to encourage himself that he can make it. Imagine, at my age, at the age of Alfred Lunt and of all such people—and not only age but our tenure of service, of office in our profession . . . Do you suppose that anyone could go up to a lawyer, to Clarence Darrow, and say you were terrible yesterday when you stood up before that—that was a dreadful mess you made there? But we take it from a director every time we go into a new play. And we must, and we want it, and we're heartsick if we don't get it. You know what happens to people—even like us? After all the time we've been in the profession, if a director isn't telling us that we were bad in this scene or that—if we don't get something like that from a director, we're terrified. We think we're so bad he doesn't know what to say to us. This is how far from conceited actors are, and I assure you that I've worked with . . . You know, Kim Stanley, with all her fighting and everything else—that's the basis of Kim's fighting. It's such a personal insecurity about herself—"Oh, how terrible I am, I can't do this." And the greater the insecurity is, the more they put on this act of bravado sometimes. I just worked in a silly television show with Jason Robards, Jr., and I saw this fellow with his haunted eyes—was he going to do right by Mary Roberts Rinehart's *The Bat*—was he going to get that right? And taking the direction, his eyes locked with the director's eyes, and I used to sit on the side and watch him and think it's extraordinary, that here he is . . .

INTERVIEWER   Acting, then, does not get easier over the years for you.

HAYES   No, but there I'm talking about young ones. You say, "How can we get more dignity in the community?" Well, I just think that people ought to have a little more understanding and dignity in their attitude toward actors—a great many people. If anyone says, of course, that actors are children and not grown up, I agree with him, because I think that an actor has a childlike approach to life because he's like somebody who's in school at the age of fifty, and taking his homework from teacher and being kept after school when he doesn't do right. I mean we can't grow up because . . .

INTERVIEWER   He's constantly being scolded—Is that what you would say?

HAYES   Not only scolded, but guided, and we can't get that wonderful kind of solid maturity when we are actors. And also, don't forget that I said another thing. We're volatile, and we're overly emotional because we are so aware of our own pain and doubts and fears in life, just as we are aware of those of everyone around us. And when you are in on those inner secrets of people's hearts and souls, you can't just become as wonderfully detached and cool-headed as a surgeon or a legal mind. I defy you to. So we are people who work with our emotions and deal with the emotions. Acting in the theatre is the most direct and effective approach to emotions that has ever been devised, isn't it? It really is, I think, above music and everything else. It just goes clean right through to the emotions. So perhaps we don't have the kind of accepted maturity, but I think we have a far greater maturity than an awful lot of these characters I meet outside.

INTERVIEWER   What part of acting is drudgery?

HAYES   All of it.

INTERVIEWER   All of it? Well, what are the rewards, apart from the monetary? What are the rewards of acting?

HAYES   That one moment of miracle when you and the audience get together.

INTERVIEWER   How do you feel this miracle?

HAYES   I don't know.

INTERVIEWER   I mean, what does it feel like? Is there any way to describe it?

HAYES   It's the moment when you have realized exactly what you meant to realize in a part—what that message was that you got when you first read it, what you thought. Then there's the drudgery of trying to get to that, to reach that, and to have it come out of you. It often doesn't, but some one time maybe it will. Maybe at a magic rehearsal—like that—this thing takes life.

INTERVIEWER   How many times during a run does this happen?

HAYES   Oh, so few times, so very few times. And the rest of the time is just trying to—what is it?—not re-create that moment but to approach it.

INTERVIEWER   To simulate?

HAYES   Yes, simulate. I couldn't think of anything but assimilate. Yes, simulate that moment—that's what you're trying to do all the time, and that's pure drudgery.

INTERVIEWER   In other words, in a long run or in a short run, that miracle doesn't happen very often?

HAYES   No, it happens only a few times and we're so grateful for that, and we are ready for all the drudgery in between.

INTERVIEWER   That's very interesting, because we tried to encourage Maureen Stapleton, for instance, about her performance that we had seen, and she said, "Oh, no, we were terrible." And then I asked her a couple of days later how it went, and she said, "Oh, it was terrible last night, too."

HAYES   I know, I know.

INTERVIEWER   What do you expect of a director when you are working with him? I mean, some actors don't want direction.

HAYES   Oh, I crave it. But I'm trying to think now what I mind about all this philosophizing that goes on. I know I suddenly, when we were rehearsing *A Touch of the Poet,* blurted out once to Harold Clurman—and this may sum up what I want from a director—"Stop telling me what everything means. Just tell me how to do it." I think that's it! I mind, I detest, the invasion of my own spiritual and intellectual grasp on the character, and on the whole philosophy of the play. I think I know about that. Well, like Portman said . . . And I may be all wrong, but once a director begins to probe and invade that particular area of my preparation and rehearsal, my courage is shaken, and when my courage is shaken, you know, like Shaw said, "God deliver me from a frightened Englishman"—well, God deliver anybody from me when I'm scared. I blew up at Clurman, so terribly, and I couldn't believe I had done it. But he was barging in there where he didn't belong. That was my business, but his business was to get me around that stage and find ways and means . . . Instead it was I who was doing that. I was saying, "Looka here, I come on here and everybody talks about me being a busy woman and I'm tired." I'll have to go into detail so you will understand. I said to him, "I'm supposed to be a tired woman, and you have me walk through this door, walk over here and sit down in a chair and sit there for the whole rest of the act, while Sara, the daughter, Kim Stanley, talks about you're (that's me) wearing yourself to the bone for him, you're doing this, you're doing that . . ." I said, "You give the audience no picture of a woman moving, you just have her walk in and sit down." I said, "How could Nora have that much freedom in the course of a morning in that inn. How could she be free long enough to sit down . . . All right, Mr. O'Neill wrote it without giving any direction that she was doing anything, but I've got to move, I've got to do something. I've got to give people a sense that I'm a woman who's busy." So here I was devising things to come in on—you know, wetting my hands, coming on wiping the dishwater off my hands. I said, "I've got to have something to move"—you know, moving about the stage and then, finally, sort of giving the sense that I have been working hard in that kitchen. So I walked in still looking around, as if to say, "Now what else is there for me to do here. There must be something else that I have to do in this room before I can sit down." Well, these are the things that I feel are in the director's province. The director should help me in my grasp on the spirit of the character. He should have those things ready to supply to me, so that my grasp of the character's whole being could be enlightened. But I think the directors are too often today taking over the actors' business of interpretation of the character and forgetting about their business as directors.

INTERVIEWER   In other words, the director should be the absolute master at rehearsal. He should be able to say, "I want you to do it this way," and he should decide whether it is satisfactory; and if it isn't satisfactory, to say, "Now do it this way."

HAYES   Yes.

INTERVIEWER   That's what you want from a director— you feel the business should be worked out between you and the director, or, at least, developed more by the director.

HAYES   Yes. I think the director ought to know something more about the mechanics of putting a thing on the stage—which is very, very important. Because, heaven help you, you can be expressing something so miraculously, but if you're way off in the wrong part of the stage, and if something else is happening on this part of the stage that detracts from you there . . . If some mechanical thing is against you, you can be acting your heart out, feeling and understanding, and everything can be happening inside of you—and yet you can never make it happen, because the director's part of it—the picture which he sees from the front, the overall picture—has not aided you in conveying that. Some directors just want you to get an understanding and let the actor just automatically do the rest. And we finally do it. But we do it as actors—saying now I'm going to go over here and I'm going to do this, and, you know, tell the stage manager that I want this prop here or there.

INTERVIEWER   In other words, some directors analyze more than they direct.

HAYES   We sometimes do what we shouldn't have to do, because we should just have a free mind to do our acting. There's a lot of that in the theatre today. George Abbott was so startled when we were working with Alan Schneider, a good director—modern school, you know. We'd go through the whole day's rehearsal when we were doing *The Skin of Our Teeth*, and then Alan would come and take each one of us aside and have these long talks about the meaning and the feel and everything else. We all though we knew what Thornton Wilder was about and everything—what we really wanted to know was where to go on the stage and how to best make the thing come off. And George Abbott said one day, "I don't understand this—I don't understand this." Well, George is old school, and a wonderful director, isn't he? So there you are. I really must call the hospital now.

Vivien Leigh

BIOGRAPHY

Born in Darjeeling India, in 1913, where her British parents were living, Vivien Leigh grew up in England. She studied acting at the Royal Academy of Dramatic Arts in London and also privately in Paris. Her first acting assignment was in the movies, as a schoolgirl in *Things Are Looking Up,* and her first stage appearance was in London in 1935 in *The Green Sash.* It was in *The Mask of Virtue,* at Oxford for the Oxford University Dramatic Society, that she scored her first major success.

Miss Leigh was soon asked to play with the Old Vic Company, and appeared in *Hamlet* as Ophelia, with Laurence Olivier (who was to become her second husband and from whom she was divorced in 1960), and as Titania in *A Midsummer Night's Dream.* Not long after, Miss Leigh won one of the most highly coveted—and fiercely contested—roles in the history of Hollywood, and one which was to bring her international renown and an Academy Award, Scarlett O'Hara in Margaret Mitchell's *Gone with the Wind.*

In 1940 Miss Leigh made her American stage debut as Juliet to Laurence Olivier's Romeo. Among the plays she has appeared in in England are Shaw's *The Doctor's Dilemma*, Thornton Wilder's *The Skin of Our Teeth*, Terence Rattigan's *The Sleeping Prince*, Noel Coward's *Look After Lulu*, and Tennessee Williams' *A Streetcar Named Desire*. During the war Miss Leigh toured the Middle East, entertaining the troops; and at other times has toured in Europe, Australia and New Zealand. She and Laurence Olivier played a season at the Shakespeare Memorial Theatre in Stratford. Her roles there included Viola in *Twelfth Night*, Lady Macbeth, and Lavinia in *Titus Andronicus*.

The last appearance in New York for Miss Leigh, before doing *Duel of Angels*, was with Sir Laurence in alternating performances of Shaw's *Caesar and Cleopatra* and Shakespeare's *Antony and Cleopatra*.

Miss Leigh has been in many movies in addition to *Gone with the Wind*, including *Caesar and Cleopatra, Anna Karenina, That Hamilton Woman, Waterloo Bridge*, and *A Streetcar Named Desire*, for which she won her second Oscar.

SETTING

Vivien Leigh had not yet returned from a Long Island sojourn at the home of friends when we arrived at the New York apartment she had rented for the Broadway run of Jean Giraudoux' *Duel of Angels*. She had recently closed in this in New York and was just about to take it on tour. Her housekeeper told us Miss Leigh would be back soon, and asked if we wouldn't have a drink while waiting. We found that we were once again in the living room of what we now decided was New York's most distinguished theatrical rooming house—Edith Meiser's duplex garden apartment in which we had interviewed Sir John Gielgud some months earlier. The room was much the same, although Sir John's phonograph had given way to a small old-type TV set.

After a quarter of an hour, a young man, Miss Leigh's secretary, pleasantly assured us that Miss Leigh would surely be right along, and, indeed, in a few minutes she did arrive, accompanied by John Merivale, young and handsomely bearded and a fellow player in *Duel of Angels*. He had driven her in from Long Island. Their entrance was in striking contrast to their stage entrances. A Caribbean extravaganza was a bit more in key with this entrance than that of the stately mood of nineteenth-century Aix of *Duel*.

Miss Leigh, with that beguiling smile that has devastated scores of stalwart heroes since and before Rhett Butler, came quickly into the room, full of apologies, and cast on a chair a straw beach hat fancifully decorated with imitation fruits. She wore a gay multicolored silk blouse, beige shantung slacks, canvas beach shoes; her hair was neatly held beneath a chartreuse chiffon scarf tied under her chin. Many bracelets with many bangles were on her wrists. About Miss Leigh one could easily use that word one can use only on the rarest occasions—delicious. Mr. Merivale sustained the Caribbean effect, with red slacks, a blue sports shirt—and that luxuriant beard.

There were apéritifs all around, preceded for Miss Leigh by a kiss for Poo-Jones, her Siamese cat. A move was made to get down to our interview, but not before her secretary called her out of the room on some bit of business, nor until various telephone calls were attended to, and Miss Leigh *did* want the secretary to get some of those *"divine"* lilies she loved so.

The interview appeared to be about to get under way, but Miss Leigh did have a question on just what it was all about—its purpose, originally explained to her agent, had obviously gotten scattered a bit in Miss Leigh's swirling life. And with the explanation, that devastating smile was on—but with just the slightest flicker of reproach, perhaps for broaching a somewhat serious subject on such a nice day. A few opening questions, and then Mr. Merivale took his leave. After getting into the interview, Miss Leigh talked with some interest, sometimes with a quiet animation, emphasizing a point with the flat of her palm brought down on her crossed leg. Throughout, the Leigh glamour never let down. Nearly all charm, there nevertheless was a hint that here could be a moody glamour.

The interview was recessed for lunch. Arriving for the occasion was Robert Helpmann, actor, dancer, choreographer and director of *Duel*. During lunch the conversation turned on directing Shakespeare; Katharine Hepburn playing Shakespeare at Stratford, Connecticut; future plans of Miss Leigh's. And Miss Leigh discussed some of the people she knew and admired, Bernard Berenson, for instance. ". . . the most elegant man I ever knew. I loved him. I think women do, men don't. My husband didn't."* Before the lunch was over,

* At the time of the interview Miss Leigh was still married to Laurence Olivier.

there were arrangements to be made for the evening. Would Mr. Helpmann join Miss Leigh and Mr. Merivale for dinner, the new Hitchcock film, *Psycho,* and dancing afterward—"I adore dancing," Miss Leigh added. And the secretary *must* get those divine lilies. And the car should come for her at six. And back to the interview. But not for long. Miss Leigh's is a busy house.

Interview

INTERVIEWER   According to one article I read, you went into the theatre as a reaction against your parents, who had sent you off to school. Is that really true?

LEIGH   Oh, no! I doubt it.

INTERVIEWER   This was not a sort of rebellion?

LEIGH   No, it's not true.

INTERVIEWER   I didn't quite believe it either. Well, then, what lured you into the theatre?

LEIGH   I haven't the vaguest notion. I was seven when Maureen O'Sullivan said, "What are you going to be when you grow up?" and I said, "I'm going to be an actress." I don't know why. I like dressing up, I think.

INTERVIEWER   As simple as that?

LEIGH   Absolutely.

INTERVIEWER   At what age did you start acting? What was the first role you ever remember having?

LEIGH   Mustardseed in *A Midsummer Night's Dream* at my convent school at Roehampton. By the way, my parents were absolutely delighted that I knew what I wanted to do.

INTERVIEWER   Well, I should think they would be.

LEIGH   And they were very pleased and they encouraged me all the way through. I had special dancing—ballet lessons—from the age of seven to thirteen. I was educated all over the place, in England, France, Germany and Italy.

INTERVIEWER   You were born in India?

LEIGH   Born in India. Came back to England when I was five, went straight to convent school—I was the youngest child there, and so I imagine I was rather spoiled. I remember I was allowed to take cats to bed with me. I've always been mad about cats.

INTERVIEWER   When you decided to go into the theatre as an actress, what training did you seek out?

LEIGH When I was at school in Paris, I had special lessons from Mademoiselle Antoine, who was an actress at the Comédie Française, and I was taken to every sort of play —which the other girls weren't allowed to go to—and so I felt very grand.

INTERVIEWER How does French training differ—what special qualities has it?

LEIGH I think it helps enormously in diction mostly. You know, English people don't pronounce, don't have very good diction on the whole, I don't think. And I think learning other languages . . . In France you have to pronounce very particularly and very clearly, and I think that learning French at a very early age helped me enormously. I think any classical training in a theatre is of enormous value.

INTERVIEWER Why?

LEIGH Just—well, because I think that classical plays require more imagination and more general training to be able to do. That's why I like playing Shakespeare better than anything else; because I think he wrote the greatest plays for people, and I think they require more to be brought to them. And I think one learns more through acting in classical plays than one does through anything else.

INTERVIEWER But there are some Method players . . .

LEIGH I don't understand. I don't know what that Method is. I've read Stanislavsky, naturally, and it seems to me that the Method is: if you say something, you've got to mean it, and you've got to say it as interestingly as possible. But that applies to life—and acting is life, to me, and should be.

INTERVIEWER It also applies, if I'm not mistaken, in the Method school here. That's Lee Strasberg's Actors Studio.

LEIGH I don't know anything about that. It's based on Stanislavsky, surely. But I don't understand. They never seem to do any comedies at Lee Strasberg's school, whereas comedy is much more difficult than tragedy—and a much better training, I think.

INTERVIEWER Why do you find that comedy is much more difficult?

LEIGH Because timing in comedy is . . .

INTERVIEWER Timing?

LEIGH It's much easier to make people cry than to make them laugh.

INTERVIEWER Why do you think that is so?

LEIGH I really don't know. I simply don't know why it should be more difficult, but it is.

INTERVIEWER   Well, now, we digressed for a moment. I wanted to get back to the schools that you attended.

LEIGH   I went to a convent school outside London, and I went to a day school in Biarritz. Then I went to a convent in Italy for a year; then I went to a finishing school in Paris for six months; then I went to a school in Germany, and I meant to be there six months and I stayed eighteen.

INTERVIEWER   What did you do about schools for your drama inclinations?

LEIGH   In Paris, as I said, I studied with Mademoiselle Antoine, and then when I came back to England I went straight to the Academy of Dramatic Arts.

INTERVIEWER   How long did you stay at the Academy? Did you complete the course?

LEIGH   No, no. I was in it only six months. Then I got married, and I went back after I was married and stayed there until I was going to have my child. But I just took the French course after that, because I liked particularly working with a wonderful teacher there called Mademoiselle Gracet—Alice Gracet was her name—and I did something in French and was abominable, absolutely shocking. And, in fact, all my reports from the Academy were very bad. I did a play called *Caesar's Wife*, by Somerset Maugham, and I remember the report saying, "Why were you so bad? Is it because you have too much sense of humor?" Well, I don't know what the reason was, but I was very shocking. I expect I didn't concentrate. But I loved my time there, particularly the fencing and the dancing and the elocution. I had two plays in French. One, Shaw's *Saint Joan*—and I remember that there was only one suit of armor, chain mail, which had been worn by Sybil Thorndyke, who is a good deal bigger than I am, so I had to stuff the toes with tissue paper. Well, I had—we all had to do various scenes. I had two scenes, the river scene and the cathedral scene. So the cathedral scene starts off kneeling down, and when I got up, my toes were standing straight up there, you know. You can imagine what kind of performance that was. Awful.

INTERVIEWER   There's a story that says you exacted a promise from your first husband that you would be permitted to continue your career in the theatre.

LEIGH   Oh, I don't think I was as severe as that. And, anyway, he was perfectly delighted that I should go on with it.

INTERVIEWER   What did you find—

LEIGH   He was a very good critic and very helpful to me in every possible sort of way.

INTERVIEWER What is it that you found so satisfying in the theatre?

LEIGH I think just making people laugh, and making them understand things. I like that.

INTERVIEWER Can you give me an example?

LEIGH No, I don't think I can. The playwright does the initial work, after all, and one is just an interpreter of what the playwright thinks, and therefore the greater the playwright, the more satisfying it is to act in the plays. For instance, Thornton Wilder—I loved playing *The Skin of Our Teeth*. And anything in Shakespeare. And the play I'm doing at present, *Duel of Angels,* I love because I think Giraudoux was a marvelous playwright. I think it's a fascinating play. Full of ideas. Full of truth. I think the audiences here have been quite extraordinary, but they're shocked by it, to begin with. They're far more shocked in this country by this sort of a play than they are in England. I can feel it. I can feel the audience being shocked.

INTERVIEWER How do you feel that?

LEIGH Well, because they take a breath before they dare laugh, for a start. They're not as quick, I don't think, with a play of this nature. I'm not complaining, because they've been perfectly marvelous. But they are—in fact, they suddenly think, "Oh, heavens, what she said," you know, and they're kind of alarmed. The very truth of the play, the sophistication of it, shocks them. And they're very fascinating to play to. They're dead quiet, and their enthusiasm is marvelous.

INTERVIEWER Have you noticed that in any other plays? The difference in the temper of an audience?

LEIGH Yes, yes, quite different. When we were here with the Cleopatras—the Shaw and the Shakespeare—they were much slower to laugh in the Shaw. I noticed that very much. And I think, on the whole, one has to speak much more slowly for an American audience. Of course, it's because of our English accent. That again—that you have to speak more slowly and make it much clearer for them than you do for an English audience—that is a very good thing, a very good challenge.

INTERVIEWER I wonder if this has something to do with the fact that we are getting increasingly used to being sort of bludgeoned on the head by some of our playwrights.

LEIGH I think that may be so. I think that may be so, very easily. But all classical plays—I mean, we play

Shakespeare all the time in England, and we play to all classes.

INTERVIEWER We're sort of coming into it now with the American Shakespeare Festival.

LEIGH Yes, and with the Lincoln Center. I think that's just the most marvelous thing here.

INTERVIEWER I'm going to ask you a question now, which shouldn't offend you—but have you found, or did you find in your early years, that your beauty was a handicap?

LEIGH Certainly I did, and it's very, very irritating, because people think that if you look fairly reasonable, you can't possibly act, and as I only care about acting, I think beauty can be a great handicap, if you really want to look like the part you're playing—which isn't necessarily like you.

INTERVIEWER As a matter of fact, it was said of you, largely I think in England, that your beauty had brought you success before you had learned the ABC's of acting.

LEIGH Absolutely true. But I remember the morning after *The Mask of Virtue*—which is the first play I did in the West End—that some critics saw fit to be as foolish as to say that I was a great actress. And I thought, that was a foolish, wicked thing to say, because it put such an onus and such a responsibility onto me, which I simply wasn't able to carry. And it took me years to learn enough to live up to what they said—for those first notices. I find it so stupid. I remember the critic very well, and have never forgiven him.

INTERVIEWER Who was the critic?

LEIGH W. A. Darlington.

INTERVIEWER Really?

LEIGH Yes. That's what he said in the *Daily Telegraph*, and I read it and I thought, "That very awful man."

INTERVIEWER Now that's rather interesting, because, on the basis of what you said, it appears that he recanted in subsequent reviews.

LEIGH Yes, he did.

INTERVIEWER You were aware of that?

LEIGH Oh, yes, I was certainly aware of it. I read all the reviews.

INTERVIEWER Because after that he began to grade you very carefully. For instance, in *The Doctor's Dilemma*, he said Miss Leigh had performed a remarkable job in that play. Shaw didn't give her too much to work with . . .

LEIGH No, it's a wretched role.

INTERVIEWER But, he went on, she came through, and

now it remains to be seen whether she has the emotional depth to carry on in the theatre. I mean, he was always waiting for you to bring something forth.

LEIGH   Yes.

INTERVIEWER   Actually, to get back to this matter of beauty in the theatre—you say it was a handicap. I'm sure you wouldn't trade that beauty for a plainer visage, would you?

LEIGH   Oh, I think Edith Evans is the most marvelous actress in the world and she can look beautiful. I mean, people who aren't beautiful can look beautiful. She can look as beautiful as Diana Cooper, who was the most beautiful woman in the world to my mind.

INTERVIEWER   They can evoke a spirit.

LEIGH   Yes—which is the important thing. Actual beauty—beauty of feature is not what matters, it's beauty of spirit and beauty of imagination and beauty of mind. I tried in *Streetcar* to let people see what Blanche was like when she was in love with her young husband when she was seventeen or eighteen. That was awfully important, because Blanche, who needn't necessarily have been a beautiful person, but she—you should have been able to see what she was like, and why this gradually had happened to her. And her sister helps by saying, "Nobody was tender and trusting as she was," and that's a very important line. And I remember I quarreled with Mr. Kazan, our director, on that, because the way it was said, I didn't approve of. I think the very words tender and trusting are words that have to be elongated because they are marvelous words, and in those two things you have to evoke this whole creature when she was young and when she was tender and trusting, as opposed to what she had become—cynical and hard, mad, and distressed and distraught.

INTERVIEWER   Now, I'm curious to know, and particularly now that you've conceded that this was a problem, what did you do to overcome this?

LEIGH   Played as many different parts as possible. A variety of roles.

INTERVIEWER   I was going to ask you—how does one, in fact, learn to be an actress? What steps did you take? And you've answered it by saying doing as great a variety of . . .

LEIGH   As great a variety as possible.

INTERVIEWER   What is required of a person who sets out to be an actor or an actress?

LEIGH   Oh, heavens! Strength.

INTERVIEWER   Strength in what sense?

LEIGH   Strength in health and imagination and courage, I think, and patience.

INTERVIEWER   Would you take each one of those by itself and elaborate a little bit for us.

LEIGH   Well, strength because it's a very hard life. The hours are different from the rest of normal living, and in order to be able to act well, you have to be in marvelous physical condition. It's very important—in order for your voice to be absolutely right, in order for you to look right, you have to be in good physical training. It's a most disciplinarian job—a disciplinarian feat, I think, as the army, you know. All day long you're really leading up to the evening's performance, and in order to time everything correctly, to breathe correctly, you have to take care of yourself—which is a very difficult thing to do, because it's highly emotional, and once the performance is over, you're inclined to say, "Oh, thank God"—a great release. And then, you just stay up too late and talk too much and that kind of thing.

INTERVIEWER   Is there that heightened feeling about every performance?

LEIGH   Every performance. The other day I was going on, and Mr. Merivale said, "Why are you shaking?" I said because I was nervous. And I'd been playing it then for ten months—nine months in London and one month in New York. Every single night I'm nervous.

INTERVIEWER   That's very distressing. But why must it be every night?

LEIGH   The audience is different. You never know how the audience is going to react, so it's different for you every night. You never know what the other actors are going to do, quite. I mean, it stays pretty much the same, but anything can happen. It's one of the hazards of acting.

INTERVIEWER   In other words, every performance is a different performance.

LEIGH   Yes, it is. You're adding something all the time, to begin with.

INTERVIEWER   And each performance is shaped by the audience, is it?

LEIGH   Yes, it is, in a way.

INTERVIEWER   Now, to make a switch to that famous role of yours, Scarlett O'Hara. Did getting the role of Scarlett O'Hara hurt your career in any way?

LEIGH   No. I think it helped it enormously.

INTERVIEWER   I thought that perhaps coming so early in your career, and focusing so much attention on you, that it might have been some kind of a handicap.

LEIGH   No, it was such a marvelous role that it helped. I certainly intended to get it, I may say. From the moment I read the book, I said, "I've got to play that," and I was laughed to scorn on it.

INTERVIEWER   And you certainly had a lot of competition.

LEIGH   I certainly did.

INTERVIEWER   Several others also were determined to play that role?

LEIGH   Yes, they were, and the day that I tested for it, I remember the costumes being taken hot off somebody else's body and put on mine. It was quite unpleasant.

INTERVIEWER   It's rather interesting, in a sense, that you had the courage to do this, because actually here was a Southern belle . . .

LEIGH   I never find accents difficult, after learning languages. That didn't bother me.

INTERVIEWER   Could that be something that any actress can do?

LEIGH   They should be able to.

INTERVIEWER   Really?

LEIGH   Well, they should be able to do anything they're called upon to do, I think.

INTERVIEWER   Well, now, that's a big, big statement. Do you mean that every actress should be able to act the entire range from low comedy to the higher tragedy?

LEIGH   I do—ideally.

INTERVIEWER   Ideally?

LEIGH   Ideally. My husband, who's the greatest actor in the world, can do anything. Look at what he did in *The Critic* and *Oedipus*. In every role he gets—he did this in *Richard the Third*—there's nothing he can't do, nothing. Just nothing.

INTERVIEWER   Is that one reason why you wanted to do *Look After Lulu,* because it was a farce and something novel for you?

LEIGH   No, I did *Look After Lulu* out of expediency, to tell you the truth. I didn't have anything, I hadn't read a play that I wanted to do. I'd asked Noel Coward to translate Georges Feydeau's *Occupe-toi d'Amélie,* and he'd done it, and then I said I wouldn't do it for months and months. And suddenly came the time when I said I should be working, because the whole point in acting is to act, you know—you can't just sit around. There's no use being an actress who doesn't act. It's one's job and also one has to make money, let's face it. And so I said I'd do it, but I didn't want to, and I despised to very much. And Noel Coward and I talked about it and he hadn't liked translating it and I hated playing it—and yet it taught me a lot.

INTERVIEWER   In what way?

LEIGH   That you can do things reasonably well, even if you dislike them very much. I've been very fortunate. I've done mostly plays in my life that I loved to do. This one, I didn't want to do. I didn't like doing it, and all the time I was doing it, I disliked it; and yet, the mere fact—the discipline—of having to do it, I think, taught me a lot.

INTERVIEWER   Sort of character training?

LEIGH   Yes. If you're in love with something, it's comparatively easy, but if you're not, then life is more difficult, isn't it?

INTERVIEWER   That's right. Now, at the time of *The Doctor's Dilemma* you . . .

LEIGH   That I didn't like.

INTERVIEWER   Then why did you do it? Was this something that was regarded as a step in the development of your career?

LEIGH   For one thing, we hadn't one single penny between us, my husband and I. And they were going to do this, the Tennant management—Hugh Beaumont, who I think is the most marvelous manager in the whole world, and that includes our own management. I think that Hugh Beaumont is just the most marvelously courageous impresario that there is. During the war he kept the theatre alive. And he said we are going to do *The Doctor's Dilemma* and would I play Jennifer Dubedat. He took me to meet Shaw—Shaw had written about Jennifer Dubedat. He wrote to the first Jennifer and he said, "This is the sort of a woman I hate, and you're going to have your work cut out to make her fascinating." And that is true. So in a way *she's* good discipline—to make her interesting. Because the real interesting part . . . All of the *Doctors* are marvelous parts and so is Dubedat, but Jennifer is really, well, she's just not an interesting woman.

INTERVIEWER   You were criticized in *The Doctor's Dilemma* for a mannered, swooping way of walking. Are you aware of that?

LEIGH   I walked according to the costume and in a

way I felt that woman would walk. I daresay it was affected but she was an affected creature.

INTERVIEWER In other words, you don't feel that this criticism had any validity?

LEIGH No, no, I don't.

INTERVIEWER I thought when I read about it that it was something that was a manner of yours which was a problem that you had to overcome.

LEIGH No.

INTERVIEWER But actually you adopted it for the play.

LEIGH I adopted it for the part.

INTERVIEWER How did you deepen your emotional power as an actress?

LEIGH Oh, I think life deepens one's emotional power.

INTERVIEWER Besides life, there are other ways, aren't there?

LEIGH No, I think life is the prime mover in that direction.

INTERVIEWER But, after all, by the time you had played that part in *Gone with the Wind,* which was a part that called for great emotional insight . . .

LEIGH But she's a shallow person, Scarlett, shallow compared to, for instance, what I'm playing now. She's shallow compared to Shakespeare's Cleopatra. She's a shallow creature.

INTERVIEWER I'd like to come back to this question of how an actress or an actor deepens his emotional power. You say "life" and you say it unequivocally. Well, let's put it this way—if that is it, can you give me samples? I mean, would you?

LEIGH Oh, that would be going into one's personal life and that isn't the object of this.

INTERVIEWER No, indeed, but . . .

LEIGH I think that every emotional experience that one goes through, whether one's in love or out of love, or whether one is totally miserable or totally happy—all those things help you to describe a character, portray a character.

INTERVIEWER Do you think that an actress or an actor should seek out life's experiences?

LEIGH I do.

INTERVIEWER What I mean is, you can't tailor your life to have a great love, or a great experience, or to know the heights.

LEIGH No, it just happens. You're just lucky if it happens.

INTERVIEWER   Well, all right, but does that mean that you feel that an actress can only be a great actress if she has experienced these things?

LEIGH   I think it helps.

INTERVIEWER   But it isn't in the power of many to do these things.

LEIGH   No. But I think the greatest actors and actresses have all been through tremendous emotional experiences.

INTERVIEWER   Reading would not be an aid?

LEIGH   Oh, yes, I'm sure it would.

INTERVIEWER   Or a certain sensitivity which transmits the same emotion?

LEIGH   And imagination is, of course, as I say, one of the most important things of all.

INTERVIEWER   Say you were an actress just beginning. I mean, would you seek out experiences?

LEIGH   But some people are more talented when they're born. Some people have to struggle. I mean, my husband, I'm sure, started out life as a most talented actor. I don't think I did. I think I have had to learn an awful lot, and, of course, living with him has taught me things. I'm very lucky. I think I'm the most fortunate person in the world— talking to him, watching him work, being directed by him.

INTERVIEWER   This is an aspect of the question of experience of living. How did you, for instance, deepen your understanding of human beings, which is also a requisite of an actor or actress?

LEIGH   I'm fascinated by people, I love them.

INTERVIEWER   What do you do? How do you learn about people?

LEIGH   Talking to them, asking questions, finding out about them. I love them. I love the audience. I like the feeling of them and I want them to understand what I have to give.

INTERVIEWER   It must be more than that, loving people. You must hate people.

LEIGH   I don't hate anybody, I really don't. I don't always admire them by any means, and I can't stand fools.

INTERVIEWER   Have you learned to overcome this?

LEIGH   No, it's just that I forget things that I don't like and I forget people I don't like.

INTERVIEWER   Is this because you've played roles in which there has been hatred?

LEIGH   Yes.

INTERVIEWER   But if you don't understand or . . .

LEIGH I understand, I understand hatred, but I don't harbor it, because I think it's frightfully aging, to begin with.

INTERVIEWER But I mean, in line with what you did say, ideally you would go through a period where you did hate. You would hate somebody and that would give you this insight when you were playing a character. Now you say you never have hated, so in a way you contradicted yourself.

LEIGH Oh, momentarily I've hated.

INTERVIEWER You say that you love people and you like asking them questions. Do you study every person, or most persons, you meet?

LEIGH Yes, anybody whom I find interesting. I love old people for that reason.

INTERVIEWER What do you get from old people?

LEIGH Their wisdom will do for a start; the fact that they've lived. I've always loved old people. My friends, when I was young, were always older than I was, and I've always liked them. And I love old men and old ladies, really. But I've known more elderly men, like Max Beerbohm, like Bernard Berenson, like Somerset Maugham, Winston Churchill—I'd put him first, anyway—what they say is so wise and so good. They know what they're talking about.

INTERVIEWER What or who has influenced you most as an actress?

LEIGH Oh, my husband.

INTERVIEWER In what ways?

LEIGH Well, I saw him about fifteen times in *Hamlet* and I thought, "That's the greatest actor in the world." And I think acting is an important profession, because acting can give pleasure and can teach you at the same time, and that is a good thing. And he taught me more about how actors should be, about how an actor should live, than anybody I can imagine.

INTERVIEWER You've mentioned before the necessity of health and strength and how one should live. Do you have any special kind of regimen when you are working in a role?

LEIGH Yes, I do. I like to get to the theatre very early, to begin with. I like to be in my dressing room early. I go through my part every night before I go on.

INTERVIEWER What do you mean you go through your part every night?

LEIGH Well, I mean I say my part to myself every night.

INTERVIEWER   You really do?

LEIGH   Every night. Yes.

INTERVIEWER   Without the cues. Just your part?

LEIGH   Well, I know all the parts anyway.

INTERVIEWER   How long does it take you to do something like this?

LEIGH   I find it essential to know my part before I start rehearsing, so I like to get a play weeks before and learn the whole thing. I don't agree at all with the new method some young actors and actresses have of saying, "Oh, I can't learn the lines before I do the moves," I don't agree with that. I like to know the lines absolutely, because then I can concentrate during the three or four weeks' rehearsal, or whatever it is, on learning more about it. If I haven't got the lines, I'm wasting all that time learning lines when I could be spending it on bringing the imaginative part of it, the creative part of the work.

INTERVIEWER   I'm fascinated by the fact that you say you go through your entire part every evening before your performance.

LEIGH   I do.

INTERVIEWER   This is very unusual. What inclined you to . . . ?

LEIGH   Well, for one thing, that gets me in the mood of the play. I don't mean by that when people come in—I like people to come and visit me all the time in the dressing room, and I love that. But I can still go through the lines, quite quietly; I don't say them out loud.

INTERVIEWER   Very interesting.

LEIGH   But I go through it in my head.

INTERVIEWER   I want to get this regimen on a twenty-four-hour basis. Now, you get to the theatre well in advance of the curtain time.

LEIGH   Yes.

INTERVIEWER   In other words, well in advance of eight o'clock. You must be in the theatre by seven, I would say.

LEIGH   I get in an hour before.

INTERVIEWER   That would be seven-thirty.

LEIGH   Yes.

INTERVIEWER   And then after theatre what do you do?

LEIGH   Well, then I like to dance better than anything.

INTERVIEWER   Do you find dancing very relaxing?

LEIGH   Yes. I like dancing and riding and swimming.

INTERVIEWER   You can't go swimming at three o'clock in the morning.

LEIGH   Now don't you worry, you can, you know.

INTERVIEWER   You have to know the right places. Then what time do you get to bed?

LEIGH   Oh, terribly late. I love sitting up. I love talking with friends, and anybody.

INTERVIEWER   What would you say is the time that you get to bed?

LEIGH   Four, five.

INTERVIEWER   And what time do you generally rise?

LEIGH   This is when I'm working?

INTERVIEWER   When you're working, that's right.

LEIGH   Otherwise I go to bed about ten or eleven.

INTERVIEWER   We're talking now about when you're working.

LEIGH   Then I get up—I never sleep more than five hours, hardly ever.

INTERVIEWER   You can get along on that?

LEIGH   Yes, I can get along. I never slept much, ever. Since I was born I haven't slept much.

INTERVIEWER   Now let's see, we've got you in bed at four—that means you're up by nine.

LEIGH   Nine. I'm awake at nine. I don't get up. I lie about and read, telephone, write. But I don't like the telephone at all. I absolutely hate it.

INTERVIEWER   Do you do anything in the way of physical calisthenics?

LEIGH   No, never.

INTERVIEWER   Then what do you do?

LEIGH   I love walking.

INTERVIEWER   Is that part of your regimen?

LEIGH   No, I don't do anything like that.

INTERVIEWER   What do you do to keep fit, let us say, aside from walking?

LEIGH   Nothing.

INTERVIEWER   Nothing?

LEIGH   Absolutely nothing.

INTERVIEWER   But do you rest during the day up until curtain time?

LEIGH   I sleep for an hour. I get into bed, draw the curtain, pretend it's night, for an hour before I go to the theatre. And then I have something very light to eat. You can't act on an empty stomach, because your breathing's all wrong.

INTERVIEWER   Yes. You don't have any social life in the afternoons if you can help it?

LEIGH No, no. I go to a movie or I go to an art gallery.

INTERVIEWER I see. You say that you read in the morning—does this have any relationship to your views about gaining new experiences?

LEIGH I don't read nearly enough. I go through periods where I can't read at all, can't read, can't do anything.

INTERVIEWER Has reading actually ever been a particularly moving experience for you?

LEIGH Yes—Dickens. All during the war when I was traveling on these blackout trains, because I used to go back to see my husband on weekends, I read the whole of Dickens. And I think that that was one of the most thrilling experiences.

INTERVIEWER Is this something which you have called on in your career?

LEIGH Dickens?

INTERVIEWER Yes. In acting a part, has it enriched your experience of life?

LEIGH Oh, yes. The Dickens characters are just marvelous. I think that was the most thrilling of all-round reading experiences. And then I read poetry quite a lot.

INTERVIEWER Any special reason?

LEIGH I just like it.

INTERVIEWER I mean, there's nothing for the ear? I mean, there's no utilitarian purpose in reading the poetry?

LEIGH No. I try to learn it as I go along. I've been ill for long periods of my life and have tried to learn a sonnet a day and that sort of thing.

INTERVIEWER Whose poetry do you read?

LEIGH Shakespeare's and Shelley and Browning and Dylan Thomas, who I think is a marvelous poet.

INTERVIEWER How did you prepare for the two Cleopatras?

LEIGH Well, every time I do any important role at all I go back to school, as it were. I go to an elocution teacher. There have been lots of different ones, and every time I do something like that. For instance, before the Cleopatras I went to a marvelous teacher. I didn't study the role with her, but I studied the actual speeches with her and did exercises. I still do. And before *Duel of Angels,* I went to a marvelous woman who Robert Helpmann told me about whose name escapes me at the moment. She was wonderful and I went to her for breathing exercises. I go into a sort of little training before every big role. I find it essential because I'm, I guess, out of practice—like you do anything else. I mean, athletes go into training, and actors should go into training.

INTERVIEWER That was the physical preparation, let us say, for a role. And I asked you specifically, in relation to the Cleopatras, how did you grasp it intellectually?

LEIGH Just read the play.

INTERVIEWER Didn't you read Plutarch?

LEIGH Yes, I did. Oh, yes, naturally.

INTERVIEWER Did you try to find out everything you could possibly find out about her?

LEIGH Yes, I did. I read about everything. For instance, Dover Wilson.* I read him very carefully and—what else did I read? I can't remember what else I read but I read anything I could get hold of on Cleopatra.

INTERVIEWER Why do you think this is helpful?

LEIGH Oh, it just gets you into the atmosphere and into the mood.

INTERVIEWER I've heard some people say that it is enough to read the play itself, because a good playwright will supply you with all you need.

LEIGH I think Shakespeare does.

INTERVIEWER Yes. You don't need anything more.

LEIGH But there is a marvelous—there is a beautiful little series of books about Shakespeare's characters before the plays start. For instance, Glen Byam Shaw† has them. They're written by a woman in the last century. And Viola, for instance, was very helpful to me because there was the whole of Viola's life before the play starts, and the fact that she'd seen Orsino when she was a small girl, so when she saw him suddenly at court—when she comes to Illyria—she's already in love with him, which starts her on the right foot. And there's a marvelous account of Lady Macbeth before *Macbeth* starts, about how Macbeth rode up to the castle when she was a young woman and how she fell in love with him. Because, to me, *Macbeth* is a great love story and I'd never found Lady Macbeth a monster. I think she's a perfectly understandable human being, and I adored playing it. It's one of my favorite roles.

INTERVIEWER And you understand her.

LEIGH Yes, by knowing something about her life before—exactly, exactly.

INTERVIEWER You had a special problem in the Cleo-

---

* Shakespearean scholar.
† Prominent British Shakespearean director.

patra undertaking, and that was a matter of voice, as I recall.

LEIGH Yes, but I went to a man called Baraldi and he said you use your voice like your boots, like climbing boots, I think he said. He said, "You have to keep your voice down for the older Cleopatra and bring it right up for the young one." He said to use your voice like mountain shoes, he said. And so I said, "Yes, well, I've got to." And he said, "Well, it will be very strenuous and you must take great care while you're doing it," and indeed he was right. It was a great strain.

INTERVIEWER You played the older Cleopatra with the deeper voice.

LEIGH Yes, just as one's voice does get deeper. When I first started out, James Agate* said that my voice was absolutely appalling, which it was—it was very high-pitched and squeaky and altogether absolutely rotten.

INTERVIEWER How did you learn to develop your voice? Only through elocution?

LEIGH It wasn't Baraldi. Baraldi was the first one I went to when I was nineteen, and then Cunelli was the other voice teacher I went to before Cleopatras. Cunelli was, in fact, a singing teacher.

INTERVIEWER Besides elocution, do you find singing lessons good—or do you take them?

LEIGH Singing lessons, I think, are marvelous for a speaking voice.

INTERVIEWER Which of the two Cleopatras was the easier one for you to play?

LEIGH Oh, Shaw was easier, and Shakespeare was much the most interesting and much the one I loved the most.

INTERVIEWER Why was that?

LEIGH Because it was a fuller character.

INTERVIEWER In what ways?

LEIGH It had more variety—an older woman.

INTERVIEWER You have said that American actors have only just started to be trained, and I was curious to know what you meant by that.

LEIGH They are only just starting, I think, to do the classics as much as we do them in England or in France or in any other country. America is younger in every way.

INTERVIEWER How does a director help an actor?

LEIGH By giving him confidence; because most actors,

* One of England's most highly regarded drama critics. Died in 1947.

I think, are lacking in confidence. By helping with his own particular gifts.

INTERVIEWER   And imagination is one of these gifts, isn't it?

LEIGH   Indeed imagination really means how to present an idea in the most interesting way, in an imaginative fashion. It may be very eccentric, it may be art, but, well—just that the imagination can take flight, and in acting every performer should take flight, so that you do things in an imaginative way as opposed to a pedestrian or an ordinary way.

INTERVIEWER   I would like to get back to, if I may, the problems of the actor. I have read that there's a danger to actors in too much intellectualization, too much soul-searching, and too little knowledge of technique.

LEIGH   I quite agree. I think all this talk about acting is—you just have to act, you have to do the thing, you have to practice the art, just like a painter practices his art, just like a writer writes.

Morris Carnovsky

BIOGRAPHY

Morris Carnovsky was born in St. Louis, Missouri, in 1898. After college, he entered the theatre, making early appearances in Boston and first appearing in New York in 1922 at the Provincetown Theatre in *The God of Vengeance*. Later he joined the Theatre Guild, remaining with it until 1930, appearing in such plays as *Saint Joan, The Brothers Karamazov, The Doctor's Dilemma, Marco Millions, Volpone, Uncle Vanya, The Apple Cart* and *Elizabeth the Queen*.

In 1931, he joined the Group Theatre. His plays with the Group included *The House of Connelly, Night Over Taos, Gold Eagle Guy, Awake and Sing, Waiting for Lefty, Johnny Johnson, Golden Boy, Rocket to the Moon, Thunder Rock* and *Night Music*. Among his triumphs with the Group Theatre was *Golden Boy*, in which he played Mr. Bonaparte both in New York and in London.

Following his association with the Group Theatre, he appeared in *My Sister Eileen* in 1940, and later in *Café Crown, Counterattack* and *Joy to the World*.

Starting in the summer of 1957, and continuing in 1958, '59 and '60, Mr. Carnovsky played with the American

Shakespeare Festival at Stratford, Connecticut, appearing in *Measure for Measure, The Tempest, The Taming of the Shrew, Hamlet, A Midsummer Night's Dream* and *The Merchant of Venice,* in which he played Shylock, a major success of his career.

Mr. Carnovsky has appeared in a number of motion pictures, including *The Life of Emile Zola, Tovarich, Cyrano de Bergerac* and *Rhapsody in Blue.* He gives private instruction in acting in New York City. He is married to Phoebe Brand, the actress; they have one son.

SETTING

Stratford, Connecticut, was the scene for the interview with Morris Carnovsky. It was in this pleasant town that Mr. Carnovsky was spending the summer, playing the season with the American Shakespeare Festival and appearing in *The Tempest, Twelfth Night* and *Antony and Cleopatra,* and teaching in the Festival's school as well.

Just as we were getting out of the car at the administration building—an old white clapboard one-time private home near the new Festival Theatre—Mr. Carnovsky came pedaling along on his bicycle, a hearty and cheerful-looking man. He had black-rimmed eyeglasses and was wearing a tan sports coat, sports shirt and slacks. He greeted us pleasantly, his manner genial but with a certain dignified reserve.

We went into the administration building, to one of the rooms used for classes. The room had once been the kitchen, and the blackboard, practice piano, desk and fifteen or so folding chairs scattered about could still not disguise it—with its kitchen whiteness, its black-and-white linoleum floor, its cupboards. But of the rest of the kitchen only one high kitchen chair was evident.

Mr. Carnovsky gave a description of himself during the interview that, if contradictory, was at least partly accurate. "I'm a rather romantic person . . . I may not look it . . . but my own bent is to romanticism." Indeed, at first glance he does not look romantic—the impression of non-romantic emphasized perhaps by the informality of manner—and the arrival on bicycle! But the splendid resonance of that voice that has been remarked upon by critics over the years, the piercing quality of those eyes when he is talking on a subject close to his heart, and, above all, the dramatic intensity he brings to even a small excerpt from a play he may interpolate into the conversation to demonstrate a point he is making—all do indeed give evidence of his romantic bent.

For the most part, though, Mr. Carnovsky talks quietly. He has great vitality, a hearty laugh. Using gestures effectively and frequently, on a few occasions he would throw himself more completely into what he was saying, such as when he was "playing" tennis to underline his remarks on the relationship of acting to sports. And when he discussed his role as Shylock—not only its meaning as theatre, but its meaning to him personally—the subdued passion of his voice, the intensity of his expression, left no doubt of the deep engagement of this man in his profession.

After the interview Mr. Carnovsky came outside to the car. Just as we were about to leave to go back to the city—taking a slightly envious glance at the flower garden, the lawns and the altogether pleasant setting of the place—one of us remarked that an actor's life is a good one. Mr. Carnovsky answered that an actor's life—when it was good—was very good.

Interview

INTERVIEWER   The dream of many actors is to become associated with a permanent acting company. In fact, as you know, a good many thoughtful people in the theatre consider the development of such companies a prerequisite to the vigorous growth of theatre in this country. To an unusual degree, you have gravitated to such companies. Which companies have you been a member of and how would you evaluate your experience with them?

CARNOVSKY   Well, there was a kind of semipermanence about the Theatre Guild, with which I was associated for about six years. The value of this experience was that it was continuous—it pointed out the value of a continuity of practice amongst actors, who met each other day after day, worked together and learned to know each other's methods, and could learn from each other. However, since the Guild was not organized on a permanent-company basis, the lessons of this six-year experience were transmuted into those which were begun by the Group Theatre. The Group Theatre is without question the great unified experience of my life. For one thing, not only did it prove the value of a permanent relationship between actors working, as we then thought, for the rest of our lives in the theatre together; but also it gave us an opportunity to be absolutely honest and down to earth about the rules of the craft that we were pursuing, that we were learning. After six years with the Guild, and even more with theatres before that, I myself came to the same kind of conclusion that the majority of our Group actors came to. Namely, we've got to be basic; we've got to go back to the fundamental rules. Find out what they are, because we were working in a kind of hit-or-miss way. Many actors, you know, go onto the stage or are plunged onto it or they're thrown onto it, because they're either good-looking or in some other way they have the right kind of quality, as you know, for certain parts. And in this way they get to have a certain excellence, a certain technique of projecting themselves, but they do not grapple with acting as an art, which it has a right to be considered. And we're still fighting that fight, in spite of the fact that the Group Theatre has long gone and the practitioners of what we learned in the Group are now mostly scattered amongst the stages of Broadway and Hollywood, and teaching. One must not forget that, that the lessons we learned in the Group are being handed on by the various people, not always in agreement with each other, by the way, which shows how the matter changes through the years. So the Group Theatre, then, was the major permanent company of my career. The present one, the Shakespeare Company, is not yet a company in my estimation. It changes too much; it has no fundamental artistic policy. It has a kind of wish—sometimes a pious wish—you know, with regard to "wouldn't it be nice to have a group of actors who work together over a long period of time?" Well, that becomes almost like a wish for a new type of church or debating society. But the thing to be said about permanence, the idea of permanence in the theatre, is the basic one which was enunciated when we first got together in the Group Theatre—and I don't want to sound like a kind of fundamentalist in a congregation—and that is that the art of the theatre reflects life. The American art of the theatre reflects American life. It reflects American life in the midst of a world which is becoming more and more one, in its hopes, at any rate. Therefore, the technique—the rules of the technique—of such a theatre has got to be terribly seriously examined; the relationship of art to life has got to be explored and understood; human nature must be studied not only from the point of view of the needs of the dramatist but also the needs of the people who are acting the work of the dramatist. And this is why the Group Theatre was important, in being, I think, the first theatre in this country to have a philosophy, to have a point of view. This is very essential for a theatre. We were all trying to say the same thing, and in order to do so we had to acquire the same craft, the same technique. This is the meaning of the technical work of the Group Theatre.

INTERVIEWER   How would you describe this point of view of the Group Theatre?

CARNOVSKY   I can illustrate this by harking back to the fact that the Group Theatre came into existence at the time of the beginning of the depression . . .

INTERVIEWER   My memories of the depression are very vivid and very sharp. I shouldn't have interrupted you, but I did want to tell you how important the Group was to me, for instance, as was the Civic Repertory Theatre.

CARNOVSKY   You did find the Group Theatre important to you?

INTERVIEWER   Yes.

CARNOVSKY   Which simply indicates that in one way or other you were looking for the same kind of answers that we were. Surrounding us in the New York streets were bread lines, apple sellers, all the poverty and horror that was associated with that period: the newspapers full of screaming headlines about millionaires jumping out of windows, and all the rest of it. And the question which naturally arose in sensitive people's minds was, "What are we doing here? In what way are we members of our time? In what way are we contributing to the contemporary theatre?" This didn't mean that we jumped on our horses like Paul Revere and galloped off spreading propaganda, although we were accused of that. It is true that our actors became very politically conscious; this was part of the learning of life that they underwent at that time. Suddenly they found that life was a rather bitter thing; it was sometimes pitched in a minor key. It was not possible then for us of the Group Theatre to accept a play like *Dinner at Eight,* good as it may be, stageworthy as *Dinner at Eight* undoubtedly was. That was not our kind of play. In other words we experienced a kind of unity of feeling about life and also a common attitude to the things that were happening around us. This is what I mean by point of view. In other words, we wanted to say "America." We wanted to say the country we live in at the time that we were living in it. And this is why we encouraged our authors to say that. Our authors sometimes came and lived with us in summertime in order to absorb some of the technical ideas that we were pursuing. And some of them wrote plays which could only be done by us. Not always good plays, certainly not. A man like Sidney Kingsley brought us *Men in White*, not that this was such a profound play, socially speaking, although it aimed at a kind of integrity which it didn't altogether fully achieve. But the kind of inner technique that we were acquiring made us the logical people to do that particular play.

INTERVIEWER   It is interesting to hear why the Group was so important to you in terms of its being a theatre with a point of view. Now, I wonder about the value of a permanent acting company to the actor as a home, and I wonder whether this is what keeps you coming back to groups that promise permanence.

CARNOVSKY   Well, yes, that's true. In the nine or ten years of the Group Theatre experience I consciously examined the materials of my craft. In other words, I attained a conscious technique. Before that I'd been an accepted, recognized actor with the Guild, but I never did feel that I had a technique on which I could absolutely depend. After the years with the Group Theatre, working in concert with my fellow actors who were looking for the same things, I was able day after day to examine my craft, to examine myself in relation to my technique, to make mistakes in common with them, and in a sense to formulate a language of the craft, which has since become pretty permanent. If you go to the Actors Studio and listen to them speaking, you'll hear them using the same phrases and uttering the same purposes that we did back there. *"Plus ça change, plus c'est la même chose,"* you know. Thirty years ago it was just as valid as it is now.

INTERVIEWER   Yet that's in direct contradiction, for instance, to, let us say, what Tyrone Guthrie says. Guthrie says that the Method is antiquated because Stanislavsky developed the Method in rebellion against a certain set of conditions which no longer exist and consequently cannot be accepted as the only valid style of acting.

CARNOVSKY   Stanislavsky did not aim at a valid style of acting. What Guthrie says, I'm in disagreement with, of course. Because I don't think that Stanislavsky aimed at establishing permanently a particular style of acting. It happened that he expressed himself realistically. He was in rebellion against the clichés of his day, just as any sensitive actor would be. And it's those that threaten the theatre constantly; the antiquated habits of the actor are always threatening the theatre. We have them today in spite of the fact that the Group Theatre has been and gone, you know. So it's necessary for Guthrie really to be fair to Stanislavsky. What I've read of his doesn't strike me as correct.

INTERVIEWER We have been led to believe—many people on the periphery, let us say, of the theatre, like myself —that the Method does not encourage technique as much as it encourages constant soul-searching, this whole quest for feeling and for truth. And Guthrie, as I recall, has said that one of the troubles with the Method is that it encourages this other thing at the expense of technique. And you, as one of the archbishops of the Method, you have just made a great pitch for technique.

CARNOVSKY Why not Cardinal of the Method? Well, the Method is technique. Suppose you were to ask an artist, a painter, what it is he is trying fundamentally to say. He will have to answer, I am trying to say "myself." I am trying to say myself in relation to the world I live in. Now this is fundamental. I want to say it in a certain way. A Van Gogh found himself expressing himself in these sharp, passionate daubs on canvas, which have since become so recognizable and so famous and so necessary for the understanding of his art. I don't care who the artist is, or whether he's a composer or a pianist or a writer—I feel what he wants to do is find out how to say himself. I as an actor want to find out how to say myself, through O'Neill, through Shakespeare, through Chekhov, through whoever. It is not a matter of soul-searching; it can be everything. We are not sacrosanct material, you see; it happens that the actor is the material of his own making. He presents himself in various aspects. That is to say, he does use his soul as well as his body. And you cannot draw any distinction between them. Technique, as Guthrie may be using the term, is not a matter of simply knowing how to cavort and how to dispose of yourself in pleasing ways, or in moving ways around the stage. Behind every movement of the actor, whether it be a movement of his hands, of his body, of his voice, of his eyes, of his face, of anything—is an inner movement which I regret to have to call his soul. If you don't like the word, well, find another, I don't care. But the two things together, body technique and inner technique, form the material of the actor's craft. And who can deny this?

INTERVIEWER But this brings up another question. Is the actor a creative artist or an interpretive artist? If you accept what you just said, that the actor must represent the truth of himself, then you are saying that the actor is a creative artist, in a sense, if I understand you correctly. But other people say that the obligation of the actor is to create or to interpret what the playwright has written, not to project himself over the character that the playwright has conceived.

CARNOVSKY   I could refer to the Shylock I played, which you said you had seen, and ask you for your impressions. What came over to you, since you happened to have liked that performance? Was it me, or was it the character as Shakespeare wrote him? Mind you, there are many ways to skin a cat, and the next actor who plays Shylock—I understand there's a very fine man in England playing it right now, along lines that I'm very interested in, his name is O'Toole—the next actor will find a different way of tackling this same material. But I can say that there's an example of a part which, when it finally became "my own," in quotes, was as much flesh of my flesh and blood of my blood as anything that I've ever done in my life. Now what comes first? Shakespeare wrote the part several hundred years ago, and I imagine how it's done and project it in my way, my experience of life. And I assure you that this matters very much in the doing of a Shylock. The vital actual experience of my life is as important a part of the fabric of doing Shylock as anything that I learned in the Group Theatre, or from Stanislavsky, or anybody. Now to me that's a creative act. You see? You spoke of interpretation. There are many ways to act, of course. Recently I had a magnificent experience watching the Italian Piccolo Teatro di Milano. What a wonderful, wonderful theatre! I can't do that. That's not my kind of theatre. I wish it were. What a wonderful life that is! Their way of doing Shylock would be quite different from mine. But—I started to say this about interpretation—many people think an actor has got to read the play and then say, "Ah, I see what the author is driving at. He wants me to do it in such and such a way." But from my point of view, what the actor has to do is to take the material which the author has given him and re-create it in his own terms. Because in the last analysis we have only ourselves, whether we are Van Gogh or Gielgud, or anybody.

INTERVIEWER   I understand that Stanislavsky felt that an actor to prepare for his career must learn life, know life, by drinking life as much as he can, for the very purpose of being able to interpret or to create and represent a large variety of characters. Without this knowledge of life he wouldn't have the insights into the characters he must portray. On the other hand, in the event that his experience has led him to consider life differently from the way the playwright did, he still is not to give this his own imprint; he still has to follow what the playwright has suggested. Isn't there a fine line—a time when your formula might be overstepping and you might be doing more Morris Carnovsky than Shakespeare?

CARNOVSKY   At this point we throw ourselves at the mercy of the public and their representatives, the critics. It's for them to tell us whether they accept what we do about a certain part or not. If they reject it because they say, "Look here, you're trying to teach me something which isn't in the play and I resent it," well, that's worth knowing, too.

INTERVIEWER   But the audience doesn't know the playwright or the play as well as the actor does. So don't you also have a responsibility to the playwright, which the audience may be unaware of?

CARNOVSKY   Yes, you do. Recently—in the last five years, anyway—Alec Guinness played Hamlet and they roasted him off the stage. They practically said, "How dare you touch this material?" And one of his replies, as I remember it, was, "It happens that I know more about this part than any critic on earth." You see, now, at this point, a man is alone with his—I don't want to call it ego—private understanding of a part that he reveres, and who is to say whether Guinness was wrong or not? I've seen pictures of Gielgud doing King Lear in Chinese fashion, you know, in Chinese make-up. Well, to me this is a little fantastic, but those are the experiments that make for life.

INTERVIEWER   You said that your interpretation of Shylock came from your own very personal, deep experience. Does that suggest your Jewishness?

CARNOVSKY   Oh, yes, certainly.

INTERVIEWER   And all the problems that go with being a Jew in an Aryan society?

CARNOVSKY   Yes, indeed, very much so.

INTERVIEWER   Does it also encompass political pressures of some kind?

CARNOVSKY   Yes, that's right. Yes, it does, it does.

INTERVIEWER   In other words, all your experiences in Hollywood with the Un-American Committee, and your Jewishness, all this went into shaping the Shylock.

CARNOVSKY   That's right. What is of interest here is, how does this come about? How does the material which emerges

from experiences like that go into the shaping of a role?
That's the fascinating thing.

INTERVIEWER   Give us an example.

CARNOVSKY   I would like to answer you as factually as
possible, the question that you just asked, but in a rather
interesting way. I'd like to try to show how the actor seeks
for material which he may shape into something rich and
strange, as Shakespeare says. But—a person has a painful
experience. Coleridge or somebody, Wordsworth possibly,
yes, Wordsworth, said that poetry is the result of emotion
recollected in tranquillity. In other words, he rejects the emotion at the moment when you're suffering, you know—the
painful emotion. This he rejects. It's only when it passes
through a period of time and can be absorbed as crystallized
experience, so to speak, then it is useful to the artist, to the
poet, or whoever it may be. It comes through mists of re-
flection, of waiting, of ruminating.

INTERVIEWER   It's precipitation, really, isn't it? In a
chemical laboratory you throw elements in, and then what
comes out is a crystal which is the result of all the elements
working together.

CARNOVSKY   Yes, yes. That's valid. But the way in which
it happens is—I don't want to call it mystic, because to me
nothing is really mystic. There are mysterious overtones about
all artistic pursuits, but the rules of the craft are very clear,
very crystal clear to me, very specific—that's the word. But a
moment, an experience, which leaves its vibrations in depth,
so to speak, in the life of a person—what happens to those
things? We've all had them. What do we do with them? The
artist re-creates them, as Heine says, in poems. And the actuality of these experiences are what the actor, for example,
must preserve. I must never, never forget that the Jews were
persecuted by Hitler in the way that they were. I must not
forget that. I must not forget the fact that I saw Ku Klux
Klan crosses on the hills one night when I was playing in a
Chautauqua tent. I must not forget that the Un-American
Committee and certain people in the theatre who are "highly
respected people"—I put that in quotes, for I don't respect
them—made it necessary for me to be blacklisted for several
years. I must not forget these things. These are part of life
and living. And because I must not forget them, they enter
into the not-forgetting, so to speak, of a man like Shylock. The
way they enter is not in a kind of vicious I'll-get-my-own-
back, although I understand that, too; the actor has got to
understand everything. It comes out differently. It comes out,

if you like, with a certain edge of beauty to it. Because what the actor tries to convey is the universality of an episode, of an experience. Because what was happening to me personally didn't matter, really. It was happening all over the country. The repression, the oppression, that was taking place all over the country at that time is something that we'll none of us ever forget. I'm sure you remember it. The feeling of a heavy smog in our thinking atmosphere. Well, this is life. I mean, we go through these things, and they become part of the artist's equipment eventually because he has been there. And he's lucky, indeed, if he gets a part like Shylock to express it through, or Prospero, in the present instance, to express it from, because Prospero is given to forgiveness, whereas Shylock is out for revenge.

INTERVIEWER   I assume this has shaped your career then —finding parts which in effect will permit you to give voice to your inner feelings, to your experiences and to your conviction that the theatre serves this role in society.

CARNOVSKY   Yes, if I understand you correctly. But I don't wait around for such parts. There are many parts to play.

INTERVIEWER   But this is something that you look for and hope for.

CARNOVSKY   In a way, this brings me to the present semipermanent, if you like, theatre that I'm with, which is Shakespeare. I think the thing that brought me to Shakespeare was that I could always be confident of playing something good. It's *great* material, and if our present-day writers are not giving me parts to play which are in the same alley, well, I can always go to this great man. And always, but always, find something to do there.

INTERVIEWER   Since we've come back to Shakespeare from a long way around, one of the reasons that your conversation about the Method is so vital here is that you are, in a sense, again, the contradiction of two other arguments related to the Method: One argument advanced against the Method is that the Method encourages, through the naturalistic emphasis, mumbling. (God knows, you don't mumble, you have one of the most beautiful voices in the contemporary theatre.) And another is, the Method is not supposed to be conducive to playing the classics. And here you are enjoying some of the greatest successes of your career, in the classics. So that—well—take off.

CARNOVSKY   First, the mumbling thing. Of course, not for one moment do I believe that anything in what Stanislavsky spoke of, or suggested, as a search for the realistic actor, was intended to emerge as unclear speech, because Stanislavsky to the end of his life studied means of making words clear—consonants, he loved them; vowels, he adored them. To him these were his beloved objects. The actor deals with such objects, these are his stock-in-trade. And, as such, speech—careful speech—the way it's pronounced, the way it issues, the way it balances in our practice—all those things —these are precious things to the sensitive actor. I must conclude, then, that the actor who is not aware of this power in his equipment is not as sensitive as he should be, and should take lessons. As for realistic approach and the diving within that people talk about in relation to the Stanislavsky method— never was it intended to encourage that kind of sloppiness. So I don't think it's worth really spending too much time on that aspect of it. It's an abuse.

INTERVIEWER Some critics say Marlon Brando had something to do with this mumbling business we hear so much about.

CARNOVSKY That's what they say. I think it's unfortunate. I've heard Brando speak somewhat in that way. I've also heard him speak very clearly in *Julius Caesar*. Some of the greatest moments in the Caesar movie were contributed by him—four or five that I could mention. In between, he wavered a little bit, but those wonderful moments I won't forget. Now the other thing. You wonder that an actor who was trained in the realistic approach to acting as projected and suggested by Stanislavsky should come to Shakespeare— how did you put it?

INTERVIEWER I said, in effect, that it has been argued that the Method is not conducive to the classics, that the Method has not proved itself in Shakespeare. And yet, interestingly enough, you, who are a Method actor, even from the days of the Group, are having your greatest successes in Shakespeare. And I am interested in hearing your reply to these arguments.

CARNOVSKY Well, for one thing it's becoming clearer to me that my own understanding and approach to Shakespeare, who is to me the greatest author in the theatre, is double. It's romantic and realistic. It happens that I'm a rather romantic person; I mean, in myself. I may not look it—and you may not believe it—but my own bent is to romanticism. I also believe thoroughly in realism, in the realistic approach to acting. Mainly because it invites utter, integral truth. Reality emerging from inner truth is the thing that Stanislavsky worked for all his life, and this is what I feel our American theatre conveys best. I believe that the American theatre has a great opportunity. I don't want to say rudely that we have the opportunity to save Shakespeare from the English. They wouldn't like it, and it wouldn't be true, because they have done, as we know, the greatest work in Shakespeare. But I sometimes do suspect that they've lived with Shakespeare for so long that there's a tendency to take him a little bit for granted. And also to insist on certain colors resident in his writing as fixed—"This is the way it's got to be, and don't tell me otherwise." You know, this is the feeling I sometimes get from them—"That's the way it has to be." Well, there's no such law with regard to a great genius such as Shakespeare was. He wrote for all of us, even Americans. And I do believe, and I say this humbly, that the American actor is by and large a mixture of romanticism and realism, and it's this cross-pollination added to some kind of understanding of poetry and of poetic speech which I think offers Americans our great opportunity in Shakespeare. I'm fascinated by it and I'm interested in it. This is what I want to bring out and pursue in my own attempts to do Shakespeare.

INTERVIEWER   Do you feel the American Shakespeare Festival is going toward developing this American style?

CARNOVSKY   In a wishful way, it may be, but it's not doing so in a conscious enough way to suit me.

INTERVIEWER   What more could it do?

CARNOVSKY   It could consciously evaluate its artistic position. It could devote itself to a period of time in which to prove that artistic position. It could choose all of its resources with relation to that objective—performers, directors, scene designers, musicians, everything; the school, the academy.

INTERVIEWER   Wasn't. Houseman going in that direction?

CARNOVSKY   Not enough. Nobody has so far. They would be the first to admit it.

INTERVIEWER   What is the fatal difficulty? Is it money?

CARNOVSKY   No, I'm not so sure about money. Money somehow or another seems to materialize around these productions. They're very good productions and they never seem to lack for money.

INTERVIEWER   The need to hold the unit together over a period of time is what I have in mind—what Houseman was striving for. To keep the group together, to provide employment, let us say, for eight months a year. Is this what is lacking?

CARNOVSKY Yes, that's right.

INTERVIEWER Perhaps, too, you're talking about an idea. It's more the idea that hasn't emerged.

CARNOVSKY Yes. I think that when you start out to do Shakespeare it's a tremendous responsibility, terrific responsibility. And we're apt to be a little bit cavalier about it. Now, don't misunderstand me, and I don't want the people who are all working so marvelously here to misunderstand me either. Good work is being done. Wonderful work is being done here—here, there, everywhere you can put your finger on. And as for the devotion, the dedication of the actor, it's fabulous. Simply wonderful. The desires even of the Board are very respectable. But I don't think that they're artistically and responsibly conscious of what one has to do to have a theatre of that kind, a theatre devoted to Shakespeare. It sounds as if I'm stepping all over all the toes around here. Anyway, you see, it happens that we were told the other day that there were going to be twenty-six weeks on the road of two plays, *A Midsummer Night's Dream* and *The Winter's Tale*. This would seem to be certainly in the direction that you mentioned of continuous life for the actor, in summer and winter. It certainly is. Yes, it is that. It will certainly have great value. But I think the lessons of that will be seen after the event. And I still maintain that the artistic plan for that kind of event is not profound enough.

INTERVIEWER Well, I'm sure that you are one of the elder statesmen of this company, and you are heard in these matters.

CARNOVSKY One has to be responsible when one is called an elder statesman. I hate the word. The way they call people dean—it's one step from rabbi. I don't like these official positions. I would rather you would think that I am passionately involved in the theatre. By the way, Brooks Atkinson has said occasionally that what he misses about our theatre—unless I misquote him—is a certain sense of style. And I've often wondered—I'd like to have asked him—did he mean because our speech is by and large not as good as English speech. It doesn't have a certain kind of flying distinction that their speech really has. And I've wondered, I would like to know.

INTERVIEWER I saw, some years ago, Katharine Hepburn in *Much Ado About Nothing,* done here in an American, a southwestern, setting. Now, maybe this was an extreme effort at finding this new form or style.

CARNOVSKY   Well, if you see *Twelfth Night* here, you'll see it done in the period of Daumier.

INTERVIEWER   And yet, in anything you've said, you don't suggest any violent change from the traditional way of doing Shakespeare. I gather you suggest a more harmonious accommodation with American forms. Is that right?

CARNOVSKY   What I would say is what I once said to someone—the trouble with American Shakespeare as I've seen it is that, not only do we do the new approach to Shakespeare badly, but we don't even do the old one well. Now, I would like to see an old *Hamlet* done with utter truth and fidelity to the concepts of the play, or *King Lear*. I would like to see the old one done well before we throw it overboard and start working for cute new ideas. You know, Michel Saint-Denis, who is a very profound thinker in the theatre, said that he disapproves thoroughly, he's fed up with the notion— "Wouldn't it be fun to do Greek tragedy as if it were O'Neill?" "Wouldn't it be fun to dress it up as if it were Toulouse-Lautrec?"

INTERVIEWER   Or do it under water.

CARNOVSKY   Yes, that's right. Now, before you asked why we aren't proceeding more swiftly in the direction that I suggested. The first thought that occurred to me was that there are the commercial needs of the theatre.

INTERVIEWER   This was going on in the back of my mind all the time. Let's see if we're thinking along the same lines. Brooks Atkinson has gone up to Stratford in Canada and he says that this is the finest Shakespearean acting company in North America. Brooks has said this several times. And it occurs to me that they have a different situation up there from what we have have here. They can take a company and keep it cohesive and bring in one or two stars for dressing, because they're providing a theatre in a country which has had very little theatre and to which people wish to come for the sake of coming. We in this country seem to have gotten . . . This is nothing new, but it seems to have emphasized itself more now than it has for a long time—we require a little of the spectacular, a little of the unusual, a bit of the star system. And we're not attracted otherwise, so we will take a star who may not be absolutely fitted for a role, but bring him or her in, let us say here, to make sure that the box office has magnetism. This may not be true in Canada; so the Canadian company has stayed together basically over the period of seven or eight years, and can strive in a more definitive single

direction. Does that make sense, in line with what you're
saying?

CARNOVSKY Yes, yes, I think it does. I think very likely
that is what happens. My regret is that we don't get a real
opportunity to examine what would happen if we devoted
ourselves to a long-term project such as I spoke of before.
I'd like to suggest that. But they would say to me, "Yes, yes,
Morris, we'll get to that, some day. Believe us, that's in our
minds too. But in the meantime we've got to live and this
place has got to go. Therefore, let's put on a bang-up production of this and slip in a quality production of a tragedy—
you've got to have a tragedy, you know—and end off with a
nice harmless fantasy play which is dressed up by so-and-so,
music by so-and-so." This is the way their minds click and
the way they work. I hope I'm not hurting people's feelings.

INTERVIEWER But there's always a touch of the compromise.

CARNOVSKY That's what I feel.

INTERVIEWER How can you go about developing the
theatre you have in mind? Is it really possible, do you think?

CARNOVSKY Yes, you've got to start—humbly—from the
grass roots. You've got to take young actors, eight or nine of
them, and say, "Let's do it. Let's devote ourselves to it for
a year." Then tack on another year, and another, and maybe
the same kind of thing that happened in the Group Theatre
might happen again. But the Group Theatre was constantly
undermined, you know, by—by . . .

INTERVIEWER By Hollywood.

CARNOVSKY Among other things, among other things.

INTERVIEWER For example.

CARNOVSKY Commercialism, in one way or another, and
inner stupidities of our own. I was guilty of things myself
that I hope I wouldn't be if we would have the experience to
do over again. There was a lack of consciousness, a lack of
understanding, so that after about nine years the thing was
worn out.

INTERVIEWER I'd like to come back, if you don't mind,
to a little bit of the basics of acting, and I would like to ask
you, of all of an actor's equipment, what do you consider most
important? Would you put, for instance, voice ahead of everything else in the equipment of an actor?

CARNOVSKY There again, the whole equipment of the
actor is such an organic composite that if you were to isolate

one you are bound to affect all the others. Salvini* said, of course, voice, voice, more voice. And from his point of view that's all that was necessary. But that particular voice happened to be backed up by one of the most majestic temperaments the world has ever seen, apparently, although I never saw him in the theatre. Therefore, he knew that in order to discharge the lightnings and thunders of his own personality he had to have a great instrument. Therefore, he said that's all he needed. And really perhaps that was all. But, intelligence, imagination, concentration—already we're getting into the technique of acting—these are things Stanislavsky speaks specifically about: concentration, the ability to relax in front of an audience, the ability to understand and to probe into the author's intention, amalgamated with one's own, on the stage. I have personally evolved—this is no discovery of mine, but I do talk a lot about it to my students—something that I refer to as the sense of self, the acceptance and use of your own individuality, no matter what part you may be playing. Now this sounds, perhaps, easier than it is. It's never easy to explain, by the way, because people insist on regarding it as some sort of a psychiatric formula—sense of self. I don't mean that at all. Really, it's a full use of your relaxed, easy state. It's the acceptance of yourself as an instrument.

INTERVIEWER   Are you saying the spine or the core of yourself? Or am I wrong in interjecting that?

CARNOVSKY   You could call it that. You could call it that. In other words, at the core of every part is the self of the actor who is doing it. You can say Prospero is quite different from Shylock, but at the vortex, or core, whatever you want to call it, of both parts is me. It's my Prospero, it was my Shylock.

INTERVIEWER   Using this word, I think it would be interesting to differentiate between the kind of self which you're talking about and the kind of self which has been greatly criticized in the Method, that is, where the person brings his own problems and interprets a role through his own problems. The Method has been criticized for this. And this is one of the abuses, I imagine, of the Method.

CARNOVSKY   No, I don't mean that. I don't go for that kind of thing. I know, I've heard stories, horrible ones sometimes, to me, of people who do not hesitate to exhibit themselves in the most naked ways in certain studios. No, I don't go for that. To get back to the basics. I think I might be

* Tommaso Salvini (1829-1916), internationally renowned Italian actor.

tempted to put imagination first of all. Because imagination implies the experience—where does imagination come from? We're not necessarily born with it. We maybe have a bent that way, but . . . It implies the experience which always has to do with comparing. What happened to me a year ago was different from what happened two years ago, which was different from what is happening now. What has happened in the meantime? What is the significance of this whole development? How may I understand a Richard III in the light of what I know about life, of what I could do on the stage in relation to him? How to encourage the flame of the author's conception, how to provide fuel for it out of the experience of my own life. See, this takes imagination. Imagination is the key.

INTERVIEWER Robert Lewis, in a lecture, said that imagination is the actor's realism.

CARNOVSKY Yes, he's written a very good book, *Method or Madness*.

INTERVIEWER Just as someone once said that intelligence is the ability to correlate experience, so in the same sense you're saying that imagination is the ability to correlate experience.

CARNOVSKY Yes. There's an example at the end of a little essay I wrote on Shylock for a new paperback edition of the work which will, perhaps, illustrate what you just said. When I was working on Shylock, I was haunted by the idea of a broken face, and I remembered certain artistic examples of this—the man with the broken nose by Rodin, a face that Picasso did, a mask, Marc Chagall's "The Vitebsk Rabbi," Ivan Mestrović's "Moses." These things all impressed me. But most of all I remembered a certain character in my youth; he was a crazy, half-demented fellow. His name was Yussel, and they called him Yussel the Meshugeneh—Yussel the crazy one. He was a terribly pathetic creature, terribly pathetic. And I recall the kids used to throw things at him, and there was no way of his protecting himself. He had a broken nose and a dirty, bedraggled beard, and now and then he would turn on them and ask them, "Why do you do this? What have I done to you?" And the pathos of this poor, demented creature being hounded by the kids came very sharply into my mind when I was thinking about Shylock. Now, where did it come from? I hadn't thought about him for many years. But suddenly in working on Shylock it was necessary that this image should come up out of the depths and present itself to me as if to say, "Here I am, if you want to, use me." And

I did. Not necessarily to make him up that way, but there was something about the identification with that image which I certainly could use.

INTERVIEWER   This is very interesting, too. Because you are talking as an exponent of the Method, but there are actors and actresses who know nothing at all, or pretend not to know anything at all, about the Method and do exactly what you do. And they say, "The Method people do this. We do this. What's the difference?"

CARNOVSKY   There is no difference, if they do it.

INTERVIEWER   It's interesting to see how much of a Method actress Lynn Fontanne really is. Or Helen Hayes, who has said that she remembered, for instance, something she had seen that made a terrible impression on her and she used it for *Coquette*. She once saw a picture of a mother standing over the grave of her son, her arms tight together over her stomach—and she used it in *Coquette*, when she hears that her lover is shot. And she felt that this was right. But this came to her instinctively, this search for an association with experience, without her having gone through the teaching of the Method.

CARNOVSKY   Well, let me try to describe—it would take a book—what the inner composition of the actor is. You force me to think about it when you ask such questions as what do you think is the most important element, and so on, and so on; then you tell me that Helen Hayes had such an experience, and so-and-so had such an experience, all of which is true. There's an element of consciousness, it seems to me, about the work of the actor, which is inseparable from the consciousness of any working artist. I think consciousness is what an artist has to achieve in order to make a mark on canvas, in order to make a sound. The word technique is not a superficial one. The word technique involves one's whole life, the inner history and set of sensibilities that the actor possesses. For a man—for an actor to exert himself in the act of concentration means that he brings his whole history to bear on the act of concentration.

INTERVIEWER   How would you relate to comedy, for instance? You've played comedy and you've played tragedy. How do you go back in your life—do you do the same thing, do you go back to the comedy in your life?

CARNOVSKY   Comedy to me is an expression of joy. Perhaps this is another reason why I love doing Shakespeare. "What fools these mortals be," you know, is one of the delightful statements of all time. And there is a certain freedom which the actor attains in comedy that he never achieves in any other branch of theatre. Through expressing his own foolishness he expresses that of his fellow man. By the way, Harold Clurman* once said about me that I was fundamentally a clown, and I'm half inclined to agree with that. And so, there's a certain pleasure, a certain gusto and release and relief, that I have from making jokes and from expressing comical attitudes on the stage and from hearing the laughter of the audience, from connecting in a kind of a satirical or ironical or graceful way with my fellow actors by means of the purposes of comedy.

INTERVIEWER Would you agree with what seems to be the consensus, that comedy is harder to play than tragedy? The reason I ask you this question is because I have a feeling that you enjoy playing comedy, and so, perhaps, you don't find it as hard to play comedy as most actors seem to.

CARNOVSKY Well, if comedy is thought of by its practitioners as a mechanical matter of effects, of attaining effects; for example, a person may achieve a laugh by the take—the well-known take—he may hear somebody say something as he's going out the door, suddenly he turns and says, "Huh"—comes the laugh. And he knows that if he turns at just exactly the right time—what is known as timing; I get kind of sick of that word, although I recognize its importance—but he knows that if he turns at exactly the right time and says, "Huh," the laugh will come and this pleases him and justifies his job as an actor. I don't despise that at all. I think all's grist to the actor's mill. But, personally, I do like for results, even comedy results, to come from the reality and the truth of the scene. The so-called "take," rightly understood, is nothing but a kind of delayed confusion with a sudden illumination. Now, that's wrapping a four-letter word like "take" in some awfully big words, but that's what it is to me, and the ability to be confused and then suddenly say, "Oh," and to be illuminated, is to me a delightful contrast. It's not at all funny as I tell it, but it leads to funny results on the stage. And I would prefer to go about it, again, in a realistic way. That sounds awfully starchy—it's no way to describe a "take," and I won't ever describe it again.

INTERVIEWER I'd like to come back—and I know you are asked this question incessantly, but it is about your voice. You mentioned Salvini. I know that one is born with a certain timbre in one's voice. I mean you have this resonance.

* Director, critic and founder of the Group Theatre.

What else have you done to cultivate this vocal equipment, this instrument that's so valuable to you? Have you done anything to help it?

CARNOVSKY First let me say I accept your description of it. I myself don't like to listen to my voice, by the way. When I hear it on tape or anything, I don't see what the shootin's about. People have told me all my life I have a wonderful voice. All right. So, fine. But I've never, not seriously or for long, studied, taken any kind of vocal lessons; I should have —and, by the way, I still have it in mind to do so. I was speaking just the other day to our teacher here. I would like for him to take me on for a bit of singing, because I do sing in *Twelfth Night* and I'd like to do what I can for that. But what I have found as a wonderful help to projection for a voice is what I've learned in the "Method"—in quotes—as relaxation and concentration. I think when a person has faith in what he's talking about and intends to pursue a certain objective on the stage and is relaxed while he's doing it, he need have no fear about his vocal equipment. I may be naïve in the conclusion, but this has been my experience.

INTERVIEWER I wanted to talk to you about relaxation because I know that in the past you have discussed relaxation and its importance to you and to all actors. What you were saying fits in with what a speech teacher has said—Marian Rich . . .

CARNOVSKY A very good woman.

INTERVIEWER That the voice represents the inner status of the personality and that the voice will reflect what a person is. If a person is nervous, disorganized, the voice reflects this. If one is relaxed, then one has the power to control what one is saying, I suspect, from what you say. How does one achieve this relaxation? What is relaxation on the stage?

CARNOVSKY Michael Chekhov, who was a very fine actor, I suppose a great actor, and who I think understood the nature of the actor more than any person since, and possibly including Stanislavsky, used to refer to relaxation as the feeling of ease. Now, the actor learns the importance of this by doing it. He doesn't know that he's struggling against tensions for a number of years, until suddenly he says, "Come on, let's get conscious about this. A tension is a tension, and if it's interfering with your speech, if it's interfering with your thinking, if it's interfering with your muscles, get rid of it." So you do various things: you go to courses in gymnastics; you study fencing; you become acquainted with your body; you realize that in certain conditions your body is interfering with your thinking; and you gradually achieve—by a mechanical pursuit of that kind—you gradually achieve an ease. Then you realize that the feeling of ease can be induced on the stage in spite of the interference of the audience, because the presence of this crowd of people is apt to be very tensing to a young actor. But you find ways and means of overcoming that presence. The primary thing an actor learns to do is to connect with an object. The fact that I am looking at one of you, and connecting specifically with you at this point, delivers me from the interference of the other—of him who might be attempting to disturb my concentration. The more connected I am with you, the less I care about his interference, or their interference. And this state of connection is capturable by the actor with ease, after a while—with great ease. And through this feeling of ease the actor is released to do those things which are prompted by the subconscious or the unconscious. Stanislavsky said that the path of the actor's technique was to the unconscious by way of the conscious. In other words, you release, you become released. Things become expressed in you and through you that you hardly planned for. So that an actor very often says to himself, "Wonder what made me do that? That was exciting. What made me do it? I made a discovery." And he can encourage that condition in himself by ease, by relaxation.

INTERVIEWER   I followed you with great interest and understanding through the mechanical supports for relaxation—fencing, athletics, physical exercise—by which you develop an ease. And I also understand when you say that by fixing on an object like myself you are able to exclude him or exclude the audience. But what specifically do you do as an actor right on the stage to find that ease or relaxation? What is it specifically? I don't think you actually told us what it is.

CARNOVSKY   It's so simple that you might think it's too simple. I was playing some years ago in *An Enemy of the People* with Fredric March—Bobby Lewis, by the way, directed it. And I was playing the brother of Stockmann, the villain of the piece. And I found it of great value to myself, when I came in, when I took off my hat, deposited my umbrella in the areaway where I came in, to relate to things. "Here is my hat. It is my hat." Putting it down. "This is my umbrella." Putting it down. "Here is the room. There is that lamp, that expensive lamp that my foolish brother bought. Here is a tablecloth. I don't have any such tablecloth in my house. This carpet is probably much finer than anything anybody in town has. What right has he to have a tablecloth and

stuff like this around?" Already, this began to induce me to
enter into the life of the play, and by means of simple objects.
So that all at once I felt at home. In spite of the fact that I
was criticizing these surroundings, it was the place where I
had to act. And, therefore, these things reassured me; so that
when I sat down on a chair, a too-expensive chair, by the way,
typical of my brother, I already had an attitude, if you like,
to the whole room—and to everybody in it. So that the animosity which then proceeded to be expressed started from
simple, ordinary objects which reassured my own being—me,
Morris Carnovsky's being—within the character. The character I didn't have to worry about, that had been worked for
in rehearsal. That was assured, perhaps, by the clothes, by my
movements, my walk, my attitude, the way I sat. These are
all things which I had explored with Bobby Lewis' help in
rehearsal. So now the reassurance I needed was the inner-
self-reassurance, which came to me from ordinary objects.
In Prospero, which I'm playing now, I come in with a magic
staff. The first thing I do is relate to that stick with my
eyes. There it is. And it can perform. It can do magic. It can
do wonders. And already, as I do so, I feel something within
me relaxing. If this is real, then I am real. If this can perform
wonders through me, then I can perform wonders through it.
And behold—thunder! Not from the stage manager who's
pressing a button, who says, "Make it, boys." But from me.
In other words, belief is encouraged by simple relationship
to objects. As I say, it's possibly so simple that people won't
believe it.

INTERVIEWER   No, no. I know why it's true, and I'll tell
you why it's true. I went out to play golf yesterday. I was
alone; I didn't have anybody to play with and I went out
alone. I came to the golf course, and there were a man and a
woman, and they said, "If you wish to tee off, go ahead."
That always puts you on your mettle, because (a) you've got
to get out in front of them fast enough so that you don't hold
them up, since they've been courteous to you; (b) it means
you've got to hit that ball right, because otherwise you're
going to be a damned fool. So I concentrated, I excluded
everything, and I got off what was for me one of the best shots
I could possibly hope for. And, somehow or other, for the
rest of the day, I had gotten into this concentration. So that
what you said, as you said it, to me was very clear and revealing.

CARNOVSKY   Absolutely. That's a perfect parallel.

INTERVIEWER   In doing this—entering the life of the

play as you described you did in *Enemy of the People*—it would have, I would think, not only the effect of this extraordinary relaxation that you described, but doesn't it also provide something of what in his lectures Robert Lewis refers to frequently as the intention, a sort of underpinning of understanding and approach to the whole part, which he considered so important in acting?

CARNOVSKY   Oh, certainly, it's related to the intention that the character is playing throughout. You see, a part is built up moment by moment. The actor playing Stockmann knows that in the third act he is going to have to justify what he does in the first act. The sense of form leads him into a development of this climactic development—that's redundant —but through the whole process, so that he knows "By the time I get there I must justify what I begin here." So if the animosity which is pursued in terms of action in the first act is correctly developed by the time he gets to the third act, the climax comes in terms of the very same action, and it will be justified. It is unified. I often tell my students, "Be aware of the objective as the target of your action—'I am going there. I know I am going there.' Therefore everything you do will relate to the final object."

INTERVIEWER   How long did it take you to learn this art of relaxation, to learn and believe in this procedure?

CARNOVSKY   Really all my life, because tension is always the enemy. And there are very few actors who are so utterly relaxed that they've lost their fear that tension may interfere with them. Personalities like Jack Benny—I even suspect him, for all his seeming relaxation—have certain fears back there that haunt them. I don't know about that. But that kind of ease is very enviable. When did it begin? One has to have faith in the processes that one finds out are good. I remember once sitting on the stage before a performance of *Awake and Sing* many years ago in Cleveland. It was a matinée, and I came on stage, as I sometimes do, to kind of think a little bit about the part, and I said to myself, "Today I'm going to relate to Stella Adler (who was playing my daughter in the play) not as my daughter, Bessie Berger, but as Stella Adler. I know it's Stella. She knows it's me. It's Morris. She knows. She doesn't have to be told that. I know it's Stella. I don't have to say that's Bessie Berger. I don't have to do her creation for her. All I know is, that is Stella." So I said to myself, "I'm going to relate to her today, Morris to Stella." It did an extraordinary thing for me. It was my own hunch, you know, that I was following. And Stella herself commented on it afterward. And as a matter of fact I related that way to all the people in the play—to Sandy, to Art, to Joe, to Phoebe, and so on. And Stella said, "What happened today? There was a—a—" I said, "What was it? What did you see?" She said, "Well, there was a certain exciting actuality about it. It was true, very true, beyond what it had been. It excited me. It made me want to—it made me wonder what was going on." Well, I made a discovery for myself in exploring this particular facet of craft. It has to do again with the sense of self, one self relating to another.

INTERVIEWER   Can you describe that discovery, what it meant to you?

CARNOVSKY   It meant greater relaxation. For example, today, in the moment that we met out there at the car, and I didn't know very much about you, there were certain tensions that naturally intruded, came between us, because of society and politeness and all that stuff. By now, we've kind of all let our hair down. We're looking at each other with different eyes. My I—ego—is encountering yours in a much more easy way than it was able to out there at the car. This is all to the good. And this is the relationship which the actor tries to fill himself with from the outset.

INTERVIEWER   Wouldn't that take away from this thing called the intent? If you accept Stella Adler on the basis of being Stella Adler—which may bring a whole host of associations to you, about Stella Adler, having nothing to do with her role, about the vacation she's taking in two weeks or that she had told you about how her feet hurt—wouldn't these take away from the whole image you were building?

CARNOVSKY   No, because those associations are not the important things about the Stella Adler which I encounter within the image of the part, Bessie Berger. You see, I'm not interested in Bessie Berger's vacation or her feet; I'm only interested in Bessie Berger, the character that Stella is playing. And within that particular image there is an essential Stella whom I know and to whom I relate with my eyes, with my ears, with my senses, with my attitude. She at the same time is doing so to me in the same way—I hope. And this is what makes a scene. This is what makes it pulse. What I began to say in the beginning—the discovery, in itself, is an important one for me. But it was necessary for me to repeat it, to do it again and again. That meant to have faith. I had to have faith in that discovery. Just as I had to have faith that relaxation really works, that ease is terribly important, that the relationship to an object is terribly important. And when that happens, action then is released, and action is the all-important thing in a play, action or intention—that thing that you mentioned that Bobby Lewis spoke of—intention—that is it, that's action; intention that gives rise to dynamic activity. Actions are inner things; therefore it has to do with intention.

INTERVIEWER   Concentration is wrapped up in all this, of course, and, you know, this is a lesson for me, too. I can't help realizing, as we've been talking here, particularly about relaxation and tension, how much relationship there is between the art of acting and sports.

CARNOVSKY   Absolutely. We talked about this very much in the Group Theatre. Lee Strasberg was a great tennis player, you know, and he was always pointing out that the ability to connect with the ball, to follow through, to shift into your next necessity, to encounter the ball again, the back-hand, the follow-through, all this, this rhythm of movement established by sport, and what we ourselves have certainly discovered— you in golf, and I in swimming . . .

INTERVIEWER   I might add again that as in acting, there are dozens and dozens of books written about the theory of golf. They tell you don't do this, don't do that; keep this arm that way, and so on. And yet, when it comes right down to it, the secret is, somehow, in the concentration, and the relaxation.

CARNOVSKY   That's right. That's right. Yes. There is no performance that I do on this or any other stage which is not preceded by a moment, a curious moment, in which the door is unlocked, as it were. It's as if I say to myself, "Now, this it it. This is it." It's a kind of marshaling of all the resources. Sometimes you don't succeed in marshaling them fully, but you try. That movement is always taking place: "Now, this is it." It is an act of concentration.

INTERVIEWER   I wanted to know what feeling you have about the relationship between an actor and a director. What should the relationship be?

CARNOVSKY   The relationship should be one of mutual respect, understanding, and love of the work—also trust. Because the director represents the eye which helps the actor to decide the form in which what he does will take place. When this trust is not there, it's just too bad—that's all. And the actor has to then supply what the director is unable to supply —and the director, paradoxically, may have to fire the actor!

INTERVIEWER   An actress we interviewed was talking about what she considered was the Method school of directing. She complained that a certain director nearly drove her crazy because he would talk about the intention of the scene and what it was meant to convey, and discuss the scene, and discuss so-and-so's psychological momentum, and so forth and so on, and she thought this was all rather unnecessary, that the director must have faith that the actress's own intuitions and intelligence will tell her this. Is that a mark of Actors Studio directing—that there is a good deal of talk and of thinking through and of analysis?

CARNOVSKY   I think that one of the most valuable fermenters—I can't think of a better word—of a good performance is excitement in rehearsal. Excitement in rehearsal can be captured by some—very often—by some good talk, and sometimes you can't have enough of it. I happen to know, on the basis of having worked, for example, with Harold Clurman, that he is one of the finest talkers in the world. In fact, I would rather work with him than almost any other director that I can think of. Bobby Lewis is another—I love working with him. And now Bill Ball, who directed *The Tempest*. He is a magnificent director.

INTERVIEWER   Is it because of this sense of excitement?

CARNOVSKY   Yes. Where some people think Harold Clurman occasionally misses is in the post-talking phase, as a *metteur en scène*. But, regardless, he's absolutely marvelous for stimulating the imagination of the actor. And that actor is poor, indeed, who cannot take from Harold something which, if he allows it to penetrate into himself, will produce a much better performance than he can do all by himself. Harold has wit, penetration, imagination, passion, and these are all things which if you set loose in the theatre can only help the actor. Of course, the actor is a craftsman and an artist in his own right, and sometimes the danger of too much talk is that the actor may feel a little bit insecure, as if he says, "Gee, I can't do what that man seems to want." That's a danger.

INTERVIEWER   I would think that for an instinctive or intuitive actor, the one who is not scientifically trained, let us say, in a set of principles—that for an actor this scientific approach could be unnerving, as you just outlined. I can see that.

CARNOVSKY   Incidentally, I would like to add, about Harold Clurman, that I love to work with him. And while we are on the subject of Harold Clurman I would like to add that he is owed an outstanding and absolute debt by the whole American theatre. Of all the workers in the theatre that I know, going back to the beginning of the Group Theatre, he, more than anyone else, has put more passion and desire and understanding and imagination into the theatre.

INTERVIEWER   I suppose you could say that his work with the Group Theatre was like throwing a stone into the middle of a lake; the ripples have gone to many shores—to Hollywood, to the theatre, to television. There are practitioners all over now. Speaking of ripples, I wonder, do you see in some of the off-Broadway theatres some new forms developing? For instance, have you seen *The Connection* or *Krapp's Last Tape?*

CARNOVSKY   Unfortunately, no, I haven't seen either of those. I saw the Tennessee Williams play *Camino Real.* That was the last thing I saw off-Broadway. I was very struck by the richness of the material and by the direction. I think Quintero is a lovely director. But the people. . . . Let me say this first. In the period before the Group Theatre, you didn't see such a rich assortment of talents in one play that you would see in that play there. There are at least nine or ten really rich, beautiful performances in that thing. I was amazed.

INTERVIEWER   Do you see any place which you could identify as the wellsprings of the new theatre? The theatre is having a rather hard time and we need some vigorous forces to open up a new way, perhaps, and I wonder what you see ahead.

CARNOVSKY   I'm sure that the young actors who study passionately, and who go down off-Broadway to find a place to express their talents—I'm sure that they are starting something down there which is very rich for the theatre of the future. On Broadway, no, I don't see very much happening there.

INTERVIEWER   You said, quite some time ago, that the theatre was daily emerging as a more powerful social force. That was in 1937. But today, of course, not only do you have the movies, but you have television and a diminishing theatre. Are you discouraged about this?

CARNOVSKY   No, not at all. I believe in the living material of the actor. I believe in the expansion of the imagination. If I was a little bit sanguine about the importance of the theatre as a social force, why—so I learned my lesson. Not too long after that came the McCarthy business, and some very depressing stuff happening in our country, and, of course, the war, and all that . . . The greatest illumination for me so far, I think, has been Shakespeare, because it has taken the lid off the actor's talent. I found it has given me a great sense of freedom, and I know it has done that for other actors who have been here with me, doing fine work, great parts.

INTERVIEWER   I'd like to come back to the director again. What is your feeling about the strong director, the director who is supposed to have his own signature dominating the whole production with his own mark? I have in mind Kazan or Tyrone Guthrie. Do you believe in the strong director, in the sense that the director is, over all, the entire king? Or do you favor the more co-operative sort of direction, more of the give and take between actor and director?

CARNOVSKY   I haven't worked with either of the people you mentioned. One of the greatest experiences that I think I've had in the theatre was the Habimah *Dybbuk*, years ago. And this was a reworking of an old production; its director had long ago passed away, Vakhtangov of the Russian theatre. And I never had such an experience. For unification of style, the only theatre that I've seen since then that was in the same alley or level was the Piccolo, the Milano people. But for a spell of creation, really like the creation of the world, nothing has paralleled what I felt with that *Dybbuk*. It laid a kind of a charm on me even between the acts. I couldn't move, you know, I just sat there thinking about it. And I didn't understand Hebrew. So here was something that was created for all time—the Parthenon if you like. Now what was this traceable to? I think it was traceable to love. Let me put it right on the table—love. I think Vakhtangov loved the material, I think he loved his actors, I think his actors loved him; I think that together they made what is to me the classic experience of the theatre. Now, I don't know—not having worked with the people you mentioned—but I would say that it is a terrible temptation to a director to minimize what his actors can do and to use them as puppets. I don't know whether those two men use their actors in that way. Certainly they're strong directors, and they do put their mark on whatever they do. I think that a production which emerges with a life of its own, which seems to say, "I am Anton Chekhov's *Cherry Orchard*. He dreamed me. He imagined me. And these are all the loving participators in the act of making me come to life"—this is the kind of production that I believe in, and I think this can only be brought about by respect for the material. For the director not to take too much to himself, not to push his ideas onto the actors at the expense of the material. Sometimes, by the way, a director can illuminate material like mad, you know. By the way, I loved very much what Mark Van Doren once said about *The Tempest*. He said that the play is of such power that any set of symbols comes to light and illuminates automatically if you bring them near this play. Ideas like freedom, love, life—all these things become suddenly illuminated in the presence of this electrical thing which *The Tempest* is. Now, if a director can do that, that's a fine director. That's a really fine director. I do believe that Stanislavsky was that kind of director, and I'm certain that Vakhtangov was.

INTERVIEWER   What leads a man into character acting? Or is this something that happens to an actor because he's not capable of being a juvenile?

CARNOVSKY   That is very likely, that's part of it. But what is the opposite of character acting? Juveniles only?

INTERVIEWER   No. All character actors are actors— that's what you're trying to get me to say.

CARNOVSKY   I knew you would say it, because it's a fact: all acting is character acting. I think the gift of identifying with objects in life is what impels the actor to become what we call a character actor. By objects, I mean people. If I see the same Yussel that I spoke of, if I remember him as an image and I have a strong identification with him, I will say to myself, "Some day I hope I'm in a play which will enable me to play him." That is to say, I won't imitate what he did and was—it's too long anyway, and I wouldn't be able to remember it all—but I will remember a certain essence about him.

INTERVIEWER   You have often played older men. Has that been particularly easy for you? Do you like those parts, or do they just come along?

CARNOVSKY   Yes, I have—the majority of them have been older men. Some author somewhere said, "Old men are always interesting." And maybe that's the thing in a nutshell. Their quirks, their peculiarities, the differences between them and the other men—even other old men—are always interesting to capture. But, basically, in all acting the aim of the actor is to seize the kernel, what you called the spine before, the spine of the character. In rehearsal we're always searching for that. What is the thing that makes all things tick? You will find that the spine of Shylock expressed itself through a phrase which is normally overlooked, and which had great meaning for me; namely, when Shylock says to Antonio, "You spit upon my Jewish gabardine . . . You that did void your rheum upon my beard." Now that statement is generally taken as, well, not a very nice act on the part of Antonio to discharge so much venom and hatred against a poor Jew. But I took it very literally, and I found a horror coming to me and an antagonism and, not venom, but a degradation of dignity coming to me out of something which Shakespeare had provided me in the script. "You that did void your rheum upon my beard." There is no insult which goes further than that. And Shakespeare meant it literally and he put it there for the actor to use.

INTERVIEWER   That goes back to what we said before; I find it amazing the insight of Shakespeare into the heart and mind of a Jew. The play is called a comedy by Shakespeare, but it's not possible that he meant it literally. He seems to have understood only too well the suffering of the Jew.

CARNOVSKY   I think that Shakespeare had something very subtle in mind when he wrote *The Merchant of Venice —A Comedy*. Indeed, as I wrote in my commentary for the Laurel Shakespeare edition of *The Merchant of Venice:* "The Merchant of Venice—A Comedy* . . . And what kind of comedy is this, we might well inquire. A succession of lyrical scenes puffed high with the words and antics of a group of men-about-town, wastrels, fortune hunters, gamblers, heiresses (by law and by theft), businessmen, and in the midst of it all, a desperately serious man galvanized by revenge, committing his life and fortune to the wild pursuit of retributive justice. An unpleasant play, Shaw would have called it. A disturbing play for the times we live in—and perhaps even for Shakespeare's time, for all that Shylock was fair game. And probably disturbing for Shakespeare himself. For one has the feeling that the mood in which he wrote *The Merchant of Venice* was a foreshadowing, tentative as yet, of the later and more bitter plays. The ideas of this play center about the acquisition of money and the corruption that stems therefrom. Its characters without exception are tarred with the same brush. Heiress and apostate, merchant and money-lender, waster and thief—to the degree that money has shaped their point of view, to that degree are they dehumanized. Perhaps Shakespeare was speaking for himself through Antonio when he wrote those first words: 'In sooth I know not why I am so sad.' For truth to tell, the alternation of luminous folderol and self-destructive vengefulness on which he was embarking promised to shed little credit on the nature of humanity. But having started, Shakespeare nailed down the bitter indictment with truthful blow after blow. 'Look,' he seems to be saying, 'you are really repellent in your corruption and your hatefulness, your pride of place and wealth—why then all these airs and graces? What triumph of the human spirit are you celebrating? And in sooth, why are you so sad?' And particularly why these class distinctions between Negro, white, Gentile and Jew?"

INTERVIEWER I don't think I will ever forget your Shylock.

CARNOVSKY Thank you very much. And I would like to say, incidentally, I did not want to play for what is known as sympathy. On the other hand, I certainly did not believe that Shylock was a villain. I wanted to show him as a human being within certain circumstances, within which circumstances he would react with the dignity of an individual, you know, a *mensch*. And in showing that it was necessary for him to go through with this business of a pound of flesh, which is terrible—no one can deny it—it's horrible; but in showing the reasons why it was necessary for him to carry through and go to law about it, I have a feeling of the affirmation of human dignity. And that, I think, is what Shakespeare intended. He did not say, however, "I'm going to show him as a sympathetic human being." Nor did he show him utterly as a villain. He showed him as Shakespeare; that's the way Shakespeare writes.

INTERVIEWER You have said that you rely upon the audience also before you set your part, and that as a matter of fact, you never really finally set it because you're always depending upon the audience, in a sense, so as to give you the rhythm of your part. Can you tell us a little bit about that?

CARNOVSKY Yes. It happens all the time. The actor learns very swiftly, in dress rehearsal when he begins to have an audience, just what is carrying out the intention of the director and of himself in the play. Sometimes, if he's playing comedy, for example, he knows that there's a laugh there—in terms of result, in terms of sheer effect, he knows that there's a laugh there. In his intentions, again, he works for it, because that is what a play like that is for. In plays which are predominantly serious, even tragic, there's a certain thickness that he experiences in the air which comes from the audience. I felt it very much so in *The Merchant of Venice*. You could tell a relationship was established between the actor and the audience, so that the audience themselves became actors in the whole event. The play was an event in which the audience participated. For me there's nothing more really shattering and moving than this particular experience—the way an audience rises to the material of the play. It's a peculiar kind of . . . It argues that the theatre was descended from the church, you know; and in the last analysis it's a curious kind of act of prayer or dedication—devotion, let's say—which is inherent in the whole act of watching a play. It happens in certain plays, of course, more than others; and, of course, in the catchpenny stuff that you see around a good deal, well, you don't expect it there.

INTERVIEWER   Guthrie has said that the theatre is a ritual, and it must be approached as a ritual.

CARNOVSKY   That's right. I agree with him there. I agree. Yes. Certainly I felt it with relation to *The Dybbuk*. I mean, there was a certain something very much out of the common—and religious, one has to say about it. And *this* is something the actor senses. An actor will come off the stage saying, "They were with me tonight. They were with me. Gee, they were nice." Something like that. "What a good audience." They are giving him something. If he's wise he will learn how to give the next audience back what he receives, in terms of pace, rhythm, what to minimize and what to accent, what they want to hear, what makes for a laugh—which sometimes is a very beautiful thing. In *The Tempest*, for example, Bill Hickey, who plays Trinculo, does a lovely piece of comedy, it's really beautiful, and the audience responds in the same way; they laugh at how funny he is, but they also laugh because they love him. They respond because they love him.

INTERVIEWER   As a teacher who sees a good many of the young people coming into the theatre—what are they like today?

CARNOVSKY   I know this: when students come to me, they're the same young people that we were when we started the Group Theatre, and they want the same thing.

INTERVIEWER   They don't just want stardom?

CARNOVSKY   Oh, of course they do, but I don't let them get away with that idea for long. And there's this to say: young actors come to the theatre, and they may have stardust in their eyes and they may think they're going to plunge in and get a big break and be gathered into the firmament overnight. But the great majority of them get, not a rude awakening, but a very important awakening to the fact that theatre technique has got to be studied; you've got to devote yourself to it. There are simple, definite things which have to be performed, some of which I've tried to indicate here. One has to learn to do these things. One has to learn to look at people, to connect with people, to find a humanity in people, so that they will bring out the answering humanity in you. And in this very act, they've discovered their own humanity, where sometimes they didn't even suspect it was there; or, if they took it for granted, it was on a level that they didn't know was possible to attain. Suddenly they begin to have hopes for this material that they themselves are; that's what induced us to say "A good actor is a good man" in the old days. It doesn't always happen. But they suddenly, by investigating their own material, find how precious they are as material.

Shelley Winters

BIOGRAPHY

Shelley Winters was born in St. Louis in 1923 and was brought to New York City at the age of eight. After graduating from Thomas Jefferson High School, where she participated in dramatics, she became a model, using part of her earnings to study acting in the evenings. Her early years included work as a chorus girl and in summer stock. She went on to small parts in several shows in New York, in which she sang as well as acted. Included among them were *Conquest in April* and *Meet the People*. In 1942 she was given a supporting role in the Broadway production of the operetta *Rosalinda*, and this brought her a Hollywood contract. She appeared in various films, including *Knickerbocker Holiday*. After her contract with a Hollywood film company expired she returned to New York, and in 1947 played Ado Annie in *Oklahoma!* in its fifth year.

Miss Winters then went back to Hollywood, where she played in a number of movies, including a role in *A Double Life* that brought her a nomination for an Oscar. *The Great Gatsby, Johnny Stool Pigeon, South Sea Sinner* and *A Place in the Sun* were among her other films.

In 1951 Miss Winters returned to settle in New York and started studying at the Actors Studio. In 1955 she appeared in *A Hatful of Rain,* and won wide critical support; the next year she was in *Girls of Summer,* and in 1959 in *A Piece of Blue Sky.* During this entire Broadway period, however, Miss Winters had been busy in Hollywood as well, filling major roles in such films as *Phone Call from a Stranger, Executive Suite* and *The Diary of Anne Frank,* for which she won an Oscar. She also made frequent television appearances. Miss Winters is divorced from her husband, Anthony Franciosa; she has one daughter by a previous marriage to Vittorio Gassman.

SETTING

Shelley Winters thought she was coming down with a head cold the day of the interview, and when we arrived she had just awakened from a nap; during our talk she downed several antihistamine pills and many cups of hot tea and coffee. She wore a plain dressing gown and was without make-up. The effect managed to combine interestingly the allure of a Hollywood star, which she is, and the outdoor naturalness of a college gym teacher, which indeed she is not.

But her conversation is very much the actress, with profound interest in the stage. During most of the interview she sat curled up in a large armchair, her conversation alternating between the cheerfully informal and the intensely animated when we touched on a subject close to her heart. Her voice is somehow not that expected of an actress; the diction is quite unstudied, at least for general conversational purposes, but the range of voice is impressive. Throughout the interview, the readiness of her responses and the concern she obviously felt for the subject gave ample evidence of the thought she has given to her profession.

Miss Winters lives in a West Side apartment overlooking New York's Central Park. The living room, where the interview took place, is large and sunny, its walls well filled with modern paintings in a variety of colors, rhythms and styles. There is a good deal of furniture, some of it rather handsome period pieces, and many tasteful lamps and vases. There are a good number of comfortable easy chairs, and a large blue sofa confronting a fireplace and separated from it by a large square white marble coffee table. On the mantel are small reproductions of such sculptures as Rodin's "The Kiss" and the "Moses" of Michelangelo, with a Japanese doll reposing somewhat informally among this distinguished grouping. Around the room are various other pieces of small sculpture, including some heads and a blue hippopotamus. On either side of the mantelpiece are bookcases, one quite filled with books, mostly popular novels and some plays and other volumes, and the other case containing mostly records—from classical to the latest musical comedy—and a hi-fi record player and radio. On the coffee table, amid various other items, were some copies of the British magazine of comment and opinion, *Encounter,* and a copy of the *Hollywood Reporter.* There is also a desk in the room, obviously well used and with a businesslike litter of papers on it; and there is a big color-television set, upon it a framed photograph of Miss Winters with Mrs. Roosevelt and a photograph of Miss Winters with her daughter and friends. A spinet piano, with some of her daughter's practice pieces, is against another wall—and at the back of the room there stands on a table a resplendently shiny Oscar, which Miss Winters won for her role in *The Diary of Anne Frank.*

Interview

INTERVIEWER   What is it that makes a person think she can be an actress?

WINTERS   I find that a very difficult question. I have days when I think I can be an actress, and other days when I think I have not fulfilled the degree of attainment that I think an actress should reach. Can you phrase it in a different way?

INTERVIEWER   Well, when did you first know you wanted to be an actress?

WINTERS   I really can't remember when I didn't want to be an actress. I think I was very, very young. I think the first time I saw a talking movie, *The Jazz Singer*—I was very little, and even before that I had been to a pantomime or something. But the idea of communicating thoughts and emotions to so many people, and moving them, seemed a special kind of art and fulfillment that I wanted. I always did.

INTERVIEWER   How old were you when you saw *The Jazz Singer?*

WINTERS   Four.

INTERVIEWER   Four—and you recall that?

WINTERS   Absolutely. I have almost total recall with films.

INTERVIEWER   What is it in you that compels you to act?

WINTERS   Well, I have a theory that an actor communicates ideas by the means of the author's words, and to me it seems a very great personal achievement. I don't mean just the money and fame. If you somehow are effective in a play that has some kind of content—in a funny kind of way, you've changed everybody's life a little bit. And that is the purpose of all art, I guess, and I guess I act because I want my life to have meaning. Between the time of birth and death we wish our lives to have some kind of meaning.

INTERVIEWER   Is that the reason you seem to lean predominantly in the choice of your roles to the more serious things?

WINTERS   I try to. But you can do it with comedy, too, I think.

INTERVIEWER   Oh, yes.

WINTERS   I mean the effort for human beings to live together better and find the best way to use this beautiful world. When you are an actress or a writer, you reach large audiences and you can communicate ideas, so when you do get something like *A Place in the Sun* or *Anne Frank* or *Executive Suite* or *The Big Knife* . . .

INTERVIEWER   Or *A Hatful of Rain.*

WINTERS   *A Hatful of Rain,* yes, that makes some kind of comment in this line; there is a degree of fulfillment.

INTERVIEWER   Your remark that each role or each play changes a life a little reminds me of an article in the *Times* several weeks ago, by Robert Brustein of Columbia University, in which he told about how he was cornered by an actress who said everybody who sees this play—he was referring to a particular play—leaves the theatre changed. And he questioned that. He queried how you can do in two and a half hours what the analyst's couch sometimes can't do in eight years.

WINTERS   Oh, but life is a continual process of change. I didn't see the article, but that's nonsense. It's a question of degree. I know that I was a different person when I came out of *Death of a Salesman* than when I went in. Maybe a lesser experience affects me. The first time I saw a painting of Picasso which had special meaning . . . I mean, you can hear a symphony nine times and on the tenth time suddenly it has a sort of meaning and does something to you.

INTERVIEWER   But it doesn't change you really?

WINTERS   Of course it does. Life is a constant process of change, for better or worse. I don't know what he was referring to, but even if you resist the ideas presented—you disagree with the playwright or the actor, or what you're seeing—that is a process of change because something new has been presented to you, and you've either refuted it or you've opened another little window in your experience. In Arthur Miller's *Death of a Salesman*—the acknowledgment about the pressure for success in our society, that the very things that we seek, we destroy in the process—it was a great examination of the means to an end. And you can ignore it and forget it, but it stays somewhere in your decisions, I think. I had that experience with *The Visit*. I don't know whether you saw that play. My first reaction to it was that I disliked it. But I couldn't forget it; it stayed with me and I had to think about it. I mean, the man and the question he posed of the meaning of love in our society and times: What is love? What we do because of it or for it or against it, and where the materialistic and the spiritual, if you will, starts and stops. And I don't think that anybody can see *The Visit*—the way the Lunts did it—and come out the same person.

INTERVIEWER   Only the other day something turned up in regard to a will that reminded me vividly of *The Visit*. What will happen because of money! What people will do! For money they will crucify a father. They will justify a man's death for money.

WINTERS   Or betray their most beloved ones—if the pressure is enough. You haven't asked me, but one of the things I think—if I wasn't an actress—I would like to be is a writer, and especially a dramatist, because I think even when playwrights aren't especially sociologically or politically aware, if they're good, they can't help but reflect their times. They're in a way the best historians. Ibsen certainly is more exciting than the history books of his time. And Tennessee Williams, for instance—I've just read his new play, and I've heard him talk about it, and maybe this is presumptuous of me, but I've read a different play than he talks about. He's written a really political play. It is called *Period of Adjustment*. He called it, once, *High Point Is Built on a Cavern*, and he called it that because his setting is a house in the suburbs that is on an underground cavern and the walls are kind of sinking, but I really think he used that symbolism for it because he's a playwright that absorbs, not maybe really meaning to point it at a certain thing. I mean, it's very difficult sometimes for a playwright to tell you the theme of his play, you know, but it is the job of the director and the actor to focus it in a certain direction. I remember *A Hatful of Rain* . . . It obviously had to go a certain way, and still, Mike Gazzo, the playwright, got furious in Washington, and said you're ruining my play (it was a smash hit). He wrote about life and death, and yet he didn't think that's what it was about. He wrote about a boy, you know, who was a drug addict, who was dying—and that's a death wish; and I was his pregnant wife who was gonna have that baby and keep that home together no matter what. But he didn't believe that he wrote that. The audience told him that's what he wrote and . . .

INTERVIEWER You mean the audience had told him what he wrote, after you and the director got finished with the play?

WINTERS Yes, but, well, the audience in a funny way told us. An audience is a fantastic instrument. Sometimes in the theatre when I see a play for the second time I watch the audience—and I always stand in the wings when I'm in a play and watch them—because they do many things besides laugh or cry. The silences are terribly important, or the coughing or the shifting.

INTERVIEWER How do you react to this on the stage?

WINTERS When you really have a subtext going and you're really aware of the audience in a special kind of a way, what happens is that after about fifteen minutes they take on the personality of one body or one person. If a play is good and you're effective in it, you suddenly hear a silence that is loud, and that moment makes the whole schmageggy business of an actor or an actress worthwhile, because you suddenly know that they are human beings like you, who are receiving something from you.

INTERVIEWER You must miss this audience reaction in making films.

WINTERS Terribly, just terribly. The films are a tool of the director. When you have a good director who has time—who can take a long time in shooting a film—then it can be a very gratifying experience. It's impossible to shoot a good film fast, unless it's the kind of film that you can rehearse for two or three weeks; and then the setting of it is such that you don't need a lot of camera movement— you're in one set or two sets, something like that—and you can do it sort of like a play, you know, long shots and stuff. The only times I've really enjoyed working in films have been with George Stevens, I would say, because you really get a chance to investigate the layers of work. I mean, you can pick up a phone and somebody says, "Hello," just that word, and you know how they feel, what they're doing. You know, you hear "Hello," and you say to yourself immediately, "Oh, I shouldn't have called now." That has to come out of—I don't want to use mysticism—that's not just intellectual things.

INTERVIEWER   Don't be afraid to use mysticism.

WINTERS   What I mean is—well, I don't like to use the word soul, because I'm not quite sure what it is, or psyche, or something. But everything in the human being creates. Languages are the means of communication. You can't learn an author's lines just saying them, and get anything valuable. You're just saying words—might as well be reciting, you know, reading. You must, as an actress or an actor—when you have a good director—investigate all the areas that make those words come out.

INTERVIEWER   Well, that raises a question about *Hatful of Rain*. You said that Gazzo did not realize he had written a play about life and death, and it seems that the actors and the director interpreted that play for him, and I was wondering whether that is the province of the actor and the director—to project their own interpretation.

WINTERS   I didn't say their own interpretation. I said the audience. That's why you go out of town. The audience tells you what your play is about. See, Gazzo really did know that he wrote about that, but he couldn't face it. A real art form comes out of a human being's guts and totality of experience. I know that the first time I saw *A Place in the Sun*—which was the first real work I did—I wouldn't talk to George Stevens. I saw a rough cut of the movie—and Theodore Dreiser's wife was there and Charlie Chaplin, and they started congratulating me. And all I could think of was that I was furious, that it was terrible exposure—how dare he expose me like that. And art is exposure. And until you've developed a degree of maturity to handle that knowledge, you are revealing what other people keep hidden. And I think that that's why Mike didn't want to face what he had written about. When we left Washington he fought bitterly, he wanted another kind . . . He didn't know what he wanted, he couldn't say what he wanted, but he saw . . . Curiously enough, I would say that he's a product of this so-called "beat" generation. I think he wanted the force of death to win, but it happened in the play that the force of life won. Actually, it's left up in the air, but to the degree that you *think* that life's got a pretty good chance. I don't think he wanted that. But he wrote it in the play, and depending on the audience, depending on the actors, the meaning of a play can change—with the same words.

INTERVIEWER   Did this play change more in rehearsal because your process is strictly Method?

WINTERS   I don't know what strictly Method means. To me, Method means a method of work, you know, not just that attitude.

INTERVIEWER   What I meant was: in the working out of *A Hatful of Rain,* I've read that you used the method of work of the Method—if that will be semantically acceptable—of probing into the lives of the characters to away back before the crisis of the crucial sequence in the play, and that at one point in rehearsal, you ad-libbed the whole action; you did not recite the lines.

WINTERS   Yes.

INTERVIEWER   And you found that you got nuances and pauses that you were not always aware of when . . .

WINTERS   When you recite the lines. You see, when I say subtext, what I mean is the thoughts in the actor that produces the words of the playwright. I don't know whether you have seen *The Connection* . . .

INTERVIEWER   Yes.

WINTERS   Because you have a sense—whether you like the play or not—you have a sense as you watch that play that they're just making it up, that the dialogue is theirs. Now, that to me is the test of an actor, because then the audience really identifies, feels that something alive is going on on the stage. When someone says to me that actor is good, or this actor is good, that annoys me. I think what is exciting is what goes on between the actors in the air, that if they're exchanging, like we're doing now—you tell me, I receive it, and back—that's the exciting life-thing that goes on.

INTERVIEWER   That's ensemble playing.

WINTERS   That's right; and the way to get at it is as you said—is through that improvisation, that period of rehearsal, when you are getting the thoughts of the actors and the motivating forces that make them say eventually what the playwright wants them to say. And then you're not just getting up and saying words to somebody, you know, and hitting a gesture, or an attitude, and saying the lines.

INTERVIEWER Now, to clarify for me something you said: when you finished rehearsing the play, the play had a certain form—it represented the combination of the company's work in collaboration with the author and the director.

WINTERS Yes.

INTERVIEWER Then you open out of town, and you say that the audience begins to tell you things that you did not see in rehearsal.

WINTERS Yes. The audience tells you how to focus the play.

INTERVIEWER In other words, in *A Hatful of Rain* you found that the approach changed after opening, is that correct?

WINTERS That's right. You see, we have an expression at the Actors Studio—it's sort of an inside joke—we say, "It's a secret." I mean, we can be doing all kinds of things, you know, with the other actors. The audience doesn't know and couldn't care less. It's a secret between you, the playwright and the other actors. The thing the audience tells you is whether it's coming over, the idea that you wish to convey.

INTERVIEWER Do you believe that an actor is a creative artist, or is he primarily an interpretive artist?

WINTERS I *absolutely* think he's a creative artist.

INTERVIEWER Unequivocally?

WINTERS Unequivocally. I've heard all of that secondary art stuff, and all that. As an example, Laurette Taylor, who with secondary plays gave audiences great experiences that we're still talking about; and in her whole lifetime she had one great play, and she was like the greatest artist of our theatre. I had a funny experience with her. I had never heard of Laurette Taylor. I went from Brooklyn to Hollywood and nobody mentioned her name, and I was on a publicity tour and I stopped in Chicago and I knew Tony Ross and I saw an ad for *The Glass Menagerie* and I went to see it, and I never, never, never can forget that night in the theatre. I would say that that and *Death of a Salesman* were the greatest nights in the theatre I ever had. The night I saw *Death of a Salesman* the audience was talking to each other and a strange man turned around to me and said to me, "Well, what can you do if you don't get the goods? What can you do?" They were talking to each other, it was so powerful—the impact of the denial or the expression of their own hopes and dreams. Anyway, about Laurette Taylor. I went backstage and I thought she'd change her clothes and become a young girl—you know, in the scene when she talks about the plantation. I never saw anything like that on the stage. I've seen other actresses do that part. That is a creative art, when it is on that level, when an actor achieves that level—because you touch people in an area that somehow uplifts them, and that I think is the purpose of art. To me, that's the only real acknowledgement of the human soul I've ever seen. Great music—and when I see people respond to each other, to the communication of art.

INTERVIEWER Why, if what you say it true, are there those who say that the actor is more of an interpretive artist, that his obligation is primarily to the playwright to interpret the character as the playwright conceived him, not as the actor conceives him, so that in that sense the actor cannot be the creative artist.

WINTERS Wait a minute. You're giving me a premise I don't accept.

INTERVIEWER But the premise exists, does it not?

WINTERS Well, I don't know. The actor first must know what the playwright wants to communicate. The actor is the means by which the playwright speaks to the audience—I don't deny that. Now, it's on all degrees, all levels of penetration that this can happen. A playwright can say war is horrible. One actor plays this part in this play where the theme is that war is horrible—the audience says, "Ych, it is, you know." Another actor plays the same part, and the audience says, "My God, I must do everything within my power to see that there is never a war again." Another actor plays the same part, same words, and somebody else can listen and say, "Wars can be fun, you get away from home." I'm using an exaggerated theme, but I have seen that happen with the same absolute role, same play. Now, to say that there is only one way to do a role is a little nonsensical. You have all levels of—of ways of fulfilling what the playwright wants to say, and often the actor and the director bring something to a play that the playwright didn't know he said.

INTERVIEWER That's borne out with what you just said about *Hatful of Rain*. Let's go back for a moment. I was curious to know how you got started in musicals.

WINTERS Oh—let me see. Well, I had a lot of *chutzbah* —plenty of gall—when I was a kid and I couldn't get a job. I had a job in a little play, *The Night Before Christmas*, which lasted—it was at the end of the war, I think—lasted two weeks, to get that first Equity card. To this day I've never transferred my union affiliation with Equity to the

Screen Actors Guild. I don't know, that's just how I feel about myself—that I'm a stage actress primarily. Although I've spent twelve years out there making movies and I still like to make them, my primary direction of work is the theatre. Anyway, what was I saying?

INTERVIEWER I had asked you how come you had gone into musicals?

WINTERS Yes. Well, what happened was—as a kid I used to hang around Walgreen's, and this play was a flop, and I was just—oh, I was just floored because I had got into Equity and I had been looking for a job since I was a junior in high school. I used to dress up and I'd go and look at the Equity board and try to get into a play—and I never finished high school. I went till the sixth term—and I still should have been in high school when I did this play, and it failed and I was pretty awful in it, too. I was scared of the audience. I backed up—the little scene I had—and Ruth Weston, who was in it, swore I was upstaging her. I just wanted to get the hell off, I was so scared of the audience. But anyway, I had done some Borscht Circuit work in the summer and I heard that Max Reinhardt was auditioning opera singers at the Forty-fourth Street Theatre, which is now the extension of the *New York Times* . . . I can't bear to see it, every time I go by I get furious—they had to tear down a theatre! And I feel personally upset about it. Anyway, I heard that he was auditioning singers for an operetta called *Rosalinda,* and I said, well, I would try that, and I went over to a music store and got a copy of "Chi Chi Castenango," which I had done on the Borscht Circuit, and I went along on this call, and Reinhardt was sitting up there in a box. He had singers from the Metropolitan there. They were singing Wagner and, I don't know, Mozart, and everything. And I walked on when my turn came—he used to talk, he used to ask your name, and where you had come from, and what kind of acting you would like to do, or singing—and I handed my music to the classical accompanist there and I started singing "Chi Chi Castenango," and Reinhardt almost fell out of the box, he started laughing so hard. It was right in the middle of all this serious music. And the guy playing, you know, had a tough time following this sort of jazzy music. And when I finished, there he was laughing. He said, "Did you know this is an operetta?" And I said, "Yes, but I'm willing to try." And he kinda looked at me for a moment and said, "There's no part in the show for you, but I am going to write one in for you." And he said, "You should be in the theatre." And I told him from the stage that my one play had failed. There was a little part of a girl that hangs on Oscar Karlweis' arm—I don't know whether you saw it—and he kinda gave me a couple of little scenes in the play, sort of a few jokes and stuff, and the show was a hit. Then I had enough money to study acting.

INTERVIEWER Where did you go to study acting?

WINTERS Oh, several places. I went to Piscator's class in the New School. Then I studied at the New Theatre School, and then I took some classes from—oh, what's his name—Geiger.

INTERVIEWER Geiger?

WINTERS Yes, and I was always working in little theatre groups.

INTERVIEWER In other words, your going into musicals was purely accidental. What you were really interested in was the serious work.

WINTERS Oh, yes. Well, I just wanted to work so I could . . . I was modeling and I hated it—and the fella said I was the world's worst model because I was always studying scenes and, you know, I could never remember the numbers of the dresses—just to get through the day so that I could go to dramatic school at night.

INTERVIEWER Then you didn't stay in musicals very long?

WINTERS No, but I got in several. I did that one. I did *Oklahoma!* but it was sort of accidentally.

INTERVIEWER And *Of "V" We Sing*.

WINTERS Yes, *Of "V" We Sing*. That was a kind of special revue, rather accidental.

INTERVIEWER I was curious about your career in the musicals. What did you find in terms of the acting requirements? Is there much acting required?

WINTERS Oh, I think musicals are great training for an actor. I did a lot of musicals on the Borscht Circuit. I see all these kids working in summer stock, and they paint scenery, you know, they don't get a chance to act.

INTERVIEWER Yes, that's true.

WINTERS I don't think they do this any more on the Borscht Circuit, but I worked at two places—one called Aaron and Pinya Pasha's Lake Shore Chateau, and I worked at Grossinger's when they had social staffs—and every week you did a musical and a dramatic play and then kind of one-act plays, and you'd get a kind of freedom that you really don't get just acting in straight plays. Acting is the development of one's own personality, too, you know. That's what the public buys in a star, shall we say, the personality thing. And I hope to go back to musicals. I like doing them. I'm studying singing now.

INTERVIEWER   I understand you've given lectures to young people on how to break into the theatre.

WINTERS   Well, yes, it sort of happened accidentally. I was asked to give a kind of lecture on acting, and I found that the kids, when the question period came, really wanted to know how one goes about getting their first job—what they do. I'll tell you what you do. You create it. You find a place to make an off-Broadway theatre. You watch the Equity boards for plays being cast. You try to find, like I did, places on the Borscht Circuit that could support a social staff and want entertainment. Maybe it's not quite so tough now with television. And maybe there is more opportunity. And you try to get with the affiliated things, like modeling, messenger boys at CBS, NBC, all the things that are closely correllated to performing. Or you take an upstairs loft and, you know, fit in a couple of seats and do plays. I know, in California, the Players Ring and the Circle Theatre and the Gallery Workshop—if you really want to act. You see, I know that these kids have had other jobs, and by each of them contributing a hundred dollars they've managed to get up the initial expense to have a theatre. They've got a director. And there is an appetite for off-Broadway all over the country. And the actual experience of performing in front of an audience is the most important thing, whether it's in the Y.M.C.A. or in lodges, you know. But what really makes me sad is when I go into Downey's* or some place and see these kids just hanging around and waiting for the jobs to come to them. It just doesn't work that way.

INTERVIEWER   You feel that you have to make the breaks for yourself?

WINTERS   Yes. You have to. There is a degree of luck, but you have to grab opportunity. The way I got *A Place in the Sun* is I read *An American Tragedy* and I spoke to Norman Mailer, whom I met at a party, and he was a protégé of Dreiser's and wrote Stevens a long letter about it.

INTERVIEWER   Is that so? You mean even at your stage of the game?

WINTERS   I had only done one picture, *A Double Life.* But he thought I was, you know, a blond sexpot. He didn't

* A restaurant in New York where young actors gather.

even want to talk to me. My agent had mentioned me. He didn't even want—he said this is ridiculous. He wouldn't even let me come to the studio. I met him at the Hollywood Athletic Club, and then I dyed my hair brown. My sister was a nurse up at Cedars and I got her dress and belt. I got there early and sat in a corner, and he walked in and sat down in the lobby and waited, and he looked at me, looked at me and waited, and waited for me to show up, and after a while he began to stare at me. I looked exactly like the character and he—he didn't even know who I was, and he walked over . . .

INTERVIEWER You say you had played only one film at that point?

WINTERS Yes, that had been seen—*A Double Life*—that's the only one that he had seen. Let me see. Yes, another sexpot in *The Great Gatsby*—another blonde, flamboyant. That's the only two, and I don't even know if that one was out yet.

INTERVIEWER You're regarded, or you used to be regarded, as a temperamental actress. I am curious to know whether it is good for an actress to be temperamental?

WINTERS Well, that's a word that covers a lot. I wish they'd take it out of the English language, because it covers all degrees of behavior and feeling. I did have a reputation for being difficult and temperamental. One, I was. That's a good reason. And two, the studio used to discipline—or attempt to discipline—me when I wouldn't do certain movies. Also, I used to lend myself to it in two ways. One, I would let the publicity department publicize me that way because it was easy to get into print that way—people like Earl Wilson or Hedda Hopper, you know, will print these jazzy kind of items. And, two, I was sold on the idea that if you got to be a public figure, then you'd get the kind of roles that your talent deserves. There's something wrong with that reasoning, because what happens is that when you get that kind of reputation, good directors, who make good films, are a little scared of you. I'm answering this in various parts. The other thing is, if you are an artist who works, as I said, with your guts or your own human experience, and makes a kind of parallel thing to what's going on in your play or part—you do generate your problems, you know. If mechanics get calluses on their hands, nobody is surprised. Now, actors work with their emotions in a movie about ten hours a day, and in a theatre for a very intense period of three hours a night—and, you know, it's an occupational disease. Of course, as you gain maturity you are able to tolerate the anxiety you've generated a little better. I hope I have. I don't know how others actors cry, or get upset, and so forth, but I know if you're not doing it mechanically—if it's really coming out of somewhere, truthfully—it's pretty hard to shut it off when they say cut, or when the curtain comes down. You're still stuck a little bit with what you've generated, do you understand? And it's very hard to go around with a sort of disembodied anxiety, as it were. You pin it on something. I've had various degrees of that happen and I really never could deal with it until I went into psychoanalysis, which I have for the last three years. I didn't even want to talk about my acting or my talent. I thought it was mysterious, something magical that would go away. Well, to the contrary, what has happened is that it has extended my range of emotions.

INTERVIEWER   The analysis has?

WINTERS   Yes.

INTERVIEWER   Well, that's interesting, because . . .

WINTERS   Wait, wait, I still haven't answered your question. You asked whether . . .

INTERVIEWER   It is good for an actress to have temperament.

WINTERS   If it is the kind of temperament that is constructive to themselves and to their fellow workers, I would say yes. I think it's impossible for an artist not to have some kind of temperament. But it can be destructive to your rehearsal periods and to yourself and your performing. Then it's very bad. I feel that every time somebody says to me, "That performer is temperamental," I feel like saying they ought to have a more intelligent director, because if an artist is temperamental it usually means that they're scared to death, and it's the object of the director to find out what is frightening to them, I think. It's sometimes hard to explain it, and to face it, but a good director usually can head it off, and knows where it's coming from and why.

INTERVIEWER   In the matter of analysis—there is a question I wanted to ask you. It's very interesting that you say that analysis has actually helped you to open up a range of emotion. Did I understand you correctly?

WINTERS   Yes, you did.

INTERVIEWER   In what way did analysis do that?

WINTERS   Well, first, I think I have to explain to you a little about why I embarked on analysis. I accepted the American credo that to be a movie star is the best thing a young girl can be in America. You get that kind of propaganda from all sides: that to be a movie actor is sort of—a kind of royalty of art, society. You know what I mean—gossip colmuns, meeting important people . . .

INTERVIEWER Yes.

WINTERS I spent a good deal of my young years trying to achieve this, and it took me a long time to really face the fact that it had nothing to do with my being a good artist or a human being, or a happy person, or even being able to keep the money. It's all an illusion, you know—you don't even get the money, with taxes being what they are. So it's a—it's a real whole kind of nonsense. As an example, just now I was doing *Two for the Seesaw* in summer stock, which is a role that I've always wanted to do because I had a kind of idea about it. And I was offered this film, *Matter of Conviction,* and I said I would only do it if they could adjust it to my summer stock schedule. So I made three trips to California, and they had to fix their production schedule to go with my summer stock. And my agent said you would have gotten more money if you had just canceled out the summer stock. Yes, I said, but I can't cancel out the knowledge that I will get from playing this role. Now, where the analysis comes in—if you are secure in a certain type of performance, you find rationalization always to play that kind of part. For me, it meant a part with an expectation of doom. Now, since I have somewhat examined my continual expectation of doom and seen what is realistic about it and what is unrealistic about it, my range is wider. I don't have to play every role the same way. I can extend my range. I think in the last years I've done a lot of comedy and I like it, and sometimes in comedy you can make the audience feel poignancy stronger than you can with tears or anguish. I think almost invariably analysis extends the range and the potential that a human being has, because the very purpose of it is to free you, not to make you operate under the limits of your compulsions and your neuroses.

INTERVIEWER How did you get acquainted with the Method? How did you get started with the Method?

WINTERS Well, this is kind of an old joke, but unfortunately it's true with me, I think. I was exposed to it in dramatic school a little, but I really didn't understand it and I had to become a star to get enough money to learn how to act. After I did *A Place in the Sun*, I was very surprised with my reaction to it. Stevens would say that he doesn't work with the Method, I think, but he does. He sends the actor on a certain kind of track and then gets the performance out of him, rather than superimposing the performance on him, which is . . . No matter how well you imitate a director's reading the lines, it's no good if it doesn't come out of your own heart and guts—you know what I mean? The audience always kind of knows, unless maybe in a musical sometimes you can get away with it. But not in a deep play or film. Anyway, after I signed at Universal and did *A Place in the Sun,* I was doing kind of jazzy gangster pictures—I always had the illusion that I did the same picture twenty times, just changing my costume. I said the same lines—just different scenery and costumes. But I came back to New York, and the Actors Studio was sort of just starting. I was here accidentally and I went to a performance of *Sundown Beach,* which Julie Harris was in.

INTERVIEWER   Kazan directed.

WINTERS   Yes. And I was so excited when I saw it. I had casually known Kazan around New York when I was sort of a kid, and I asked him—I had heard that they had started this Studio—and I asked him if I could come. He said, "Well, you can be an observer, but you really live in Hollywood, you have a contract." So I said I'll come whenever I'm in New York. You know, it wasn't like now that it takes five hours—I made about twenty trips this year—but then it was a big deal, you know, very expensive. But I was here for a week or so doing interviews and publicity and stuff, and I managed to go to about four or five sessions and I did a scene from *The Children's Hour.* Kazan had set a very interesting problem, I remember—*Hedda Gabler,* with various suggestions, different themes, the same play with different themes. Kazan set it for three directors (Marlon Brando directed one of them) and it was like. . . . Up to that point I never really believed I was an actress. It didn't matter what they said to me about *A Place in the Sun.* I thought it was a fluke, that it was the publicity jazz and the blond hair and bosom. And up to that point I thought it was an accident. I still had several years of the contract to finish. But from then on, I came here as soon as I could. Every time I got through with a picture I'd be here. As soon as I could, I would come and live at a hotel and I'd go to the Studio. Then, as soon as my seven years were up, I started to look for a play to do. But I—I only got into the Studio the year after *A Hatful of Rain.* I was an observer for six years.

INTERVIEWER   I've been to the Studio, I think, only

twice. And one of the times I was there I saw you doing an exercise.

WINTERS No kidding.

INTERVIEWER And I remember you sitting there and saying, "But I don't feel it."

WINTERS Well, I had a big thing to break, which was— I played what you call results.

INTERVIEWER What does that mean?

WINTERS You sort of know it's going to be effective, so you just do it that way without any of the internal work. And it took me a long time to break that. In fact, I only really did a couple of years ago. I had a scene to do from *A Piece of Blue Sky*. I did it with another actor and he just wouldn't do anything that was necessary for the script. Like if I said sit down, he was already sitting. He just was so free, that he, he—none of the obligations of the playwright would he adhere to. And that morning I called up—I called Lee and I said I didn't want to do it. He said he didn't care, but he said, "If you can get up, and whatever he does, use it without planning in advance what you need, or what's going to happen with the scene, you will have broken the biggest barrier to your talent." I didn't quite understand what the hell he meant.

INTERVIEWER I'm not quite sure I understand it either.

WINTERS Let me explain it to you. You get up in a play and you kind of know what's gonna happen—you plan it. But the essence of a play is that you don't know what's gonna happen. That it has to look that way to the audience. You, as the actor, are supposed not to know what the next line is. You're not supposed to know how the play is going to come out, right? Well, that is—that is what the theatre is— fresh every night. It has to be as if it's the first time you ever said that line, the first time you ever heard it. Now, when you see actors who are boring—they have everything planned, they do "takes" . . . Do you know what I'm talking about? It's—so the audience knows, too.

INTERVIEWER These are the tricks of acting?

WINTERS That's right, and they're kind of—in some ways they can be effective, and they have a place, but they shouldn't be a method of performing. It's a difference. I saw Olivier do this once. I saw him do *The Entertainer* at a rehearsal. He was acting a failure. I saw a rehearsal he did where he started out by walking over to the proscenium and spitting on it. That was his adjustment; and he was no more acting a failure—he was. The difference was like—I just can't tell you. The English theatre is a little scared of that kind of emotion. They feel it's too raw. Yet it's slowly creeping into their work. Richardson, when he's good, is that kind of a performer.

INTERVIEWER   I am sure that Richardson, however, wouldn't admit that he's an actual Method actor.

WINTERS   Well, you know, it's such a funny word. Laurette Taylor was a Method acress—Stanislavsky saw her once and said so. They don't really know and they can't articulate what the Method is. Stanislavsky observed fine actors in work and questioned them and figured out what it was that they did.

INTERVIEWER   That they did instinctively.

WINTERS   Or found out through years of experience.

INTERVIEWER   Or intuitively.

WINTERS   That's right, and there are many aspects to it. Where it gets so out of line, you know, is when kids do in performance what they are only supposed to do in class. But when I finally was able to do that—what Lee was trying to get me to do . . . Now an actor on the stage can do anything, it won't bother me in the least. I use what they do—it doesn't bug me at all. And sometimes it makes my performance richer, where before I had to know in advance and plan what was going to happen or I'd be thrown higher than a kite.

INTERVIEWER   In other words, you find that the Method gives you a relaxation on the stage which enables you . . .

WINTERS   And a stimulation.

INTERVIEWER   To do anything under any circumstance.

WINTERS   And a control of the role. You're really able to live on that stage because you've got an inner human being going on who would . . . Like in real life, if I drop my cigarette, you'd pick it up. You see actors—something unexpected happens on the stage, they're dead.

INTERVIEWER   In other words, they're mechanical.

WINTERS   That's right.

INTERVIEWER   Why is it that the Method has gotten such a bad name in terms of audibility and scratching?

WINTERS   When you say a bad name, I doubt this, because when you see fine directors cast plays, they are usually looking for the people from the Studio or people who have been trained by Lee Strasberg. Just examine who are the new young stars in Hollywood. I would say that ten out of eleven are trained in the Method, so the proof of the pudding is the eating. People who give the Method a bad name are people who are set in their ways, scared of something, and don't really understand what it is. Now I'll tell you what audibility and mannerisms are. Marlon Brando and Jimmy Dean started a whole new style and they were, in a way, spokesmen for their generation. I think the existentialists and beatniks are all connected, which is a kind of the bomb's-going-to-fall-so-to-hell-with-everything-anyway, you know. That's the reason for Marlon's, I think—outside of the tremendous sexual power and drive and that kind of interest. But the very fact of his slovenliness and inaudibility, the I-don't-care-ism, captured the imagination and the identity of the youngsters watching—and Jimmy Dean, too. Now, a whole bunch of kids, as they do in every generation, I'm sure, imitate—I hate to use this term, but I don't know what else to use—imitate the sex symbol of the time. Thirty-five years ago, I'm sure, they were imitating Rudy Vallee—I don't know—and they started imitating him—Brando—especially, the actors, the young actors. They kind of mixed up one of the things and they did it on the stage and in auditions, which makes Lee very mad. But I think the youngsters confuse classroom work with theatre work.

INTERVIEWER That's an interesting point. Helen Hayes was telling me that when she was on the summer theatre circuit doing a play, the kids would stop rehearsals for half an hour and complain they couldn't "feel it." And she would finally say, "Get on with it, let's work, let's do it." Are you in favor of halting rehearsals for discussion and theorizing?

WINTERS If it's necessary. And my feeling about Helen Hayes is she would have been the greatest actress . . . Now, don't misunderstand me, I still think Helen Hayes is one of the finest actresses in our theatre. I didn't mean to qualify her achievement. But sometimes I think she feels a great responsibility to the play and the audience, which interferes with her depth. I don't know whether that's clear.

INTERVIEWER In what sense does it interfere?

WINTERS Well, if you are not involved in ensemble playing—as the star carrying the burden of the play, you have to make the points of the plot and the theme clear. And this can interfere with what you are allowing to happen to you. Let's see if that's clear. Acting is allowing things to happen to yourself, not editing it, so that the audience shares the experience. When you weep, you allow yourself to weep—you set the gears in motion and it goes. And, really, a fine actress . . . I've seen this happen to Helen

Hayes some nights when she's a little rattled, or something, and she's absolutely magnificent—when she's a little out of control. I saw her do it with—what was it?—the play about the South?

INTERVIEWER   *The Wisteria Trees.*

WINTERS   Yes. I saw her on a night when something seemed wrong, and she wasn't so in control. You understand what I mean?

INTERVIEWER   In other words, when you use the word control you mean that you think that too much of what she does is planned.

WINTERS   That's right.

INTERVIEWER   She's depending very much on technique —is that what you're saying?

WINTERS   Well, you need some of that, too. There are some nights when you had a fight and you're empty and your dinner doesn't agree with you—and you have to perform. You need technique. But given all things equal, if you have a technique of Method work, every performance is somewhat different and has a kind of life and a reality that is fascinating to an audience. They know it. It still doesn't mean that you should mumble—I want to get that in.

INTERVIEWER   Is there any difference in your preparation for a role in the movies and your preparation for one on the stage?

WINTERS   Well, I feel—or I hope—that I'm learning all the time. The movies—most of the time you don't really have enough time, and you just do a scene from the end of the picture, or the beginning, and you don't know where you are emotionally, and it's just very tough. I have a definite method for the rehearsing of a play.

INTERVIEWER   I wish you would describe it, sort of step by step.

WINTERS   I find when I rehearse properly I never have to study the lines. Not once. If I rehearse properly.

INTERVIEWER   What do you mean, rehearse properly?

WINTERS   Well, say you've got a good play. Like I just did *Two for the Seesaw,* which is a big role. I don't think I drilled those lines more than once. What I do first is I read it with the other actor and the playwright and we discuss the theme of the play that we're after. In this version of *Two for the Seesaw* we used *The Seesaw Log.** We attempted

* The book William Gibson wrote following the successful Broadway production, in which he recounted the pre-production and tryout tour problems.

to achieve what I think Gibson felt was missing in the Broadway production. We used that version that was published, which was somewhat different. I had an idea that he wanted the audience to feel what two human beings contributed to each other's development, not just that the man had used her. He says so. And with Frank Corsaro, the director, we discussed where the specific places in the play were that she learned through the man—his speech, his ideas. You see me in the first act eat in a very sloppy way, and then you see me make a real effort to handle a knife and fork—like him—although in one place I give up, when I say it's too difficult, the hell with it. The audience got it all. The realization that she tricks him in a way. She figures out when she hears him talk to his wife, she says, in a sense, you're never going to say that to me, I got a hand inside of you. And in a way she can't resist using her illness to trap him. But then she realizes that she's got nothing. At the end of the play she says, "I want somebody who's mine to take care of me." She has learned this from him, what the real meaning of love is—not, you know, sex or companionship or an antidote to loneliness, but a real ability to give, not just to take. And at the end of the play, what I do is I come in, and you see that the girl's going to become a real person—a *mensch;* that she's learned something of her potential from this man. When we did it, one of the reviewers said he understood why Gibson wrote *The Seesaw Log.* And a woman said to me in New Jersey, "I was afraid at the end of the play she was going to marry him." Not that he wouldn't marry her, which they, the audience, got from the Broadway play. And in many ways Anne Bancroft was much better in the role than me. She's funnier, she's more Gittel than I am in personality. But I was trying for another kind of aspect of the play. Anyway, as we investigated these things, we decided on this train of behavior and subtext. Then I got an image of someone I know, who's not dumb but who is emotionally blocked from learning, and who is shrewd and cunning. And I thought about her—it's somebody I knew in my past—I thought about her as much as I could. The girl was almost an idiot, but it was a kind of defense and I realized it, and I thought about her and wrote out all her history, as much as I could about her. And then we started to rehearse. The play staged itself. We did what comes naturally to human beings with those kind of backgrounds. Nobody has to tell you to sit over there. You do what is right for you. And we found activities which the script called for. When a director sets his actors in motion that way, he doesn't have to tell them where to stand or what to do. They will invent things automatically. And his job then is to edit what is valuable, what carries out the theme of the play and what doesn't. He doesn't have to give them directives. Now, by the time we got through staging the play—we did it in a week—I practically knew the lines. And if I went up in the lines, I spoke my own lines till I got back to where the lines were. Then after we went through that stage, I sat down one day and I drilled with a girl, that is, I went over the lines.

INTERVIEWER   Of course, you have that great facility that you mentioned before, of total recall.

WINTERS   No, you see, I can't memorize. You give me a script and say memorize these lines—you know, I don't know two pages. I can study one page for four years. I have to get the inner life of the character, what the lines come out of. I could never do a soap opera—I wouldn't know what to do. I have to first get at what is going on in the human being. When you've got a good playwright, like Gibson, there's only one thing to say.

INTERVIEWER   Is this true when you work in Hollywood, too?

WINTERS   I try to make it true. It was true, I think, in *Anne Frank*.

INTERVIEWER   What I mean is—you don't memorize the lines, you first have to understand what the character is about?

WINTERS   Yes. The first person I got this from was George Stevens. He didn't mention it this way, but the first time when we started on *A Place in the Sun,* I said, "Now, what do I do in this scene?" And he said, "I don't know. Let's find out." And he said, "If you were such-and-such, would you do this?" Then I did a scene—you remember the abortion scene in the picture, when I go and ask the doctor? He sprang that on me one morning. You see, the danger is, actors go right to the lines as if that's where they're going to find the performance—and that's where you're not going to get it. The lines are the last thing to learn, in a funny kind of way. Anyway, I did the scene and I was crying, and I thought I was great, and he sat and thought for a while and then he said, "Now, Shelley, let me ask you something about this girl. What is she here for?" And I said, "She's desperate to get the doctor to help her." And so he said, "What she wants in this scene is for the doctor to help her." And I said, "Yes." And he said, "If she does what you just did, would he help her?" and I said, "No, she would scare him." But I was angry at him, because, you know, I thought it was so great if I started crying away like crazy. And so he said, "Then the problem in the scene is for her not to cry." And I said, "Yeh." And he said, "All right. Now let's do it again. And you get this doctor to help you." I started the scene, and I wanted to cry, and I had to wait—I don't know whether you remember it, but there were long waits while I got myself under control, and I just sat there and looked at him. Well, it was ninety times more effective than the other. Now, if I'd just gone to the words and picked up the cue . . . The words were secondary, you know. Stevens hates dialogue; he hates sound pictures. And he's right. Television is the sound medium, movies are visual. His favorite trick is to rehearse you with the lines and then take the lines away and say now do the scene—just looking at each other. And in some ways, it's more powerful because you communicate thoughts.

INTERVIEWER You know, everybody works differently. I think, if my memory is correct, the Lunts first learn the lines—this, they've got to learn. Then everything else comes afterward. But your approach is also interesting.

WINTERS Yes, but I think eventually what they do is what I was just talking about. Because I've seen the way they play to each other, where they listen to each other with their hearts almost as it were. Yes, some actors do have to learn the lines. They have to be secure in the lines and then from the lines they get all the thinking.

INTERVIEWER You said before that you wrote out a whole history of this girl.

WINTERS I also write out the lines in my own handwriting. Every night after we've staged a scene I come home and I write out—Stanislavsky recommended this. I don't know whether you've read his book or not—you know, the Russian actors, they didn't have copies of the plays, I guess because of the revolution, so they all had to write out their parts. And in a peculiar kind of way it becomes part of your guts when you write it out in your own handwriting. And I do that. But I don't do it till after the scene has been staged. And I go home and I write it out.

INTERVIEWER But you mentioned that you wrote out everything you knew about this girl whom you used from life.

WINTERS That was fitting for Gittel.

INTERVIEWER Is this a process you do regularly?

WINTERS I do it where it's applicable for the character

I'm playing. In *Anne Frank* I did it. Of course, I had to gain weight and everything. I played a Dutch housewife. I was very concerned with the Dutch aspect of it. And I studied it. In the character it is indicated her father was a rich farmer, and I did some investigating into Dutch agriculture. And did you know that in Holland a man starts to make a field a hundred years before it's going to be used. So—how to make a field. First you push back the ocean. Then for five years every year you sift the sand, get the salt out. Then you bring in earth from . . . It's a process that goes on for a hundred years. Now, a woman who has watched her father do that is a special kind of woman. What I tried to achieve in it was a woman who is scared, who's had a bourgeois life, who's namby-pamby. But when the chips are down, the strength that is inherent in her background comes out. Her husband is the weak one—Remember when he steals the bread and everything and the way she holds on to the fur coat, the mink coat. Well, I played that—the fear, and then through danger, the courage comes out, as a kind of crucible. And I think the audience saw it, and wanted it. Now, that comes out of knowledge of the background of the human being, which sometimes the playwright gives you and sometimes he doesn't. And when you do this, you can discuss it with the director. But the best thing is to show him, especially if he is a non-Method director. If you talk about it, you scare him. They don't know quite what you're—they say, "That's not in the play." But if you show them that it adds dimension . . . And maybe even the playwright didn't anticipate its being there—but if it fulfills the message of his play, he'll want it. But if it distorts it, then it's wrong. That's the funny thing, that Method actors get trapped—because a thing that's effective for a scene, sometimes it doesn't work for the play.

INTERVIEWER   In other words, it must always be true for the play. Whatever you do, the play is the controlling factor.

WINTERS   That's where the weakness is in the Method. We assume that all the directors will have the right kind of knowledge and training. And it's just not true. Especially if you are up against a strong star who wants to do it. Sometimes the directors let them do it and they don't know quite what's wrong until that curtain goes up. I think Kim Stanley is the best actress in the American theatre—even better than me, but (laughing) I'll give her competition. But really, she is remarkable—she's a great actress. And she, unless she has a good director, can do things which while in themselves are magnificent, they have nothing to do with the play. And the

audience says, "What? What? What happened?" Like—well, I
don't want to cite examples, but I've seen her fall into it.
Now, when she's lucky, she has a good director who can edit
out and say, "No, you can't do that there, do it here," so that
the audience can follow the logic of the play. Another thing,
a technique which I've learned from Lee Strasberg, which
has been very useful to me—you see, method of work means
a method for you. Certain things are meaningful for some
actors, and for some they have no use. And some actors just
learn the lines and get up on the stage and God gave them
the talent and everything they say falls into place. There are
actors like that. And if you monkey around with them—if they
start thinking, they're lost. I think they're few and far between. I think they learn by trial and error and they learn
to know what works. One of the most interesting things I ever
saw at the Studio—it didn't happen to me. I saw an actress
get up and say to Lee, "I have become phony. I used to be a
good actress." This is a terrible admission for a girl to make.
She said, "What has happened to me? I just know I'm not an
actress any more. How can I fix it?" "Well," he said, "I
wouldn't have said this to you." (Despite everything that you
hear about Lee, he's very kind. He's only tough with people
who can take it and who are successful. I've never seen him
clobber somebody who isn't strong enough to take it. In my
own early days at the Studio, he was very kind to me. Now
he'll get very tough if I'm lazy or I won't work, and he'll
criticize me in the areas where I need it very sharply and
question me if I've achieved it.) And he said to her, "I
wouldn't have said that to you but since you bring it up and
you're aware of it . . ." She said, "Why am I false?" He said,
"Well, during the course of years I think somehow you have
made up a personality for yourself." She said, "Yes, why do I
carry these mannerisms and behavior into my work?" And
he said, "Well, in a way, they're inseparable. I'll do an exercise with you called 'Effective Memory.' Stanislavsky speaks of
it." And he said, "Now sit down on the chair and you think
of the most powerful thing that ever happened to you in your
life. Don't tell us what it is. Just describe the sensory memories
of that time." And the class was very quiet—we'd never seen
this done before. And she was quiet for a while and then she
said, "Well, the night air is very cool. I can feel my dress on
my skin, I can smell the flowers. The lights on the road—the
car lights . . ." And she was just describing sensory impressions. And we became terrified. I don't know what happened
to her, but she communicated absolute terror. We were sweat-

ing. We were shaking. And she was shaking. And he stopped her. And he said, "That is where you find the truth in yourself. When you prepare a role, you don't do it so much with an intellectual decision of how you're going to play this scene or that scene. You have to find a parallel experience in the role that . . . I mean, if you've got to kill somebody—you're never going to kill somebody, but you've wanted to kill, you've hated. There are many ways of getting at this kind of truth for yourself—not the director's truth, not the playwright's truth, but your truth. That's one way of checking yourself." I use this in very important spots in a play.

INTERVIEWER   In other words, you go to life.

WINTERS   Yes. As much as I can.

INTERVIEWER   You go to life, your own experience.

WINTERS   My observations of human beings.

INTERVIEWER   Do you make notes of people you see in a subway or on the streets or in the parks?

WINTERS   I did when I was in dramatic school. Then I stopped for a long time. But then I found . . . I'll tell you, an actor does something that's just horrible. They're always storing stuff up for a role.

INTERVIEWER   Writers do, too.

WINTERS   I mean, you could be in the middle of the most horrendous fight and you say, "Oh, that's very good." You don't even know you're doing it. Sometimes I'll be weeping and I'll look in the mirror and I say, "Why do I twist up my face?" I'm right in the middle of agony and I'm sort of remembering how I got to this feeling of agony. I mean, I am like in the middle of an operation, and I can remember, "Now this is how you go under ether, this is how you come out of ether," as if . . . I'm not sure that this is good, in fact, I think it's bad, but maybe you can't help it if you're an actor. I have the strange illusion when I'm in a play and enjoying it—it's like the rest of life is the preparation for those three hours. And in a peculiar kind of way I have the feeling that when I open the door to walk on the stage that that's real and the backstage is unreal. It's such a heightened thing. Anyway, when you're in a hit play, your whole life takes on the discipline and the rhythm of those three hours. I start getting ready at three o'clock in the afternoon. I walk, and exercise, and take a nap, and eat dinner. I eat dinner at five and then I rest afterwards.

INTERVIEWER   An extremely intense experience.

WINTERS   The level of energy, the concentration. That's what's so terrible about movies, too. I mean, everybody gags it up in between shots, they want to, but in the picture I just made, they wouldn't allow it. John Frankenheimer just shut the people up. Stevens' sets are like death, they're so quiet. And the crews know it. They move scenery quietly. He knows the actors have to stay quiet, and sometimes he jars you out of the mood purposely because he knows it's getting too long, like he will turn up the air conditioning till you freeze, when it's a scene that you have to be cold in. In the dead of summer, in August, he'll put the heating system on if he wants you to be hot. And sometimes he has a thing that's just wonderful—I wish there was a way to use it in the theatre. You know, he's from silent pictures and he has a kind of thing—it's a gadget that's next to his chair, and he knows what music works on you, and he pushes the button and he finds the kind of music you respond to; and in preparation for a scene, when he says, "Roll 'em," before you start acting, he will play that music, sometimes he'll play it during the scene. Like when I was doing a scene where I was being very courageous, he'd turn on a thing with German boots marching and Hitler talking, and he said, "You are not scared, you are courageous"—he gave me something to push against, you know.

INTERVIEWER   What is the role that you're going to play in the Laurents play? *

WINTERS   Well, it's quite a jump for me. It's a woman by the name of Camilla Jablonsky. She's a woman who has come to terms with life, who has humor, who has depth, who has not gotten what she wants, has her own set of values. She has an illegitimate child; her values aren't like other people, she wanted to have that child. She's of modest means, but enough for her. She doesn't dress, act or behave like any of the mores of our society, like you're supposed to. And what Arthur is doing is setting up an examination of what we think makes a happy and successful life. That's why he calls it *Invitation to a March*. You know, where everybody is marching along with this—that what we are taught is the way to be and the way we will achieve happiness. And he has among all these people this woman who says, who twenty years ago said, "No. You wanta march, go ahead, I've got my own rhythm, I'll listen to my own music."

* The play referred to is *Invitation to a March*, written and directed by Arthur Laurents. Subsequently, Miss Winters and Mr. Laurents disagreed on the role's portrayal; she left the play and was replaced by Celeste Holm.

INTERVIEWER   And how are you going to prepare for this?

WINTERS   I don't know. I'm really having a very tough time with it, because these kind of women are very rare. I've known one, but I only knew her when she was much older— a woman by the name of Salka Viertel; she was Peter Viertel's mother. When I first went to Hollywood, she had a salon there. She was a friend of Chaplin's. She's got a run-down lovely house down at the beach and every Sunday she used to make Hasenpfeffer, and Christopher Isherwood and Dylan Thomas and everybody that came to Hollywood used to be at her house, you know, the writers—and Thomas Mann—and also the talented actors and composers, and lawyers, engineers—people with interesting ideas and ability. Now this woman was married to Peter's father and she had four sons, and then they were divorced and she never married again. She's still alive, she must be in her late sixties; I guess I knew her when she was in her late fifties. And she lived a special kind of unconventional life with great warmth and love for ideas, and I still don't really have an image of her as old— there's something about her that is young. Now that's the clue —it's a very tough thing. I don't quite know why Arthur cast me in the role. He believes I can play it, but I'm really having a tough time with it. And I procrastinate. I've read the script about three times and I'm breaking down the scenes. Because I really don't have a handle, and until I really do have a handle on it, I'm going to be very difficult and cranky.

INTERVIEWER   I can see you getting tense over it, even at this moment.

WINTERS   Yeh. And I wake up in the middle of the night and say, "Now why did she say that?" You see, I've read it three times and I know all of the important lines she says, I mean the lines to her character.

INTERVIEWER   It sounds like an interesting play.

WINTERS   I hope so. I think so.

INTERVIEWER   What attracted you to it?

WINTERS   Well, number one, Arthur is a very stimulating writer, even when his plays don't come off. The things that he tackles are very ingenious. And, number two, I would like to play an un-neurotic woman.

INTERVIEWER   Un-neurotic?

WINTERS   Un-neurotic. This woman has had a very tough time with life, and yet she came to terms with it, and enjoys even the bad things that happen and have happened to her. She enjoys the process of living. And she's funny in a special kind of way. She's earthy and connected with the human race—and enjoys everything.

INTERVIEWER   Have you spent much time with Arthur talking about this?

WINTERS   Oh, yes, for three days—when we were out at Quogue, Long Island, last weekend. But what the play says I like, because that's what I did—somebody said Hollywood contract and I signed seven years of my life; I accepted those values and they're wrong. They just are. They have nothing to do with happiness or real personal achievement. Acting is a secondary art when you're involved with secondary plays or films. When you're involved with junk, then you really feel like, not a secondary artist, but a twentieth-degree artist, because you're communicating false ideas. Now, how do you find a truth to communicate false ideas? It's tough unless you do it very superficially. I don't think it's possible to be good in a bad picture. I don't think you can. You have little moments of something interesting, but . . .

INTERVIEWER   How does that apply to the stage?

WINTERS   Oh, I think it's the same thing on the stage. I think you can have more artistic license because the cutter isn't out there cutting. So sometimes you can communicate something more interesting.

INTERVIEWER   I understand that in preparing for *A Hatful of Rain*, you did a great deal of research in narcotics—that you read up on narcotics, that you read up on the disease, and you spoke to people.

WINTERS   Oh, I went out with the Vice Squad and saw . . . Well, I'll give you an example. Mike, when he first wrote the first scene, where my husband says to me, "I'm hooked, I'm a junkie," and she says, "That's silly"—when we rehearsed it Mike said that's not a good line, and I said, "Mike, don't you dare take that away, your instinct was absolutely right." You know, a woman sitting down to dinner and her husband says, "I'm a junkie," and she says, "That's silly." She can't—well, you just can't swallow something like that; you can't absorb it. Now, realistically, in the play, I don't have time to find out about the reasons for the disease, but I must come to grips with that, even in the space of time allotted, so that at the end of the play I know that the best thing I can do for my husband is to pick up the phone and get the police and get him into the right hands, where he has the proper treatment. That's the only chance of his survival, or otherwise death is the answer. So I wanted to learn as much about the behavior, and the reasons why, as I could. It came in very good stead anyway. In the picture I just did, *Let No Man Write My Epitaph,* I play a drug addict.

INTERVIEWER   Nothing ever is wasted then?

WINTERS   Well, I used it to some degree there, but I used it to greater degree here. I've got very strong feelings about that subject. I feel that it belongs in the hands of the medical authorities, not of the police, and I think it's dreadful that we don't do something about it in that department—there's too much graft involved in it.

INTERVIEWER   I'm coming back to the Method again. I have a note here that Tyrone Guthrie has written in the *Times* that there is too much emphasis in the Method on self-analysis and too little on technique. What would your reply be to that?

WINTERS   Yes. I agree with him.

INTERVIEWER   Heresy?

WINTERS   No. I don't think they're mutually exclusive and I don't think he thinks so either. I would be very surprised if he did. I've just finished reading his book.* There is the thing of talking—and I'm sure that writers have this problem—of talking the subject out of existence, using up all the energy, as Helen Hayes said, wasting it in analysis and not doing. Now, there is a point when you set it, and then you've gotta stop talking about it and do it. And there is the temptation—since acting is a little scary, you know—to plunge into analysis, because, especially in rehearsal periods, it's uncomfortable. Also, that's why actors have such difficult times with each other, with the father-director, because it's a very personal rejectful time when you're using things that disturbed you.

INTERVIEWER   What about the criticisms we hear of speech training, stage movement and so forth?

WINTERS   They're trying to correct it now at the Studio. American actors don't know how to speak properly, don't learn enough about body movement. I believe that the theatre should be a beautiful place. To get to something else for a minute. I get very angry when I see plays that are unnecessarily dirty. If they make a point, like *The Balcony* does, which is quite extraordinary, that's something else. To me, the theatre—I don't like to say it, but I'll say it—is a temple, in a kind of way, where human beings go to be elevated.

INTERVIEWER   Why be afraid to say it?

WINTERS   That's right. Now to get back. And, being a

* *A Life in the Theatre.*

performer and being a trained Method actor are the same thing. One enhances the other. You are more of a performer if you've had this kind of training. One without the other is no good. Have you done a story on Gielgud?

INTERVIEWER Yes.

WINTERS Gielgud to me is a great example. To me, he is the greatest Shakespearean actor there is. I saw *Ages of Man* five times. Yet when Gielgud gets on the stage with other actors, in certain kinds of comedies, he does not allow things to happen to himself, as he did in that recital. He truly used himself, every element—what he thinks he is, what he thinks he isn't. It was so rich and so full that it was stunning. And yet he will get on the stage, where he isn't just involved with himself, but with other actors, and he doesn't go the route—he edits, he stops himself. And he's acting what he thinks should be there, not what happens. It's a subtle difference. And he isn't as effective when he does that. But when he really uses himself, like he did in that recital, he's the greatest English-speaking actor—he really is.

INTERVIEWER What training in technique have you yourself had in terms of body movement and in terms of voice control, and things like that?

WINTERS Never in any consistent fashion, unfortunately.

INTERVIEWER And you miss it?

WINTERS Terribly. My dream is to go work in Stratford. I've done Shakespeare here and there, I know the speeches, and I once played *The Tempest* and I did *The Taming of the Shrew*. And I mean, these are the greatest plays ever written and we can't handle them—Greek drama and the Shakespearean plays. It's a thing of vocal projection, of sustaining a role through that kind of exhaustion with the costumes and the mannerisms and the behaviors, which is necessary to carry them off in grand style. We can't do it.

INTERVIEWER Well, then, would you say that someone like Morris Carnovsky, who has achieved some of his greatest successes in recent years in Shakespeare, is an exception as a Method actor?

WINTERS Yes, yes.

INTERVIEWER But you feel that classical training is essential, really.

WINTERS Oh, yes. I wish there was a way of combining . . . We're trying to at the Studio now. Last year we had, let's see, the teacher of Marccau—you know, the pantomimist —I can't think of his name.

INTERVIEWER Etienne Decroux.

WINTERS That's right. And we have a very fine speech teacher now. Well, I think I had better get ready. I've got a date to see a play in Westport.

Bert Lahr

BIOGRAPHY

Bert Lahr was born in the Yorkville section of New York City in August, 1895. His early days were spent in vaudeville and in burlesque, where he developed the comedy routines that brought him to the attention of Broadway producers. He appeared at the Shubert Theatre in *Delmar's Revels* in 1927. There followed a great many musicals and revues, with an ever-widening public for Mr. Lahr. In 1928 he appeared in *Hold Everything,* and followed this with such shows as *Flying High, Hot-Cha, George White's Music Hall Varieties, Life Begins at 8:40,* and *George White's Scandals of 1935; The Show Is On,* with Beatrice Lillie, in 1936; *Du Barry was a Lady,* with Ethel Merman, in 1939. In 1944 Mr. Lahr appeared in *The Seven Lively Arts,* and in 1946 he entered the non-musical theatre as Skid in *Burlesque.* In 1951 he was in the revue *Two on the Aisle.*

The year 1956 saw Mr. Lahr make a radical departure from anything he had done before, when he played Estragon in Samuel Beckett's *Waiting for Godot,* a role which brought him critical acclaim as a serious actor. In 1957 Mr. Lahr played in the farce, *Hotel Paradiso,* and in 1959 he teamed with Nancy Walker in the revue *The Girls Against the Boys*. In 1960 Mr. Lahr introduced another new phase into his career: he played Bottom in *A Midsummer Night's Dream* during the American Shakespeare Festival Company's national tour.

Mr. Lahr is not a stranger to Hollywood. His first film there was *Faint Heart,* but his best-known role by far is that of the Cowardly Lion in *The Wizard of Oz.* Mr. Lahr has appeared frequently on television, both in variety shows and in plays.

He is married and has a teen-age daughter and a son in his twenties with his present wife, and an older son with his first wife.

SETTING

Although Bert Lahr, with a demonstration of the Lahr double take or the Lahr leer, can break up an audience of two interviewers just as easily as a packed theatre, nevertheless an interviewer need have no fear of losing precious words in gusts of laughter. The fact is, Mr. Lahr takes comedy quite seriously, and a conversation with this comedian is serious. As Mr. Lahr says, he's a serious man, and most comedians he knows are fairly serious fellows.

We talked to Mr. Lahr in a dressing room just off the stage of the Lyceum Theatre one Sunday afternoon during the final rehearsals of the American Shakespeare Festival's touring production of *A Midsummer Night's Dream,* in which Mr. Lahr played Bottom. Mr. Lahr sat in an easy chair. He was wearing a brown sports shirt and khaki slacks, having changed from the blue suit, white shirt and tie he wore on arrival at the theatre. Adding to this informal rehearsal attire, he donned a beautiful and stylized ass's head when Director Jack Landau called him on-stage to rehearse.

Although it was the star's dressing room, it was a rather grim—and grimy—room, with its dirtish gray paint, dusty and spotted gray rug, and a single overhead light casting a baleful glow over all; it was windowless. On the dressing table were piles of scripts, some first-aid supplies and left-over make-up prerequisites. On a cardboard carton, which served as a table and around which our chairs were drawn up, were an ashtray and a pack of cigarettes—Mr. Lahr could nearly qualify for a chain smoker. There was also his little transistor radio kept handy for the ball-game score. "These Yanks under pressure—they come through." (This was the double-header in which the Yanks beat Baltimore and practically clinched the pennant.) There was also room enough for a container of coffee for Mr. Lahr and a roast beef sandwich, which constituted his lunch. "Don't know why they gave me roast beef —always eat corned beef." Nevertheless, he ate with evident relish.

Alternating between rehearsing on-stage and the interview did not faze Mr. Lahr in the least. He appears to be an actor with little temperament when there's a job to be done, and he was unruffled by the change in pace from a stage visit with Titania in her bower to a discussion in the dressing room of burlesque's contribution to comedy.

Mr. Lahr's mood, if not sunny, was informal, interested. He spoke earnestly and easily, although he was sometimes concerned lest he was not making some point clear, reiterating that he was no theoretician, but that he knew what he had learned along the way.

His voice was even, gaining emphasis when he felt strongly about a point. An intensely expressive face lent even more meaning to his words. Although his face is that of a worrier, he claims to be a reformed worrier. He used few gestures, smiled infrequently, and apparently reserves those famous Lahr guffaws for the stage.

Between the time spent on rehearsing and conversing with us, nearly seven hours elapsed, but Mr. Lahr was not one bit tired. He only regretted, he said, that we hadn't started even earlier. "I've been up since nine this morning. Doing the crossword puzzle in the Sunday paper."

Interview

INTERVIEWER   We don't usually find you keeping company with the Bard. Any special concerns about appearing in Shakespeare?

LAHR   No, I'm not worried. But those songs! Well, this is the first time I've done them on my feet, and the damn lyrics. I'll get them. But they're so stupid, you know. They don't make sense. The doxie on the dale, the pug in the tooth, or whatever it is.* I don't even know the words yet.

---

* Here Mr. Lahr's scorn is inspired by lines in *The Winter's Tale*, which Mr. Lahr was also rehearsing, in the part of Autolycus, although this play was not retained on the tour with *A Midsummer Night's Dream*.

INTERVIEWER   I'd like to return to Shakespeare, but to go back in your own history a bit, what was it that impelled you into show business?

LAHR   Well, I was a lazy kid and I wasn't a good student. I had the capacity to be, but I loathed school, I hated it, and I couldn't hold a job. I was just irresponsible, let's say—dreaming about something. I don't know what. But one thing I did have was a good handwriting, and I'd write letters when the *Times* advertisement column wanted a delivery boy or something, for which I'd get the munificent sum of four dollars or four dollars and fifty cents a week. But one day a fella in my neighborhood called Charlie Berrado, an Italian fella—he played a little Jewish comedian in school acts—he said do you want to join a school act, a kid act? I said fine, because I used to like vaudeville and the burlesque shows. The comedians intrigued me, you know, and I used to think I was funny when I was a kid—at least I was funny-looking—and it just intrigued me, so I joined this act. We got very little work, but I got the bug—I could sleep late, you know? And it was kind of a nice life and I stayed with it against my parents' wishes. Then I got into a school act, which was quite popular in those days, called—let me see, what was the name—"Nine Crazy Kids," and that played the small-time theatres, naturally. In these kid acts I would be the teacher—the Dutch teacher, like the Dutch comedians I'd see in burlesque. I was born in Yorkville, which is a German neighborhood in New York, you know, so I got the accent. Then I got a chance to take Jack Pearl's place. Jack was a little Dutch comedian in an act called "The Boys and Girls of Avenue B"—a fella by the name of Irving Becker had it—and Jack left to go into a burlesque show. I got eighteen dollars a week. I sent my mother ten dollars out of that, and saved a little on the side. On the bill at the Olympic Theatre in Brooklyn, which was a small-time vaudeville house, was an act called Billy Wells. He was a monologist, and he also wrote for burlesque shows, and he asked me, he said, "Young fella, do you want to go into burlesque?" Well, that was steady work, you know.

INTERVIEWER   Did vaudevillians in general want to get into burlesque?

LAHR   Some did—those that didn't get much work, and this was steady work. But burlesque in those days was quite different from the burlesque of today. Your big comedians were there. Comedy was the predominating thing.

INTERVIEWER   Yes, Fanny Brice among others.

LAHR   Well, fifty, sixty big names came out of burlesque.

So I joined a burlesque show at thirty-five dollars for the first ten weeks and forty dollars after that. I was the third comic. And after the opening show they made me the second comic; then, after two years, I became the star comic.

INTERVIEWER   Top banana?

LAHR   Yes. And when I was seventeen years old, I was the youngest star in burlesque.

INTERVIEWER   And it was the comics that always intrigued you.

LAHR   The reason for that was, I guess, they amused me, and the girls were around them all the time. So I was in burlesque, and that's where I married my first wife, who was the soubrette later on. In the summertime I played vaudeville with her. Then, when I left burlesque, when my contract expired, I did a vaudeville act with her, which was Lahr and Mercedes, which became a recognized, big-time vaudeville act. Then the Shuberts signed me, but after six or eight months they didn't do anything for me, and I asked for my release, which they gave me—and afterwards regretted. My first show on Broadway was *Delmar's Revels,* which was a flop show, but from that Aarons and Freedley signed me up and I made a big hit in *Hold Everything.* That was my first big Broadway hit, and from then on I've been going fairly well.

INTERVIEWER   It has been said that it is harder to make people laugh than to make them cry. Would you agree?

LAHR   Oh yes. You see, the reason for that is—if the situation in the play is right, and you're physically right for the part, the play plays for you. Do you see what I mean? If the situation says that you come home and find your father dead, or your mother, and if you've created enough sympathy through the show, and the part is right for you, that's a simple thing. Now the play is working for you. But if you come into a scene—in a revue, let's say, where the situation is contrived, and then, say, the scene itself has a light thread of situation —then you must contribute a lot to that; you sort of conjure up things and contrive things for it. But I found it easier to play a legitimate play, where you stay in character, than to make people laugh. I have found it that way.

INTERVIEWER   So it really is hard to make an audience laugh.

LAHR   I think so, in general, but I haven't found it so for myself. You see, it's very complex. Everybody in show business, everybody is a specialist. The majority of them are. There's character people, and there's comedians—light comedians, low comedians, monologists. There are all different forms and everybody's taste varies. Some people say, "I like him," others, "I can't stand him." It's the same thing as people's taste in art, or anything. If fifty percent of the audience like me, I'm very happy. What was the question?

INTERVIEWER Is it harder to make people laugh than to make them cry?

LAHR Well, you're equipped for both. Let's put it this way, if you're equipped for both, they're both easy. But you will find that a comedian—a good comedian—has to be a good actor. And the reason for a comedian being a good comedian, he creates a sympathy. He immediately creates a warmth in his audience, so, once you do that and the audience roots for you, it's a very simple matter to make them cry. I think you laugh at a great comedian because you want to cry. Laughter is never too far away from tears. You will cry at a peddler much easier than you would cry at a woman dressed in ermine who had just lost her whole family, let's say.

INTERVIEWER What is your secret of getting the sympathy of the audience?

LAHR I think it's a physical and chemical thing, the same as if you go to a party and somebody comes in a room who immediately attracts you. So a person comes out with a manner on the stage that makes you say, "Aah, he's a sweet guy"—do you see? Which I don't think you can acquire, and I don't think you can acquire good taste—I think you've got to be born with that. You know what not to say, what not to do. I think it's his manner, his general attitude, a humbleness.

INTERVIEWER You must have done something to cultivate this. Let's start with the fact that you have the basic equipment.

LAHR It isn't a question of cultivating. You cannot cultivate a humbleness, it becomes phony. He's either a humble fella or a brash fella, do you understand what I mean? There are tricks to it, too.

INTERVIEWER And that's what I'm interested in. What are they?

LAHR Well, the tricks are this. In order to get sympathy, there are little tricks which have become trite—patting a baby on the head, let's say, or patting a dog, or picking up a bird that had just hurt its wing and petting it. That's the very obvious way of doing it, but I used to tell the writers, when I did musicals, I'd say I don't want any laughs at first—if they come, fine, but let them bounce the laughs off me, ridicule me. Do you see what I mean? Say I have a dragon of a wife who's browbeating me, and there I'm a sweet fella—do you understand my point? Now let's take W. C. Fields, as an example. He was a rogue, a knave, a thief, a cheat. He was everything. But you liked him. He knew what he was doing. He would always have a wife that would ridicule him, or the brother-in-law, or a kid, a child—he would hit a child on the head and you were glad he did it, see what I mean, because he saw to it that the kid would kick him in the shins, or stick pins in him or something.

INTERVIEWER   What would you call your woodman sketch?

LAHR   That's the ridiculous. That was a satire on the baritone. That's ludicrous.

INTERVIEWER   But even then there was a likable quality.

LAHR   Well, the likable quality came about because they were making a fool of this guy—throwing chips at him, and he's duckin' them, and they'd . . . It was ruffled dignity, do you see?

INTERVIEWER   So perhaps you can find some element of that in nearly all the things you've done.

LAHR   There has to be; you just don't acquire that. Now you take a little Willie Howard, who was, God knows, not a handsome fella—a little wizened ugly man, Willie. No matter what he did on the stage, you would never resent— He had a mien, a manner—you just don't acquire that. You can help whatever you've got by knowing what to do. You're either a sweet guy or you're a bum, understand what I mean?

INTERVIEWER   Okay. Accepting the existence of this special quality and of this talent, how do you improve the talent?

LAHR   Application. It's the same thing as a violinist has to do—practice, which is application; doing it every day, learning what not to do.

INTERVIEWER   Can you be specific?

LAHR   Just one word, one action can change a man's performance. I throw things out, for instance, that the heavies would do, the heavies in the theatre who you hate; and your leading men, they save the girl and they always do the right thing, you see. It's all impressionistic. An audience, when they're in the theatre, they're wrapped up in this thing. They live it. They love. They hate. And they always go for the underdog and they root for the underdog—and it's only natural. You've done it. You say, "Oh, that s.o.b., I hope they get him." And it's all make-believe. I think if an actor has talent, he can broaden his talent by different roles. I think reading helps an actor, and that goes for a comic, any-body . . . Not that I'm a well-read fella.

INTERVIEWER   Oh, I know that you are.

LAHR   I think reading is a great asset. But most impor-tant, working at perfecting your performance, which is noth-ing but practice, and having the opportunity to go out there, thinking about it—and don't take your talent for granted. It's not easy. It's also knowing what you can do. There are dif-ferent types of comedians. There are comedians that'll never play, couldn't possibly go through, a whole show; it's not their business, they're quipsters—good, understand, they're very good in what they're doing. There are comics today that wouldn't last—wouldn't know how to play a part. That's a different type of a business. Of course, times have changed. The type of comedian that I am, or Bobby Clark, or Ed Wynn—there are very few of those fellas. It's the fast talker, the monologists, what they call stand-up comics. The majority of those fellas, you put them in a play, they wouldn't know what the hell to do, they'd just flounder around.

INTERVIEWER   I'd like to follow up on your reading, be-cause I know that you do a lot of reading and that you've al-ways felt that it was important to you. What is it in reading that is important for you in relation to your comic work?

LAHR   It's knowing what you do. Situations may arise where a certain manner, or a certain phrase or even dress—now when I did King Louis in *Du Barry Was a Lady*, certain things arose where I got laughs, without their being written in. I just can't explain it now. But I do know this, that it helps you, helps you on Broadway, but I just can't explain it.

INTERVIEWER   You really don't want to become a theo-retician—is that what you're saying?

LAHR   I certainly don't. I just—I'm giving you honestly what I feel. I may be wrong on a lot of things.

INTERVIEWER   To go back, I gather from what you have said that you feel that the kind of person you are and the kind of comedy you play, are really very closely related. As you say, you're either a good guy or you're not a good guy, and this reflects itself in the performance. Is that right?

LAHR   Well, he's gotta be a hell of an actor if he's really innately a bastard.

INTERVIEWER   So in a sense your own training started at your home, the kind of things your parents admired, or didn't.

LAHR   Well now, I wouldn't even say that. I'd say it's—it's something unexplainable. It's a manner.

INTERVIEWER   Something that's inside of one?

LAHR   That's right! If a fella is sincere, facially, you can
tell. An audience is very sensitive to that. The majority of
your audiences, they'll pick you up.

INTERVIEWER   Learning about human nature, then, is an
important part of your preparation.

LAHR   Well, that's one of the reasons for reading. Like
Kerr* said—I say this modestly—in one of his reviews: I
portrayed life itself in *Godot,* and he was amazed, he said,
"Where did he get it?" Well, you get it even if you're a
burlesque comedian; if you've got any intelligence, you know
what's going on.

INTERVIEWER   In your reading, do you have any specific
tastes?

LAHR   Don't misunderstand me. I don't read fiction. And
I'm not an avid reader, I'm an observing reader. I do the crossword puzzle, and I have a lot of reference books, you see,
and through that I get a smattering of French, and a smattering of Latin; and then, if the thing interests me, I'll read up
on it because I have all the reference books. And I used to
read biographies, all your classic authors practically. I can't
quote them, but I did get something from them.

INTERVIEWER   Are there any that you can think of now?

LAHR   I used to be a great lover of Dickens. If Dickens
were to write today, he wouldn't sell a copy, because he was
too convenient, too pat, but his character writing—I don't
think anybody today can touch him.

INTERVIEWER   Do you find when you get a new role that
you draw on your reading?

LAHR   No, I'm not that technical about it, or I'm not
that erudite.

INTERVIEWER   It's part of your inner experience then,
let us say.

LAHR   It's just, as I said before, application, watching,
instinct. I guess I have a little talent. That's the basic thing in
show business. If you're in the chorus and if you can't do the
dances, you're out. The chorus girl has talent or not, she's
either good or bad. You're not gonna make an actor if you

* Walter Kerr, drama critic for the New York *Herald Tribune.* Mr.
Kerr said: "His anticipatory chuckle as he begs to be told a funny story
he has already heard, his forcibly raised eyebrows as he positively
assures himself that he is happy, his passionate insistence that he is not
listening to a word that is spoken—these are the rhythms of an artist
with an eye for God's own truth. All of them, I think, are the rhythms
of musical comedy, of revue, of tanbark entertainment. And they suggest
that Mr. Lahr has, all along in his own lowbrow career, been in touch
with what goes on in the minds and hearts of the folk out front."

can't act. You're not gonna make a violinist if you can't play. A fella is gonna be a quack if he's not good, hasn't talent.

INTERVIEWER   On other occasions you've said that a comedian has to be a serious person.

LAHR   Not necessarily. But I think all your great comedians were.

INTERVIEWER   Why would that be?

LAHR   I don't know. I guess that's a Freudian question. I couldn't explain it. But all of the comics I knew in my day were serious people: Ed Wynn, Bobby Clark, Charlie Chaplin, W. C. Fields. They all had a sense of humor, don't misunderstand me—Sam Bernard, Louis Mann, Raymond Hitchcock. You go down the line, all the great ones.

INTERVIEWER   I wonder why.

LAHR   I guess it's an interest in their business. I think a comic, a great comic—there's a very thin line between tragedy and comedy. It all reverts back to that sympathetic thing. You've gotta have a sympathy for greatness. The audience must like you personally.

INTERVIEWER   I was going to ask you, what was the value of burlesque in your training?

LAHR   The value of burlesque was this—it was the breath of the theatre. You learned to dance. You learned to act scenes. You learned your trade. There was a first comedian, second comedian, third comedian, fourth comedian, and if you had it, you could make it. If you didn't, you'd be the third banana or the fourth banana; in other words, you had very little talent.

INTERVIEWER   What was the best teacher in burlesque— the other comedians, or the audience, or what?

LAHR   Observance. Observance. A capacity to pick it up, and a capacity to edit yourself. You could learn to be an acrobat if you were strong enough; you could learn to take falls. Or if you wanted to be a comedy acrobat, you'd put on funny clothes, and have gags, pull the wigs up and down, which the audience would laugh at, but that's—we're talking about other standards, right?

INTERVIEWER   When you first began, you said that you studied other comedians. How did you study them?

LAHR   Observing, watching what they did. I'll tell you the truth, I copied, we all copied. I mean everyone in those days—kids—you either were a Dutch comedian, if you were in burlesque, or a Jew comedian. We did emulate somebody, but then later on I forgot that, and I think I created a character that was never done before, one which was natural to me. How I ran into it, I don't know. I was a Dutch comedian when I went into *Delmar's Revels,* and then, when I did *Hold Everything,* I just had to do this fella—I played a bellowing sort of guy, and then I worked on that thing. It just, as I said, came naturally. You're not gonna learn how to sing, are you, if you haven't got a voice? You can improve what you've got, but if you haven't any voice you couldn't, even if you had operations on your vocal cords—you've gotta have that talent. I don't know, I can't explan it. I did it. Perhaps what I did was physically right for my physical appearance, you understand?

INTERVIEWER   Did this gradually build up; you'd find here and there something, like your very wonderful laugh— you know, that special one?

LAHR   Well, I did that one day in burlesque, and how I don't know.

INTERVIEWER   Just did it?

LAHR   Just did it. You're either funny, or you're not. Of course, for me the situation has to be right. I'm mostly a situation fella, I'm not a gag man. I know what to do in a situation if it presents itself. The gag itself may not be funny —you could say, "Oh!" and it would be a belly laugh, if the situation is right, you see? Look, there was a forum on the other night, and I understand . . . I didn't see it—this forum on Channel 13—what is it?

INTERVIEWER   David Susskind's "Open End"?

LAHR   Yes. And they had a lot of gag writers around and they were going after the comedians, and I understand in it I was mentioned, that I was hard to work for. Well, perhaps. My standards are different. I'm not a tough guy. I have very little trouble with writers, but I certainly red-pencil a lot of things. Now, if that is the case, perhaps I've been spoiled by such gag writers as Molière, Shakespeare, Shaw, Beckett, Cole Porter, DeSylva, Brown and Henderson. Maybe I'm spoiled, you see, because of my standards, and maybe when I see things that are trite, I don't like them. Well, that doesn't necessarily mean that I'm a tough guy.

INTERVIEWER   No. As a discouraged television viewer, I would say for heaven's sake keep up your standards.

LAHR   You see what I mean. It was quite a surprise to me, because I certainly haven't had much trouble with writers. But I guess *all* gag writers think that their gags are incomparable.

INTERVIEWER   You are supposed to have spent a good

deal of time practicing making funny faces in the mirror—is that true?

LAHR   No, no. Sure, when we were kids we'd all do a lot of mugging.

INTERVIEWER   I think there are writers who have made up things about you.

LAHR   I think so, yes.

INTERVIEWER   Well, in other words, lots of the mannerisms, the rolling of the eyes and the gahng, gahng, gahng*—these are things that *you* hit upon.

LAHR   These are things that I . . . They were not studied, and it reverts back to what I told you. It's you! We all have peculiarities, all have a different walk, we all have a different method of using our hands. They're not all alike. You have a different manner of speaking.

INTERVIEWER   In other words, what we're getting at here, is that you're on the stage in a given situation, and a flash comes to you, you don't know where it comes from, it's part of you—"Do this, try this."

LAHR   Well, your audience is your barometer, naturally. Sometimes, if I'm working in a show, I'll think out a scene. I'll say if I do it this way or if I do it that way—but I can't explain it to you. I just can't say how you do it. A kid five years old gets up at a piano and plays. Nobody taught him. Like I have a daughter who paints beautifully. Nobody taught her. It's instinctive. It's the same as a beaver. I just saw a little baby beaver. I don't think the mother showed him how to build a dam. I think they do it all by instinct. I don't think anybody showed them how. I don't think anybody can show you how to act. I think they can say, "If you do it this way . . ." and that's the trouble with kids today. They all act alike, because the teacher says one, two, three, four, five, move. Very few have individuality.

INTERVIEWER   What is the difference between your day and today?

LAHR   In my day you just went out and did it. You developed it yourself. Years ago in show business the audience would discover you, but if you worked like anybody else on Broadway, you never became a star. They would pick out individuals. Now I'll mention you names, and they were all individuals. They worked differently, had different methods. Take Bill Fields. Have you ever seen anybody work like Bill Fields when he was a star? Chaplin? Ed Wynn? Leon Errol?

* A marvelously comic and uniquely Lahrian sound which simply cannot be adequately conveyed in print.

You had to have it, or you weren't a star. The audience would find you.

INTERVIEWER I wonder if that has something to do with the whole present-day aura of conformity.

LAHR Well, all the youngsters sing alike.

INTERVIEWER Now, over the years you naturally developed certain things that you can rely on, that you know are tried and true to get a laugh. What are these things that you know you can always fall back on when you need to?

LAHR That gahng, gahng, gahng—I don't do that anymore. You see, it isn't only laughs that count. There are other things. As far as I'm concerned I would much rather hold interest and get respect from the audience, and the sympathy. Many a time I'd throw out a big laugh if it was the wrong kind of a laugh. I didn't do that years ago, but I'm a little more discerning today. You take Chevalier. He gets very few laughs, but he has a tremendous charm and a tremendous interest and a tremendous magnetism. You see, I would like to get laughs if the situation called for it, but I would also like to have them say, "Well, this guy can act pretty good too." Of course, there are funny men, naturally funny men, and my definiton of a funny man is a fella who comes on the stage, no material at all, physically funny—I don't mean deformed— and says hello and gets a laugh. I know fellas that can do that. Or you giggle. Bea Lillie can do this (twisting head sideways) and make an audience laugh. No material. I can do this (closing eyes, as if in pain) and make an audience laugh.

INTERVIEWER What do you think it is?

LAHR It's what I told you. You're either funny, you've either got it, or you haven't got it. You can't learn that.

INTERVIEWER You mentioned Beatrice Lillie. I wonder if you'd talk a little bit about the women comedians.

LAHR Well, I think Beatrice Lillie is the greatest woman comedian I ever worked with. Bea needs very little material. She's a funny, basically funny, woman, and I think her humor comes from incongruous dignity, do you understand what I mean? (Mimicking) "But, my deah." You see what I mean. It's making fun of that particular type of person without being bitter. But that's Bea Lillie.

INTERVIEWER Who else of the women comedians? You worked with Nancy Walker.

LAHR Nancy is a very funny little girl. Let me see who else I like. There was Edna May Oliver, who was a character woman, an actress, basically an actress—and her own manner was humorous at times. Bea I laugh at. Fanny Brice I thought was fine. I think Lucille Ball is fine. She does all the hokum, but she's a funny gal. But Bea has a more literate aspect. I guess her humor comes from phony dignity and her tremendous sense of satire.

INTERVIEWER   I think that she is able to pinprick a human foible to satirize.

LAHR   She didn't study that, you know, you don't study that. You can see a fella walking down the street and you turn around and he's funny-looking. He may have the wrong kind of a hat on, but if he were a big handsome fella with the wrong kind of hat and wrong kind of a shoe, you'd say isn't he a ridiculous s.o.b. and you wouldn't laugh at him, but if it was a little peddler . . .

INTERVIEWER   Menasha Skulnik would be a sample of the little peddler.

LAHR   That's the difference. It's the physical difference. You never laugh, you never feel sorry for a football player when he's carried off the field. You'd never feel sorry for the tyrant, the heavy, if he gets killed. It's something psychological.

INTERVIEWER   Then with the comedian it's sheer instinct above everything else, is that it?

LAHR   I don't know about anybody else, but that is how I feel about it.

INTERVIEWER   Aren't there certain things, though, that all comedians have in common, aside from being funny men —for instance, a sense of timing?

LAHR   I don't know what timing is, and may I explain that to you. There's another instinct. It is rhythm. The ear must be attuned. That comes by application, practice, being out there. I mean, what the hell is timing? It's a rhythm. I wish somebody would explain timing to me. They say timing, how he times! It's knowing when to come in when the laugh dies.

INTERVIEWER   With you, then, it's all instinct?

LAHR   Instinct. Always has been. And practice.

INTERVIEWER   Have you discussed these problems of the comic with other comics? Have you found that they worked the same way that you do?

LAHR   No, no. Ed Wynn—he worked on his mechanics, his tricks and things; he'd conjure those, develop those. Ed had a manner of delivery and, I guess, his rhythm and timing —he knew what to do. I never delved into that.

INTERVIEWER   Are comedians likely to talk among themselves about their comedy?

LAHR   No, not very much, I don't think—how they do it, or how they don't—I don't think so. I don't think those that I talked to plan it. They may instinctively know how they are gonna do it.

INTERVIEWER   In approaching a new role, do you first plan it in your mind?

LAHR   Sure, I plan how I will play it, how I'll play the character. And the moment you get the lines, then you put your personality into it.

INTERVIEWER   So your first problem is to learn your lines.

LAHR   Yes. Then you get the sense of it. I don't know how others do. There's a lot of people who analyze the scenes and then they know how to go on. But the way I work is getting the lines first, then analyzing it and getting the sense out of what I'm doing. I'm never right till about two, three weeks after the show opens on the road. It all has to be clear to me. Then one day I wake up and there it is. I have to do things instinctively; and, naturally, you take direction. A director can see certain things—like this fellow Landau* is very fine, very good.

INTERVIEWER   What do you admire in his directing?

LAHR   The suggestions he gives you. You don't know what a certain thing means sometimes. And sometimes I can help the director, which I've done many times.

INTERVIEWER   When you get a sketch, for instance, in a revue—what is your procedure in working on that sketch, in figuring out what is going to be funny, how you're going to handle it?

LAHR   Well, you never know what's going to be funny, your audience will tell you that. Then you edit it, like the paper picker . . .

INTERVIEWER   Oh, yes, in *Two on the Aisle*.

LAHR   The situation was basically right, I knew it was right, and they were gonna take it out of the show because it never went over. We rewrote it, and—well, there you are, it was one of the great sketches. The idea was right, but the construction and the words were wrong, you see. Now we took a different slant.

INTERVIEWER   I wanted to ask a little bit more about whether you studied people or studied human situations in perfecting your comedy.

LAHR   No, no.

* Jack Landau, artistic director of the American Shakespeare Festival, who directed Mr. Lahr in *A Midsummer Night's Dream*.

INTERVIEWER   It all comes from inside?

LAHR   Well, you observe. I guess we're all parrots to a certain extent. You observe certain mannerisms of people if you're playing a certain character, perhaps. But make a study of people, no. No, I haven't.

INTERVIEWER   Then you don't do what some actors do. They sit in subways and they study faces, or maybe they go to parks.

LAHR   No, I think that's a lot of nonsense.

INTERVIEWER   Now I think we would like to spend a little more time on trying to find out what your procedure is when you get the script of a play.

LAHR   When I get the script of a play, I read it. If I like the play, and I think I can do it, then I'll accept it. My first procedure is to have the play explained to me without wasting time in delving into the details. Then I learn my lines by rote. Then when I know the lines, I analyze what I'm saying. I may change inflections. I get the sense of what I'm saying and it comes to me much easier that way. I find it easier to learn it by rote, and then the conception of the part and the meaning of the words come easier for me.

INTERVIEWER   Taking some particular sketch or play, how do you decide on which pieces of business to use?

LAHR   Well, as I said before, you take direction, and if the sketch is funny—of course, in revues nobody knows, you may rehearse ten sketches and all can follow the wind— and if I think of a piece of business, I'll ask the director what he thinks of it, and invariably it goes in. And sometimes after it's gone in, we talk it over to see if it fits. It's the usual procedure. Naturally, an actor needs help from a director in editing, and I've usually helped the sketches by injections of lines and pieces of business, and then I let the audience edit it for me, you see. That's why we go on the road.

INTERVIEWER   I guess you can't quite use that procedure in this show?

LAHR   Oh, no, no, no. This is cut-and-dried Shakespeare. It's a little strange to me—the phrasing, the way the English language is written in the Elizabethan way, which isn't contemporary at all. It's strange to me; therefore the words don't come easy, but they eventually will.

INTERVIEWER   Have you had to do anything special, different from other plays?

LAHR   Oh, I've injected a few little things into this, because it is flexible enough so that you can do it. But you stay within the script. I don't change any words. You can't you see, because if you do you're not true to Shakespeare. Understand, I don't profess to be a Shakespearean actor. But it's quite a departure and it'll be a lot of fun, I think.

INTERVIEWER   Aside from the language problem, which is a departure, what else do you find?

LAHR   What else do you find with Shakespeare? You find a tremendous sense of travesty that the man had. You find that his characters are well written, and there's no question that he was the master.

INTERVIEWER   In other words, he provides you with plenty of things that you can embroider upon.

LAHR   Well, you can use your own conception of what he does. You can't, certainly, as I said before, change the language, not that there aren't different ways of expressing— same as in any contemporary playwright. One fellow will play it differently from the other, but that's for the audience to decide, if my conception is right.

INTERVIEWER   What is your concept of Bottom? How are you working on that?

LAHR   Bottom is a—a layman, an artisan. He's a weaver who portrays ninety percent of the people in the world, with an ego, an exhibitionistic complex—we all have. You talk to anybody, they'll either say I've wanted to be an actor, my daughter is gonna be an actress. I think that's a natural trait, and it must have been that in that time, too, they had amateur groups that were bumblers, you know. And that's the main comedy vein of this thing, but I think it's basically a story of love. Even the laymen, the artisans, they have a love for the Duke and they want to do something for him. But it's travesty, it's burlesque. And I imagine from his writing that the comedians in those days were low comedians—and the same as we had at one time here—Hebrew comedians, dialect comedians. They used to make fun of the masters, you know, the workmen—the same in this day. I can imagine these workmen would, by comparison, be Brooklynites or—or characters that didn't speak the language quite literally, or literately.

INTERVIEWER   Which of all your creations have you been fondest of?

LAHR   The thing that I'm proudest of and I've done a lot of things, the most gratifying was Beckett's *Waiting for Godot*.

INTERVIEWER   Why was that?

LAHR   Well, it was such a strange play, and it was such a departure, and I think although the general consensus was sort of split, there were those critics that were enthralled, and others that were puzzled by the play—but I think I got unanimous praise.

INTERVIEWER   Oh, yes.

LAHR   Then the second thing is the Lion in *The Wizard of Oz*. I think that will outlive many pictures, I mean the picture itself. And I did get the Critics Award for that. I think I liked all, everything I did, with the exception maybe of two or three shows that when we got on the road, I wasn't too happy, I misjudged the material. Then, *Burlesque* —I loved doing that very much, the show *Burlesque*. And *Hotel Paradiso*, which was sort of a tour de force.

INTERVIEWER   Do you have any particular direction you'd like to go in now?

LAHR   I never thought of it. I never think of it. My main thing in this stage of life is to keep going and, naturally, do good things. I never really had any ambition to do Shakespeare, but I was flattered when they asked me. There's one job I was offered, in opera—and this very few people know, because I gave Mr. Bing my word that I wouldn't give out any publicity—but I turned it down. It wasn't lucrative enough. I mean, they offered me twenty-two performances in twenty-six weeks, or something like that, to appear in a Strauss operetta. I had a meeting with Mr. Bing and some of the others and they were all enthused, and I said I'd let them know, if I didn't do a musical, and I held off for a couple of months and then I finally said I'm not that wealthy that I can do a thing like that.

INTERVIEWER   It appealed to you nevertheless, because it was something new?

LAHR   Well, the reason is that then I would have touched every phase of the theatre, you see.

INTERVIEWER   Was that one of the things that appealed to you most about *Godot?*

LAHR   Well, yes. I knew I could do it. I don't attempt anything I can't do, with the exception of television—and that's a question of money. The money is that good that you just do it. And I've made mistakes, like this last show I did. But that *The Boys Against the Girls*, that wasn't our fault, I assure you—little Nancy's and mine—we had very little help. But what we heard at the start, the way it was explained to us, it looked exciting.

INTERVIEWER   How could you have used more help in that show? What do you need to make a success?

LAHR   There's lots of things to decide in any show, besides the stars. A well-rounded cast, the material, the type of material—and revues today are especially difficult to do unless your material is above average. They've done everything on television, the revue type of entertainment. A revue has to have an idea that is very novel. It's a very difficult form of entertainment today. The same as vaudeville, it sort of went out.

INTERVIEWER   And did you find that in this particular show none of these components were present?

LAHR   I have had my doubts about a revue anyway for many years. I knew that it sort of went out of vogue, and I wouldn't advise anybody to do a revue unless the material is so novel and so good that it's far above the average.

INTERVIEWER   You said before that you don't do the gahng, gahng, gahng any more.

LAHR   No, very seldom. It fits in this. I sound like a donkey braying or a donkey laughing—that's the only reason I put it in. I may change it, I may find another noise.

INTERVIEWER   How do you look for these noises?

LAHR   I don't look for them. In burlesque, years ago, everybody was identified with something, either a catch line or some individual trait, and this happened one day.

INTERVIEWER   You say that you put the gahng, gahng, gahng here in the role of Bottom because you felt that it fitted. Yet you may change it—why?

LAHR   You see, the reason I may change it is this. I don't think that Shakespeare, when he wrote this, ever figured a fella would do that. I understand that whoever played Bottom made noises like a donkey or some sound that conveyed that it was a donkey. I may not even do that. I may make a sound like braying, or something, but I will let the audience decide and let the critics decide. They're liable to say what the hell is he putting that in here for.

INTERVIEWER   Have you made a study of all sounds of animals?

LAHR   No, no. I've made a study of nothing.

INTERVIEWER   You just neighed like a horse.

LAHR   Well, you hear a horse, you hear a horse! I did it one day and it sounded all right. I never neighed like a horse before.

INTERVIEWER   But when you say that you may find another noise, are you thinking about another noise?

LAHR   I'll find it out there, I'll do something. I may
come in the dressing room and try something, maybe ong,
ong, or some damn thing. If it fits, the audience will tell me.
I certainly won't give a Bronx cheer, or anything like that.

INTERVIEWER   You have said that taste is very important in your work.

LAHR   As I said, I don't think you can acquire good
taste. I don't say good taste in clothes, I mean good taste
in living, in saying the right thing, in being tactful—of course
we all make mistakes at some time. But where it is most
necessary is when you're on the stage. Certain people can
say certain things on the stage and they're accepted. Other
people whose personalities don't fit what they're saying, the
audience will resent it. Now, as I said before, there are
tricks in this business. If you play beneath an audience, if
your character is a lowly character, do you see, the audience, although they like you, doesn't take you too seriously.
"Oh, he's a schmo," they'll say, but they let you get away
with it, you know what I mean. I have done things on the
stage that I don't think any other actor has ever done and
the audience never resented it. I say this modestly. In *Flying
High*, I had this skit—it was about a urine test—and it was
the biggest laugh; it's known in the history of the theatre,
in this country, and you can check that with anyone. Now,
if a wise guy were to do that, a fellow with the wrong personality or that the audience did not respect, they could
resent it very much and it could be shocking. It all reverts
back to how the audience feels about you out there, if they
accept you as a guy that bumbles into something—and that's
in the writing and in the playing. It's a matter of maintaining
an air of innocence. You can do almost anything on the
stage, if you do it as if you haven't the slightest idea that
there's anything wrong with what you're doing. Some comedians can do that particular thing, but a lot of comedians
make it vulgar and dirty, and the audience won't accept it.

INTERVIEWER   What was it that you—what was it about
you and your taste that kept it from getting vulgar?

LAHR   Well, let me explain it. I don't like to hear a
woman swear, or get dirty in any sense; certain girls when
they do it, they rankle, but others you accept, your personality is right for it. I know, I won't mention names, but I
know a little gal that'll say the filthiest things in the world,
and I'll accept it and laugh like hell. For others it just won't
fit them, and that holds good on the stage.

INTERVIEWER In general, do you find that audiences change in what they like?

LAHR Oh, of course. Audiences today are so satiated with entertainment that you just don't know. They'll accept one thing for a year, and then let it alone. Years ago it was an event if your father took your mother to a show once a year to see a certain star they liked. Today they have a hundred stars a day. The product now is thrown in their faces, you see. Stars come up quicker. They come up overnight, whether they have talent or not. Today it isn't a question of talent as much as it's a question of personality. That holds good especially for television. God knows, I won't mention names, but there's a lot of people that are big in television that couldn't get arrested on the stage, if you judge it by talent, but they sell the product. They have a certain personality and they have a flair for the oral expression, you know, and they're nice-looking. But if you take it from an acting point of view, they couldn't get arrested.

INTERVIEWER Do you go through much agony in the creation of a role or a sketch?

LAHR No, no. What I do is learn the words, and I may take my car sometimes and drive, and as I'm driving, I'll think and think how I'll do it, and maybe a line suggests itself. We all go through agonies before the opening. I don't know of anybody that doesn't, that has any integrity or any imagination.

INTERVIEWER Agonies of what?

LAHR Of doubt!

INTERVIEWER About the way you're doing it, or the way the show will go?

LAHR No, how you will be accepted—do you understand? Now, you see, certain actors when they reach a stage in life, if they do something that isn't quite as good, critics who have seen them over a period of years will make excuses. Some who are vicious won't. I have been fortunate. I don't believe that I myself on Broadway—and this is an open book, you can see it all—have ever had an adverse criticism. They would say, well, the play wasn't right, or why don't they give Lahr better material, and so on. But at the opening you're selling yourself. You take any product. If an automobile comes out and it isn't too hot, their sales go down, it's not as salable, but if they come out with a good car— the same as you could come out with a good play or have a good part—you ride. Just before I did *Godot* there was nothing around. I've always made a pretty good living. I do a picture, maybe television, and I kept going. But there was nothing around. Then, when I did *Godot*, after that things got easy for two or three years. But I've been around a long time. I remember when I first got into the business—I mean, first got recognized and made a hit—the old fellas weren't working so often. Great stars in their day. You've been seen, the new people come in, tastes change—which doesn't hold true in England. I'm very fortunate. I'm one of the few that, at least at this stage of the game, can get jobs, although not as many. When I was doing musicals, I'd do a musical, and they'd be writing another one, do you understand? So that's something, too, and I realize that—that you've been around, and they've seen you and seen you and seen you. But these are some of the things I mean when I talk about doubts. But you still have fans that are loyal, you know. And what I would advise a fella to do is get along with the times. When I couldn't get jobs as a low comic—they weren't writing for them any more—I took *Burlesque*. I took *Godot*. I took straight things, and fortunately I could do it, you see. But you have to be ready to change, to change your acting. When I got to be a little more discerning and when I realized that the obvious things that they used to laugh at years ago—tangle talk, malaprops—became a little out of fashion, I stopped doing it, as much as I could. Now, I did a little thing with a boy called Eddie Hodges, a television show, where we did all of this, but I was the old vaudeville actor teaching the young kid. It was all right there, it was in a situation, you see, and I think there are very few around of our type. I'm talking about Wynn or his type. I know a lot of fellas, and if they would have changed years ago and not stuck to their method, they would still be working today—but you get dated, you know? Which is a horrible thing. In England once you've made it, you're there forever.

INTERVIEWER   What is it, according to your observations, that people don't laugh at any more?

LAHR   At the obvious things they've heard so often. All the jokes. They won't laugh at a joke they've heard twice. I don't think they'd laugh at a song that I did when I was a Dutch comedian, "Oh, How That Woman Could Cook," with malapropisms like her soup was malicious, do you understand?

INTERVIEWER   In those days they laughed at that, that's right.

LAHR That's right. Tangle talk. I think the pun has
gone. They will laugh at it if you make fun of it, you see.
I did a sketch with Bea Lillie. We did a burlesque sketch.
We were burlesquers. She did Gypsy Rose Lee and I was
the comedian, and I could use old clichés in the situation
that we were making fun of, such as, if the audience didn't
laugh, I'd say, "Is the curtain up?" Well, that's been said a
million times, but in that situation they'd laugh. But if an
actor would come out today and do it on the level, you see,
they'd say, "What does that man want, we've heard this."

INTERVIEWER How else have you found the times have
changed as far as your comedy, or your shows, go?

LAHR Well, there was a time when you were a bastard
comedian. By that I mean you went out there for laughing
purposes only, you didn't care. And that was the vaudeville
days when the comedian'd come out and talk about Swiss
cheese, and the next minute he'd say, "Well, I was down
at this corner and another thing happened to me," and then
they'd sing a song—with nothing that was connected. Well,
the same went for burlesque shows. The same went for
musicals. Now, when I did musicals, the love interest was
secondary. They were just out there to do the love songs,
like in *Flying High,* when the girl was in a tenement she
sang, "Oh, if my . . ." I don't know what the exact words
are, but she sang, "If my lover would come." And the
guy came down in a parachute—do you understand what I
mean?—which was accepted. If the audiences were entertained—pretty girls, jokes, and the scenes were there, no
matter how thin the story was, it was acceptable. But today
the play has to be well written; it has to be probable, not
contrived. Years ago you could take writing liberties. And
if you'll notice, that's why all your farces are dying. Noel
Coward did one. We did one which got rave notices—and
died.

INTERVIEWER You're talking about *Hotel Paradiso?*

LAHR *Paradiso.* We ran about fourteen weeks and we
thought we had a hit. But the audience left us. And I think
pictures have done that.

INTERVIEWER Why should that be?

LAHR I'll tell you why. Years ago you'd put a back-
drop out and a rock or somethin', and that was a forest. But
today, through pictures, when you go into a forest, that is
a forest. If there is an oil painting on the wall, that is an
oil painting. If it's a picket fence, that is a picket fence.
If it's grass, it's real grass and not a grass mat. It has to

be the real thing, and I think pictures have done that. Your situations have to be real, and a play has to say something. They must get something out of the play. There's another reason why *Hotel Paradiso* was sort of an enigma. It left the audience with nothing. The story line itself was distasteful—a man trying to have an affair with his friend's wife, you see, which is acceptable in France, where the play was written. It was one of the first farces written. And no matter how well it's done—and believe me, the night of the Actors' Benefit with *Paradiso,* they stood up and bravoed, it was an actor's play—no matter how well done, you'd have a tough time. So, as I say, the times have changed. The same with the advent of radio. The public got attuned to a mechanical sound. It wasn't ocular any more. The jokes became the thing. Now with television, your situation is back, which goes to prove your comedians were the backbone of pictures at one time—your two-reelers, all your money-makers. But the audience became satiated with the low comedy that left them nothing here (pointing to his heart), with the exception of Chaplin, who lasted, do you see? And boom—it wasn't slowly, it was boom. The same thing happened in television. The audience got nothing from it. They became a little more literate, but in the early days of television, they used to laugh at the pie in the face, which they brought back. Now you take what they call sick comics. I like them. Some of their humor is very intelligent. They speak about things today that comics wouldn't have dared to years ago. The audience wouldn't have known what the hell they were talking about. But their humor is biting. I've heard some that are very, very good. Some people resent them, but I think that humor today is a little more intelligent. So times change, with the exception of classics, which will always be accepted, the same as your books are still accepted today.

INTERVIEWER   You're recognized as a pantomime artist, who without lines can reach people. What is it about you that people laugh at?

LAHR   I don't know. Maybe I'm funny-looking, maybe my mannerisms are ludicrous, maybe over a period of years by practice and application I found out that they'd laugh at this (rolling his eyes), and then I would do it, or a movement or something. But those things haven't been planned or studied. Maybe some other fellas do, but I don't.

INTERVIEWER   Chaplin created an image, a picture.

He was the little man who was always getting kicked around by the world.

LAHR That's right, that's right, and that goes for nearly any comedian. Charlie Chaplin was a tremendous craftsman, and he knew, as all comedians know, that you have to get a sympathy, and he used different gimmicks. He would be a fella that was hungry—"Oh, the poor fella." You see, you can kick a woman in the pants—like in *Taming of the Shrew*—if she's a dragon, if she's distasteful to an audience, if she's a shrew. That's when you can do those things—when you can be rough to a woman, or even a child, if the audience doesn't like 'em. And he knew that. He would go along and take a piece of sugar and give it to a horse as he'd go, or pat a little baby on the head. "Aw, isn't that a nice fella," they'd say. Well, that's the secret of any comedian, if the audience immediately . . . I won't mention any names, but I saw a comic with a tremendous talent that did the wrong thing one night. Instead of doing what he should have done, he came in and frightened a bird, but he didn't do it once, he did it three times. He went "Boo." Well, he was dead. Nobody wants to frighten a bird. You know who did that, the heavies years ago. When they made a study of what the audiences would hate—like a man would come in and there was a child in the crib, and he'd flick his ashes on the child—hisss—hissss. It was as simple as that. You play on the sensibilities of the audience, and a good playwright will keep that in mind.

INTERVIEWER That reminds one of the skit in which you're a baseball player being interviewed, and the interviewer will hardly let you get a word in edgewise.

LAHR Well now, that's simple. Here was an obnoxious radio interviewer that wouldn't let this fella talk. If I'd of spit in his eye, the audience would have accepted it. If I'd of hit him on the head with a bat and walked out, they would applaud—do you see?

INTERVIEWER Yes. Well, did you study ballplayers in order to develop that character?

LAHR I didn't. But I saw some of them on the Wheaties hour.

INTERVIEWER So you do, on occasion, go to life for your material.

LAHR Well, you burlesque it. I just don't go into some particular person's mannerisms or anything like that. You put your own personality in it.

INTERVIEWER   But what I'm getting at is, there are characterizations that you have developed which have their basis in some person that you have seen, perhaps, or some situation that you have noticed.

LAHR   Oh, I guess that's natural to anybody. You see a man drunk, staggering down the street, you don't say I'm gonna do it that way, but you know that he went like this.

INTERVIEWER   In that sketch of the baseball player, did you have anything to do with writing or creating it?

LAHR   I put a few things in. No, no, I did with other things. But Abe Burrows* did that.

INTERVIEWER   Well, how about the paper picker?

LAHR   I did have a lot to do with that.

INTERVIEWER   Did you go to Central Park, for instance, and watch a guy picking?

LAHR   No, no! Geez, I'm not that academic. Anybody that does that must . . .

INTERVIEWER   There are actors that do that.

LAHR   Well, maybe that's the way they . . . I'm not that—how can I say?—enthusiastic!

INTERVIEWER   In other words, you want us to believe you're still basically lazy?

LAHR   It's not a question of being lazy, but I'm not that type of an actor. There are some actors . . . Now I've seen a fella that's done some tremendous things, and I think he's a brilliant actor—his name is Rod Steiger. He has a great talent for what he's doing, which is characters, and evidently this man studies the mob. Well, that's his type of work, but I don't lean that way.

INTERVIEWER   Incidentally, for a lazy man, a self-confessed lazy man, didn't you get in the wrong line of work? Isn't it pretty hard?

LAHR   Oh, I never liked what I was doing before. I like what I'm doing, you know.

INTERVIEWER   But it's hard work, isn't it?

LAHR   It isn't easy. But it's the only thing I can do.

INTERVIEWER   What actually is the hardest thing about being a comedian?

LAHR   Keeping your audience interested in you, keeping the producers interested in you, making a living. You have to keep going. You have to make money. You try new things. I'm not going to stand on a corner with a tin cup, it isn't a question of that. But, as you know, today when

---

* Abe Burrows directed *Two on the Aisle*, in which the skit was seen.

you have children and you can't send them to a public school—you wouldn't send yours, I don't think, today, if you lived in certain neighborhoods—and want to send them to college, and with the tax situation the way it is—you've gotta keep going, because you can't live on capital any more; you've done that for many years. So if you acquire dependents and a mode of life—well, you may cut out a few things, but how much? No matter how much money you make you're always even, unless you're tremendous or have a faculty for investments and things like that where you can get a capital gains.

INTERVIEWER   Getting the parts that "keep you going," as you say, is one of the main problems?

LAHR   Well, for myself, there are very few good parts around. I've reached the stage where you get a certain amount of money. Sometimes producers say, "Well, this part, although it's a very good one, if we get Lahr, he gets a certain amount of money and that's too much for us." And some of them say, "Oh no, he's had it, he's tired, we've seen him. Let's see who's somebody new." Well, the only way to get them interested is, as I've said before, you do something like *Godot*. This may interest them again.

INTERVIEWER   How important is a good agent?

LAHR   Very important, *very* important. You see, what's happened to the theatre today, I mean to the agency business, is this: the big boys have the entrées, with exceptions, naturally. They have directors, producers, they have writers on their staff, and naturally they're going to protect their own people. They also have "packages"—where they do their own shows. My agent isn't a big agent, he's well known, but he isn't big. It's Louis Shurr and Lester Shurr in New York—but they haven't got that. They have a few actors; some of them you know very well. They've got Bob Hope. Now, Bob is a comic, I'm a comic, and they can't say to Bob, "Now look, I want Lahr on there"—see? But an agent is tremendously important today.

INTERVIEWER   It has been said that the comedian of all entertainers, must have the closest rapport with the audience. Would you agree with that statement?

LAHR   Oh, I agree with that, if he's out on his own, if he's a stand-up fella and goes out there. But Shakespeare said, "The play's the thing," didn't he? If you have the right words, and you're right for the words. See, some fellas, their manner is right for a particular part. Now, I would no more think of going in and playing the leading man or, let's say, any part that Rod could do. Well, maybe I could play a few of them, maybe not as well; but there are certain things that I'm not right for—vocally I'm not right for it, physically I'm not right for it. And I think casting has a lot to do with the success of a venture; that's why a casting man is very, very important.

INTERVIEWER What are some of the qualities you would look for in choosing a comic?

LAHR I think every comedian has to have a certain amount of intelligence. I think he has to be witty, has to have a manner, personality, deportment. There's a lot of good things go into a comedian. And I'll say this again—good taste. I have a certain standard that I go by—a lot of comedians I think are great, others that the public are crazy about I don't like, and it's a matter of taste. But all the comedians that I knew have been intelligent men.

INTERVIEWER What are the special problems for the comedian in television?

LAHR Material.

INTERVIEWER How about the time element for preparation?

LAHR You see, that's another thing. I think the most essential thing for a radio or a television comedian is to be a quick study. You'll never get perfection out of television for a comic. The only way you're going to get perfection is if a comic goes on and he has done his material before, even in a dramatic play. Helen Hayes, if she'd go out and do Victoria, she's done it, then it's perfection. But even a good play that's been rehearsed for two weeks and put on television could be a hundred percent better if they had perfected it and edited it on the road. But from your television standards, considering the amount of time utilized, some of them are pretty good. Now, nobody is gonna come in and tell 'em how to do television, because naturally—it's ten years now—they've found out what's good and what's bad. But a quick study, that's the most essential thing. There's some people can look over a part and know it. I did a picture with a fella called Jack Carson. It's amazing. Geez, he'd come in the dressing room, look the thing over, come out and do it.

INTERVIEWER He must have a photographic memory.

LAHR Yeah, that's right. That's most essential in television, I think.

INTERVIEWER Haven't you liked your movie work?

LAHR I did a few things in pictures that were pretty

good. But, unhappily and unfortunately, I came in at the time they were utilizing the comic as a friend or a guest, you know, or Charlie's friend. In later years—unless you were a light comedian that would carry the love interest—the funny man was out. I did some straight things which were pretty good, but I never amounted to much in pictures.

INTERVIEWER You've said in the past, that the minute you get out on the stage you can tell the mood of the audience. How do you tell that?

LAHR I don't say the mood of the audience. You can tell if they're receptive or not.

INTERVIEWER If you sense that they're not being receptive, or it's a tired audience, what do you do?

LAHR Well, I don't say I used to do this years ago. I was very ambitious, you know, but I found out it's the same thing as a fighter, or any athlete. When you try, and you're tense, you're just twice as bad. What I found out is you have sign posts, you have certain lines, maybe two or three, maybe it's a subtle line, maybe it's a piece of business—and when you make your entrance, and you have a few things to say that have been laughs, perhaps different pieces of business, and if they don't laugh, you know, you've got to work on them. But instead of working on them, the easiest way to get an audience is to take it easy, to fool, have fun—if you're not in a straight play—ingratiate yourself to an audience. Instead of working hard, relax, take it easy, have fun. Make it appear spontaneous, and invariably it works.

INTERVIEWER Do you have a problem in order to be able to relax that way?

LAHR I have a reputation of being a worrier and a nervous fella. I don't say that years ago before an opening I wouldn't be in a terrible state, but I'll explain it this way. After a doctor's tenth operation, it becomes—I don't say that I'm not nervous going on, but not one-hundreth of what I used to be. And you build up as a defense a certain philosophy. You say to yourself, "What the hell, what have I got to prove, now!" For a defense you say to yourself, "So they don't like me, the hell with them. The curtain comes down at eleven o'clock, I'm alive, I'm breathing. What the hell am I worrying about this for!" But subconsciously it's, "Geez, if I'm not good, I may not get a job in the next one, I'm through," which is a horrible bugaboo.

INTERVIEWER How do you get over that?

LAHR   I don't think any actor, unless he's tremendously wealthy, gets over it.

INTERVIEWER   Or deal with it, I should say.

LAHR   Well, it has to happen sometime. You know, I'm not a doddering old man, don't misunderstand me—but I know an actor today who's great, but people are afraid to take a chance with him because he's very old. He just doesn't get jobs. He can't get jobs. And he was one of our great comedians. That's in the back of your mind unless you're very secure, by which I mean money-wise. That's a thing a lot of actors feel and that's where they get the fear. That goes for a ballplayer when he's through, or anybody, you know. It's perfectly natural. I try to throw it out of my mind, but I guess that's the reason for insecurity in actors. "How will the audience like me? If I don't do this thing good, maybe next season will be rough, another flop"—do you understand?

INTERVIEWER   You said that a person has to be something on-stage of what he is off-stage, that the fabric of the person runs through his acting.

LAHR   Oh, you can play a character. If I play a heavy, I'd play at being the heavy, I'd be a mean guy—but I'm talking about a comedian.

INTERVIEWER   Yes, I understand that, but the theatre as a rule is a pretty tough business, and as you're outlining some of it, it's a hard business.

LAHR   This sure is a business today. You see, when I started on Broadway, you had a lot of producers that had a love for the theatre. That came first. They loved it—Ziegfeld, Belasco, Dillingham, Sam Harris. First it was the love. Then if the thing paid off, fine. But today it is a business. It's a matter of economics. Times have changed. Unions have become very strong. So today a producer, with exceptions, is first a good businessman, and second a producer. The business comes first. I know Arthur Hopkins did a couple of things for love. He said, "I like it. It's going to be an artistic success and I'm not gonna make a quarter." Arthur and I were very good friends. When he did *Burlesque* he produced that for eleven thousand in 1927. When we did it in '47, it cost us sixty thousand. Today that same production would cost you a hundred and twenty-five thousand or a hundred and fifty thousand. So times have changed.

INTERVIEWER   Has all this taken some of the fun out of the theatre, because of the pressures?

LAHR   Yes, it has taken the fun out of it. Years ago a

Broadway actor could make a living. You could play vaudeville, if you didn't have a show right away; you could pick
up a season of vaudeville and you were paid very well for
it. There were stock companies. There were night clubs,
lots of them. Today—and I'm talkin' from a Broadway point
of view—an actor who is a good actor, and there's lots of
good ones and lots of good leading ladies around, can't
get jobs—and where are they going? Maybe they'll get a
job in television. It's not as easy; therefore it's not as much
fun. I'm talking about making a living. I know years ago
I never worried. I'd work over at the Palace and knock off
five thousand. Take Ed Wynn. Now he's a real actor. You
can't learn that. You've either got it or you haven't. He's
not a poor man, but I mean he loved what he was doing,
and he was a very unhappy man. I did a television show
with Ed. We were very good friends and we were discussing
the situation. And he told me what he went through. For
two or three years he couldn't get a job. He couldn't get
anything. He accepted a Red Skelton show for twenty-five
hundred dollars, where he used to get fifteen thousand or
twenty thousand, and then Gobel's, and then he got a break
with a good part.

INTERVIEWER   If a young man wanted to become a
comedian today, what advice would you give him? And I'm
not talking about the so-called stand-up comedians, or the
sick comedians. I mean the true clown comedian.

LAHR   Be honest with himself. We all have an ego,
but the audience will tell him if he's funny enough. And if
he isn't funny, he's not gonna learn how to be funny, so
forget it. If he's naturally a funny man and people laugh at
him at parties, he should give it a try and be honest with
himself. Let the audience tell him if he's funny or not.

INTERVIEWER   In the absence of vaudeville and burlesque, where would this young fellow go today to develop
his comedy?

LAHR   Well, I'd say there's only two places. Night
clubs or television. Or college plays. I don't know how the
hell you can learn how to be a comedian. You're either funny
or you're not. You have a sense or humor or you haven't.
You have the personality to be a funny man or you haven't.
There's no in-between. You've got to have a talent for it.
I can't tell anyone what to do. The only other advice I can
give is that if he's funny he should look at somebody that he
admires, watch him, study him and emulate him, and then,
perhaps, if he learns this fella's tricks and his methods, maybe

he can finally drift away and find his own. I have a daughter and I think she has talent; but if she said, "Daddy, what do you think I should do?"—now this is my opinion. If you want to be an actress, learn languages—French, Latin, Greek. Study semantics, English, elocution. Then find a place where you can do your own plays in school. Then, practice, practice, practice, practice. If you haven't got a theatre, practice in a parlor, get your relatives over. That's the only good thing I think that acting schools today do—they give the actor a chance to do it. What I'm talkin' about is, to be great in your business, and I think that holds good for painting. If an artist has a style, nobody teaches him how to make the lines. He has a certain style, but what he studies is colors, and so on. You know, if it's a straight line, it's a straight line. Nobody can teach him you don't make a straight line that way, do you understand? Now, I may be crazy in my analysis of this.

INTERVIEWER This has come out of your experience, and that's the valid thing.

LAHR And let the audience be the judge, let the audience be the judge. They'll tell you soon enough. They'll let you know. They'll tell you if you're funny or not. If they don't laugh, fella, you'll know it damn quick. If you hear a mumble during a scene, you know damn well you're not holding. I can sense an audience, if I'm holding them.

INTERVIEWER What is the reason for studying languages, except for elocution?

LAHR Speech, knowing what the hell you're talking about.

INTERVIEWER Why would French, for instance, or Latin be important?

LAHR To talk your language, which is a mixture. English is really a bastard language, as you know. It is a mixture of Greek, French, Norman invasion, German—the Teutons—you know, a bastard language. I don't say just learn a lot of other languages, but have a smattering. Know what the hell you're saying. I'm talking about dramatic actors. One reason why your Englishmen are so impressive is because the first thing they learn in school is English, and what the hell it's all about, and they speak it beautifully. Some of them are pretty bad, but I've seen some English actors that are great. I think that especially holds good for a woman; if she speaks good English out there, she immediately gets respect. I'm not saying this about everybody. I'm not saying it about Brando, who by the way I admire greatly. He came out of that school. He had a distinctive personality, which he followed. Now, a lot of 'em came out of there, but if they didn't have talent these people wouldn't have taught it to them. As many as made it from the school —two hundred to every one that's made it didn't make it. But each individual that made it from that particular school . . . What's its name?

INTERVIEWER Actors Studio.

LAHR Well, he has individuality. I don't know what the hell Stanislavsky is. I don't know what the hell that is, but I do know this, that Herbert Berghof and Stella Adler— and I say this modestly—they send their pupils to see me. You can inquire from Berghof. I don't know what the hell acting is. I don't profess to be an actor.

INTERVIEWER Why do they send them to watch you, do you think?

LAHR I don't know. Instinctively, maybe, I do the right thing. Maybe I have an innate talent for it. Like Berghof in an article said, "He does everything against the rules, but it comes out." He said, "He's a genius, God help him"— do you understand? I'm sorry, I don't mean that, but I just know less about acting . . . I know what's good for me and I know what would be good for my daughter, and what I would tell her to do, because I see what's happened to a lot of these kids. This is a rough business on kids, what it does to them psychologically. It affects them terribly because there's not enough jobs to go around. It's their ambition. It's their goal and they study. I see it. They go to school and nothing happens. And they work in the summer jerking soda, and they hang around, until finally they're thirty-five or forty, and it's the same damn thing. They've wrecked their lives. I was fortunate. I just stumbled into this thing. I evidently loved it. Everybody wants to be an actor. But I do know this. I've seen a lot of these kids that the schools turn out. I've worked on the stage with them and I wanted to break their hands. The scratching they do and no idea of deportment. "What motivates me to do this or that," they say. I said, "You go over and get the pot. You want to get the pot, that's what motivates ya." Everything is cerebral—you go over and pick it up. "Get me that drink." "What motivates me? How will I pick the cup up?" "Ya pick it up! Bring it over here." How would you pick it up? How do you pick it up every day? But you don't scratch your ear when you're pickin' it up or make a big thing out of it. So they got these kids all distorted with these theories of acting. I don't think Helen Hayes ever took a lesson, or Shirley Booth or John Barrymore. They had an innate talent and they practiced their talent. They served an apprenticeship. People, actors told them what to do. "I wouldn't do it that way. Never turn your back to an audience. Wait for the laugh." That you learn, but nobody can teach you how to drink a glass of water. You drink a glass of water, it's not a big deal. They make it so difficult. If you have talent, everything is easy. I mean the performing of it, if you have a talent. It's easy for a good piano player to play piano, but if he's a half-baked piano player, then it becomes hard. Then he's got to work at it. What I'm trying to say is this: Some kids don't even have to study a book. They read it and the next day they've got it. They're geniuses, you know that. Well, that holds good in life. One guy's a good carpenter, the other guy stinks. The fact is, you can't make an actor unless he's got talent and don't let anybody say you can.

INTERVIEWER   You made a certain gesture just before. Did you do this for the first time while you were sitting here?

LAHR   Maybe I did, I don't know. It wasn't studied. It isn't a question of learning. I put something into *Godot,* instinctively I knew that was right. I never saw it before, but I knew I could—do things with my face. And if you remember it, it was a shock, and Kerr wrote about it, everybody wrote about it—and I put it in. It wasn't studied. I think, maybe, subconsciously, I saw a picture of a clown, crying or something, and instinctively I knew that would go in that situation. If you remember, it was with the little boy, and I shook him, and the fella says, "What are you doing?" And I put my hands in front of my face, and then when I took them away—you remember that?

INTERVIEWER   Yes, indeed.

LAHR   And then I went away sobbing. Well, that was like an electric shock to an audience, you see. I just can't explain it to you. It just so happened I was lucky. I had a talent—if I do it bad or good, but I have, let's say, a little talent for what I am doing. I was born with a funny kisser and I had a manner that was a little different when I was young, maybe.

INTERVIEWER   In other words, you don't have a philosophy of comedy.

LAHR   No, no, I'm not *that* academic. No, no.

INTERVIEWER   I mean, you don't worry about the comic sense or anything like that.

LAHR   Oh, that's just a lot of . . . I don't, I don't. Maybe it's good for somebody else.

INTERVIEWER   You have said that a comedian is not a comedian if he can't make an audience cry as well as laugh?

LAHR   He's not a great comedian! I don't know of a great comedian yet that didn't make an audience cry. Your most successful comedians were sad little men. That goes for Grock* the clown. Their general make-up was sad, their demeanor, their way of doing things was sad. Other guys are brash and fast and arrogant. But the little man, Menasha Skulnik—do you see? "Vill you please give me dot." Immediately, "Oh, what a sad fella." Now, Menasha can tear your heart out if anything happens to him, and the audience loves him. Your personality, it's a very simple thing.

INTERVIEWER   Do you find a greater satisfaction in a role which permits you to do both—make an audience sad as well as happy?

LAHR   I love to do both, if the humor comes out of the character, where you make an audience both cry and laugh, which I did in *Burlesque* and in *Godot*. It's easier for a comic—I'm talking about great comics—to make an audience cry than anybody else, because the sympathy of the audience is with them. It's the poor little girl, or the poor little fella, do you understand? Everything happens to them.

INTERVIEWER   Is there any chance of the kind of shows coming back that would utilize comedians the way they used to be?

LAHR   No, I think I will say there won't be, but I think what's happened is this, and I told it before, that the audience wants reality, the truth. You cannot do things today that you could do years ago. I don't think contrived humor will entirely go out, but I don't think it's as acceptable today unless it's part of the play. And I think Rodgers and Hammerstein did this when they came in with *Oklahoma!* The humor comes out of the characters in the play. I really think, and sincerely think, that not in my time or in many years to come will the clown come back. It's an artistic loss. Now, you take Marceau . . .

INTERVIEWER   Marcel Marceau.

LAHR   Well, that's a form of art. He's the only one left, practically. The art is gone now, out of show business.

* Internationally famous French clown, first quarter twentieth century.

The only thing that's left is the ballet. You see, there's an art in everything. There was an art in being a clown. Your circuses—as far as your public is concerned—are not salable the way they used to be. I guess from maybe a hundred circuses you've got now a handful, and I think it reverts to entertainment for nothing. They've seen everything. I think it's the same thing as eating the same thing every day. You finally tire of it. Well, that goes for your entertainment. I think the clowns are done.

INTERVIEWER   It's a shame, because the clowns had a comment on life.

LAHR   I think vaudeville's gone. The opera certainly is not as lucrative as it was. But there's been a new interest in Shakespeare. And I hope it isn't just a momentary thing.

INTERVIEWER   It'll be interesting to see what the tour does—I mean, when you go out on tour. Have they talked to you at all about appearing up in Connecticut at the Shakespeare Festival in Stratford?

LAHR   They said something about it. Before, I said I haven't any ambition to play Shakespeare. I really don't. This is a job and I'm doing it and it's something different, and I'm pretty sure I'm gonna do it pretty good. There's one part I would most like to play in Shakespeare—not Hamlet, because God knows I'm not physically right for it—and that is Falstaff in Part Two of *Henry IV*. I saw it played, and I would like to play it my way. Have you ever seen it?

INTERVIEWER   Yes.

LAHR   All right, see if my analysis is right. The way they play Falstaff, he's a lascivious, lecherous old sot, but by the time he gets to the last scene, which should tear your heart out, the audience doesn't give a damn about him. That's the way it was played, you know. I think if you play Falstaff with a twinkle—he could look at gals, but he could look at them in a cute way, it doesn't have to be like this (leering). If he plays him a little more—instead of the swaggering guy—a little more whimsical, so that the audience forgives him his faults, when he gets to that last scene the audience is gonna cry. Do you agree with me?

INTERVIEWER   Yes. Yes, that's very interesting. Did you see Larry Gates play it up in Stratford, Connecticut?

LAHR   No. I didn't.

INTERVIEWER   He came close to that, you know.

LAHR   Well, that was my analysis of the scene, maybe.

I never had any ambitions. Don't misunderstand that. I analyzed that. I think I explained it to you.

INTERVIEWER Well—here's hoping we'll see the Bert Lahr Falstaff.

Sidney Poitier

BIOGRAPHY

Sidney Poitier was born in Miami in February, 1927, but his parents took him almost immediately to the Bahamas. At fifteen, with a total of a year and a half of formal schooling, he returned to Miami, where he lived for a short time with an older brother who was married and had a home there. He then went to New York City's Harlem. For a few years he worked as a dish washer and kitchen worker, then did a stint in the Army. Returning to New York he did more dish washing, and more heavy labor. But during this period he saw an advertisement for the American Negro Theatre. When he first applied for entry, he was turned down. He persevered, however, and on a subsequent try was accepted. He then studied acting at night and pushed a hand truck in Manhattan's garment district during the day.

His first part was in the all-Negro production of *Lysistrata,* which, though it ran on Broadway briefly, was the start of a career that in a short time brought him starring roles in Hollywood and on Broadway. After *Lysistrata* he became an understudy in *Anna Lucasta* but took over a leading role when the play went on the road. His first movie, in 1951, was *No Way Out*. In 1952, he made the film version of *Cry, the Beloved Country*. Among his other important movies are *Blackboard Jungle, Something of Value, Edge of the City, The Defiant Ones, Porgy and Bess,* and *Paris Blues*.

In 1959, Mr. Poitier returned to the stage as the star of *A Raisin in the Sun*, for which he won additional acclaim. Recently, he starred in the film version of this play. Mr. Poitier is married and has three daughters.

SETTING

It is true that Sidney Poitier arrived for the interview in a sleek white Cadillac, but that was the first, and last, bit of the Hollywood touch evidenced by this star of stage and screen who has had such a spectacular rise to recognition. A dignified simplicity and directness seem to mark him in a way which precludes any shades of Hollywoodism.

Mr. Poitier, who lives in an interracial section of Mount Vernon, a suburb of New York City, chose to be interviewed at the home of Lewis Funke, also in Mount Vernon.

On arriving, Mr. Poitier strode briskly from the car to the house, and as he came into the library, where we were to talk, he said with a warm smile, but nonetheless determinedly, that he had only one hour for the interview, not the two we had requested. He said he was leaving for Paris in two days to make a film, *Paris Blues*, and that he simply could not spare more time just now.

Mr. Poitier settled his tall frame into a sofa. A trifle tense at first, he soon relaxed, and the momentum of his interest sped ahead—with our talk going along for nearly two hours!

Mr. Poitier was dressed in brown slacks, a white shirt open at the collar and a brown cardigan. A big man, Mr. Poitier is extremely expressive—his voice, his face, his whole body responding animatedly to his mood as he sits upright or leans forward tensely to make a point, perhaps snapping his fingers, or settles back in relaxation. His voice is rich, used often with markedly dramatic effects. His gestures are wide and sometimes extravagant. Mr. Poitier is obviously a man of "soul"—as he himself defines the word as used among jazz men: a man wholly and passionately engaged in living.

At the end of the interview we accompanied him to the car, and just as we were saying good-bye we helped him make a decision for the afternoon. Should Mr. Poitier take his children to the Fair in Danbury, Connecticut, or Free-domland in the Bronx, for this final family afternoon before his trip? The Danbury Fair won out.

Interview

INTERVIEWER   What made you decide to be an actor?

POITIER   What made me decide to be an actor? Well, I decided to become an actor because I had tried a great many other things. I had no skilled trade, so the things I tried all were of a—working-with-your-hands style. And it bored me quickly, all of it. I was a ditch digger, a dish washer, a car washer, a porter—and these are, for me, very boring activities, always have been. One day I found in a newspaper, a Negro newspaper, specifically the *Amsterdam News*, the New York *Amsterdam News*, on the advertise-ment page, an ad saying, "Actors Wanted," and I figured, having tried everything else, you know—and I was quite young—I figured what the hell, I'll give this a go. I went ahead and I told them I was an actor, and they said read something for us. Well, I read—very poorly. They threw me out promptly. My pride was hurt, terribly hurt. I had never been rejected so, so *forcefully* before, and I said to myself, "Well, dammit, I'll show them. I'll read good for them." So I set out on a six-month campaign of trying to orientate my speech, of trying to gather a kind of one-di-mensional understanding of the theatre and gather certain catch phrases, theatre phrases, such as whatever you use if you are an in-person in the theatre. And I went back, and that's how I became an actor.

INTERVIEWER   Why is it that acting had appealed to you at all? Had you been to plays?

POITIER   No, I had not been to plays. I thought that actors made good money, and I wanted to make money, and I also wanted to do something other than manual labor, you see. I was ill-equipped to do anything else but manual labor. I thought here is a field that probably I could take hold in, you know, if I'm lucky, rather than having to ex-pose myself to five or six years of training in a school for a special craft or trade for which I didn't have the money or the time. I figured I would have a go at this. Also I was foot-loose and fancy-free. I was moving about in the world, you know. I had no great responsibilities, I was young, and I had the—I had the freedom and the prerogative to walk off a job as a porter if I didn't like it or it bored me to tears. I was a great daydreamer. I would wind up leaving the job and going and sitting near the water, or in Central Park, and just dream all day.

INTERVIEWER   About what?

POITIER   Oh, about things, people, and mostly about . . . I think our dreams are usually made of the yearnings and needs unfulfilled, you know, so we go about trying to fulfill them.

INTERVIEWER   I understand that you bought a radio and for six months you studied the diction of people you heard on it.

POITIER   I studied the diction of people on the radio because my speech was obviously West Indian and not as clear or as cultivated as one needs to have it for theatre work. I couldn't go to a school. As a matter of fact, I didn't know there was such a thing as a school for speech. So I bought magazines and I would listen to the radio and I would repeat what I heard on the radio, mostly news broadcasts. And in time my speech began to lighten in the areas where it was particularly broad.

INTERVIEWER   I was told that when you returned for an audition, you brought one of the magazines you had studied to read from.

POITIER   Yes, *True Confessions* magazine. And I read it, I read a paragraph of it, as an audition, as a scene. Plays and all that jazz—I was fairly ignorant about the theatre. All I had was a passion to show . . . See, in all my life, although it was only a poor one and fierce one, I had always had great pride, and in the Caribbean a young Negro is never robbed of his pride, as he is in some parts of the southern United States, so that at the age of fifteen, sixteen, I was—I was fierce, crude and very alive in many, many senses, many important senses.

INTERVIEWER   So the rejection at the theatre was a blow to your pride.

POITIER   Yes, yes, the rejection was a blow and a challenge, you see, and one that I had to accept. I was told to get out of the theatre. This was the American Negro Theatre near 135th Street.

INTERVIEWER   Yes, I know.

POITIER   I was told to get out and forget it, to go back

and just get a job. And you see, the image of what—the image of the rejection to me was this: I saw my life, every subsequent year of my life, I saw it in the drudgery of manual labor. I saw a limit placed on my potential. Had I accepted the rejection as my fate, then I would have been ordained to a kind of one-dimensional living, circumscribed by my limitations and hung in a kind of abyss of never really being able to reach beyond my grasp.

INTERVIEWER   What else did you do to train yourself, besides the reading and the radio during that six-month period?

POITIER   Well, I did a great many things. In the Caribbean I had gone to school for a very brief period, for a year and a half, and I could barely write or read. However, I knew certain little—I had acquired certain little hints of reading, such as the phonetic way of pronunciation, and if a word puzzles you, you do not know its meaning, you start with the first three letters, et cetera, et cetera, so that you, in turn, will be able to pronounce it fairly accurately. And I began to try to improve my reading, you see, by sight, which was very hard for me, but it began to improve. The reason I went to a *True Confessions* magazine primarily is because they were—aside from the fact that I didn't know anything about bookstores—they were always very simply written and I could understand what it was saying. I was not often overwhelmed by words in its structure. I studied reading and I listened to the radio for speech and I used to read newspapers a great deal. I didn't always know what was in them, or what the articles were all about, but I did know some of the words, and a constant exposure to these words helped me to develop a familiarity with them, so that sight and reproduction became synonymous.

INTERVIEWER   Did you use a dictionary, too?

POITIER   No, I did not. I had a strange way of holding words that I could pronounce but did not understand their meaning—holding them in abeyance for a time when I did find a sentence with the word in it so structured that I suddenly knew what it meant.

INTERVIEWER   How many hours a day did you spend at this radio to rid yourself of the West Indian accent?

POITIER   Many, many hours. When I was working, and I worked throughout this period—I worked various places. I was working in the garment district for the most part. Evenings and mornings and whenever I could get to a magazine or a newspaper. The reading was constant, because I had no time for much else. I had no friends. The small salary from the district, or wherever I worked, was such that the small room I maintained and the food and the few dollars for clothing—well, that was all I could afford.

INTERVIEWER You've made the statement that you were an actor made exclusively by friends over the years, and I was curious to know whether this was a correct statement and who were the important influences upon you.

POITIER It is a correct statement, in part. I am made, in terms of my success, by my friends, people who at one time or another did me a good turn. Who are the friends? They are varied, they come from many walks of life, they are people who permitted me to use them as studies, they are people who are interested in my work or interested in me, or interested in helping—they are directors and writers, producers and work-aday folk. So this, though it's true in part, is not a definitive statement.

INTERVIEWER Did you study other actors? Did you go to the theatre to watch actors, our leading actors, work?

POITIER It was only in later years that I developed a kind of interest in watching other actors work in the theatre. But I watched many actors work because I was always involved in classwork and group work and various theatre groups. That was my life, you see, that's where I did most of my learning. I was in and out of groups and little theatres and projects. I, first of all, couldn't afford the legitimate theatre often, but I didn't take advantage of the times when I could afford it. It used to bore me. Broadway theatre used to bore the daylights out of me, until finally I became interested in certain actors. There were certain actors who were my kind of actors, people with great power, and I would go and watch them work.

INTERVIEWER Did you have any formal training, or are you now taking formal training?

POITIER As an actor?

INTERVIEWER As an actor.

POITIER Oh, yes, I took many years. From 1946 I took formal training. Which is what now?—fourteen years. I took formal training at the American Negro Theatre. It was training of a kind, adequate for that period, totally inadequate for now. In 1947, '48, '49, '50, I was always taking formal training from various people; sometimes actors, sometimes from a group, sometimes from—sometimes for free, sometimes you pay a small fee. And then I eventually wound up—in the '50's I wound up with the Paul Mann Actors Workshop, after having taken many, many years of formal training, helter-skelter, of course, but formal training.

INTERVIEWER   Paul Mann, as I understand it, follows the Stanislavsky approach to acting.

POITIER   Yes.

INTERVIEWER   Are you then one of the Method actors in your work, or do you amalgamate Method with your own methods?

POITIER   I am not a Method actor. I study Method and I work Method before I perform. To explain: The Stanislavsky Method is intended, I believe—and if I'm wrong I use it this way, nevertheless—I think it is intended to be used as a method of preparation for work, not as a method employable in the instance of work. So I used the Stanislavsky Method in preparing my work, something which I am privileged to use over a *long* period of time before I go on the stage, or before I go on in front of a camera. Which means that instead of employing the Stanislavsky Method for two hours a night in a theatre, I employ it for two or three months in the preparation of that work, so that when I go on the stage, or in front of a camera, my function becomes organic and instant and natural, spontaneous and full, because I have a frame of reference for every want, every need, every desire that is registered on my emotion boards.

INTERVIEWER   Could you be specific here, and just take us through a single part you prepared for?

POITIER   Well, let's take the last thing I did on the stage; let's take *A Raisin in the Sun*. I received the script almost a year before we went into production, right? And I read it, naturally, many, many, many times and I knew, generally, after ten or twenty readings, what the circumstances of the play were. I knew what the individual characters were like, generally. I understood my character kind of generally. Now I needed time to make my understanding of my character specific. In so doing I must understand all of the contributing elements that go to making up this character. First I must understand what are the driving forces in the man. In order to understand that, you must find out what are his political, social, economic, religious milieus, and how they contribute to the personality idiosyncrasies or whatever. And in so examining, I find that this, first, is a Negro man thirty-six years old, living in Chicago on the South Side—which of itself is quite significant in the building of a character, because only a particular kind of Negro lives on the South Side in this particular kind of circumstances, see? So that narrows the field already. And then we take: Why is this man living here? Is he here by choice? What is his relation to his community? What is his relation to his religion, if he has one? What is his relation to his economic disposition? Is it one in which he finds enough elasticity to function and maintain his manhood or is it a constant badge or remembrance of his inadequacies —you follow?—and all these things can be found in the script, or at least if they're not there they can be made compatible with what is in the script at one point or another. So that— after months of actually making specific this man in his milieu—then I come to the final conclusion of what are his wants. And when I find what are his general wants, I find what is his most specific want or wants. And they aren't many —so with his most specific want, I now have the man in total. I know what his reaction would be to everything done and said in the play—see? I know what and how he feels about his neighborhood, so that any question or reference to it strikes a certain chord in a man. Now with this kind of information, I then proceed to familiarize myself with the pros and cons of his life and his wants. I try to experience them, so by the time I'm ready to perform, I don't go in a corner—at least I don't have to go in a corner and concentrate and conjure up some mysterious magic. I walk on the stage and it happens. And I don't work Method because it's too late now to work Method. If you're not ready, forget it. You walk on the stage and you perform, because what begins to happen out there is that you find that you have taken on the milieu of the character, and you then begin to seek out and fulfill the very wants that are burning inside *you* now, which are his wants. Once you're on the stage you have no time, because the stage is to experience—you follow?—the stage is to experience . . . Once the curtain goes up and there is an audience out there, you, the artist, your responsibility is to experience, and only through your experiencing are you able really to transmit—you follow? There are many kinds of actors. There are actors who can get on a stage, but they can never quite enthrall, nor can they ever quite involve or hypnotize, but they can give a workmanlike job. Well, if they're not gifted, they don't enthrall and they don't involve, because they themselves are not able to involve on the level required by the artist.

INTERVIEWER What is the difference between these two?

POITIER There is a basic difference to my mind between the two. And ofttimes it's not because of the difference in talent. It's sometimes—it always is the difference in the humanity of the individual, you see. There is a phrase used by jazz musicians, and they call it "soul." It is a reference to a certain kind of humanity—of the sensitivity of humanity—that is overstocked in one person. They use the word soul because there are certain gifted, brilliant musicians who have a kind of human compassion that—they are so inarticulate in every other phase of life, they can only express through their music, and hence they are terribly important musicians and gifted. With actors, I think—there are some actors who have a great degree of "soul power." There are actors who have not as much and there are actors who are void of it. Now, the fine actors who are void of it are called technicians. They are quite capable of making you *realize* you are in a theatre watching a terribly gifted technician at work, and you say, "Ahh, he's marvelous." If he had the added gift of soul, you would forget you're in a theatre, that's the difference.

INTERVIEWER   What is it that you find you like about acting?

POITIER   That I like about acting?

INTERVIEWER   Yes. But if you prefer to talk about what you don't like about acting, you can do that, too.

POITIER   Well, I—you know, that's an interesting question. I don't know how I can answer it.

INTERVIEWER   What do you get from acting that satisfies you?

POITIER   That's a different question. I can better answer that. From acting I get a sense of—of worthwhileness. I feel, for instance, there were times in my past when out of sheer naïveté and modesty I was afraid to accept the fact that I was a gifted actor. It was only in later years that I realized that the gift of an actor does not belong to him, that I accepted that I am a gifted actor—and cannot point to any one or group of efforts on my part that created the gift. I was born with it. Let's be honest and let's be factual. I was born with a gift. I had nothing to do with it. When my mother conceived—that moment, the combination of genes carried inherently whatever there was that I suddenly found at the age of seventeen or eighteen. So what I get from acting is using it for others, using it for people. I find that when I work well, people enjoy it and they—things happen to them. By that I mean, when I use it well, they share it, you see, and they share it in good ways—you follow? And that's what I—that's what I get from it.

INTERVIEWER   You have this gift, but you must do

something to make yourself a better actor or a better human being or whatever—or am I wrong? I mean, is the gift there and that's the end of it?

POITIER   No. It's your responsibility to nurture it. It's like a seed. It's like a flower. It's like a plant. It's like a child. You feed it, yes, you nurture it, you care for it.

INTERVIEWER   How?

POITIER   Well, I've tried to care for it for fourteen years. First of all, it is important that the actor recognize that his gift is an entity, the human entity—in that package. So the package must be cared for, not only cared for, but it must be cared for in ways that become advantageous to the flowering of the gift. The mind and the body are the only two tools that the gift can use. The mind and the body, therefore, are to be cared for, kept not under glass, but kept in good working condition. Above and beyond that it must be exposed to its limits constantly—to life. Because it then acts as an absorption board. So that when the gift has to be placed in motion, you are not trying to click it over a void. You need to call on experiences. When you are in the process of working on a part—for instance, in the preproduction, in the preopening periods of a part—when you say what kind of life did this guy lead, your conclusions must be not only theory—you follow? You must be able to bridge the gap between theory and experience sometimes. So that, in other words, to play a coal miner, you can read all you want about coal mining, but just to know what the feel of the area is at the entrance of a coal mine is experience that's worth more than the ten volumes you'll read about it. So that I don't mean that the gift is there and it just begins to kick over. No, you nurture it and you work with it and it's your responsibility. Now, if you're going to be an artist—and this is where you say this is my function—then that's what you are in life. If you are going to be a carpenter, and you go through the growing pains of learning how to measure and cut and saw and nail, and then, if you walk away from it—after you learn it—you can't go back to it in ten years and build a house. And also, when you walk away from it, it is because you are not—you have not committed yourself to it. I commit to the theatre. I commit to art, that's me. I'm thirty-three years old, I have no place else to go—you follow? And the only reasons I know I am—that are of importance to me—are the reasons I get from my work, from my milieu as an artist, and from my contribution.

INTERVIEWER   But success tends to put you in a hothouse, in a comfortable hothouse—doesn't it?

POITIER   Success tends to put the American artist in a hothouse, and it is a—just one of the many temptations, potential indulgences, that the artist has to face up to.

INTERVIEWER   But how do you grow then?

POITIER   I live in a certain way. I make a great deal of money and I live in New York. I live in Westchester. I live in a lower-middle-income community. I am not ghetto-ized here, I can live anywhere I want to live in New York State. And if they won't sell me a house, I'll buy the land and build a house. I am not ghetto-ized. I live in a certain way, I move in every circle—I have to. I am interested fortunately in many things. I'm interested in politics, I'm interested in economics, I'm interested in art, see, I'm interested in hunger, and I'm interested in—in oppressions. I'm interested in the independence of the African and Asian states. I'm interested in the power of the Church. I'm interested in the lack of civil liberties in the Soviet Union. I'm interested in a lot of things —birth control and old-age pensions, assistance for the aged. I'm interested in a lot of things. And I'm not—fortunately I am not trying to force an interest. I am genuinely interested in these things, so I don't—I mean, the success is not an end.

INTERVIEWER   How do you choose your roles? Do you choose them because of the acting opportunities that are available to you, or do you choose them in combination with their significance to you?

POITIER   I choose my roles now—I must differentiate, because in the past I was always selective, only not for snobbish reasons. I was always selective because most of the parts offered me were of no interest to me and I refused them and that was that. The difference now is that the parts that are offered to me, if they interest me and they are not quite right, I get help to fix them. I look for certain things, not in the part only, but in the play. If a play or a film has a comment— mind you, comment is different from a statement—if a play has a comment that transcends itself, then I will be interested in doing it. Now, what do I mean by a play that transcends itself? If the play's comment can be made dimensionally, clearly, forcefully to everyone who sees it, whatever their country, whatever their language, as long as it's a man or a woman or a child of this milieu in our contemporary world— then the play has significance *for me*. I do not wish to make a comment that is peculiar only to a section of this country or of this world. I do not wish to make a comment that is peculiar to Negroes only, or on behalf of Negroes only. I am not interested in the comment that is on behalf of Americans only. I cannot any more be thusly interested. I want to say, if I'm able, something about people, and I believe that basically people are the same everywhere, if they are literate or not, if they are sophisticated, rich, poor, Russian, American, black, white—basically they are the same. And art can touch them all in the same place, you see. The same piece of art can touch them all. That which touches *only* the black man, not understood by the white, is really not accomplishing much, because ofttimes that which is understood by the black and not by the white is poison, and in and of itself it becomes contradictory to the purposes intended.

INTERVIEWER   I was going to ask you, what if any difference do you find in preparation for the stage and for the films?

POITIER   There is a difference in the preparation and there is a difference in the performance. On the stage, in terms of the preparation, you have two months or more, depending on how soon you get the script, or whatever your working habits are, and how important you are. Sometimes you get a script three, four months in advance. You begin working then. Then you have the four-week period of rehearsals, and then you have a tryout, usually, and then you come in prepared to work two hours a night and twice on Wednesdays and Saturdays. In the film, your preparation, at least mine, takes a different course. There are different demands made by the two mediums. The stage's limitations are of a nature that they make certain kinds of demands which require adjustments in the technique or in the approach to work. The film makes similar demands, according to its needs and limitations. In the film, I prepare pretty much the same way, and when I am done—after the two months or three months of preparation—when I am done I have to begin to work in bits and pieces on what is in essence one performance, which carries over an eight- or ten-week period. So what I do is, I begin to experience each day the total up to the point I am performing, so that there is a flow. Now, how to experience it? I don't sit and go through excruciating pains, I just review in my mind the flow, the natural flow of events involving me to this point so that I can segue into this moment, this three minutes they intend to shoot today. But naturally and connectedly.

INTERVIEWER   You find the movies harder than the stage?

POITIER   Yes.

INTERVIEWER   I understand you have said in some

earlier interviews that you find that the technical intrusion of cameras bothers you.

POITIER   Well, that's only part of it. You see, the film is—well, the best way to give you an example: I came here at ten o'clock. Let us assume that this is a stage, and it's a performance, and I come in and I spend an hour here and all that we have done this morning in this interview was actually a portion of a play. But I came in and I had one *continuous* hour in which to perform, or experience. If it is a film, the total, when it is done, will be the hour similar to what we spent here, but it does not flow in that manner. I will come here every day for thirty-six days and I will work with you and you will work with me, and in the course of *one* day, our total, the aggregate of our film time, will be three minutes— you see? And each day I come I must—through whatever senses, awareness I possess—I must thread yesterday's needle with today's thread, so that it would seem that no time has elapsed. That is difficult. Now, we are able in films to get around it easily, because it's a very technical medium and you can cut up film and nobody really cares about the performance, you know, unless you yourself are interested. So to make a whole—that in life, in a lifelike experience, will unfold in an hour or two or three—to put it together bit by bit is like patchquilt work. The job of the artist, if he is interested, is to make it seem that this is a total experience when it is done. That makes it more difficult than the stage, infinitely more difficult. But, by the same token, it is in films where if someone is not interested—the medium is a haven because he can hide behind other things. The medium permits an actor to be lazy, if he wishes. If he has a winning personality and a nice face to look at, and a not displeasing voice, he can read words and move around in an attempt at playing and get away with it easier than he can on the stage. Because on the stage he has only one frame, you see. On the screen he has the two-lens and the four-lens and a fifty-lens and a seventy-five-lens, so that his image comes to us in gears. It comes that way, this way, you know, and we see all kinds of images of him, and he comes so close to us we can almost touch him. On the stage he remains in the same dimension, so there's nothing going for him there except his work.

INTERVIEWER   You've been playing serious roles. What about comic ones? I understand from what I've been reading about you, that you have a talent for comedy.

POITIER   I would like to try that very much and I am going to. I am sure that it will have to be as a result of my own efforts, because I am now used to being thought of as a "heavy" actor.

INTERVIEWER What do you think are the prospects for the Negro actor in America?

POITIER Ah! Good question. I think they are good, if the Negro actor is a gifted actor and he develops himself. He will work, cannot help but work. There will be very few limitations on the Negro actor, truly gifted, in the future. The country—the pace of change socially in America has accelerated so that the Negro actor of today is experiencing more hope and more involvement in the theatre and in pictures than ever before. Television and the radio are a little— still behind the times. But picture-wise, it's coming marvelously, the stage also. In music and theatre and art generally, the power of the gift is what counts for the most part. Another artist who is white, if he is committed to art, and he finds a gift in a black man or woman, he *has* to use it, he *has* to work with it—you follow?—because that is his commitment. Like in music—I don't care how *sick* a white musician, who is dedicated to music, is on the race question, he would go out of his skull to play with Miles Davis. He would go out of his skull to play with him. So that directors and writers, producers even, who are really interested in working on a certain artistic level, if they find an actor who is a Mexican actor or a white actor or a black actor or a Chinese actor who has great power, they have to use him. Now on a workaday level, lots has yet to be accomplished for the actor who is just so-so. The so-so Negro actor will not work with the consistency that the so-so white actor works, because the Negro is unfortunately still in that kind of social thing. But there is hope, there is *much* hope. The salvation of the Negro actor also will be realized through the realization of Negro writers in the theatre. All kinds of good things are pointing to it.

INTERVIEWER What advice would you give to the beginning Negro actor in terms of training for the stage?

POITIER I would give him the same advice that I would give to the beginning actor of any other race, and that is to study hard and long and fierce. If you control the methods of work, then you can, in essence, control your growth or help to control your growth. If you are unable to control the body or the mind under certain work situations, then you'll find that you'll never be able to play any one part completely. The only tools you have are—is the body. How you move, how you speak, everything you do with the body becomes the essence of your work. Aside from learning the other aspects of acting, controlling the body is the most important.

INTERVIEWER   I would like to extend the question a little bit. I accept the fact that the advice you would give would be regardless of color, but I wonder, in terms of psychological or philosophical approach or attitude—how would you guide a young Negro actor so that he doesn't become embittered, let us say, at lack of opportunity?

POITIER   Let him become embittered. I think that bitterness is also a fruit of life. If bitterness was an end result directed toward no one else, then we wouldn't mind bitterness. We object to bitterness because we don't wish to be the object of it. I think that bitterness is an absolutely correct reaction to some of the absurdities perpetuated on Negroes in this country. I will not say to a young Negro actor, "Don't become bitter." If he earns the right to be bitter, by God let him be bitter. I do say to him, earn the right to be bitter. Go and prepare yourself to be an artist, and if you become an artist—if you are on your way to realizing your potential as an artist—and some bastards superimpose restrictions on your efforts, get as bitter as you want—you follow?

INTERVIEWER   On the other hand, bitterness in your own private life can be a disturbing element. Isn't there some approach to peace with yourself . . . ?

POITIER   Are you asking if there is a way to tranquilize oneself against the intrusions of all the injustices? No, there isn't any way to tranquilize oneself. What the Negro actor should do, or the Negro person per se should do, is not to be concerned about bitterness. Because it is an experience, and out of it usually comes some very profound, constructive, philosophical attitude—usually, you see. And it is not essentially an adjustment, because if the persons who are so busy creating these obstacles for minorities in this country, if they themselves ever were to experience what those people, the minorities, go through, they would be better human beings themselves. I believe that you cannot be full in this life until you know what pain is, until you know what joys are. And instead of spending a lifetime, like most whites in this country, running from pain, setting up an antiseptic life, struggling and working and closing out, nailing out, all the adversities—pain and a little hardship and struggle—and becoming essentially antiseptic . . . I think that the more antiseptic they become, the more lack of soul becomes evident. So I have no great horror for bitterness on the part of Negroes. Negroes are becoming less bitter and it's marvelous that they are, but the experience of bitterness has been—will be—used by them in marvelous ways, you know. The venom of a snake can kill and it can also be an antidote, correct? So I don't want to say to Negroes, "Don't be bitter." If they are in a situation that provokes the bitterness, let them be bitter. And when the situation, through their effort, or through the collective effort of both sides, is overcome, when they overcome the bitterness, then they have a frame of reference. Then they've had that experience, you see, and it is the experience that will make of them the better man—if they overcome it, if they get through it. Do you follow?

INTERVIEWER I was going to ask you, do you think that a Negro star, of your stature, has problems different from the problems of a white star of your stature?

POITIER I'm sure that some of my problems are peculiar to Negroes, but I don't—I don't let them bug me. Sometimes some of the things are painful—not too often. Sometimes they hurt—not too often. I don't worry about it. It's an experience now, and usually I am able—through my transcending my bitterness—to some extent I am able to view very compassionately the inadequacies, the *gigantic* limitations, that enmesh the perpetuators of these moments of pain for me, and I *do* dismiss them, for they are afflicted infinitely more than I.

INTERVIEWER Living here in Mount Vernon and raising your children here—how do you equate this experience?

POITIER I have an interest in not losing my balance and I also have an interest in keeping my children in a certain kind of multiracial cultural milieu. And I fear antiseptic living. I *fear* it. It leads to alcohol and nicotine and a kind of stagnation intellectually, and I'm not interested in that.

INTERVIEWER I read also that you don't let them know too much about your success. Is that true?

POITIER Yes. The magnitude of my good fortune, commercially, is nothing whatever for them to be dealing with at this time in their lives. I wish them always to have a frame of reference for everything, and if they have a father who is so unlike other fathers, it will begin to give them a kind of orientation that can be unhealthy. It's my feeling that my children—first let them be children, and let them be children as fully as they can be children, you see, and they'll deal with what their father is and they'll have to—probably have to—overcome it at a later time.

INTERVIEWER What are the frustrations of the Negro actor—that is, in the ability to use the full range of his talents?

POITIER   What are the frustrations of the Negro actor?

INTERVIEWER   I mean, have you yet encountered frustrations as a Negro actor in being limited, let us say, to certain roles?

POITIER   No, honestly, not yet. I am entering now into an area, career-wise, where I am sure I will be—I will be involved with the frustrations. Because I am now interested in the kind of work, as I described to you before, of a certain reach, and if I am not offered it, I will have to try to bring about its realization by myself. Meaning, I'll produce it myself. So I haven't really experienced it yet. I've been busy building a career and trying not to make too many outlandish compromises. But now I'm interested in moving on to another level.

INTERVIEWER   What is that level actually?

POITIER   Well, first a level of work—and a level of comment. They are not necessarily compatible if you must mix them, but they each represent individually a step up from what has been the pattern for many years. On the artistic side, there is now an urgent need to do better work. I think I have the potential for better work, so I now must stretch . . .

INTERVIEWER   What do you consider better work? How do you consider an actor should progress in his career?

POITIER   Better work for me now would be—at least, I've thought it would be—to reach for a level of work that is commensurate with, say, another dimension. In acting, as in all art, there is a constant reaching for another depth. Well, the frame of reference for your trying to plumb the depths is to bring about a dimension that is almost indistinguishable from reality, you see, so that . . . And that is a big task, but it is interesting enough to me. If I never come close, it would at least permit me—cause me—in reaching for it, to stretch myself artistically. There is a dimension not yet tampered with, at least by me, and that is to be able to work on a par —in such a way that when the experience happens it has about it an encompassing effect on an audience. Encompassing, in that they become a part of the total, so that there is not a theatre and there is not a stage. Now, this is done in many other fields, you see. It is done quite often by musicians. You can sit down and listen to music and in no time your mind stops thinking about business. It stops, and it isn't even concentrating on the music. It sort of suspends itself, and for a while there is nothing but a kind of total moment with the music and you and the nothingness. It happens when we are speaking about something that interests us fiercely, and especially when someone is saying what we want to hear. We become hypnotized with our eyes wide open and we are—we are hung, you see. I think actors can weave this spell, because in the old days storytellers wove these spells in market places all over the world, hundreds of years ago, thousands of years ago. Not with the aid of lights and sets and all that jazz. So the actor can do it.

INTERVIEWER Going back to *A Raisin in the Sun,* I recall that Mr. Atkinson, in the *Times,* said that you were as effective when you had words to say as when you were silent. Obviously you conveyed that excitement. From many directions you have much encouragement in achieving your goal.

POITIER We'll see how the next step goes.

INTERVIEWER I gather that you are studying Shakespeare, that you have hopes to perform in Shakespeare, is that true?

POITIER That is no longer true.

INTERVIEWER Why is that?

POITIER Well, I am, I was, interested in Shakespeare—very—and then I found a very interesting truth and it is this—I found I was interested in Shakespeare because of a kind of coercion.

INTERVIEWER A coercion?

POITIER Yes. I was coerced into an interest in Shakespeare by the awesomeness of its reputation, by the correctness of a man of my position having to, at one point or another, say that I would like to play Shakespeare. It is the thing to do, and it is the comment to make. And I started reading it and I kept saying I'd like to play Shakespeare, but it seems to be actually a status symbol to—to reach a point where you can say all right I want to play Shakespeare. I *don't* want to play Shakespeare, essentially. First, because I am not trained sufficiently to play Shakespeare. Most of Shakespeare's stuff bores me to tears. I enjoy infinitely more to read the words, because the man was, indeed, a genius—just to read the structure of his sentences. I lie in bed with a Shakespeare book and have a ball! To play it, I'm not interested. It's that simple.

INTERVIEWER That's a very sound confession. I think that even in writing, to reach beyond your interests is purely a form of snobbism.

POITIER Now it would be reaching beyond my interests. If I do change my mind because of additional information, or because of additional changes in my values, I'll play it. I will begin to prepare again to play it. But as of now, I am in a period where I would much prefer just to read it, just to read it, because to read it is an experience. It's very wonderful, it's relaxing, and it's—it's a kind of freedom you experience reading it to realize that a *mind,* or a man, was so gifted to put *words* together in this order. It is fantastic.

INTERVIEWER Why is it that you've concentrated your energies—and this may be an obvious or rhetorical question or maybe even naïve, but I think that it should be asked, and I think I know part of the answer—but why is it that you've confined your interests to Hollywood, in opposition to the stage?

POITIER Because I have three children, and one on the way, by the way, and a wife, a mother and father, a mother-in-law and various and sundry other relations who are not as fortunate as I, and who, in some manner or other, depend on me for livelihood. I cannot work long under the constant pressure of, or the call of the economic, so I am doing my two years in Hollywood style. My deals are so constructed that two more jobs and my relatives and I will not have to respond economically to pressure—meaning, that it's a tricky business and I understand it very well, the business of it. If I have no money and wish to remain in the theatre, I must fight a constant battle of integrity versus the icebox, you see. I find it disconcerting to do that. If I have to do it because
y circumstances are such, then I would do it. But I have seen
⌐ way to circumvent its being a constant thorn in my side. When my success came, as fledgling as it is, my representatives and I sat down and we determined to get me a work relation with the people I work for of a nature that I can be paid over a long period of time, rather than to take monies up front; so my monies now are—and it's all legal, tax-wise— paid to me in a livable sum on the first of January every year for twenty-five years, which leaves me free of that consideration. So that after the picture in Paris, and one additional job of work, which is in early spring, I can do as much theatre for as long as I wish anywhere in the world.

INTERVIEWER Can we expect you next season in the theatre?

POITIER You can very well expect me next season.

INTERVIEWER There is something on the way?

POITIER There are some things being talked about. I do want to go on the stage, but not to the exclusion of films. I want . . . But see, simply, if you are offered one hundred fifty thousand dollars for a job, that's an awful lot of money.

And they give it to you. And the government gets sixty thousand dollars, your agent gets fifteen thousand dollars—that's seventy-five thousand dollars. The State of California gets three or five, and the State of New York gets and this gets, and that gets. So you wind up with about thirty thousand dollars or forty thousand dollars. Now the forty thousand dollars, if you live at a clip of ten thousand dollars a year, lasts you four years. But if you have one hundred fifty thousand dollars, and the government permits you to spread that money and you take twenty thousand dollars a year, that's seven and a half years. Then you do another film for the same company and you stretch the seven and a half years to fifteen. Then you work for another company, and you take ten for fifteen—you see?

INTERVIEWER I know you rejected a role in a film—that *Phenix City Story* role—and I wanted to know a little more about why you rejected it.

POITIER The role was a cheat, in the context of what the film dealt with. The part was a cheat and a compromise. It was a lie, an absolute out-and-out lie, and they used it in an uncourageous manner. It was the part of a young Negro father, during the political and criminal holocaust in Phenix City, Alabama, or Phenix City somewhere in the South. And it's an open city, gambling, and corruption; and this father, because he worked for somebody or did something, his daughter was killed and thrown on the lawn—a five- or six-year-old girl, thrown on the lawn. And the father goes out hunting for the killer, and toward the end of the film he comes across him and he's got him in a shed and he's gonna kill him. And they put in his mouth the most ugly compromise. If it were an honest change of heart the man had, it could have been beautiful, because it would have shown great growth, you see; but they put in his mouth such crappy words like, "I suddenly realize that the Lord doesn't want me to do this."

INTERVIEWER And they wouldn't change it to meet your ideas?

POITIER I was at that time a seven-hundred-fifty-dollar actor for the whole thing—you know, three weeks for the seven hundred fifty dollars. I was making two hundred dollars a week or three hundred dollars a week.

INTERVIEWER What has been your favorite role?

POITIER My favorite? There is no such thing.

INTERVIEWER Then which was the most challenging role, let's put it that way, and why?

POITIER Again there is no such thing. There is no easy

part to play, really. I used to think there was, but there isn't. During the work, every part, even when you're having a miserable time, is an important part because it is a challenge to you. Whatever the extenuating circumstances are—such as a bad director or a disinterested group of fellow actors—the product, the finished product, becomes a challenge because you have a job of work that has to be done, that has to be good, and you know that you can work good. So that each job has to, like, be up to snuff, you know. You must notch up another. So, however you feel about the part, there is that kind of sense of—you have what you have to do, and if you fail it's sickening. So each part—even the ones that you look back in retrospect and say I didn't like it—at least the working on it was as honest as any other. There is no enthusiasm for a part only, when you have no interest in the play, you see, and I don't work like that. I work with enthusiasm because I am interested in the things I do, and when I work at it I work as fully as I can.

INTERVIEWER　You said before that it's important for the artist to experience and to live. Do you make it your business, for instance, to study people of all colors and races? Do you return to Harlem to refresh your memory and experience of what life in Harlem is like? Do you go out to Chicago or go down South to keep in touch with the problems and experiences of people of your race?

POITIER　I do. Not only with people in Harlem—I go to Harlem almost every day. I have friends there and I am there almost every day. I go in two guises. I go as myself and sometimes I go—I go as anonymously as I can. And it's an experience, but it's a very rewarding one; it keeps me alive in certain areas of my consciousness. Let me explain Harlem to you. In Harlem I am not a stranger, nor am I a film star as such. I was in business in Harlem and I lived there many years. And when I return to the community now, there is a small element of awe on the part of the people, and there is also an element of looking at a movie actor. But it's a movie actor they know very well, you see, so that there is not often much time spent on those amenities that would ordinarily ensue if it were a movie actor that they didn't know and stood in awe of hour after hour. I walk around in Harlem, I go into the bars, I go into the churches. I move about freely and I'm never bugged. People will come and ask for autographs, but they ask for it with a kind of casualness, knowing that they're going to get it. They call me by my first name. Because it's a community that knows me well, I'm able to go to it and refill my cup, so to speak. In other communities, strangely enough, in white communities, I am really looked at with awe—dig? But no one makes any fuss about me in Harlem. I am a part of the fixtures, so to speak. So, as I said, there is that awe thing, but then it's gone, and next I am with the guys in their milieu and they have no defenses up against me, so that I can swing with them on their scene, at their speed —you dig?—which is important to me. I do this wherever I go in Negro communities, with the exception of the Deep South. I have a particular aversion to the Deep South and I don't go around down there. I go other places. I move in New York, in the midtown area, in the restaurants, in the theatre circle, and from time to time I go into the night-club circle, but actually that is a little off my path, because I don't dig that scene at all.

ACTORS TALK
ABOUT ACTING—II

PART II

Cast in Order of Appearance

Lynn Fontanne
and
Alfred Lunt

BIOGRAPHY

Lynn Fontanne was born in Woodford, England, the date being her special secret; Alfred Lunt in Milwaukee, Wisconsin, in 1893. Miss Fontanne got her start—after being a protégée of Dame Ellen Terry—in a West End pantomime of *Cinderella* in 1906. Mr. Lunt got his start in Boston with the Castle Square Players, in a play called *The Aviator*, in 1912. Both were stage-struck and dedicated; both took every part they could get—walk-ons and bits.

After seeing her abroad, Laurette Taylor brought Miss Fontanne to the United States to act with her. Miss Fontanne's first big personal success was as Dulcinea in *Dulcy* in New York, although she had already made a mark in England. It was the title role in Booth Tarkington's *Clarence* that first attracted major attention to Mr. Lunt.

11

Lynn Fontanne and Alfred Lunt were married in 1922, and they played together for the first time, in *Sweet Nell of Old Drury,* the following year in New York. But this was not the play that made history. It was a year later, in *The Guardsman*—by Ferenc Molnár, presented by the Theatre Guild—that they set out along their unique road. Of the more than a score of plays they have appeared in together, it is hard to choose those in which they are remembered best. *Elizabeth the Queen,* by Maxwell Anderson; *Design for Living,* by Noel Coward; *Reunion in Vienna, Idiot's Delight* or *There Shall Be No Night,* by Robert E. Sherwood; *Amphitryon 38,* by Jean Giraudoux; and, most recently, *The Visit,* by Friedrich Duerrenmatt.

The Lunts have appeared in England in many of these plays, some originating there, for England's claim to the Lunts is as great as America's. They have taken most of their productions on tour in the United States.

Mr. Lunt has directed several of the plays he and Miss Fontanne have appeared in, including *There Shall Be No Night, The Pirate, O Mistress Mine* and *Quadrille,* as well as several plays neither he nor his wife appeared in, and one opera, *Così fan Tutte,* the Mozart work he directed for the Metropolitan Opera House in New York City. The Lunts appeared together in a movie version of *The Guardsman* and briefly in the film *Stage Door Canteen* during the war. They made a single telecast, an adaptation of their production of *The Great Sebastians.*

SETTING

Interviews with Lynn Fontanne and Alfred Lunt were held on two days. The first interview was with Mr. Lunt alone in his dressing room prior to an evening's performance of *The Visit,* in which the Lunts were playing a return engagement in New York after a cross-country tour. The second was at their house on Manhattan's Upper East Side, just opposite Carl Schurz Park, which borders the East River. (They also have a home at Genesee Depot in Mr. Lunt's native state of Wisconsin.)

The interview at the house was scheduled for 1:30 P.M. and we were requested to be there promptly. We arrived some minutes ahead of time and were admitted by a maid into a tiny vestibule, then ushered upstairs to the living room. The house is small, but decorated to a jewel-like perfection. The living room—with its air of eighteenth-century elegance, its muted gray and yellow tones, crystal chandeliers, faultlessly arranged flowers—might well serve as the setting for one of the Lunts' more sophisticated comedies. And, indeed, it turned out that the room was decorated with the help of stage designer Stewart Chaney, who drew inspiration for it from ideas used on the sets for the play in which the Lunts were appearing when they were decorating their house—S. N. Behrman's urbane comedy, *I Know My Love*.

Every piece in the room obviously had been chosen and placed with exquisite care—this is not a room to scatter the Sunday papers in. But it is comfortable, with deep chairs and two sofas—one for each, it is said, as in *I Know My Love*, to provide good vantage points for the Lunts, who can spar offstage as well as on, and equally adroitly. On one wall, over a lovely mantelpiece, is a collection of china figures. The fireplace itself is flanked by delicately colored panels of oriental scenes. The opposite wall is mirrored. While there is a chastely monogrammed silver cigarette box on a low coffee table, there is a certain impersonality about the room, but no lack of warmth.

Mr. Lunt met the visitors on arrival, friendly and hospitable. At precisely one-thirty Miss Fontanne made her entrance—an entrance worthy of the setting, and of Miss Fontanne. Radiant, Miss Fontanne's charm seems to flow before her. Her grace is striking, from the raise of a hand to the tilt of her head with a smiling greeting. Her appearance is one of stylish perfection: the faultless coiffure of her brown hair; the elegance of her afternoon dress, black silk with a red pattern, enhanced by a multitiered necklace of black and red beads. Her poise and perfection of appearance needed no reassurance, but still she gave an almost imperceptible glance toward the mirrored wall. No moment is left to chance here.

Miss Fontanne seated her guests. Mr. Lunt was opposite her. Coffee was served by the maid—who had been with Mr. Lunt's mother, we were told. The conversation was animated and easy and as entertaining as—well—as the Lunts! Perhaps the interviewers' only problem was to make sure that there were not too many voices at one time, a problem somewhat simplified perhaps by Miss Fontanne, who on occasion takes a wife's prerogative—usually discreetly, sometimes pointedly—to take stage center.

The setting for the first interview with Mr. Lunt was in striking contrast: a harshly lighted and thoroughly dismal dressing room in the New York City Center, where *The Visit*

was playing. But Mr. Lunt's charm and hospitality were not
one whit dampened. It was two hours before curtain time,
and Mr. Lunt—in a blue dressing gown, a rather nondescript
one—was putting on his make-up with the aid of his valet.
His expertise as he applied eye shadow or hair blacking was
impressive. He worked busily, but never missed a beat of the
conversation. On the long dressing table before him—it was
really more of a shelf—and amidst the usual jars and pots
was a silver pig salt shaker. Mr. Lunt explained that it had
been given to him many years ago during the London run
of Robert Sherwood's *Reunion in Vienna* by an inveterate
first-nighter, a woman who wanted to give him a good-luck
charm. It has been the first thing his valet has put on every
dressing-room table since, and apparently the silver pig
has carried out its assignment superbly.

Lunt
Interview

LUNT (as he began applying his make-up and getting
ready): We went to a party given to the company in San
Francisco, and I had never seen them dressed up before. We
were so surprised.

INTERVIEWER That is a fact. The get-up you wear in
this play is really something.

LUNT Is it good? I'm awfully proud of it. (Speaking
to his dresser) Show them the back of my shirt. There it
is—I wouldn't change that shirt for anything in the world.
It doesn't show, but somehow or another I suppose it helps
me feel the character.

INTERVIEWER Did you deliberately tear it apart?

LUNT No.

INTERVIEWER Where did you get the shirt from?

LUNT London. It's a very old one. It was the most
beautiful material—once, once long ago. Jules dips it at the
end of the week, squeezes it out—we can't have it washed,
it would fall apart. But this has nothing to do with your . . .

INTERVIEWER As a matter of fact it does. This is part
of your preparation for a role. It fits in with what we have
heard about the Lunts over the years, that you two are the
arch perfectionists of the theatre. (During this compliment
Lunt kept mumbling, "Well, well.") Anyway, I am going to

ask you how it feels to have this tremendous response here at the City Center? I was talking to Morton Baum yesterday and he was most excited, said that last week you had just missed fifty thousand dollars.

LUNT He did! I am glad he said that, because I was afraid you were going to say fifty. It was forty-nine thousand, seven—forty-nine thousand, seven— What, Jules? Yes, that's it, forty-nine thousand, seven hundred and thirty. Broke our hearts.

INTERVIEWER And he says this week he is sure you will hit sixty.

LUNT Oh, he couldn't possibly.

INTERVIEWER He says you are going to. He is most pleased, and . . .

LUNT My God—fifty-four—three—in Philadelphia. It really is exciting. Well, you know, you hear it. But what does it mean to you, you know? It's just a lot of figures. But really there is a lot of satisfaction.

INTERVIEWER Well, of course, the implication is clear. Those figures represent approval—approval for the play and of the Lunts.

LUNT No, no. It is the play. Don't kid yourself.

INTERVIEWER Well, all right, but how do you think the play would be without the Lunts?

LUNT It would be fine. It can be played in many ways, you know. The way we do it is just one way of doing it. It could be played in many ways. This way is the way Peter Brook wanted us to do it. We tried out everything he told us, you know. I have tremendous respect for him as a director. We put ourselves entirely in his hands.

INTERVIEWER Do you always take direction that way?

LUNT Oh, I make a suggestion now and then. After all, if you have directed plays as I have for many years, you are bound to have some ideas. Talking about directors, I must mention Philip Moeller. We worked with him for years, when we first were with the Theatre Guild. I don't know whether Philip was a great director but he had—in doing comedy—a great and valuable quality. He would sit out front and he would laugh a great deal. Well, if you are playing a comic part, if you are playing a comedy, and the director sits out front and goes into fits, you immediately respond in your playing. It wasn't a trick. He meant it. There are directors out front who don't go into any fits and, if I might say so, don't even know what's going on, and that isn't much help, is it? But Philip laughing—that was wonderful. You knew that your timing was right, or that a piece of business you or he had invented was right. And what's more, Philip was a very witty man. I must tell you—we were doing so many translations, you know, in those days and he would write very funny lines of his own and stick them in. Made it great fun and exciting—trying, too, at times, you know.

INTERVIEWER   Were there any rough times with Philip?

LUNT   Oh, yes. We didn't always agree. We had terrible hours with Philip.

INTERVIEWER   Over bits of business?

LUNT   Well, yes. For instance, when we did *The Guardsman* I thought I'd wear a Cossack uniform in black, and he said, "You can't play comedy in black." And Lynn said, "Listen, Mr. Moeller, if the lines are worth reading you can play comedy inside a burlap bag, inside a closed piano —if they can hear you and the lines are good!" Really—and she was right. She was right. It's true. And Philip, well, you know.

INTERVIEWER   I was wondering why it is that you and Miss Fontanne, unlike so many present-day actors, still go out on the road and get such enjoyment from it?

LUNT   I would never use the word "enjoyment."

INTERVIEWER   But you wouldn't be doing it if you didn't get pleasure or recreation from it, would you?

LUNT   We said in some interview before we came into town: We have been brought up in that school; there is an obligation to the author. That is where our living comes from. It is not the brilliant producer, but from the dramatist, isn't it? And so you are under obligation to the dramatist to keep his play going as long as you can. That's why we have played these plays for so long. We played *There Shall Be No Night,* you know, about fourteen hundred times. It is a long time. But, as I say, the playwright has every right to expect you to continue in his play as long as you can in New York, and then on the road. He needs those royalties. And where would we actors be with*out* the playwright, I ask you?

INTERVIEWER   Well, what is it in our younger people —this refusal to go out on the road? Is it a lack of responsibility?

LUNT   I don't know. They don't have to do it, perhaps. They can make money some other way, I suppose. But, of course, we like to make a living too, you know. I suppose we could stay in town and do television, but I'd rather not. We are—what would you say?—you could call us old hat.

INTERVIEWER   Well, it's good for the theatre. Anyway,

how come you don't, as so many other actors do, complain about your long runs and getting stale and so on?

LUNT   Oh, no. Don't be silly. I don't understand that. I don't get bored. I don't think I have ever been bored in my life, except shaving and washing my teeth and before going to bed. That bores me, really bores me.

INTERVIEWER   You have made a rare statement. It's nearly always the reverse—actors constantly say they get tired, become bored, absent-minded. They can't go through another performance. And yet you, who have had more long runs than most, don't say that. How come?

LUNT   Oh, I get tired. On Sunday I was so tired, I didn't honestly think I could make it—you know we have two Sunday performances. I just didn't think I could make it. It worried me very much. And Cathleen Nesbitt came backstage and I said, "Oh, Cathleen, wasn't it wooden—forced?" You know, you force when you are tired. And she said, "No," which was a relief. But I also forgot we had such a good play. You forget that, you know.

INTERVIEWER   What is it that does keep your interest in a play during a long run?

LUNT   Oh, it's because you never feel you make it anyway, from the beginning. I mean you never give a satisfactory performance from the time you start. Something always goes wrong.

INTERVIEWER   You feel that each performance is its own challenge.

LUNT   Certainly. And there is always a different audience out there.

INTERVIEWER   And this is the secret of not going stale?

LUNT   For me it is. Perhaps, you know, if I had only one line, I'd get bored.

INTERVIEWER   There is a case of one leading actor in a play who claimed he got so bored and tired—and reflected it in his work—that they finally closed the play with the audiences still coming. What is the difference in your attitude?

LUNT   Well, I don't think I am good enough, for one thing. And that sounds false. It isn't really. It sounds like one of those phony statements, but it isn't.

INTERVIEWER   No, I understand what you mean. Perhaps if one didn't know your standards, it would be. But we know that this renewal is something that has been constant with you and Miss Fontanne. We had sort of hoped you'd give the answer you did.

LUNT I guess it's a simple statement, rather childish, isn't it? But it's the truth.

INTERVIEWER I think it displays the proper modesty, as a matter of fact, in relationship to one's art: to feel that one is never good enough. It must be rough, however, on the psyche.

LUNT It is. You know, sometimes you wake up, and think you are fine. You think you are really going to give a fine performance tonight. I don't know, but you don't for some reason or other. Then you can come into the theatre feeling perfectly awful, dreadful, and some chemistry takes place and you're brilliant. It is exciting from both sides. What that is, I don't know. You feel that particularly in comedy.

INTERVIEWER Is it one of the apocryphal stories of the theatre that Miss Fontanne got a desired laugh on a curtain line on the last night of the show, a laugh she had been toiling all along to get?

LUNT True! True! Oh, she had an awful time of it. It was in *Reunion in Vienna*. She had a line she thought would be amusing. Well, she tried it for two years, you know, three years in fact, but she didn't get it until the last night. But she got it.

INTERVIEWER Which certainly is proof that the Lunts keep working on their roles.

LUNT Oh, yes. And let me tell you, rather show you, what can happen. I had a line in *Quadrille* in London that I thought was amusing. I was playing this American railroad man and I had to say, "Well, perhaps after all I will have a cup of tea," and actually, you know, he should have had a shot of bourbon. To me it was amusing. It did for a little while get a sort of smile—vaguely amused, not a great guffaw. But then I lost it. And I said to her, "Why have I lost that laugh?" "Because," she said, "you are not asking for a cup of tea, you are asking for a laugh." You see, I had sort of slipped up. That's why you must always keep working.

INTERVIEWER What is the secret of your teamwork?

LUNT I don't know. I guess each of us is interested in the other. That's one thing. And, of course, there is our way of speaking together. We started it in *The Guardsman*. We would speak to each other as people do in real life. I would, for instance, start a speech, and in the middle, on our own cue, which we would agree on in advance, Lynn would cut in and start talking. I would continue on a bit, you see. You can't do it in Shakespeare, of course. But in drawing-room comedies, in realistic plays, it is most effective. How can I make that clear? We what is known as overlapped...

INTERVIEWER Without waiting...

LUNT Yes, in the middle of a sentence. This is exactly what I mean, what we are doing right now. We are talking together, aren't we? You heard what I said, and I heard what you said. Well, to do that on the stage, you see, you have to work it very, very carefully, because you overlap lines. So that once I say the line, "Come into the next room and I will get ready," your cue really is "the next room," and you say, "All right," and I continue and say, "and I will get ready," underneath, as it were. Of course, I must lower my voice so that she is still heard. Is it clear?

INTERVIEWER This interaction is presumably what every actor dreams of.

LUNT They thought it couldn't be done. They said you will never do it. And when we first played *Caprice* in London, they were outraged because we talked together. Really outraged, the press was. But it was a great success. And I think it was the first time it was ever done. I don't know. It just happened because we knew each other so well and trusted each other. Although sometimes I have been accused, and I accuse her, of stepping on a line or a laugh or a bit of business. "Why do you come in so quickly?" "Why don't you . . . ?"

INTERVIEWER Is this something that is inseparable from your personal lives? You are used to each other, your cadences, your thought processes.

LUNT No, I don't think so, because the lines are not ours. They belong to somebody else.

INTERVIEWER How do you study your roles together?

LUNT Well, when we were doing this, for instance, the first forest scene, she learned her lines and I learned mine, and I might say that it was a very difficult scene. It is a very strangely written scene and—well, you stumble along until you know it, and then you begin—when you really know it—you begin playing to each other, into the eyes, as it were, until it has some reality. For instance, there was a line in this play, *The Visit,* and for some weeks I could never get it, when Lynn said, "And you married Mathilde Blumhard," and I thought I should say, "Oh, don't be angry with me for marrying Mathilde," in a kind of German sentimental hurt way, you know, it was an awful thing to do—but it wasn't any good because it lacked the intimacy of the old days. Then one day I decided I'd become angry, and that was true. It had the right ring. It had more truth in it. In effect I was saying, "Don't blame me. Just think of what I did for you," because I'm also protecting my home—self, too. I feel like I should protect myself, do you understand? The problem is always to arrive at some truthful—truthful expression, manner—what is the word?—more truthful . . .

INTERVIEWER   Feeling?

LUNT   Yes, a feeling—a true feeling. And that is the way it comes. Does that mean anything?

INTERVIEWER   Yes. You don't adhere to any one method?

LUNT   No, I just try to be as real—say I try to act with as much reality as I can. I once had a class of G.I.'s after the war, and they said, "What is technique?"—you know, acting techniques—and I said, "I haven't the slightest idea, I'll go home and ask my wife." And I did. And she said: "You just read your part with as much reality as you can—truthfulness—a little louder than in an ordinary room and don't bump into each other, that's all." Noel (Coward) has picked that up and uses it. It's true. But there is much more to it than that, I suppose.

INTERVIEWER   In this play—how do you find the truth, the reality of these very vicious people whom you portray?

LUNT   For me, a man I know in Genesee Depot immediately came into my mind. (Turning to his valet) You know who I mean. This man in Wisconsin was not quite as bad as Schill, the character I play. But pretty bad, and I tried to look like him and walk like him.

INTERVIEWER   You mean you related your character to that man?

LUNT   Yes, although, mind you, he wasn't as bad as Schill. Schill is an awful man. Yet, you know, there is also a temptation to try to make him something of a hero, but he isn't, and so, maybe, I make the mistake and pull it the other way. I suppose I could look better, but Peter, our director, didn't want me to and I didn't want to, either. I suppose I could be a little more attractive and still give you the idea of what he was and yet . . . I sometimes have to bring out a picture when I am doing this, and look at myself and say, "When I was a young man, I wasn't so bad."

INTERVIEWER   You start feeling very sympathetic for Schill. As a member of the audience I did and then suddenly you realize that . . .

LUNT   He's forgotten. He's forgotten what he did, it's been fifty years.

INTERVIEWER   How did you develop the scene in the

store when your anger and fear begin to overcome you? When you realize you are likely to die—it must be so hard not to overplay it, I should think.

LUNT Well, originally, in the play, the minute Schill saw the shoes he began to scream; he screamed right on to the end of the play. But Peter didn't want it to be done that way. It was, I might add, the way it was written, too. And I said at the beginning, "But I can't do it any other way, Peter, that is the way it will have to be. I'll try it, but we'll never get it the way you want to." It was pulled back all the time, always pulled back for control. And that is due to Peter. Anything you see that is good is due to Peter.

INTERVIEWER We can't quite accept that.

LUNT Oh, no. It is true. Well, I don't know. Maybe I have done it all, and maybe when we do it again in England he will redirect me, he will find something. You never get bored. That's what I mean.

(Here the discussion turned on similar problems of writing: interpretation, variety, and the ability to communicate precisely and clearly. It is a matter of current interest to Mr. Lunt, who is writing a book on a hobby to which he brings highly professional skills.)

LUNT I'm supposed to be writing a cookbook. I want to tell you! What can you do? It's the same thing over and over. Put it in the oven. Take it out. How many words are there? It must be the same. Stir and spoon. And after a while you look at the goddam thing, for it is no great literary effort, you know. It is so boring. Yet it must be clear. And I asked Truman Capote. I said, "Will you tell me how, when you make pie crust . . . ? Just describe this. I want it in words. How would you do this, now do that—in a few words?" I asked. "I could show you how, but put it in words . . . " And he couldn't.

INTERVIEWER You had a pretty good ghost writer there.

LUNT Or kneading bread. I want you to describe how you knead bread. Well, you can take a "pillow" and fold it down and press it—but it sounds so dull, you know—until it feels elastic. Well, what may be elastic to you is not to someone else.

(Returning to the theatre, the conversation centered on Stanislavsky.)

INTERVIEWER   What is your feeling toward the Stanis-lavsky Method, as it is being used today?

LUNT   I've seen some perfectly extraordinary perform-ances. We had a boy in this company—a Method boy. He was marvelous. Simply marvelous. And we saw *The Rose Tattoo*. Wasn't it mostly Method acting? What's wrong with that? I think it was extraordinary. Let me tell you a story that will illustrate how I feel about it. Some years ago Miss Fontanne had a maid who was going to join us in the coun-try for a weekend. I said to her, "Will you want to go to church on Sunday?" And she said, "Yes, I'd like to go to church." And I said, "You're a Methodist, aren't you? You know there is only one church here, and it is a Catholic Church." And she said, "Oh, that doesn't bother me. We're all heading for the same place." I often think of that in con-nection with acting. We're all just heading for the same place.

INTERVIEWER   Trying to develop the reality of the character you're playing.

LUNT   That's right. How we get it may vary maybe. What counts is the end product. Actually, I would say that no good actor is bound by rules, really. You do the best you can, and then every so often, something happens you hadn't counted on at all. You plan one piece of business to get a laugh and it lays an egg. Something you hadn't thought of at all brings down the house. I remember when Lynn and I were in *Amphitryon 38*. We had finished the New York run and we had gone to London. They were laughing at the play in London, all right, you know. But I still felt that some-thing was missing in the third act. We didn't feel it so much in New York because the laughs had been a little faster. But in London the third act was—what shall I say?—just dull. And then, mind you, without premeditation, I stumbled on a bit of business that was just wonderful. In the play I am just about to leave Alkmena after she has persuaded me against my will to be her friend and not her lover. On this particular night, as I faced Lynn, taking leave of her, I hap-pened to keep my body toward her and turned only my downstage foot. It seemed that I appeared like a little boy who had just been scolded by his mother, standing there, twisting his foot. Several persons in the audience laughed and Lynn knew something new had happened. She saw the foot gesture and immediately stopped fussing with her hair and leaned forward a little and stared at the moving foot. Every-one in the audience followed her. The laughter swelled and the scene turned into one of the funniest in the play. So, you see what I mean?

INTERVIEWER   Yes. You have done such a variety of parts. One comes to me now that I would like to ask you about. How did you prepare for Harry Van the hoofer in *Idiot's Delight?* How did you go about creating him?

LUNT   Oh, I went to night club after night club after night club. And of course you know I played in vaudeville, once with Mrs. Langtry, years ago. And I'd go to see M.C. after M.C., you know, studying that forced bravado, that gay camaraderie. I pieced Harry together from these experiences and observations. Well, isn't that the way the Method people go about it?

INTERVIEWER   I recall that the critics said at the time that you captured the essence of the man.

LUNT   Well, Bob Sherwood wrote the character. Bob wrote it, and you can't do it unless it is written for you, can you?

INTERVIEWER   Coming back to Anton Schill—and some of the business you invented for him—for instance, the retching there at the station after his failure to board the train to safety. How did you hit on this?

LUNT   Oh, that happened in Boston.

INTERVIEWER   How did you come upon . . . ?

LUNT   I'll tell you. At first I sort of used to lie there on the floor. I just lay there on the floor and did nothing. And then one night in Boston it occurred to me that a man like Schill—all sorts of men, in fact, if they were dreadfully frightened, if they knew that in short order they would face being murdered—would be frightened out of his wits. In this condition Schill would either vomit or mess his pants. So, one night, I leaned over and retched. Peter—my back was to the audience, I had turned away—came up afterward and said, "Did you vomit?" and I said, "Yes." And he said, "Oh, I like it."

INTERVIEWER   So it was in the play when you came to New York.

LUNT   Yes. It is true to the character. And maybe you will be amused to know that sometimes it goes on, because once you start to—and you can't get your breath—you have to belch away. You know, I thought it had never been done before, and I said to Larry Olivier, "It has never been done before," and he said, "Yes, it has." And I said, "When," and he said "You did it in *Elizabeth the Queen.*" I did, too. Essex was a baron; he was a very sick man. And I had no lines for a long time at the beginning of the scene. So I used to take a big glass of water, and then turn my back —and was most realistic. They adored it.

INTERVIEWER   I noticed in one scene in *The Visit* that you have a way of picking at your trousers, which was so true to the part, also.

LUNT   Oh, that probably came out of nervousness at rehearsal and I just kept it there. That's the way it sometimes happens. I don't know. That's what I tell you. I don't know myself.

INTERVIEWER   Your not knowing is in itself illuminating.

LUNT   Oh, by the way, I must add that whatever you do you must keep it within the frame of the play. You understand? I think that a lot of things must be kept within the frame of the play. The actor is an interpretive artist. His one and only job is to give life to what the playwright has written. It's the play that counts, and the actor must not be so goddam individual that he can just do anything and kill everybody else's lines that are important. You have to stand still sometimes, too. You see, in the first act I have almost nothing at all to do.

INTERVIEWER   That's right, you stand off there on the side.

LUNT   No, nothing at all, and that's why Peter wants me to be put in the back of the chorus. I have nothing for minutes and minutes, and I should be part of the scenery.

INTERVIEWER   You must recall with pleasure that one critic remarked about the eloquence of your pantomime.

LUNT   Yes, with pleasure.

INTERVIEWER   When you are not good, what are the factors behind the situation, would you say?

LUNT   I don't know. I don't know. I don't know! I may be too loud, I may force too much. I may overact.

INTERVIEWER   Where you have felt that you have not done as well as you should have—how do you get rid of this dissatisfaction with yourself?

LUNT   You just hope to God that the next night will be better, that's all.

INTERVIEWER   Does this throw you into any kind of mood?

LUNT   Oh yes, it's very disturbing. You know, I try as much as possible to keep it to myself. Sometimes I don't— and it is not such a pleasant home life. It happens to everybody. This is not unique in the theatre. I mean, any wife, any husband . . .

INTERVIEWER It must be intensified in a creative art such as the theatre.

LUNT And, of course, she sits on that goddam balcony all through the second act. And she can hear everything we do!

(Here Mr. Lunt is referring to a scene in *The Visit*, during which for a considerable period of time Miss Fontanne sits on a balcony, silently observing what is going on below—including, it happens, the acting of her husband!)

INTERVIEWER I'm glad my wife doesn't have the same advantage! As a matter of fact, this implication had not occurred to me. The other night I was just thinking, when I saw the play, "There's Miss Fontanne, looking so lovely; she's relaxing and everyone's working hard down there."

LUNT Well, she is listening, and after the play she says, for instance, as she did the other night, "Why are you throwing in so many ohs and ahs and Gods before you speak? Why do you do that—to give yourself leverage?" She's right. I do.

INTERVIEWER Are you very critical of each other all the time?

LUNT No. Well, you can't, when you're remembering your words.

INTERVIEWER What do you consider is the hardest role you ever played?

LUNT I don't know what you mean. Physically or mentally?

INTERVIEWER I would link them together, or if there is one that you think is harder mentally, the hardest mental plane or the hardest physical, then there would be two.

LUNT They're all tough, it seems to me. If you have more than a small part, it's always tough. The easiest and most satisfactory part ever—the surest—is Dubedat in *The Doctor's Dilemma*. Oh, boy, there he doesn't get in until the end of the second act—and then he has that marvelous death. Well, that's all he has. Boy, that's the dream. The doctor's is much more difficult than Dudebat, and Dudebat is the best part in the play. The cast—they work themselves to death. And then Dubedat dies in the end of the second act—very good.

INTERVIEWER What would you say you have found harder to play, comedy or tragedy?

LUNT I think that comedy is more taxing. I think any actor will tell you that.

INTERVIEWER What is it that is so much harder in playing comedy?

LUNT You have to make your feed line clear, in order that the other person tops you and so that the funny line gets the laugh. You must feed—do you understand what I mean?

INTERVIEWER Yes.

LUNT And then you have to wait for the laugh when it comes. And when it doesn't come, you must go ahead anyway; and then if the laugh comes, you have to cut it off before it dies out. This is not something you can learn. Call it a sixth sense. Certainly it isn't technique.

INTERVIEWER In other words, the timing is of the essence.

LUNT Yes. They'll all tell you the same thing. All good actors of comedy. Well, I've got to stop now. It's twenty minutes of eight.

Lunt-Fontanne
Interview

LUNT Would you like to have a cup of coffee?

INTERVIEWER Why yes, that would be very agreeable.

LUNT I was going out this morning to a place on Lexington Avenue. They have awfully good coffee cake, you know; it's fresh. Well, I didn't get there and I suppose I'm going to hear about it.

INTERVIEWER And if I may be so bold as to ask, do you, as you say, hear about it when you forget something on the stage?

LUNT I most certainly do. Believe me, though, there is nothing personal about it at all. But if, for instance, I should jump in on a line, I hear about it, and vice versa. There is nothing personal about it, mind you. Nothing personal at all. It's strictly impersonal, it's business.

INTERVIEWER A sort of difficult matter, isn't it?

LUNT Well, yes. But it has to be, we couldn't live otherwise. Oh, I must look up a word for Lynn—technique. Oh, here she comes now.

(Miss Fontanne entered the room, Mr. Lunt went for the dictionary. After the exchange of greetings we sat down. And she began to read the definition of "technique.")

FONTANNE "Manner of artistic execution or performance in relation to formal or practical details (as distinct from general effect, expression, sentiment, etc.); the mechanical or formal part of an art, especially of any of the fine arts; also, skill or ability in this department of one's art; mechanical skill in artistic work . . ." Like lots of words in the dictionary, it doesn't make it plain to us. To me, anyway. So what I think it means is the mechanics of your part, as far as acting is concerned. I think it means the amount of breath you take for one whole sentence, and the more breath you can take, the better, especially when you are playing comedy.

LUNT Or Shakespeare.

FONTANNE Or Shakespeare. And I think it means also your expertness in delivering that plate (pointing to a plate on the coffee table) to you on a given word. And you must do it exactly right and slick and also look as if it's perfectly natural—do you see? That I would say was technique. I don't think technique is the art of acting. I think the art of acting is a complete imagination—an imaginary thing. You imagine yourself the person that the author has written, and you sink yourself into that. Then out of your throat comes, perhaps, quite a different voice. And you don't think it out. But it is a mental thing, it is done with your mentality and your imagination. There!

LUNT What was it that Ellen Terry said? "Think of the meaning of the words . . ."

FONTANNE Yes, she gave me the key, I think, to acting. She said, "Think of the meaning of the words and let the words pour out of your mouth."

INTERVIEWER But this means then a very deep understanding of life, because according to this interesting prescription you wouldn't be able to evoke that person unless you had the feel of him.

FONTANNE You get—if you are an actor—you get the feel of a person by completely understanding what the author has written. Yes, there is need for complete understanding. The author has to understand the person. The author has to understand the person and present him clearly. And then the actor has to understand what the author has written—perfectly—and present him clearly.

INTERVIEWER The analysis makes sense. Now, there is a matter about which we've been most anxious to ask you, Mr. Lunt. In our interview with John Gielgud, we talked about some results of the Method school and the fact that Method actors mumble and turn their backs on their audience. Mr. Gielgud paid you a grand tribute. He said, "Only Alfred Lunt could turn his back on an audience . . ."

LUNT   Oh, that is not true. It is not true. I have been doing that as long as I can remember. I had a letter last year from a boy I went to school with. He said, "I remember when you were a boy at school"—this is when I was literally fourteen and fifteen, on up from then to nineteen—"that you used to play a lot with your back to the audience while the people you were talking to were upstage."

FONTANNE   I really have a theory about Alfred's back, and it's this. Alfred is one of the most highly nervous people I've ever known. And I think he is shunning the audience, and shutting himself away into the scene he's playing. That's what I think it is. I am certain that that is what the reason for his back is. As a matter of fact, in scenes where it is very important, Alfred gives the scene all that the scene should have. He faces the audience then, and gives himself the best position for what he has to say—if it is important to the play. I have seen him do that. But very often, and especially in an emotional scene, he will curl himself in, away from the audience. He feels more concentrated, then, I think.

LUNT   Well, I don't know, I don't know why. But I don't think it makes any difference . . .

FONTANNE   Now wait a minute . . .

LUNT   Excuse me . . .

FONTANNE   I don't know what I was going to say now. I forgot.

LUNT   Oh dear, there I go.

INTERVIEWER   That's all right. We will pick it up again, I am sure.

FONTANNE   Yes, sure.

INTERVIEWER   Well, to get back on the track—what about some of our younger actors who insist on thinking that because they are presumably living the role so completely they can mumble their parts?

LUNT   Oh no, no.

FONTANNE   No, no, no. That is what is known as technique. Voice control is absolutely essential. It is a basic technique of acting. You learn to pitch your voice to the size of the theatre, and an experienced actor does it—mechanically.

INTERVIEWER   How? How do you learn this?

FONTANNE   How? How? I don't know. That, I think, is a mystery. All I can say is that it requires long and arduous training.

LUNT Somebody just comes back and says, "I couldn't hear you." That's how. And you lose your job if you don't speak up, that's how, and ...

FONTANNE Now wait a minute, Alfred dear, because I have something to say. Often somebody comes back and says, "In back of the theatre we can't hear you." Often, you can imagine, in all the theatres that we play in, there are pockets in the theatre. And all that is "cased" by somebody belonging to us, you see, who lets us know if there are pockets in the theatre and if we have to up it a bit, do you see? Make it more brilliant. Now here's another thing—before you ask another question about that. There is something about the Method school that I would like to say. They have had who? Marlon Brando—who else?

INTERVIEWER Eli Wallach, Maureen Stapleton.

FONTANNE Yes, Maureen Stapleton.

INTERVIEWER Shelley Winters.

LUNT I haven't seen her.

INTERVIEWER Ben Gazzara.

FONTANNE Yes.

INTERVIEWER Jane Fonda and Susan Strasberg.

FONTANNE Yes, Susan Strasberg. Well, that is enough for us, isn't it? Now then, what I want to say is that whenever these young people would have gone they would have become wonderful actors. A wonderful natural-born actor also has a mind back of what he is doing, and he can take it or leave it and has done so all his life since he was eleven. So, he goes to the Method school and he takes the best of what the Method gives him. And the Method, I should say, has a lot of very good to give, you know. And also he practices his art. He does it *day* after *day* after *day,* which is the best teacher of all. (Bangs the table in rhythm)

INTERVIEWER I was going to ask you why ...

FONTANNE Also, another thing is—excuse me—they have many untalented ones in their school. I suppose Strasberg doesn't take them unless they show some semblance—isn't that true?

INTERVIEWER That's right.

FONTANNE Well, he has some who have lesser talents than these people we've mentioned. They are not the best exponents of his Method, are they?

INTERVIEWER No.

FONTANNE Then another thing. If Marlon Brando and Miss Stapleton come to the theatre and play parts and are not heard, they very soon will be heard or they will be fired. They have to be heard. They have to be heard—because they are criticized at rehearsals, and because if they don't bring it to the opening night all the critics tell them they couldn't hear them, and by that time they know it is necessary to hear the author's words.

INTERVIEWER I know, but they don't pay enough attention. The *Times* runs letters in its Drama Mail Bag and it seems to do no good. In fact, George Abbot recently said in an interview that he wished that the custom would develop again in the theatre, where if people didn't hear what they paid to hear they would yell, "Louder, please!"

FONTANNE Yes, they do in England.

INTERVIEWER Good.

FONTANNE And they yell other things, too.

INTERVIEWER If you were asked, and I am sure you are many times, by a young actor starting out, what he should do to develop as a person—because you cannot be a good actor, I think, unless you are a full person—what would you say to him that he should direct his attention to primarily?

FONTANNE (slowly and deliberately): I think that he should not form a habit of drinking every day. I think that all his life long he had better be careful of that. He should not think that "one drink a day won't hurt me." And then when they begin to near fifty and they haven't quite the excitement that they had when they were eighteen, then they take another, saying two drinks a day won't hurt me, you know . . . And now I sound like that hatchet woman—what was her name?

INTERVIEWER Carrie Nation.

FONTANNE Yes, Carrie Nation. Also, don't do too much during the day. Because that "too much" dulls the excitement that you should give to a part in the evening. Sociability is composed of the very essence of what you give to the theatre, what you give to a part. For instance, this interview is going to take it out of me for tonight. Yes, it will unless I stay quiet all the rest of the day. If I stay quiet all the rest of the day and don't go anywhere, and don't do anything, don't talk excitedly on the telephone, then I can bring excitement to my part, because that is the essence, that is the cream in the coffee—that aptness, that terrific force that you bring to the theatre.

INTERVIEWER This is the sense of dedication that one must bring to his art.

FONTANNE Yes. Then this actor of whom we're talking should cultivate honesty. He must know the value of honesty. Honesty is tremendously important in acting his part, for one thing. For another thing, he takes the money at the end of the week. Therefore, he better be quiet during the day and give everything he's got to the evening, because he takes a great deal of money, and I think a great deal more money than he generally is worth.

INTERVIEWER   You are going to be read right out of Actors Equity.

FONTANNE   I'd like to be.

INTERVIEWER   You say it is necessary to save yourself. Is this in an emotional sense, because you have to provide an emotional bridge to your audience?

FONTANNE   I think that if you have a stale audience, a dull audience, or an audience that has had too good a dinner and is a little heavy at first . . .

LUNT   And on matinées, has had too many banana splits, tuna-fish salads and sandwiches . . .

FONTANNE   You have to be able to wake them up. You must be ready for that challenge. You must have the energy and the spark.

LUNT   Lynn said, when she was auditioning people—which she did years ago—she said to them, "You can have that much talent as a young person, and that much character, and, eventually, your talent will come right down to your character, and vice versa." And it's true. We have seen it over and over again.

FONTANNE   You have to cultivate strength of character. You have to cultivate a very good sturdiness all around—and health.

INTERVIEWER   Actually, this would be generally true for any profession.

FONTANNE   Yes.

INTERVIEWER   This would be the heart of the advice that you would give to a young actor?

FONTANNE   Oh, yes. And I would say, if they are to go to a party in the afternoon, never drink anything. Never drink anything, because drink, when it wears off, it has—what do you call it?—a soporific—is that the word?—effect on you, and you are a little bit less fresh.

LUNT   I think we ought to say something, too, about discipline and alertness—how important they are for an actor. For instance, I don't understand anyone missing a cue. It drives me mad. I mean an entrance—late for an entrance. This, I have never understood—ever. I mean, they are paid to be there. Why should they be called? This does not mean anything to the layman, however. As Lynn said last night after we left the theatre, you can talk about the theatre and it generally only means something to an actor. It doesn't mean anything to anyone else. It does not mean anything to the layman, only to the actor.

FONTANNE   Well, for instance, you can say that right on the middle he "blew . . ." You know what I mean?—it means that he went up on his words. That is funny to the layman, but it is excruciating to an actor. Tell them the story of the understudy who went on . . .

LUNT   He came on—a couple of weeks ago—and he made a most wonderful entrance and he looked simply superb —he looked like a gopher . . .

FONTANNE   Let me describe him, do let me describe him. He has a very small, round face, like a baby. He's not terribly young, but he's young—and that small, round face, like a baby. He had on a great big loose cap, you know, a golfing cap with a visor. He was wearing . . .

LUNT   Oh, awful clothes, we all wear—dreadful . . .

FONTANNE   Awful clothes, as they do in the play, you know. Shabby and poor and old.

LUNT   Well, he came on. I said . . .

FONTANNE   Alfred said he came on like D'Artagnan.

LUNT   I was absolutely thrilled, because he was the essence of indecent poverty. Indecent he was. It was marvelous. He came over to me and, suddenly, went absolutely pure white. He couldn't think of his words, and I said to him, "Well, what do you want?" And he said, "A bottle of tobacco." And I said, "Brown or black." And he said, "Cognac."

FONTANNE   It was absolutely divine.

INTERVIEWER   When something like this happens, what do you do?

LUNT   You try to get rid of him as fast as you can, that's all.

FONTANNE   You maneuver. I tell you what you try to do—the other actor tries to give him a cue, and he gives it usually in a most unnatural way. For instance, I had one the other day, who got the cue to make his entrance, and didn't come on.

LUNT   As Lynn said, he didn't believe his ears.

FONTANNE   (annoyed): Oh!

LUNT   Did I spoil your story?

FONTANNE   Yes, you did. You going to do that? You want to tell the story?

LUNT   No, I don't.

FONTANNE   Well, then. He didn't come on. So I gave the cue to him again, very firmly, and the cue was, "What an extraordinary passion!" And I said, practically shouting, "What an extraordinary passion!" And I would have said it again and possibly gone out and got him if he hadn't come on. But he popped on at last, frightened, you see, like that. Well, I said to him after, "Why didn't you come on when you heard your cue?" And he said, "Well, I heard—and I couldn't come on!" And I said, "You just couldn't believe it was your cue. You were waiting for something else—me to come and get you, I suppose."

INTERVIEWER   Many of the things that you find essential in technique, as you described it, and in good acting, require training. As you say—acting and acting and acting. And yet, today, there is less and less opportunity to act.

LUNT   Quite true.

INTERVIEWER   So what I would like to know is, what reflections have you on this situation? How does, how can, an actor develop?

FONTANNE   What can the poor actors do who are out of work and have no jobs—you mean. Well, in the first place, I think you go slowly mad. You do really. And you become quite peculiar and odd. An actor out of work is quite a special person, you know. And all actors rather sympathize with him. They say, "Oh, don't worry about him, he's bitter, he is out of work," and things like that. Well, I was out of work for eighteen months here in America, and I was terribly difficult to deal with. And I was out of work for a long time in England and only got sparse jobs. Fortunately, I had a tiny income. I will tell you exactly how much it was. It was two pounds a week, which in those days came to ten dollars a week. I am talking now of when I was very young. Ten dollars a week, then, kept me in rent and food, and I froze, of course. Now, I would supplement that by going to Chelsea and sitting for different artists. And that helped enormously, but how I got experience, I don't know. But I never refused a job. I couldn't afford to.

LUNT   Neither did I.

FONTANNE   I took everything that was offered. So we got experience, finally. On tour, of course—that's a wonderful way to get experience, because that is a very definite run, you see. For instance, any actor in our company—any small-part actor—got a whale of an experience. We were on tour for six months in this play.

INTERVIEWER   Just being in the theatre is important. Is that the idea? Being able to get on the stage, no matter how long or how short the part.

LUNT   That's right, how else can you learn your business?

FONTANNE   Yes, that's right, because if you're even just

a walk-on with some fine company—well, look what you can do. You can stand and watch. You can also learn a lot of what not to do—that is, if you have selectivity, if you have judgment, if you have taste.

INTERVIEWER   What, convinced you—you two, I should say—that you ought to play as a team?

LUNT   We didn't.

FONTANNE   No, we never decided that.

LUNT   Never.

FONTANNE   It was decided for us. After we both appeared separately, and both made some successes separately—in leading parts and in secondary parts—then we had six offers in one season.

LUNT   All at once.

FONTANNE   Six offers in one season: David Belasco, Harris . . .

LUNT   Lee Shubert . . .

FONTANNE   Gilbert Miller, Lee Shubert and . . .

LUNT   There were five of them.

FONTANNE   There were six, I remember.

LUNT   Anyway, we chose *The Guardsman* out of these.

FONTANNE   Oh, the Theatre Guild, don't forget the Guild. The Guild gave us *The Guardsman*.

INTERVIEWER   What has been the secret of your playing together so well? What have you done through the years, and what did you do at the beginning, that made you such a wonderful team?

FONTANNE   I think that that is something that grows with two good actors. I think if two good actors play together long enough, it gets that way. Also, we had ideas on the subject, as Alfred told me he told you last night. About talking together—we thought it was natural to talk together because people do, as we have done today. But we did it a little differently. We dovetail it like that, you know.

LUNT   Not in this play. We can't—you can't in Shakespeare, but you can in *The Guardsman*, in *Reunion in Vienna*.

FONTANNE   We dovetail it in. We slip the word in so that the both of us can be clearly heard. Because I've seen some people do it and they jam. You know, they jam. But Alfred and I dovetail, and it requires a great deal of rehearsal.

INTERVIEWER   In other words, you are constantly working together.

FONTANNE   Oh, yes.

INTERVIEWER   Dovetailing different inflections.

FONTANNE   Oh, yes. When we have finished our rehearsal in the daytime, then Alfred and I always rehearse our particular scenes over again that evening, so that we really, during rehearsals, work at least twelve hours a day. What's Equity going to do about that? Well, there—as I was saying, we work and work at home and slowly you get into the character of the person you are playing—the walk, the gestures. I try not to think too much about my role, that is, my character. But, gradually, I become more and more acquainted with her and then as the days go by I sink deeper and deeper into her, discovering traits and things about her I did not know existed when I began to rehearse. Inflections, intonations become sharper and truer, and the false notes are corrected. This is a process that continues all during the run of the play, even after it has opened.

INTERVIEWER   Yes, I've heard that you rehearse up until the final performance, that you still try to develop things that occur to you that are new, that you feel will help the performance.

FONTANNE   Yes, yes. And I remember the most triumphant thing that ever happened to me—and I thrill now when I think of it. I think Alfred told you about it last night, about *Reunion in Vienna*. I had this line—I knew it was funny, but I couldn't get the audience to think so. I don't know what it was. Perhaps I went too fast so they were too interested altogether, or perhaps it was too sudden for them to catch quickly—because you can't wait for them, you know. So one day, and I think it was the matinée, at the end of the run—it was the Saturday matinée and we were going to close that night—it came—I got it. I was beside myself. I think I even was a little foolish in my excitement.

INTERVIEWER   What did you do?

FONTANNE   I don't know now, exactly. It was so long ago. But I can still remember that elation of winning out in the end. And I think that is true of every good actor. He is always trying to improve his role. And if he is a true artist, even though his performance may never be perfect, it, at least, will be better at the end of the run than it was on opening night.

INTERVIEWER   I see. Miss Fontanne said before—and this seems to be legendary now—that Mr. Lunt is a very nervous performer.

FONTANNE   Yes. So am I. I am very nervous, indeed, at almost every performance, but not quite as bad as he is. And I think that comes of the English "thing" they tell you when you are three years old: "Self-control, don't show it, don't show it." You know, you are told you mustn't show it. And that is even when you know that you are frightened.

INTERVIEWER   This is a slight digression. But in line with the English self-control, there is a story of a busload of Englishmen and Frenchmen who were traveling over the Alps and came very close to hurtling over the side of a mountain. The French went crazy in the bus, hollering, screaming and hysterical, but the English sat very stoically as if nothing was going on. Finally the bus was righted and everybody quieted down. When they got to the destination, the French got off, completely happy and relaxed, while all the English had nervous breakdowns.

LUNT   That could be.

FONTANNE   Wonderful story. I think that's true. We nearly crashed in the air the other day, and I know that feeling. Yes. We were coming from Toronto and we left the field and we hadn't got our full height when—this is what I found out happened after—some small aircraft, a lighter aircraft, privately driven, was coming dead on to us. All I saw—I was there on the right-hand side of the plane—all I saw was our plane doing (tilting hand and arm upward) that—and that —and then going on, going on, and I looked down, straight down to the ground, while the plane was turning upside down, and the aircraft went under our left wing, and we bumped quite a bit coming back, bumped, and then leveled out and then went ahead. While it was happening, honest to God, I knew that we were gong to crash, I knew it and I wasn't frightened. I thought, "Well, we are not too far from the ground. I think we'll make it." Do you see? That's just my mind. My mind hadn't reached fear yet. And when we got back into position again, I had to have a stiff one quickly. Because I was really shaking all over. Perhaps it isn't self-control. Perhaps the English are slow in the mind.

LUNT   The first thing I heard was—Myles* said, as we straightened out and went on, "Well, it almost meant three minutes of silence at Sardi's, didn't it?"

FONTANNE   If Sardi's could arrange to give us three minutes, I'd be highly honored.

LUNT   She had just come to like flying, you see. It's a shame.

INTERVIEWER   Have you tried anything to overcome this nervousness?

LUNT   Me?

FONTANNE   Me?

* Myles Eason, a member of *The Visit* touring company.

INTERVIEWER   Well, both of you.

LUNT   No.

FONTANNE   No.

LUNT   There is nothing to do.

INTERVIEWER   This must be a torture ever night.

FONTANNE   Alfred was never as frightened as I was, never.

INTERVIEWER   No, I mean about performance.

FONTANNE   Oh, the performance. Oh, no, there isn't anything to do. It quickly goes as soon as you get on, you see.

LUNT   It's better when you are on. But there are moments when you do want to just run, literally run. All actors have that, I am sure they do.

INTERVIEWER   I thought it true mostly, if not entirely, on opening nights. I was under the impression that once a run got under way you didn't have that every time.

LUNT   Oh, yes you do. Yes you do.

FONTANNE   Oh, yes. Oh, yes. And I think that the older you get the worse it gets.

INTERVIEWER   Really?

LUNT   Oh, yes. You ask any actor. He will tell you the same, if he is truthful.

INTERVIEWER   Is there a sense of challenge every night about the part?

FONTANNE   Certainly.

INTERVIEWER   What has been your major problem, Mr. Lunt, in this play?

LUNT   I have an awful lot of movement in this play, and some nights I am not very—what shall we say?—agile. My left foot doesn't seem to make it, you know.

FONTANNE   That isn't true.

LUNT   Well . . .

FONTANNE   That isn't true.

LUNT   Yes. At the end, when I have to stamp my feet. You know, where they strangle me—and it is a very bad position . . . It is damned uncomfortable. Hard. And some nights I just can't stamp my old feet. They won't stamp. I am too damned tired.

FONTANNE   Oh, it isn't because your feet are old, darling. It is . . .

LUNT   I'm tired.

FONTANNE   You are tired for one thing, and another thing, possibly you would find more groans from a younger actor, because he hasn't got the muscles to do it with.

INTERVIEWER   Yes, I suppose it must be very awkward.

LUNT   Oh, I stamp away, but it isn't very loud some nights.

INTERVIEWER   Do you have any problem of concentration in your roles, regardless whether it is *The Visit* or any other play?

FONTANNE   No, I don't think we've ever had trouble . . .

LUNT   I have to tell you a very amusing story. Once when we opened in San Francisco—we had closed Saturday night in *Idiot's Delight* and opened Tuesday night in *Amphitryon*—the clothes had been made by Valentina and hung, and, you know, silk jersey stretches. Well, she had in the second act a flesh-colored dress, and to my horror in the second act, as I looked over she was completely bare. (Indicating deep, deep cleavage) And all through the scene I kept worrying and worrying. But the audience had no idea it seemed—the dress being flesh-colored. Anyway, I said to her when the curtain came down, "Do you know you played the whole act bare?" She said, "Don't bother me with things like that until I know my lines." And she meant it.

INTERVIEWER   You've never had any problem in concentration? Nothing distracts you?

FONTANNE   I don't know what you mean.

INTERVIEWER   I mean, suppose there is a noise off-stage?

FONTANNE   I hear it.

INTERVIEWER   You hear it?

FONTANNE   And how!

LUNT   In all the quiet scenes on opening night at the City Center—you must have heard it. The steam pipes were playing, "God Save the Queen," or something, back there. It was maddening. And what do you do? They went on for so long, at such an even beat, that you would sort of pause and say your lines in between the banging. You do, you know, when it's bong—bong—you get on to it after a while, but it is very disturbing.

INTERVIEWER   I assume that there is no such thing as immersing yourself in the role, so that you don't hear anything, you don't know what is happening.

FONTANNE   No, no, no. That's another thing that an experienced actor has—he has an outside eye. A very good actor has to have it, or acquire it. How you do, I can't possibly tell you. You can look at yourself. For instance, you know exactly where your arm is, so that it is graceful, you know. And anything like that, you learn. You have to have an outside eye, and you also have to have an outside ear, so that when you say something, your outside ear tells you that it is the wrong inflection, just as you, yourself, in life, if you say something irritably and you are not at all irritable, but it comes out irritably, you say to yourself, "Now that sounds as if I were cross," and you explain to the person you are talking to, "I am not cross." You see? Well, that's it. Same thing, exactly. And that ear also guides your timing, which is vital in comedy, in speaking the lines of, say, Shaw or Coward or S. N. Behrman. But the timing must not be methodical or deliberate. Too much precision is worse than none. Better to be offbeat a bit than too deliberate. A good actor cannot be so self-conscious, or so shy or so nervous and tightened, that he can't hear. A good actor hears and a good actor sees.

INTERVIEWER   When you get a role—you can use *The Visit,* if you wish, or any one of your plays—what is the first thing you do, and the second thing you do? This can get involved and I don't want you to get involved too far, but . . .

LUNT   We'd go on forever.

INTERVIEWER   What I mean is, when you read a script— what are the steps that you formulate in your mind?

FONTANNE   When I read a script, I read for readability. If I find it very hard going, I know the audience is going to, as well. And if I can't put it down from beginning to end, then I know I've got a good play, at least a play the audience will stay in their seats for. We sort of visualize a play in its entirety.

LUNT   May I give you an example? Bob Sherwood sent us *Idiot's Delight.* He always did, you know, to see if we wanted to do it. He wrote it for us, but even so—he was charming . . .

FONTANNE   A great friend.

LUNT   Yes, a great friend, and so he let us have it. Lynn went into another room to read it. And a bit later I called out, I said, "Where are you?" and she said, "I am at the beginning of the second act, and we must do it." And by the middle of the second act, she announced, "We've got to do it, Alfred, we really must do this, it's most interesting and exciting." I said, "How is your part?" She said, "I haven't come to it yet." And it was true, she hadn't. She had simply walked through at the beginning, you know—you remember the play?

FONTANNE   I came on toward the end of the second act.

LUNT   That is a good example, I think, and rather unique I might add. And I also might add that this wasn't always the case. In her less experienced days Lynn used to read with her eyes on her part only. It's a matter of maturing as an artist, I believe. What's important is the play, not the size of one's role.

INTERVIEWER   When do you get down to building the details?

LUNT   You have to learn the lines first.

INTERVIEWER   All right, you learn your lines first. Then what do you do? Do you start building from within first, after you have learned your lines?

LUNT   Actually, you sort of do it all at once. Once we have the lines memorized, then we work like mad, especially at home. We'll do scenes over and over again, throw out what we do not like, keep what's good, and then we polish, polish, polish.

INTERVIEWER   In other words, the details—how Miss Fontanne lifted her arm before and looked into the mirror to see whether it was graceful—whether it was exactly where she had intended it to be. And it was. When do you get to things like that?

LUNT   Oh, way on.

FONTANNE   I will tell you when you get to things like that. When I played my very first great big part in a play by Marc Connelly and George Kaufman, called Dulcy, somebody said to my sister, "Even her bandy legs are an asset." My sister said, "She hasn't got bandy legs. She's got beautiful legs. What do you mean?" I realized that I turned my toes in, see? If I stand like this and turn my toes in, it looks as if I've got bandy legs. I turned my toes in. Well, I never turned them in again, to my knowledge. I started on that. I got my heels together, too. If you stand like that, it is very ugly. I only stand like that on certain occasions, for certain things. Well, I tidied that up. And then I made awkward gestures—I was an awkward girl. And I looked in the glass and I learned, oh, quite a good many perfectly natural, good poses. I learned them off so that I could do them without looking in the glass, you see, and then I used those in every part. I extended them, I used them all, until now it's perfectly natural for me to be graceful. I have a subconscious mind that is doing it now. And actors, if they are ungraceful, women especially, must learn to be graceful.

LUNT   If the part requires it.

FONTANNE   Men should learn to be graceful also. And it is a thing you can learn especially if you have a good eye, yourself, you know. If you have a good eye for beauty and for the look of a thing and the line of a thing.

LUNT   Oh, while we're on this subject, I must tell you a very funny story about Larry Olivier. I think it was in one of the *Henry's*. And Larry spent hours on this reddish wig and beard, and he worked for hours on the pose he was taking with his lady love at the curtain going up on the second act.

FONTANNE The curtain went up with him having a foot on a chair, a stool—like that. It was all spotlighted. It was a beautiful picture.

LUNT Oh, it nearly killed him—what happened. It was during the war, and in the first act there was an old major, and he was awfully tired and a little soused.

FONTANNE He was a little tight and he had thought it was a musical comedy. And when he found out it was not, you see, he was furious.

LUNT And the curtain went up on this wonderful picture of Larry. The curtain went up and Larry heard this old major saying, "Oh, God, there is old Ginger again."

INTERVIEWER Sometimes it doesn't pay to practice, does it?

LUNT Larry, of course, works like a dog.

INTERVIEWER How do you develop laughter?

FONTANNE What do you mean? I don't understand what you mean.

INTERVIEWER The ability to laugh at a given moment.

FONTANNE Oh, you can laugh at will. You can laugh at will. You can cry at will.

LUNT Oh, yes. You can make the tears pour out of your eyes.

FONTANNE Now, the Stanislavsky Method has you go off down in the cellar and start a fight, and you come up the stairs fighting with this person. And you come on to the stage fighting with this person, and it is good and hot by the time you get there. It's a wonderful way to do it. And if I were directing, I would like them to do it that way, you see—but not in the cellar. Perhaps I would have them start off-stage, quietly fighting until they got really hot, and come on doing it, you see. But, crying and laughing— Suppose you have to make your entrance laughing. If young people are involved, young actors, that is, I would have them think of something irresistibly funny and get themselves into a hysterical mood and then come off, and time it so that they were there for their cue. That's what I would have them do. As they grow older they can stand in the wings. They really shouldn't talk to anybody for two or three beats before they go on. It is better not to. It's better to be concentrated. You are apt to miss your cue, for one thing, if you are talking to anybody up until the last second before you go on. I never do and never have. Any old actor can turn it on, laughter or tears, like that. All their emotions are very facile by the time they have become experienced actors.

INTERVIEWER   This is the technique that becomes part of one.

FONTANNE   The technique is that you break up your emotions. You get yourself emotionally easy whether you are or not. A good actor—a good actor usually has a little fund of emotion, you know, which he can enlarge.

INTERVIEWER   You mean, he's got to relax himself, but then call upon his emotions to come into action.

FONTANNE   Well, I don't know. As soon as he goes on he is in his part—a good actor. He gets into it quickly. An experienced actor gets into it quicker than a young, inexperienced actor.

INTERVIEWER   Do you summon any image, for instance, for tears? Do you summon any recalled joke that will always evoke laughter?

FONTANNE   No. No. No.

LUNT   No, it comes.

INTERVIEWER   It just comes?

LUNT   You start out that way and then it becomes part of you, doesn't it?

FONTANNE   You start out that way.

INTERVIEWER   In other words, you can teach yourself to cry at will by simply practicing.

FONTANNE   Yes, there is a school of actors who play an emotional scene without any—I don't know whether it is without feeling or emotion or without tears. Certainly without tears. They think that—they watch actors and the more they cry the less effective they are. That is one school of actors. That is the Helen Hayes school of acting. And, of course, God knows, she plays an emotional scene divinely, you see— and is very moving. So, I don't know, but I must, for myself, if I feel a thing, it does something funny to my voice, and I think that is a good thing. I don't know. I let it do it. My judgment on it, my own personal judgment on it, is that it is good to do that. I imagine Helen does that, too, that she lets it come to her voice. She must do it. And it is a real thing, like that curious swelling of the throat. That happens when you cry, when you are going to cry—not when you are crying actually, when you are going to cry, you know. That curious swelling of the throat. And if you forbid it, you get an ache there. But when your voice comes out, when it is swelling like that, it is very good, it is full of hurt and tears and whatever you wish to convey.

INTERVIEWER   All this can be very fatiguing. I can see that.

FONTANNE   I used to think that. I said to a doctor once, "Why is it that actors who go through an agonizing scene and convey such agony can come off and throw it instantly—and they are perfectly all right. For an emotional—a screaming, emotional scene they do it eight times a week. Why aren't they ruined by that? If human beings went into such a fit of emotion eight times a week, they'd die. They would not be able to live. They would certainly go mad." And he, this doctor, said, "Well, I think it's because—and I thought it was a very wise answer—"I think it is because an actor comes offstage and knows he has done well, and that supplants the emotion."

INTERVIEWER   The satisfaction of the emotion.

FONTANNE   Also, his grief doesn't continue, you see, it is not a real grief. It is the grief of an imaginary man. So when he comes off he is himself again.

INTERVIEWER   There is a school of acting, and this is closer to the Stanislavsky people, who presumably get so caught up with the character that the grief continues.

FONTANNE   They are not allowed to speak to anybody but as the character, off-stage—as the character would speak. I think that is still for young ones. And I think that is how Stanislavsky developed that wonderful company.

INTERVIEWER   Do you as artists study people constantly—as models for roles in which you might sometime appear?

FONTANNE   Yes, let me answer that. I find that all the things that I think were the best things—whether they were or not, I don't know—but I feel that all the best things I have done I have got from life. I have got very few things from seeing other actors on the stage. I got one thing from Ethel Barrymore and it was only in its essence. I didn't copy it exactly. You wouldn't recognize it. You wouldn't recognize it now if I told you what it was, you know.

INTERVIEWER   Can you give me a sample of what you say you got from life, for instance, and relate it to your role?

FONTANNE   From life—yes. I remember once somebody being given a piece of bad news. And that person was quite silent for a long time, and then he said, "I see," and no more—there was no more—and it was the most moving thing that a person could say. Haven't you heard people do that?

INTERVIEWER   Yes.

FONTANNE   It was dreadfully meek, so awful and so accepted. That man saw; he literally meant what he said, "I see," and took it and didn't cry, or anything. It was perfectly awful. Alfred has to do it in this play.

INTERVIEWER   I was thinking of that.

FONTANNE   Yes. He has to do it in this play, and whenever he elaborates on that—which he does sometimes when he is tired and feels he has to give all, you know—and he says, "Oh, I see," or he says, "Yes, I see," or he says, "Oh ... yes ... I see"—if he says that, it isn't as good. If he just says, "I see," it is wonderful. Over a long run, you lose your eye and you lose your ear. And I have to keep watch over him as he does over me.

INTERVIEWER   You act as guardsmen to each other.

FONTANNE   Oh, yes! We do! And I think that is very possibly one of the reasons, if I might say so, for our success. I think that we are terrifically critical of each other. And we've learned, the both of us, to take it. We've learned to take it.

INTERVIEWER   When you know that you have arrived at something like the "I see," and you know that this is effective, you see to it that he continues to do it this way. You take the place of the director, who probably has gone off to other assignments.

FONTANNE   Yes, yes.

LUNT   Yes, yes. She's always watching me from that goddam balcony.

FONTANNE   Yes. From that goddam balcony I can see and hear a lot. Actually, I can't see much because I have my back turned, but I hear a lot, and that really is even better because when you hear, it must be true.

INTERVIEWER   But he does that for you, too.

FONTANNE   Oh, indeed. Indeed, he does.

INTERVIEWER   It seems to me in *There Shall Be No Night* there was ...

FONTANNE   For instance—excuse me—for instance, in this part the minute I'm not hard as nails—if I'm tired and it gets into my own voice—I hear about it from Alfred. Make no mistake, I hear about it. I play this part in a much lower register, which makes it stronger, you know. I play this part in that voice—low down like that. I very seldom rise above it. But my own natural voice is rather a light voice and I often cannot make myself heard in a room—which is very often.

INTERVIEWER   You've been so co-operative. I think our time is up.

FONTANNE Well, have you got anything else you wish to say quickly? Anything you want to ask quickly?

INTERVIEWER Well, yes. I'd like to ask you a question we asked Mr. Lunt last night. What have you found more difficult to play, comedy or tragedy?

FONTANNE I think comedy, and I'll tell you why. Because if you are capable of playing tragedy it means that you have a great well of emotion in you—and you just push yourself off and roll downhill. That is what it is, in a scene. But, of course, you have to learn how not to spend it all at the beginning. Nurse it along so you don't wear out or get thin at the end—that you have to learn. Comedy—you really have to have that ear out and that eye on yourself. You really do. You have to be very up and very brilliant and faster, much faster than you are when you play tragedy. And that, of course, is very tiring, very exhausting. Also, in comedy, breath control comes in more than it does in the other kind of thing. If you take a deep breath you can play with a sentence. There is no doubt you can get your laugh, you know, if you say it right. But if you don't take your breath—and you have to take a breath during the line—it is as if you'd gagged on something. It isn't as funny and you often miss your laugh. Mysterious, isn't it? Because you would think that the line would be as funny in any way, wouldn't you? All comedians will tell you that.

INTERVIEWER What would you say was the hardest role you played?

FONTANNE I wouldn't want to pick out one. I will say, though, that Kate in *The Taming of the Shrew* wasn't easy. You have to really keep going in it to make it last—the play. *Shrew* isn't a great play, you know.

INTERVIEWER Which of your roles gave you the most satisfaction?

FONTANNE Well, I've really found Claire Zachanassian in *The Visit* a most interesting role. But I always think that one of my favorites was that part I had in *Idiot's Delight*. It never was—as it was written—a part that was entirely clear to audiences—what and who was this woman who said she was a Russian aristocrat. Was she a phony? Well, I injected a few hints of cockney and a song that suggested she wasn't a Russian noblewoman. And the character took on a fullness it hadn't had. It was rewarding indeed.

INTERVIEWER What do you think of dramatic schools as training grounds for the young?

FONTANNE Oh, I think anywhere you go where you can

stand up and speak the lines, and walk about—anywhere—
is better than being by yourself in a room, isn't it?

INTERVIEWER   And may I have one last question?

FONTANNE   Yes.

INTERVIEWER   This may sound a little grandiose, but
what is the most rewarding thing about your life in the theatre?

FONTANNE   The most rewarding thing and the thing that
was the most exciting thing is—Alfred wants to answer
that, too—was—oh, yes, we both agree about this—was Bob
Sherwood's *There Shall Be No Night* and the particular moment that we did it.

INTERVIEWER   Why?

FONTANNE   Because the whole audience, wherever we
went, swung with us. Most of them were with us politically—
we were not at war, you know—and yet some of them were
wildly against us. But there was a meaning to that play. It
was glorious, unforgettable.

José Ferrer

BIOGRAPHY

José Ferrer, who was born in Puerto Rico in 1912, set out to be an architect; he studied at Princeton University and did graduate work at Columbia University. Soon after completing his studies, however, he turned to the theatre, starting in summer stock in 1935 and following this alternately with minor roles on Broadway and on tour. Soon more promising parts were given to him, in such plays as *Brother Rat, Missouri Legend;* and in 1939 he made an important advance in his acting career in Maxwell Anderson's *Key Largo,* which starred Paul Muni. But it was in 1940, in *Charley's Aunt,* that he was catapulted to Broadway prominence.

Vickie followed in 1942, and the next year he succeeded Danny Kaye in the musical *Let's Face It.* Mr. Ferrer went on to play Iago to Paul Robeson's Othello in a record-breaking run of the Shakespeare tragedy. One of his best-known Broadway roles followed, the lead in *Cyrano de Bergerac,* a role he repeated on the screen to win an Oscar. He later brought Cyrano to television. Mr. Ferrer went on to play *Volpone,* and in 1950 he directed and starred in *Twentieth Century.* In 1951 he was represented on Broadway by *Stalag 17,* which he produced and directed, and by *The Fourposter,* which he also directed; in 1952 by *The Chase,* which he produced and directed, and by *The Shrike,* which he presented, directed and starred in.

Mr. Ferrer has had a full career in Hollywood—as actor and director, for such films as *I Accuse* and *The High Cost of Love;* in *The Shrike* and *The Great Man,* for which he also shared writing credits; in *The Caine Mutiny* and as Toulouse-Lautrec in *Moulin Rouge.* Mr. Ferrer made his debut in still another medium, opera, in 1960, in *Gianni Schicchi;* and in the same year he sang in a television show with his wife, Rosemary Clooney.

Mr. Ferrer has been married three times, the first two marriages—to Uta Hagen and Phyllis Hill—ending in divorce. He and his present wife have five children; he also had a daughter with Uta Hagen.

SETTING

Mr. Ferrer is a dynamic man (he was represented on Broadway in one season by four plays, serving variously as producer, director or star)—and something of this dynamism becomes known well before an interview is likely even to begin. Making the arrangements provides the clue. Mr. Ferrer's pleasant and crisp-spoken British secretary, on the day set for the interview, was hard put to find Mr. Ferrer to confirm the exact evening hour of the interview. He was to fly to San Juan either that midnight or the next day; he was to talk with a leading lady of the stage about a play for next season, as well as to a producer—and among still other appointments there was his singing lesson!

But as is customary for Mr. Ferrer, he managed to be at the right place at the right time. The time was 9:00 P.M., the place his home high over New York City's Central Park in the Dakota apartment house on Central Park West. One of the earliest apartment houses built in the city, the Dakota houses a flock of celebrities of New York's stage world. Mr. Ferrer's apartment has large rooms, high ceilings, halls and foyers wonderfully wasteful of space. In the living room, with its long windows giving onto the city lights across the park, there is a mixture of antique and modern furniture—some rather handsome pieces, but the accent is apparently more on comfort than on decorative effect. There are some prints on the walls, but dominating them at the time were two large and colorful paintings—unfinished Ferrers, one still on an easel. There are two well-filled bookcases. A couple of fish tanks, one very large and both gurgling with fish-tank machinery, happened to be in the room because, as Mr. Ferrer explained, a friend had asked him to keep them for a while.

This apartment is the Ferrers' New York City place. His wife, Rosemary Clooney, and their youngsters were at their home in Hollywood. But Mr. Ferrer does not seem to be very far away from them even in New York. There are photographs of Miss Clooney and the children all around the room, and a proud father brought out a handsome album of family photographs. During the interview a call came in from "Rosie" in Hollywood.

Mr. Ferrer was dressed in a checked sports shirt with sleeves rolled up, slacks and bedroom slippers. He remained seated on a sofa, sometimes with hands clasped at the back of his head, but was not relaxed for long. He threw himself into what he was saying, giving enthusiastic emphasis to a point he was making; or, talking about a movie which had moved him, his eyes filled with tears. He seemed to live life very fully indeed—and with gusto.

Interview

INTERVIEWER   An elementary question—when did you start acting?

FERRER   I think I started acting about three or four times in my life. I started acting when my father—who's a lawyer, but a great, great storyteller and I think one of the finest actors I ever knew, always in the living room—would come home in the evening and tell us stories about what had happened during the day, even if it was only a walk down the street. When I became old enough to start telling anecdotes myself—whether it was at the age of six or eight or ten—I started telling stories, and I sort of enjoyed imitating him and re-relating some of his experiences and relating some of mine. Then when I was older and went to high school and college—and you start out with these dirty stories that you hear as a kid in high school, and then you carry on with wittier and more amusing stories you hear and enjoy when you're a little bit more mature. I sort of had a repertoire of funny stories in college—which led to my third acting debut. One day the president of the Triangle Club at Princeton University, who was in the architecture department with me and had a drafting table next to mine, said, "You ought to act in this year's show." And I said, "I don't know anything about acting." And he said, "Well, come and try out." I did try out, and I was so bad that they only let me go on to the next elimination out of courtesy, because he had asked me and they felt that they ought to give me, not a flat refusal, but an easier refusal. I heard about it and got mad, because I figured that although I was pretty bad, everybody else was worse. By getting angry, I overacted, which is what I needed to do as a beginning actor, because all the acting had been inside my head and nothing was coming out in the first tryout. Anyway, the second tryout I got the comedy lead in the show, and one night I opened in the McCarter Theatre in Princeton as an undergraduate, and that was my sort of third acting debut. Then there came a time, in 1935, when I came on as a second policeman in *A Slight Case of Murder* at the Fifty-eighth Street Theatre, and said, "What's going on here?" and went off. That was my last acting debut.

INTERVIEWER You have said that you love this profession. What is the essence of the satisfaction that you derive from acting?

FERRER I think the satisfaction that I derive from acting is, to put it as crudely as possible, helping to tell a story. To put it a little less crudely, I have one basic philosophy: I don't think there's anybody in the business who believes more sincerely than I do that the play is the thing, so everything I say is always in terms of what I call "the creative artist," namely, the playwright, with his agent or interpreter, namely, the actor, and of course with the aid of the director. To put it more stubtly, I like to tell the author's story. That's the satisfaction of acting to me. In other words, when I play Iago, I'm telling one of Shakespeare's stories, helping to tell it. When I play Charley's Aunt, I'm helping to tell Brandon Thomas' great, successful story. When I play Cyrano de Bergerac, I'm telling one of Rostand's stories. And I, on the stage, feel that I'm telling a story about once-upon-a-time these things happened, and then he did this, and then she did that, to which he said, and they lived happily ever after, or then he died, and so the story ends—whatever it is. But first of all, I'm telling the story, if I'm playing the leading role; and in the second place, I am telling the story that someone else dreamed up, without which I would not have a story to tell—unless I became a writer myself.

INTERVIEWER William Gibson—you know, *The Miracle Worker*—said in an article that every time you got a play going there were three stories being told: the playwright's, the director's and the actors'. And in the end it was a matter of who won, because each was pulling his own way, each was interpreting his own life's experience into this work. I gather you don't think that this need be the case.

FERRER No, I don't think so. I know that a great many people in the theatre feel that it is a contest and a battle. The only contest and battle that I recognize in the theatre is when I think something—and, you know, I'm like everybody else, I think I'm right and I may very well be wrong—when I think something is being done that damages the play or, what sometimes happens, that the playwright himself is damaging his own story, either through lack of experience or through wounded pride or through trying to save his face, or trying to say, "Well, so-and-so is taking the play away from me. By golly, I'm going to show him who wrote the play." Whatever the reason, the only time I ever fight with a playwright is when I feel that the playwright is not serving *his* own best ends. But as a director and as an actor, naturally the play is refracted through the prism of my personality—it can't help but be. I cannot play a part the way somebody else would play it, nor can I direct a play the way someone else would direct it. The fact that my direction and somebody else's direction can coexist, and each one have its own validity, is one of the wonderful things about the theatre. Surely, Rembrandt and Goya can both paint a woman or a tree, and one doesn't cancel the other out, they're two versions of the same thing. All right. But in my own mind, I'm convinced—and I may be deceiving myself—but I'm convinced that as an actor or as a director, I'm knocking my brains out for the playwright whose play I once read, cold and dead on a page, and which made me laugh or made me cry, or made me sit on the edge of my chair. If I'm not doing that, then I'm simply glorifying myself, which bores the daylights out of me, and I'm sure it would bore the daylights out of anybody else. As I say, I may be deceiving myself, but this is certainly the frame of reference that I . . .

INTERVIEWER An excellent statement.

FERRER I think that I'm an agent. You see, I think that Jascha Heifetz is a great violinist, Fritz Kreisler . . . Pablo Casals is a great cellist; Horowitz, a great pianist. If these people had never been born, there would still be Beethoven and Brahms and Bach and Debussy and Stravinsky, and anyone else. If I'd never been born, if Larry

Olivier had never been born, if John Gielgud had never been born, if Barrault, Henry Irving, Burbage had never been born—I don't care whom you name—there's still Shakespeare, there's still Ibsen, there's still Chekhov. *We* make a very valid contribution but we are not the essential; we are the circumstance of a certain period or of a certain century, but without the fellow who took the blank page and put words on it, where would we be? We would have to start telling stories of our own, and at that point we become playwrights first and actors later. Certainly that's what happened when the goatherd told that funny story on the slopes of a Grecian hill that we always hear about. I feel that I am the fortunate representative of somebody who put something on paper that is good even when he's been dead three hundred years, but when I'm dead five minutes I can't act anymore, I can't direct any more.

INTERVIEWER   When you started acting, did you study other actors?

FERRER   Yes, I used to go to the theatre and I still do. If I found a play that excited me, either as a play or a performance, or if I found a series of performances that excited me, I used to go over and over and over again whenever I could. Naturally, when you're acting, your availabilities are limited as a spectator unless you have an actors' benefit, which they give on Sundays. But there are periods when you don't work, and those periods increase as you become more and more successful. When I was beginning, I was always in great demand as an assistant stage manager because I was always willing to run up and down stairs and stay up all night typing sides, and so on. But, anyway, I used to do something that I still do, and it's a habit that I've developed through the years—I find my muscles take me to the back of the orchestra and I stand. I think that I'd rather see a play standing up at the back of the house than almost any other way that I know. I don't the first time I see a play, because I call up and say have you got a couple of good seats, and somebody in the management very kindly gives me house seats, or one of the stars does, or something, so I usually see a play the first time down front there, but that's usually because I go with Rosemary. If I go alone, I'll walk into a theatre and happily stand in the back. There's something about standing there and seeing the audience and the entire stage—and not being caught up in the detail of performance, or facial expression, or scenery, or props, or anything, but seeing a total picture—which pleases me enormously. And I suppose that is the director's side of me that would rather see the entire canvas than any particular corner of it.

INTERVIEWER In studying actors, did you have any particular actor that you studied more than any others?

FERRER Yes, there were several whom I studied a great deal.

INTERVIEWER And they influenced you.

FERRER Yes, enormously. And at one point, I would say, any of my performances was in one way or another an imitation of one of these men. I think that the sources are still there, but now they're snowed over by the development of my own personality and they're less perceptible. I don't know that anybody could say—any young American actor or American actor of my generation, not young but youngish— that he was impervious to the influence of John Barrymore. I, personally, get very mad at John Barrymore, and if John Barrymore were alive today and I knew him, I would scold him because he did so many bad things to his own genius, and to his own opportunities—his brilliant talent, his magnificent voice, the opportunities he had, this extraordinary beauty of face and figure that he had—that he didn't eventually respect it enough to live up to his obligations. He sort of thumbed his nose at himself, and I think this is tragic. I think he should have been spanked by somebody he loved enough to listen to. I was naturally profoundly influenced by Alfred Lunt, profoundly influenced by Paul Muni, influenced by Osgood Perkins, and influenced by a man whom I consider a contemporary today but who started acting and was very successful just enough years before I did so that when I started he was already almost a star, and that's Larry Olivier. Today I think of Larry as my contemporary, but when he was doing *Private Lives* with Noel Coward and Gertrude Lawrence and Jill Esmond, I was still in college. And when he did *The Green Bay Tree* in 1933, I was a graduate student at Columbia University. So Larry is only four or five years older than I am, and I think of him as a contemporary, and yet he was established long before I was. And he was a big influence.

INTERVIEWER Could you elaborate just a little on how, for instance, Alfred Lunt influenced you?

FERRER Oh, yes, certainly. I'll finish the list, because I have many sources of mine, actually I'm shameless about them. I think that for my particular taste, the actor who satisfied me more than any actor in the world—it's terrible to say one actor, but to a question like this, you know, if you have to pick one, who would you pick, it's an academic thing—but Louis Jouvet was my particular baby. I just think for my taste there was nobody ever like Louis Jouvet. I saw him in every movie he ever made, over and over and over again. I saw him in Paris in *Ondine,* and I saw him here when he did *The School for Wives,* I believe it was. And, as a matter of fact, I was his interpreter at the Drama Desk* at one lunch. And then Jean-Louis Barrault also, I admired very much as an actor. The other actors who affected other people, like Spencer Tracy, Leslie Howard, have not affected me that much. They affect, naturally—everybody you see affects you —but they haven't affected me as much as the more vivid personalities. I think I lean, I guess, toward more vivid ones, like Alfred Lunt, Paul Muni, Larry Olivier, and so on. And Jouvet himself, with all his quietness in acting, was very, very vivid. And I saw Helen Hayes and everything she did over and over and over again. I can't tell you how much I owe to Helen Hayes from the standpoint of just acting lessons. And Ruth Gordon also.

INTERVIEWER   In what sense did they, did these acting lessons, affect you?

FERRER   They seemed to shed a particular and specific and unique light on a play or scene that they touched, as though it had never been seen before.

INTERVIEWER   And how would something like that influence you?

FERRER   My imagination was touched off. I simply thought—well, there are personal skyrockets, you know, and eventually you have to come to the conclusion that maybe you have some of your own. And it isn't that I go around looking for effects, but I encourage letting intuition take off, because of these people who seem to me to have—well, the same thing that Ed Wynn used to do as a comic. Ed Wynn's comedy created a logic of its own; it had nothing to do with the way the world thought, you know. He took you into fairyland. Bert Lahr did, Bobby Clark.

INTERVIEWER   For instance, when you saw Alfred Lunt, what did you learn from him—or from Helen Hayes, or whomever you like? How is learning transmitted that way?

FERRER   Well, I'll tell you. They created in me a feeling of such blown-up compressions, as though you took a one-quart bottle and tried to jam two quarts of good acting into it. And boom—just as though there was a vitality, an explosion. Brooks Atkinson—who has, time and again, said a

* An organization of newspaper and magazine drama editors and reporters.

memorable thing in one sentence and a great many of whose criticisms of other actors I remember—once said, and I think it was about *Reunion in Vienna*, that Alfred Lunt took a funny line and sort of pursued it around the room until he cornered it where it couldn't escape, and then he just took it and shook it like a terrier until there was just nothing left of life and he had gotten everything out of it. And this is what Alfred did—he would just take something and he would trap it, you know, and nothing funny could escape him; and he just squeezed and squeezed and squeezed and threw away the dry sponge when the last drop of conceivable humor had been squeezed out of a joke. I was quoting Brooks again today; I was talking to somebody about acting, and they said, "Well, this is the kind of part I've never played and I don't know if I dare." And I said, "I want your particular kind of insanity in this play." And then they said, "Well, the word insanity frightens me." And I said, "You know, after Noel Coward and Gertrude Lawrence left *Private Lives* their replacements gave very, very good performances, but when Brooks Atkinson reviewed them, he said, 'They're fine but something of insanity has gone out of the performance.'" And I said, "He cherished the wrapped, twisted, refracted, prismatic view of life that Gertie and Noel brought to the play, and rightly so, because that's like the drawing of Daumier or the drawing of Goya; it's not the way anybody else in the world sees it and the minute you put something normal and sort of straightforward—well, we have that in life. Why pay money to see what you see when you walk down the street or ride the subway?" And that's what Alfred did, and that's what John does, and Larry does.

INTERVIEWER   It's less a matter of technique that you get than an inspiration.

FERRER   Yes, that's right. It's really inspiration, and it's a vista of the possibilities that lie before you.

INTERVIEWER   Well, I might suggest here—I begin to get a comprehension of what you're saying . . . When I was very young and playing the violin but with no intention of being a concert violinist, you know, but nevertheless when I went to hear, let us say, Elman or Heifetz, I would come home and for weeks I'd practice like crazy because they had done something to suggest the potential of this instrument. I could never be them, I never wanted to be them. But the point was that . . .

FERRER   That's right. That's right. But they made you want to be yourself; that's really what it boils down to: they made you want to be *you*. They gave you a glimpse of yourself. Because the creative impulse is conceited and is vain and is arrogant and says I can do it too. And you do it wrong and you fail, and you still say I can do it. That's the only way you get to be anything.

INTERVIEWER   What influences you in the choice of a role?

FERRER   I was talking to an actor yesterday, and he said, "I only read my lines when I read a play." I really in all sincerity have never, never been that way. I read the play, and if the play thrills me, then I say. "All right now, I'll consider the role." Now, if the role is one I think I can play, then the next step is: Is it a role that I want to play because it will show me off well enough, because it will increase my opportunities, or will it satisfy my vanity and everything else? And I'm not sidestepping the ego problem, I'm simply saying that that is not first with me. I certainly would never ever play a role because I thought that it was a great role and a lousy play. A play like *Edwin Booth,* for instance, was a disastrous failure everywhere. It was a failure in La Jolla, a failure in Los Angeles, a failure in San Francisco and a failure here. But I liked Edwin Booth because I liked the play. Right or wrong, I liked the play, not because I liked the part but because I liked the play. And within the framework of the play, I liked the part. But I certainly never did it because I liked the part and despised the play. I liked the play first.

INTERVIEWER   Once you've decided on a role, what are your procedures before the commencement of rehearsals; that is, what and how do you go about finding what we call the underlying truth of a role? In other words, how do you determine your motivations and your architecture?

FERRER   I can never do anything in a vacuum and I've never been able to do the things that all the modern hotshots recommend. I've never been able to sit in a room and say, "Now, here, I'll feel this," and just read a play over and over and over again and come through with pages black with notes. I just can't do it. I can't do it as a director and I cannot do it as an actor. I read a play often enough to make absolutely certain that I know what the emotional impact is on me, and if the emotional impact on me is one that I respect, then it is certainly the emotional impact I hope to create on the audience. And if it's one that the audience doesn't want, then its' my tough luck. Once I'm sure of this sort of thing I forget all about it until the first day of rehearsal, and then I see how the director affects me, how the cast affects me, how the author talks about the play, and I feel my way through with intuition, but I never come in with these voluminous prefabricated conclusions. And I speak with a certain amount of contempt, because I think the people who come in with their notebooks black with handwriting—and are always talking about letting things flow freely—have frozen everything long before it's time to freeze it.

INTERVIEWER This, I imagine, comes down to some discussion of the Stanislavsky system.

FERRER I think if they were a lot truer to Stanislavsky than they really are, they'd be a lot better off. I think the Method, the Group Theatre, and the whole dictatorial, arrogant people who say this is the only way to act and this is the only way to go to the theatre—I think they are rigid and dogmatic and unfluid and inflexible and everything that Stanislavsky was not. Because everything Stanislavsky ever wrote proves that he was a man who believed in improvisation at all times, who believed in the changing opinion of the creative artist—that if on Monday he felt something was true, on Tuesday he might feel the direct opposite was true. And these people are dogmatic to the point of . . .

INTERVIEWER Where do you think these Method people went off the track?

FERRER I think the Method people are merely a manifestation of something that has always existed: which is, the pedantic point of view as against the creative point of view. I think they call themselves the Method . . .

INTERVIEWER But they come from Stanislavsky.

FERRER So what? If Stanislavsky had never been born, they'd still be pedants. They'd have found another label.

INTERVIEWER Yes, but they use the Stanislavsky . . .

FERRER All right, so I'm not going to blame Stanislavsky for their incompetences. I think that they are using him and trying to make him small, but when their names will never be heard again, Stanislavsky's will live, because Stanislavsky was a vital force in the theatre and not simply a dogmatic . . . By definition, how can Stanislavsky's so-called Method, which was created for the period of 1890 in Russia, be valid today, seventy years later, in a period that has television, has the atom bomb, has radio and media of communication for actors that didn't exist for him.

INTERVIEWER Because, in a certain sense—and I like to take the devil's side—his influence on the theatre, on acting . . .

FERRER All right, then surely we did not need to wait until 1890 to have it. So you've defeated yourself. The thing is that the principle has always existed. If we had to wait until 1890 for Stanislavsky to be born, then acting didn't exist before, and if he hadn't been born, acting wouldn't exist today. This is baloney.

INTERVIEWER But his innovations in removing acting from the restrictions of a confining form were highly original and came out of his own approach.

FERRER No, it was a manifestation of realism that fitted in with Maupassant and flowed there in the novel, with Ibsen and Chekhov in the plays, with the whole painting school, with Debussy and the impressionists in painting and in music. He was part of his period of getting to a degree of realism that had been unknown before, because the industrial revolution and the changing political scene had brought the common man to a level where he was interesting, whereas before then kings and princes and so on had been interesting in the tragedies. This is an absolute economic and political factor, and he reflected his time, his values reflected his time, not that he invented something new. He was the *right* director for his period in history.

INTERVIEWER Then would you say that the Method people, instead of grasping their natural heritage, have taken a dead tack?

FERRER I certainly would say so. I would also say that whatever of life was left in it, they have very carefully tried to stamp out. I don't agree with the Method people that the Kim Stanleys and the Shelley Winters and the Marlon Brandos are their product. I think these people would have been there anyway, and the proof of the pudding is that most of these people went to the Method after they had established themselves, not before. They don't create. They say, "I gave Jason Robards his first job. I gave so-and-so his first job." So what? If you hadn't given Jason Robards his first job, somebody else would have given him his first job.

INTERVIEWER What do you think Stanislavsky can give today's actor?

FERRER I think he can give an enormous amount. Do you know that Stanislavsky—now Lawrence Langer told me this, so it's not my invention—came here and the Theatre Guild offered him a chance to direct and they said to him, "You can have as long to rehearse as you want. Equity allows twenty-eight days. You can have six, eight weeks, three months, and we'll foot the bills." He said, "I don't want that." He said, "I want two weeks or a year." Now, can you imagine any Method actor saying I'll put on a play in two weeks? And you know what Stanislavsky meant? What Stanislavsky meant was: "Let them learn the lines, we'll block out some movement, and then we'll get in front of an audience and we'll find out what the audience wants and we'll work with the audience, which is after all part of the cast." This is what he meant. Or, "We'll take the play and rehearse it in a lab, in a sort of workshop, for a year and really kind of dig into it and find things while we're playing at night and doing other things, and then we'll start putting that together and feeling our way." But it was never the arrogance. And there's another Stanislavsky story I'd like to tell you. Somebody said to him one day, "You wrote this and I read it and I don't understand what you mean." And he read it and he said, "I wrote this six months ago and I imagine I meant it then. Today it doesn't make any sense. I haven't a clue as to what this means." Now, this is a truly great man talking, not because he has humility but because he has honesty.

INTERVIEWER   Now, fundamental to both Stanislavsky and the Method, if I understand the matter right, is the development of character from the inside: understanding motives, studying the period in which the character lives, studying the reactions to his mother, his sister, the postman, and so on. It's an intense study of the character and putting yourself into that track. Is that not valid?

FERRER   Of course it's valid, but I think most of the Method actors apply the jargon and don't really do the job.

INTERVIEWER   For lack of their own insights?

FERRER   For the lack of talent, lack of talent. I would like to answer your questions. Since you're challenging, I would like to challenge you. What Method actor do you admire?

INTERVIEWER   Maureen Stapleton, for one.

FERRER   All right. Let us say that Maureen Stapleton had never heard of the Method, had never heard of considering the business about the aunt and the grandfather and the uncles, and so on and so forth. Do you think that Maureen Stapleton could ever give a truly bad performance with her gifts? No. Now, Laurette Taylor, who is rather like Maureen Stapleton, never heard of all this junk, but of course, if you come in the door and you have to say to yourself, "I was in a snowstorm," or, "I just saw my wife murdered," or, "I've been working all day and I'm tired," you just don't walk in blank unless you're the dreariest kind of a ham. So these great revelations that the Actors Studio takes on to itself as kind of the new coming of something or other, are standards. Surely, Hamlet in the corridor, when he sees the ghost of his father—the background of the character is built into anybody with talent; it's just unavoidable. The only thing I resent about the Method is not that I think the Method's methods are bad per se, I simply resent their arrogance. I have nothing against the Method. Of course, memory training and talking about the . . . This is all stimulating, but they seem to feel, or at least they imply—maybe I'm doing them a terrible injustice, and if I am, I apologize—but they imply that they *invented* acting, and I think they are just one more group of actors, nothing more and nothing less. And they have wonderful things, but dear Lord, they have a lot of dreadful actors who jargonize their way into a drawing room and look down on people who can earn a living, simply because they can say Stanislavsky this and Stanislavsky that and we're superior and we know. And they don't; they're just like everybody else. Talent is talent. What I'm saying is common sense. I'm not attacking the Method. I'm attacking the shabby exponents who use it as a shield to cover up their own shortcomings.

INTERVIEWER   When you're working on a role, do you relate your character to situations that you have observed in life or to experience?

FERRER   I'm sure I do. Even when I'm directing I talk at great length about things that have happened to me and about my memories of my father, who was a very great influence in my life, a man of whom I always felt that if I could ever live up to what I thought of him . . . Not that he ever tried to impose himself on me—but I'm always recalling examples of things he did. The only yardstick I have is the yardstick of what I have lived through, what I have read, what I have seen, what I have experienced, and I use it continually to stimulate myself and the people I work with.

INTERVIEWER   For instance, in the interview we had with Gielgud, he told us about his mother's death, as I recall it, and that when he would reach a certain line in a reading, he would think of her death and it became a real motivation for tears.

FERRER   Sure. Well, when I played . . . Do you remember *The Shrike*, that famous last scene*—I say famous, not

---

* A climactic scene in which Jim, played by Mr. Ferrer, at last acknowledges that his one escape from the horrors of a mental institution in which he has been incarcerated, is to be released into the custody of the scheming wife he hates—"Knowing in his heart he has simply exchanged one evil for another."

because I thought it was famous, but because people always say to me, even today, "When you made that phone conversation and you walked off." Well, I had to do that eight times a week, twice on Wednesday, twice on Saturdays. And you should know some of the things I did to myself in my own mind. At one point or another, I think I killed every single person that I loved—and I saw them lying there bleeding before me on their deathbeds—to work myself up to the point where I was moved. Because along about the third or fourth month of eight times a week, I can't be as stimulated by the situation as I was the first month; and I killed my father and my daughter and my best friend and his wife and my pet dog and my rabbit and my canary. Anything. I ran over strangers, I re-created how . . . Anything that would move me to the point where I was susceptible to an emotional impulse—and then I could, you know. Because I'm very, very honest. Just as I said, there are ten or twelve actors whom I imitated and was inspired by, I don't lie about these things. And you have to, eight times a week, week in and week out, month in and month out, use things like a junkie, you know—three jolts is no longer enough, you need four, and there you are. And the audience paid six dollars a seat, and what are you going to do—say, "I wasn't as good as I was on opening night. I got the notices, so stick it"? You can't say that, you have to give them their money's worth, so you use anything. And secretly you do terrible things to the people you love, if that's what you need. I think what John said is wonderful, but it's true you do, in a kind of a shameful way, use any tool at hand, and it isn't anything that you mean, but you use anything that moves you, you try to get it to move you again, too.

INTERVIEWER Again, Helen Hayes was telling me that when she was working on *Time Remembered,* she just couldn't get the duchess correctly, to satisfy herself; the director apparently wasn't helping or was not getting through to her. And she said she happened to turn on the radio in her room—at the Ritz in Boston, I believe—and she heard a discussion of the virginal, and someone played the virginal; and suddenly she got the whole spirit of this whacky duchess that she was going to play and the whole mood and tempo and imagination came to life. Have you had similar experiences?

FERRER I'll tell you something that I did which is not similar, but is similar at the same time. When *Othello* opened in the fall of '43 at the Shubert Theatre—and I enjoyed, you know, a very gratifying success in the role of Iago

—I read in the paper a week or two later that the Metropolitan Opera House was going to begin their season with *Boris Godunov* and that Pinza was going to sing Boris. So I wrote Pinza a letter and said, "Dear Mr. Pinza: I read that you were going to do Boris. This is to wish you good luck and to thank you for the many, many performances that I have enjoyed at the Metropolitan, and to tell you how often I went there to study your acting"—which I did. And I said, "Sometime, now that we are a hit, if you would like to see *Othello*, it might be interesting for you to see how much my Iago is your Don Giovanni." And that's how I met Ezio Pinza.

INTERVIEWER   Did he see, in what you did, anything you got from him?

FERRER   He never asked me, he never said. Pinza was a very modest man; in spite of his reputation, he was a very modest man and a very exquisite man, and the stories you hear about him I cannot reconcile with anything that I ever saw him do. They must be true, because you hear them on all sides, but my impression is that Pinza was just one of the most glorious people I have ever met and a man who is truly, truly, truly modest despite his fame, his position, his good looks and his many, many feminine conquests. I adored him, and I think he was a great artist, as an actor, certainly as an operatic actor, as well as a singer. But I, fumbling through my first experience with Shakespeare, used him definitely to—as a kind of stylistic yardstick. I don't think my performance was like anything Pinza would have done, but in my mind it was a translation. And when Helen says that she heard a virginal and—somewhere there is a parallel.

INTERVIEWER   For instance, when you prepared for your role in *The Shrike*—or take any example—you read the play, obviously, and as elements of the acting suggested themselves, did they come from your experience?

FERRER   I think so. I think *The Shrike* is very close to my experience.

INTERVIEWER   For instance, I know Anne Bancroft, for *The Miracle Worker*, studied at a blind institute, et cetera. Does that ever come into it?

FERRER   I think that's good for some people. But I, too, like the Actors Studio, have my own arrogances, and they consist in the fact that outside of specific techniques, like, for instance, if I had to play a radio operator, I would want to learn the Morse code or at least understand the bloody thing, because you know, you can't imitate. But short of that, I don't know. I think that just the way Shakespeare wrote about islands in the Aegean and wrote about Milan and Syracuse, and so on, and Cyprus and France and everything else, that if the basic concepts are true, what the hell. Now, techniques are different. When I played Toulouse-Lautrec, when I played Dreyfus, when I played people like that, I did an enormous amount of specific research because there I was dealing with some very concrete things, you know. But if I had to play... Well, in the case of Bellevue and *The Shrike,* I talked to Joe Kramm, the author, at length about his experiences in Bellevue and other hospitals, where he worked as a technician, as a consultant, and then I purified my own thinking to the point where I realized that a mental hospital for the character in *The Shrike* is not a hospital, is not a place where you're cured, it's a prison that you want to get out of. So I just said, "What do the doctors do, what do the nurses do?" and how do you give injections and then the rest is just... The hell with it, I'm going to play in prison, I'm not going to play, you know... Now, the funny thing is—this is a funny story—one day I said to Joe, "Listen, I'm going to go down to Bellevue." We were in rehearsals, see. And Joe's a good director. So I said, "Run all the scenes that I'm not in and I'll go down to Bellevue and just sniff around. I want to listen to the sounds and look at the faces and get the smells and the feel of the place. And I'll be back in an hour or two." And he said, "Fine." So I started out, and as I was going out the stage door an actor was coming in, bringing coffee for the cast, and he said, "Where are you going?" And I said, "I'm going down to Bellevue and look around," and I made the same speech. And he said, "Boy, wouldn't it be funny if you took the wrong turn and a door clicked closed behind you and pretty soon the word came downstairs, 'There's a nut up here who says he's José Ferrer'?" I said, "That's all, Jack." I walked right back into the room. I suddenly got terrified. That's the amount of research—it took me as far as the stage door.

INTERVIEWER You said before that *The Shrike* was very close to you. Would it be personal asking you what you meant by that?

FERRER It wouldn't be personal because I don't know why it was close to me, but it was close to me. I've never had any mental disturbance other than saying, "I've got a flop," or, "Where's my next job coming from?" or, "I'm unhappy at home," or something, you know. But I've never been truly, deeply nervous—I don't know what it is, but somewhere along in my background, I had sufficient insecurity to understand this trapped man and this trapped feeling. I don't

know why, because there's nothing in my life that's parallel
to it, but I sure as hell . . . I was out on that wave length,
boy, very close, very, very close. It wasn't an invention, that
performance. That performance was a true identification.
And I don't know—I suppose if I dug deeply enough I would
find the answer—but I sure as hell . . .

INTERVIEWER   Does that make it easier or harder?

FERRER   Oh, it makes it wonderfully easy. Easy from the
standpoint that you know you have the tools. Now, you still
have to do the hard work, but, boy, when you tune in on
something like that! But believe me, I feel the same way
about Iago—something in my background—(he made a popping sound) there it goes. For the same reason, I am as close
to Iago as I was to *The Shrike,* and can you imagine two
characters more diametrically opposed?

INTERVIEWER   How important is technique to an actor?
And what are techniques, by the way?

FERRER   Techniques are the following: First of all, I
believe in techniques. To get back to the Actors Studio—a lot
of these people say, "Well, I'm going to go out there and feel
it." Well, I just say you can't feel anything eight times a
week for six months or a year. I just don't think you can.
I think you can turn talent on and off. I think you have to
have techniques. Surely—and again to relate to you as a
writer—there are times when a story excites you more
than another story does. When you say, "By golly, I'm going
to really write the piece or column of all times." Or at other
times you say, "Jesus Christ, I wish I didn't have to do this
story tonight." Well, all right, but as a pro you have to do it,
and that's what I mean about techniques. Techniques hold
you up. Techniques give you a high basic minimum below
which you don't fall. In the case of certain people, it's here;
in the case of others, it's up there. But somewhere along
the line it's a platform below which you don't fall. That's
what a technique is. As an actor, I have to play a matinée
of Iago or Cyrano de Bergerac, two very, very taxing roles,
or *The Shrike,* and then come back three hours later and,
boom, do it all over again. And then I have to do the same
thing again on Saturday, when I've got the weight of six performances behind me with no rest. I've got to be good for
matinée ladies who might not be interested in that aspect;
I have to be good for drunken whozits; I have to be good for
a sharp audience that demands only the best; I have to be
good for children; I have to be good for whoever it is. I
may have a cold, I may have a hangover, maybe I couldn't
sleep the night before, maybe my wife left me, maybe my

child died, maybe my lawyer said, "You are broke and you are in bankruptcy." Who knows what happened to me?—my voice, my body, my everything has to work for me. This is what techniques are. I mean, if you go to Carnegie Hall—again, I keep using Heifetz and Horowitz and Toscanini—what the hell do you care about what happened to Toscanini in Riverdale that morning, or to Heifetz, you know, the fact that he was on a plane and didn't get any sleep. You paid your six dollars to Carnegie Hall and you want to hear da-da-da-di-da, and that's all you care about, and it's the only time maybe you're ever going to hear Heifetz for the next five years. If he feels lousy, that's his tough luck.

INTERVIEWER To be specific . . .

FERRER Techniques are methods of producing automatic results, which therefore liberate your intuition and your inspiration. To be concrete: Before Caruso can sing a high C, he has muscles that he has to warm up and exercise and make sure in what condition they are that day for the high C. Before Pancho Gonzales can serve an ace, he serves a lot of practice aces and hits a lot of practice balls on that court, and before that he's been practicing on another tennis court for a couple of hours that we haven't seen. Before Horowitz walks into Carnegie Hall, he's got a piano in his dressing room and he does scales, he looks over the difficult passages of the Chopin or the Grieg or the Bach or whatever it is he's going to do. Before Joe Louis or Sugar Ray Robinson walks into the ring, he flexes his muscles, he's been training for weeks. The techniques are the automatic habits that you develop, which without thinking stand you in good stead so that no matter what is assailing you, your guard goes up, you rush to the net. If you're in the water and drowning, you do this (gasping for air), and you keep on breathing until the lifeguard gets to you. Techniques are good, good, good habits that save your life. They're the key to the door that lets you into the room of inspiration. I don't know how else to describe it.

INTERVIEWER How do you develop those techniques?

FERRER Well, by watching the guys and the people who know how to do it, and saying, "How do they do it? It looks so easy." You try it. "I can't do it. They did it easily. I'm doing it not at all." And go back and go back and then find the exercises, and exercise and exercise. And I think the key to techniques is really relentless self-criticism and saying, "I failed, I failed, I failed." Because as long as you say I failed, if you got what it takes, you'll try to succeed, and one day you'll find it. Again back to the Actors Studio—if one of these people would admit once that they are lousy, they would be ten times as good as they are. I sound rather unsympathetic to the Actors Studio, but the only thing I'm rabid against is the arrogance of these babies.

INTERVIEWER You evidently have encountered this in the direction . . .

FERRER I've encountered enough, and I've been treated like a flunky by these people—which doesn't make me lose face, it makes them lose face. But at the same time, I'm troubled if a child of mine, or a child of anybody's, says to me, "You're crazy," after asking me a question. I would say, "There's something wrong with that child, because he really thinks he knows more than I do about something he's only experienced once or twice." And I have always been both humble and arrogant. I've felt there wasn't anything in the world I couldn't do if I wanted it bad enough. But I've also said, "I don't know how to do it yet." And I'm still at that point. At the age of forty-eight, I still say there isn't *anything* I can't do, but also I say if I try and can't make it, I admit to that. That doesn't mean that I'm not going to make it some day, but I haven't made it yet. I think these people talk as though they had reached the goal. They know the answers to everything, they are contemptuous of other people. I think their methods are fine, but they themselves don't do what they claim to do. That is the big beef.

INTERVIEWER Do you see this when you are rehearsing actors in your own play?

FERRER I haven't had many shows lately. I see it in their performances. I think their performances are ridiculous, most of them.

INTERVIEWER Now, you worked with Herbert Berghof, for instance. Berghof is a Method disciple, isn't he?

FERRER I don't know what he is. He's a combination of a lot of things. A kind heart and other things. He's not just Method.

INTERVIEWER When you're acting, do you have a set of different habits in contrast to when you are not acting? That is, in terms of keeping yourself in condition?

FERRER Yes. When I'm acting, my day begins at eight or eight-thirty—or two-thirty whenever there's a matinée. Normally I get up at around six-thirty in the morning, and I treasure those quiet hours before the noise begins and I work, and I generally go to bed early at night. But when I'm acting, my dressing room, strangely enough, becomes a drawing room and I almost never leave the theatre—and every year it becomes later and later—until twelve-thirty or one, one-thirty in the morning. People come and see me, and I bring out a drink, and I take hours to unlimber, and I then go out and get some food, and I get to bed about four or five and I sleep as late as I can, and then I go back to sleep at six in the evening and sleep for an hour before I go to the theatre. My day must begin at eight-thirty at night—so I must come in charged with energy. So my habits change to the point where I can bust out of bed and I say, "I'm going to lick the world today." This is very important.

INTERVIEWER There was a time when you were producing something and directing something else.

FERRER No matter. I always went to sleep at five or six in the afternoon. Everything stopped in the afternoon; I slept an hour or two before the performance.

INTERVIEWER Do you change your diet at all when you're acting?

FERRER No. But I always eat steaks and sliced tomatoes.

INTERVIEWER When do you find that you enjoy working on a part most?

FERRER After I've learned my lines. The nightmare of learning a part is learning the lines—for me. That's just a terror period when I just lock myself in a room with either myself or myself and somebody else and just read them over and over again. And then suddenly there's one morning when you wake up and know all your lines and then the *real* fun of rehearsing begins. I think the period of rehearsing, after you know your lines, when everything begins to sort of flower and things come to bloom and grow—that's the glorious thing. And the first month or two of playing for New York audiences is also marvelous. But I think the rehearsal period is the most thrilling period of them all, for me as an actor.

INTERVIEWER I gather long runs are difficult for you.

FERRER They're difficult for me because for one thing I don't know how to remain fresh for a year or two. It's a complicated question and a complicated answer. For another thing audiences change. In your first month you have the audiences who are habitual theatregoers and who know about plays and acting, and so forth and so on. This is something that's never said, but it's true. You have the subtle values in the first month. Then you have very good vital audiences for two or three months, who come from not the "21" Club set or Sardi's, but people who still have access to the tickets in the first rows. Then you begin to get audiences from more outlying districts, and surely after four or five or six months the audience taste-level is different. I won't say it's lower, because I'm not a judge of values, but it's certainly not the same. It is not the tastes of Brooks Atkinson or Walter Kerr, and it is not the taste of the people who go to first nights. And the things that they demand of a comedy are different. They laugh at different things in a comedy; and in a tragedy or serious play, a drama, they react to different values, and to those of us who are in the profession the values become coarser and cruder and blunter. And it's all very well to say, "I will give the same performance every night." This is baloney! How are you going to play a comedy the same to an audience that laughs at one thing as you would to an audience that laughs at another thing. You can't. At least, I can't.

INTERVIEWER I once heard an actress say that she found her role got richer all the time, because she found new things in it.

FERRER I think that's true. For me, this is true up to, I would say, five or six months, and then I stop finding new things in it. Now, I know in the case of *Othello* we played for a season, and then we laid off for six weeks and started again in September. And in September I came back to the role as if I'd never played it before, except that it was a deeper and more wonderful and significant experience for me. The layoff had helped me—the rest had helped me. An I think we were much better for several months, and when I say "we" I mean Paul Robeson, Uta Hagen and myself. And I would say that certainly, now speaking for myself, by the time May rolled around in the second season, I had gotten back into the doldrums, and I know when I played the City Center in June of the same year, I was justly criticized for not being nearly as good—and I wasn't nearly as good because two years of the same role had robbed it of its mystery for me, and I said to myself, "Well, we're sold out, and I'm bored to tears, and I know they come to see . . . Well, what the hell, I'll throw up the imitation smoke screen and most of them won't know the difference and the ones who do, saw me when I was good." And I say these things, but I don't know how many actors are willing to be as honest as I am being now, as I have been, because I know that I just don't do the job after a long run that I do at first. And this is why I don't want long runs—not because I'm lazy, not because I'm capricious and want to throw power around and say, "I've had a hit, I'm successful and therefore I want to . . ." It isn't that. It's that I know that at a given point my particular personality and my particular temperament begin not to be able to do the job that has to be done, and if I go on pretending to do it, I've got to pretend. It's not the real thing. When I was in *Charley's Aunt* I played until May or something like that, and I remember I went to Florida for two weeks and then came back and played the Bronx and Brooklyn and Maplewood in June or July. Well, just the two weeks—when I came back, gosh, everything was back, the freshness was back, the enthusiasm was back. And in May, my performance was really wilting, you know. I didn't see the mystery in the comedy any more.

INTERVIEWER The awful thing now, with the economics of the theatre, is these long runs are a necessity for anybody who's going to make money. I don't know what the answer is.

FERRER Right. I don't know what the answer is at all. I don't know.

INTERVIEWER Has your experience suggested to you some ideal world in which you would like to act? And what is that?

FERRER Yes, it did.

INTERVIEWER Repertory would be one, wouldn't it?

FERRER Repertory would be one. But if the American theatre doesn't want repertory, as maybe it doesn't, I always dreamt of—I remember I once used to talk very bravely, and I still look back with regret that I couldn't pull it off—when I thought I would play a six-month season on Broadway every year and then go out and tour for six months, and that every two years I would do a different play so that the investors and the producers and the playwright had a good crack at it. I would say that I would rehearse in August, play Boston and Philadelphia in September, open in New York in October, and if we're successful, God willing, close in April or May, take the summer off, then, boom, September start touring and tour again until April or May and cover the country. I always dreamed of playing a play a season in New York and then touring it. I always find touring very stimulating. But, of course, a home and children—all those things—affect your judgment. This is my little old dream of repertory which I didn't think anyone in my time could pull off in New York. Because Eva* tried, and other people have tried, and I tried at the City Center and, you know, we just never did. It's foolish to kid ourselves, we didn't. I don't think the taste of either the public or the

* Eva Le Gallienne's Civic Repertory Theatre.

critics will permit true repertory. You know, it's all very well to say that the Old Vic did *Oedipus* and *Henry IV, Part One* and *Henry IV, Part Two* and *Uncle Vanya,* and it's all right to say Jean-Louis Barrault did this and that. But let's just have the Old Vic and Jean-Louis Barrault around here for two years and see what happens to that fine, lovely acting company. They would not be written about in those glowing terms. We would get used to them and bored with them.

INTERVIEWER   There is a theory that actors must never stop working, they must continue to cultivate their minds and train their talents systematically. What has been your procedure along these lines?

FERRER   I have always felt that almost any human experience contributed to an actor's experience. I was born in Puerto Rico, came to New York at the age of six, and then shuttled back and forth between New York and Puerto Rico, and then at the age of twelve began sporadically to live in Europe. I speak three languages well, two others badly. I play two or three musical instruments. I majored in architecture in college and started to prepare for a master's and a Ph.D. in modern languages and all of these strange, unrelated, curious things have helped me as an actor.

INTERVIEWER   Do you see any correlation in other performers, between the rather rich life such as your own and their own?

FERRER   Indeed I do. Orson Welles, for instance, who certainly—I'm not talking about what he's done, I'm talking about what he's capable of doing, which are two different things—Orson Welles is one of the most enormous talents, one of the most gifted human beings of this or any other generation as a director and a producer. I think that his concepts of a production—certainly to my knowledge—have never been matched. And my knowledge is not all that extensive, but he is one of the most visionary and hugely scaled directors and producers of all time. He is a citizen of the world. Orson draws very well, knows all literature, knows a good deal about politics—and Orson sitting still at a café table would be investigating human existence. He could never stop training himself. Larry Olivier in *The Entertainer* sang, you know, with great musicality. As I remember, in *Romeo and Juliet* he composed music, designed costumes, designed scenery, and directed and everything else. And the fact that *Romeo and Juliet* was a failure does not detract from the fact that he has all these capabilities. I've mentioned two sort of Renaissance men, universal talents, who can do anything. But the fact remains that anybody of any real talent whom you mention is always doing something, always gardening or reading or writing or painting or manufacturing little things or walking down a country lane or something. The creative artist is a restless person, and whatever he does to interest himself in his spare time adds to his fertility and brings to his work a range of references. And, you know, the older you grow the more you realize that all things in the world are the same anyway, so that whether it's an astronomer looking at Mars or a guy saying that he hopes he'll grow prize-winning peonies in this year's Mount Kisco garden show—they're part of human experience. And I think it's the intensity of desire and the enthusiasm for participation in life that I think really—I'm fumbling a little bit and I'm being terribly general—but what I'm saying is that the feeling of waking up, walking into the theatre, or the curtain going up and coming onto the stage, with some kind of desire that is passionate, is really what it is all about. I think that kind of a person is always doing something to develop himself as an artist. Just reading a book is one way to develop yourself. Thinking is another way. But I think that when Tallulah Bankhead and Ethel Barrymore watch baseball games and go to the prize fights or . . . I once saw a picture of Rex Harrison on Long Island, when he was in *My Fair Lady*, and he had on the dirtiest, oldest pair of slacks and a moth-eaten sweater and a pair of sneakers—and I looked at this picture and said, as a fellow actor, I said, "This is why he is a great actor, because he can wear this kind of sloppy . . . This is one way he recharges himself." I think for that kind of a person almost everything you do is preparation.

INTERVIEWER And I suppose a certain sensitivity and ability to get out of any experience the essence of the experience, like Emily Dickinson, who as a poet had such tremendous wisdom although she stayed in one place, but her ability was . . .

FERRER Her wisdom is terrifying. It's a shaft, isn't it?

INTERVIEWER And to draw out from the very simple experiences, whereas another person would not have found that at all.

FERRER I think if you do the things that you care about and you love, then you get something out of them. Surely an actor who sits around in a café and flashes his dimples at the ladies who stumble into the restaurant for lunch or for dinner—and that's all he does—well, he'll bring these shallow experiences to the theatre.

INTERVIEWER That extends to drama reviewing.

FERRER   It extends to everything. We're all in the same racket, you know, whether it's acting or writing or anything else, and it does ... Your concern for the quality of these interviews is an example of a desire for something that satisfies you, whether it sells or not, as against someone who says that he's going to try something that will fit the public taste of the year 1900 and X. If this book—your book—never sells more than twenty copies, you'll still be proud of it because you both know you did your best. And now I'm looking at you as a director, and this is what you're doing. You're profoundly concerned with doing the very best you can. You're not ad-libbing this. It's a carefully prepared thing, and, therefore, it means something to you, and your whole life brings to bear on this moment—the standards that have been created for you and those you have created for yourself. It's true of actors.

INTERVIEWER   What have you done about cultivating your voice?

FERRER   I have spent thousands of dollars on good voice teachers, phony voice teachers.

INTERVIEWER   These lessons are for singing, I understand, but is this with the planned idea of developing your speaking voice?

FERRER   Yes, speaking voice. When I opened in *Brother Rat* in Baltimore in 1936, I strained my voice or I caught a cold or something. I don't remember what it was. And by the end of the week I thought I was going to have to miss performances. And I sort of croaked my way through the week in Baltimore, and I hoped my voice would come back to me for opening night in New York. It was my first big role on Broadway. My voice wasn't there opening night before the show. The curtain went up and I came on, and, I had that extra cupful of adrenalin—it wasn't anything conscious, it just happened. And suddenly, boom, my throat opened up and, clap, there it was. And then it disappeared again for another ten days afterwards. But at that point I became acutely aware—talking about techniques, this is technique —I became acutely aware that I didn't have the technique to say, "I know how to use my voice, I know how to rest it, I know how to protect it." And so that's when I started taking singing lessons. And I've taken them ever since, and I'm still taking them.

INTERVIEWER   You have proved to yourself and to theatre-going audiences that you can speak admirably. What more do you want?

FERRER   You can never speak admirably enough. You

can hit this note, but there are notes higher that you can still hit. I—again in my total honesty—I don't think I have an instrument comparable to Maurice Evans' voice, which is a great, great speaking voice, and I know that I can't do the things vocally that he can do, but on the other hand I don't despair of one day being able to do them. And I may die without being able to do them, but I still bank on the hope of being able to do them. And it's all like somebody who lifts five pounds and says I can lift ten. He lifts ten and then he says he can lift twenty and one day he'll say he can lift one hundred, and so on. And so some fellow runs the four-minute mile, and Valery Brumel jumps the seven-foot high jump. Well, you dangle before yourself ever increasingly difficult horizons as you develop because instead of defending a mediocre bastion, you always want to be reaching for the impossible. Because there is no impossible; you won't make it, but you have the stepping stone from which somebody else will make it, you know. And you're part of the thing. And this is why I'm spending a fortune training my voice. My voice will never satisfy me, I see only its faults. Other people hear its virtues, but I only hear its faults, and I see how much better than my voice Gielgud's is, and how much better than my voice Laurence Olivier's is, and how much better than my voice Maurice Evans' is. Well, maybe they hear things in my voice that they . . . Well, I don't know, but the point is I—when the day comes when I feel I can't grow, that's the time when I leave that particular art, because then I'm saying, "All right. Come on, you bastards, I'll fight you off. I'm defending my corner." I don't want to defend my corner. I want to be in the open market and I'll spend my life taking my hat off to other talents. I admire talent, I think the world is full of great wonderful people, and I feel privileged to have been in their company and to be numbered as kind of a successful actor. But, boy, if I could do half the things I think I should be able to do, wow!

INTERVIEWER What do you think you should be able to do?

FERRER I think I should be ten times the actor that I am, ten times the anything that I am. If I ever wanted to make an inventory of my faults, I would confound my critics, because I would show them things that I can't do that they never dreamed I couldn't do.

INTERVIEWER When you say that, what are you aiming at? I don't mean in specifics, but are you aiming at giving a performance which will knock hell out of the audience?

FERRER There are two things. You want to please yourself and you want to please the audience. And if you please the audience, you're grateful that you pleased them, but unless you're a jerk, you don't deceive yourself as to the things that you set out to do and didn't do, either.

INTERVIEWER I mean—I guess every writer has some model. He would like to have the impact, say of a Dreiser, or a Zola, for instance, or would like to be known for his style.

FERRER Or like to be Ernest Hemingway or Joseph Conrad.

INTERVIEWER Yes, and as an actor, do you have some ultimate ...?

FERRER No, you see, there's a difference. When you write, you are digging something out of yourself. When you act, you are using someone else's material. I could aim at somebody else's success. I could say, "I wish that when I arrived in England the Queen wanted to meet me," or, "I wish that when I arrived here, there, or elsewhere, I had the acclaim that so-and-so had." But if you say to yourself, "I wish I could be as good an actor as he is or she is," then what you're saying really is, "I wish I could be as good as I can be." And that's a different thing. And in order to be as good as you can be, you have to, again, go back to Shakespeare, Ibsen or Chekhov, or Robert Sherwood, or Tennessee Williams. And it's a different thing. At this point no writer ever had to say is my *Hamlet* as good as so-and-so's—unless he decides to write *Hamlet* again, which is not the case. But I don't wish to be as good as anybody else. I have, naturally, been human and envied the success of other people. I wish that Sam Spiegel and MGM and Warner's and everybody else wanted me instead of Alec Guinness or Marlon Brando or somebody else, but they don't. I don't think any the less of myself for that. I regret it, and I know that on Broadway I'm still very desirable, and so forth. But I do, when I have a success, say to myself, "I did these things well enough so that they praise me. There are other things, other aspects of this particular role that I didn't do so well." You know, if I were to make a list of the things I think I did wrong in *Cyrano* and still think I would do wrong and don't know whether I'd ever be able to do right—it would make a ... You know, the film of *Cyrano*, which got me an Academy Award, I've seen once, and I own a print of it and my wife runs it every so often. I leave the room. I can't bear to see it. I suffer.

INTERVIEWER You really want perfection in your art, don't you?

FERRER I know the things that I do well before anyone else does. I also know the things I do not do as well as I should, and I always say to myself that I should be able to find a way to do them.

INTERVIEWER Because you've played such a wide range of roles, you are a particularly apt subject for discussing the playing of comedy, drama and farce. What are the differences and what are the difficulties?

FERRER I don't find any difficulties, and I don't think anybody who has a sense of humor, and who has talent as an actor, does. I find the same problems in any play, whether it's *Charley's Aunt* or *Othello*. I think that—going back to the two actors whom I most admire on the English-speaking stage, John and Larry—they're both wonderful comedians. They both have a magnificent bubble of humor, burbling away inside of them with their own secret laughter going, when they come on the stage in a comedy role. And they are both great tragedians. And I don't think that either form is easy or difficult for them. I think both forms present the same problems. To me, it's a play. The curtain rises at eight-forty and goes down at eleven, and I have to keep my end of the interest alive during that time. And one is just as difficult and just as much fun as the other. If I'm moved by the play to begin with, then my problem is to convey what I feel.

INTERVIEWER Then you don't find it harder to play comedy or drama, because theoretically . . .

FERRER They're both exhausting.

INTERVIEWER But theoretically it's supposed to be more difficult to play comedy well, than it is to play drama. O'Casey has said that, and someone . . .

FERRER It's only more difficult because it's easier to cry than it is to laugh. Most people have a sense of sorrow but very few people have a true sense of fun, not at laughing at a joke, but fun. How many people do you know who will walk down the street and see somebody picking his nose, for instance, and who will laugh for the next week because of the expression on the man's face. Now this is really—you know, I'm pulling something out of the air—but this is really the sense of fun where . . .

INTERVIEWER The sense of the ridiculous, in a way.

FERRER That's right, and where you'll laugh at somebody else, as you'd laugh at yourself, because you see yourself in them. Not just the cruel laughter of slipping on a banana peel, which is the property of the envious man, who says, "Well, by heavens, the banker fell on his rear, so I'm straight." I'm not talking about that. I'm talking about the thing that makes you just chuckle and chuckle and chuckle even if it's at your own expense, because you know it's so doggoned funny that it deserves to be laughed at for the rest of your life. And for those actors, comedy is no more difficult for them than anything else. But certainly, for a square, let us say, who doesn't have that capacity, then comedy is very difficult indeed. It becomes gim-cracky.

INTERVIEWER What do you regard as the most complex role that you've ever undertaken on the stage? What has been the toughest one, the most complicated?

FERRER Probably Iago.

INTERVIEWER Why?

FERRER Well, Shakespeare's the greatest playwright that I've ever worked for, and, believe me, I've worked for them all—and gratefully. Iago had concomitant difficulties for me. Until I started rehearsing in *Othello,* you know, Shakespeare's language was gibberish to me. Today I pick up Shakespeare for relaxation. I read *Titus Andronicus or Pericles, Prince of Tyre* or *Timon of Athens* or *Troilus and Cressida,* or any of the obscure plays, the way I might read Dashiell Hammett or anything else I read for fun, because Shakespeare's language has become my vocabulary through the years and it's a pleasurable experience to taste that succulent meat, which are his words. But when I went to rehearsal in *Othello,* I didn't know what the hell I was saying and Margaret Webster, the director, had to translate, as it were, *"la plume de ma tante"* for me. Also, you know, Cyrano is an operatic role and therefore fascinating and graceful, but, psychologically, very simple compared to a Shakespearean role. *The Silver Whistle* I adored as a role and it's a performance of mine that I respect. I would dangle that as one of my kind of little crown jewels. But, you know, the motives of the Shakespearean plays and the tragedies are so enormous and so big in scale that they dwarf the *Shrikes* and the *Silver Whistles,* which, from the standpoint of the actor, are just as taxing except that you can do them the way you would sing. After all, a Rodgers and Hammerstein song is a great, great musical experience, but they are not writing Verdi operas, and that's the difference, I suppose. I don't say that one is better than the other. I just say one gives you more, demands more, and you work harder. I'm not passing moral judgment; I'm simply saying which one taxes me most.

INTERVIEWER Which of your screen roles would you say was most complex?

FERRER That's somewhat difficult to answer. One thing about the screen—any medium that can have Veronica Lake or Gary Cooper or people like that as a star—it's not an acting medium, it's a personality medium. I'm not taking anything away from it, because, you know, I think Marilyn Monroe and these people are fabulous talents when properly used, but it's not an acting medium, it's a personality medium. So, therefore, to a trained actor, acting on the screen is not difficult.

INTERVIEWER Would you care to talk about the difference between acting on the screen and acting on the stage?

FERRER Sure.

INTERVIEWER You know, I've never heard it crystallized in that way, that the stage is an acting medium, whereas the screen is a personality medium.

FERRER People tend to look down on certain forms and to look up to others. I don't have any snobbishness about anything. I don't look down—I suppose by mentioning it, I imply that. But I will use somebody else's yardstick. I don't look down on burlesque, for instance. I don't look down on an opening act in vaudeville or an acrobatic act in night clubs. I think that they have a tough row to hoe, and, if anything, harder. Somebody who comes out and juggles six balls on the edge of his nose while a lot of people are walking into a night club so that they can hear Lena Horne—who's got a tougher job, Lena Horne or the poor bastard with six balls on his nose? Well, the answer is obvious. Screen acting is not the same kind of acting as stage acting. In stage acting, you have to reach the second balcony with your voice, you have to do it live from beginning to end eight times a week, you have to play to an audience that comes in on time, sits in numbered seats, can't smoke, no teen-agers—a whole disciplined thing of the stage audience, which I am naturally in favor of, as against the stumbling in and out of mothers with children, you know, and the Safeway market and the A & P and delinquents and everything else in the movie theatre. Now the greats of films, barring a few exceptions, are great personalities rather than great acting talents. Naturally, a Leslie Howard, a Spencer Tracy, a Paul Muni, a Monty Clift, a Gregory Peck, a Jack Lemmon, Kirk Douglas, Burt Lancaster—all these people in my opinion are tremendous acting talents and would be successful actors in any medium they chose to act in. But they are also great personalities. This is where they are fortunate. Then you have the Lana Turners, the Marilyn Monroes, the

Gary Coopers, et cetera, et cetera, who are not so much great actors as great personalities. But because they are great personalities in the right medium, it permits them to give wonderful, wonderful, wonderful performances. Certainly nobody can say that Gary Cooper in *Mr. Deeds Goes to Town* was anything less than great, and after all, Gary Cooper got an Academy Award for *High Noon*. Marilyn Monroe in *Bus Stop*—I challenge any actress that ever lived to give a better performance than Marilyn Monroe did in *Bus Stop*. To me, it's one of the great, great woman performances of all time. And when people remember Jean Harlow, they think of her as a first-rate actress, which she was not in stage terms but which she was in film terms.

INTERVIEWER   As a personality.

FERRER   That's right, and a personality with acting talent for that frame. And why do we remember Rudolph Valentino, Wallace Reid, Tom Mix and William S. Hart and, if I wanted to say it, Hoot Gibson and Ken Maynard? Because their personalities were vivid for the purposes of their films. Now, acting is a different thing entirely on the stage. I don't think that a stage actor, a good stage actor, can give a bad performance on the screen. But, on the other hand, unless his face and romantic appeal and so on are pleasing in our country, in America, he doesn't have too much of a chance to become a big, big star. In France, in England or in Germany, a Walter Huston would have been the biggest star in the country. And, indeed, certainly Walter is one of the greatest actors who ever lived. We don't have a Raimu, we don't have a Fernandel, we don't have that kind of a star. And, you know, it's significant that Alec Guinness is a star in England and not really here—*River Kwai* notwithstanding. Let's just see how many starring roles Guinness is given again in America. He had a couple of cracks at things here and he didn't make it, he didn't get it, because we don't want that kind of a star. They do in Europe.

INTERVIEWER   In films, you mean.

FERRER   Yes, in films.

INTERVIEWER   Why do you say Walter Huston was one of the greatest actors? I'm interested in the concept of a great actor.

FERRER   Just because every time I saw him do anything he just hit me sort of deeper in the pit of the stomach than most actors ever did. I just thought that he was the end. In *The Barker* and *The Treasure of the Sierra Madre*, and even ... I will never forget, I was on tour with *Othello* in Detroit, and way up Jackson Boulevard somewhere they were playing something with Jane Russell, you know, and I went up there just to see what this low-cut dress was really like—and I want to tell you that when Walter Huston came on the screen, I was paralyzed with the impact of his talents. *The Outlaw*—did you ever see that film? Well, if it ever comes within your range, go and catch half an hour or forty-five minutes and see what Walter Huston could do in a shoddy . . .

INTERVIEWER And yet he failed in *Othello* here.

FERRER I didn't see it. He shouldn't have failed in *Othello*. Maybe the direction wasn't right. Maybe his range didn't include the heroic. I don't know. But I think that Walter Huston . . . I think we've had several great actors that we never . . . I think Frank Morgan was a great, great actor who is not remembered as a great actor. I think Richard Bennett was a great actor.

INTERVIEWER When you say great actor—again, to try to pin this down a little more—is this because of the impact that he is able to make upon an audience, a somewhat mysterious quality, perhaps?

FERRER The impact, impact, impact. If you are supposed to cry and he makes you cry more deeply . . . Let me just give you an example of what I think. The secret of great acting, I suppose, is that somewhere inside the actor something happens that just hits the audience so hard. Now, naturally, one of my arrogances is that if I'm in the audience and I'm hit hard, I don't care if nine thousand other people are not hit hard. I was hit hard and I'm damned if I'm going to ignore my pain, you know. Now Henry Fonda, for instance, is to me one of the guys whose capacity as an actor, emotionally, is limitless. I think Henry Fonda is capable of fantastic things, but the fact may be that either the world in which he lived or his own particular predilections didn't lead him to it. I remember I saw him in a picture one time, and I saw a trailer of the picture and there was a scene—I don't know what the picture was, I never saw the picture—but there was a scene where he was married to a young girl and he came to his father's house and his father was a sort of millionaire and a privileged tycoon, and Hank came in dressed in dirty clothes and said, "This is my wife," and introduced her, and so forth. And a scene developed between him and his father, and the father struck him across the face, which was a terrible thing to see happen on the screen if you felt about your father the way I felt about mine. And this man hit him, and Hank just stood there with his kind of gaunt, flat face and his deep eyes, and the father said, "You are talking to your father," and Hank said, "You are talking about my wife." And I just went to pieces. I feel like crying now.

INTERVIEWER   You still do?

FERRER   I sure do, and this is twenty years ago. The capacity that Henry Fonda has to affect an audience . . . There was something so deep because it somehow got in the stomach. And I think we have had enormous talents as actors that we have not respected or recognized. Henry Fonda is a talent that nobody will ever know—the capacity of this boy—because he's a deep, turbulent . . . Really, it's a marvelous thing. His position is not what his talent merits.

INTERVIEWER   There are people who don't see this intensity.

FERRER   He has not carved out the career for himself that he should have. You see, it's a two-way thing.

INTERVIEWER   It does, I suppose, mean something—the roles you choose.

FERRER   You have to fight for a certain identity, and this is where your own thinking comes into play.

INTERVIEWER   You just opened up a very important vein in the life of an actor. You said that a man has to fight to carve out a career and an identity. Now, exactly what do you mean by that?

FERRER   You have to have the courage to do things that are obviously going to be failures, and say, "I don't give a damn. I'm going to do it anyway." You have to have the courage to say, "This is an opportunity which looks desirable and lucrative, except that in all honesty I can't accept it and be true to my employers and to the salary I'm earning and to myself in my dark room at night when I lie in bed." You have to, just have to, face up to making mistake after mistake after mistake out of conviction.

INTERVIEWER   Can you cite examples from your own experience?

FERRER   I have a very vivid example. I was a struggling young actor. I was just married to Uta Hagen and she was much more successful than I and I was just chauffeuring her back and forth from Mount Kisco. And one night in the middle of a play in Mount Kisco, a guy came out and said, "Where's my taxi?" And I was sitting up in the outer office and reading a book and I said, "What's your problem?" And he said, "I've got to catch a train. I've ordered a taxi." And I said, "Well, I'll drive you to the station." And I drove him down, and he said, "What is your name?" And I said, "Ferrer." This was 1938 or '39. And he said, "Are you José Ferrer?" And I said, "Yes." And he said, "Well, my name is Eddie Sobol. I'm very grateful to you for what you've done for me." A year or so later, Eddie Sobol called me up and said, "Look, I've found a play that you must do." And he presented me with a script called *Heaven Can Wait*, I think, which eventually became *Here Comes Mr. Jordan*. He was the only man who had ever offered me a lead. I had always been the friend of the guy. Now this fellow Sobol says, "Here it is. You're on a plane. You get killed. You go to heaven." I read the play and I thought the play was lousy. And this guy offered me a lead. I was a young actor who was never going to be offered a lead, as far as I was concerned. You know, my funny face. And yet I said, "I can't in honesty accept it. I don't know how to thank you." And he said, "You drove me to the Mount Kisco station and I thought of you." And I said, "Mr. Sobol, as long as I live I'll remember you, but I can't take this because I think it's a terrible play." And he said, "Well, kid, I've been in show business for . . ." And I said, "I don't care. You're right and I'm wrong, but I don't like the play." And I turned down the lead. Now, for a starting young actor— I don't know how you can understand, but turning down a lead, especially a guy like me with a character face, well, you know . . .

INTERVIEWER   And you've done this consistently throughout your career?

FERRER   By the same token, after La Jolla—*Edwin Booth*, everybody hated it. And I will say that I said to Roger Stevens, "Well, now you're here, you saw it, shall we drop it?" And he said, "No, I think we should keep going." He was putting in the money and he said keep going. But everybody said don't do *Charley's Aunt*. Don't do *Stalag 17*. Don't do *The Shrike*. They said don't do *Cyrano de Bergerac*.

INTERVIEWER   What does something like that Booth play do to . . . ?

FERRER   In the final analysis, after a while, it doesn't do anything. It's one more show, although at the time it is a bitter experience.

INTERVIEWER   The question I was going to ask in connection with *Edwin Booth* was how much attention can or should an actor pay to the critic? Now, Brooks Atkinson was rather rough on you in his review of *Edwin Booth*.

FERRER   I didn't read it. There are two reviews I didn't read. I didn't read *Oh, Captain!* and I didn't read *Edwin Booth*, because people who read them first said to me that both of these reviews . . .

INTERVIEWER   That's two Atkinson reviews you are talking about now—*Edwin Booth,* in which you starred, and *Oh, Captain,* which you directed. And you kept away from those reviews?

FERRER   Yes. I said I don't want to remember hurt, and I don't want to be discouraged. And Brooks' review of *Oh, Captain!,* which to this day I have not read, was described as a very personal attack on me. *Oh, Captain!* particularly, not *Edwin Booth* so much, but *Oh, Captain!* So I've never read either of them. I understand that in *Oh, Captain!,* for instance, a couple of the phrases that were quoted said that I'd been away from Broadway too long, and that I should have learned by now that Broadway was a big town, no longer a small village. And I considered these remarks contemptible. And my only beef with Brooks, whom I never see and have no occasion to talk to, is that I don't think I should be spoken to in those terms, or spoken about in those terms, and I think that is petty and wrong and petulant. I've done too much good work, and certainly sincere and honest work. If the work is inferior, that's the luck of the game, but to be told that New York is now a big town and that I've been away too long is nonsense. So I've never read those because I heard a couple of these sentences, and I said, "Well, why should I remember them? They'll rankle and they'll stay with me, so . . ."

INTERVIEWER   You've sort of rhetorically answered a question of mine. How much attention should an actor pay to the critic? You've indicated that in some instances it's better not to pay attention.

FERRER   You have to pay attention in accord with your degree of tolerance. When I was younger and tougher and was on the way up, I read everything and kind of fought back. At a given point I would never speak contemptuously of Brooks Atkinson, no matter how foolish or bad a review he might write, as he is entitled to—after thirty years of reviewing—because I think that his service to the theatre is too important for him ever to be treated lightly. By the same token, I would like to have something of the same courtesy extended to me, because I don't think I can any longer be treated as a fly-by-night ego. I think I've done too many—not good things, but good-intentioned things. I mean, I've done too many sincere and hard-working things for someone to just say, "Well, we just slap him on the wrist because he's fooling around." I don't fool around. This is my livelihood, that is how I foot the bills for my meals and the meals for all my kids. And if I fail, I fail. If I make mistakes, I make mistakes. And if I guess wrong, I guess wrong. I do the best I can every time. And if it isn't good enough, fine. I'll lick my wounds and go home.

INTERVIEWER   I once heard that Hume Cronyn said something like this. He'd been in a play, *The Man in the Dog Suit*, and one of the critics said, "You should have known enough not to bring it in." And he, at a Drama Desk luncheon, said that's nonsense. I had a dedication to that play. I furthermore had a commitment to that play, to every actor in it, to the producer, and so on. And in short, who is anyone to tell us?

FERRER   Of course. You know *Our Town* was a disaster in Boston. It did eighteen hundred dollars the first week and eleven hundred the next week—not thousand, hundred a week. And Jed Harris was going to close it, and Marc Connelly went up and said, "Jed, you're crazy. This play is going to win the Pulitzer Prize. Let's play poker." If it hadn't been for Marc Connelly, *Our Town* would never have come to New York.

INTERVIEWER   Would you see any merit in a youngster who is trying to get into the theatre spending his early time in college, working in the college theatre, for instance, rather than trying to hit New York?

FERRER   I think it's never too late to get into the theatre. Joseph Conrad never wrote a novel until he was in his forties. People have started painting late in life, composing late in life. I think the longer you spend—unless you're talking about a muscular activity where your body ages, which is a different thing—the longer you spend in a wide range of experiences the more you will bring to your art. This is my point of view—again, very subjective.

INTERVIEWER   Having gotten around to talking about the young people—if we were to ask you what advice you would give to the young actor today, what would you say?

FERRER   Seek experiences, always.

INTERVIEWER   What would you say then are the basic requirements for the actor?

FERRER   First of all, he has to have talent. And I suppose a lot of actors think they have talent who don't, and a lot of actors think they have a big talent who have a mediocre talent. But only time can tell that, because you can put three young actors on a stage and they will all be vivid, and one of them will have the character to carry him on to true stardom, one of them will have what it takes to make him a mere star, and one of them will vanish three or four or five years later. And who can tell what that is? I think that's a character component. Once, in a moment of slightly drunken introspection, I said, "Goethe, when he was dying, said, 'More light,' and somebody else when he was dying said something else. What will I say when I'm dying?" —if anybody is around to listen and cares and has a pencil in hand—and I thought I would like to be heard to say, "Character is all." Because I think the world is full of talent but the world is not full of character, and I think that kind of pure metal, that true gold, that survives fire and is there in the bottom of the pan when all the sludge is drained off, is what makes a great human being or a great artist or a great anything. And when I say great human being, I don't mean one who is written about in the history books. I mean a person whose life is fulfilled and who has done his duty by his contemporaries, his profession and his family, and so forth and so on. And I think character is all. And I think that the difference between two vivid, exciting talents, age twenty, and what happens to them at forty and forty-five, is that one had character and the other didn't. One could run the mile and the other got tired after four hundred yards. And I think certain young talents in show business today obviously have what it takes. Obviously, I would say that Tony Perkins, to me, is a very thrilling, outstanding example of talent, and not only talent but also the real kind of McCoy, relentlessly torturing himself until he comes up with the best that he can deliver. I think that George Scott, for instance, is a brilliant talent and an exciting sort of meteoric talent. Whether he has the character to live up to what he is capable of is something else again. There are always young people coming along. Method or no Method, Stanislavsky or no Stanislavsky. There's always a forum for a talent. The real guys come along and they've got it and they'll make it, because they have the muscle and the moral fiber to sweat out all the rough going. And at the moment I'm thinking of Tony. I talked to him a little while ago—I scarcely know him, but I'm certainly fond of him as an artist. The advice I have is work, work, work and work.

INTERVIEWER   You've gotten rather pensive. Perhaps this is a good time to ask a tough one. What is the function of the actor as an artist?

FERRER   Go back to Heifetz. His job is to play the Beethoven Violin Concerto as well as he possibly can for the audience that is in Carnegie Hall that night. Somebody else played it better, somebody else will play it better, but he's got to play it as well as he can, and above all he's got to love Beethoven and love the audience and love himself. If he loves those three people, he can't do wrong—if he's got talent. If he hasn't got talent, God help him. If he doesn't love Beethoven, if he doesn't love the audience, if he doesn't love himself, then he's in trouble, too. I think you've got to go through the world with hat in hand for the world. I respect the world, I respect people, I love people. I wish I could live to be five hundred years old so that I could never miss a moment of the experience of being alive. I'm thrilled to be alive, and I'm rather subjective, but what the hell else can you be? I can't talk in terms of X. I can only talk in terms of myself.

Maureen Stapleton

BIOGRAPHY

Born in Troy, New York, "about" 1925, Miss Stapleton went to Catholic Central High School, where she joined the drama group for her first appearance on-stage. After graduation she worked in the State Arsenal, saving enough money to get to New York City in 1943. She attended acting classes with Herbert Berghof, and did clerical work at night to support herself and finance her studies.

Her first professional appearances were in summer stock, and after two summers she got small parts in New York in *The Playboy of the Western World* and in Katharine Cornell's production of *Antony and Cleopatra*, later touring with Miss Cornell in *The Barretts of Wimpole Street*.

Back in New York she assisted Herbert Berghof, continued her training at the Actors Studio, and appeared in *The Bird Cage*, by Arthur Laurents. This was followed by more non-acting jobs, but her big break was soon to come—as Serafina in Tennessee Williams' *The Rose Tattoo*. A week after the opening, Miss Stapletons' name was up in lights.

Plays now followed one another more quickly. Among

them were *The Emperor's Clothes,* by George Tabori, *The Crucible,* by Arthur Miller, Chekhov's *The Sea Gull* and, in early 1959, *The Cold Wind and the Warm,* by S. N. Behrman. At the time of the interview, Miss Stapleton was appearing in the 1960 Drama Critics Circle Award winner, Lillian Hellman's *Toys in the Attic.* Miss Stapleton has appeared on television a number of times, notably in *All the Kings Men* and *For Whom the Bell Tolls.* Her movies include *Lonelyhearts* and *The Fugitive Kind.*

Miss Stapleton's one marriage to Max Allentuck, general manager for producer Kermit Bloomgarden, was terminated by divorce. She has custody of their two children, Danny, aged ten, and Cathy, six.

SETTING

It is, in this case, a dramatic exit which merits first attention. For Miss Stapleton this exit was down two flights of stairs carrying a large bicycle belonging to her son Danny, two luxuriant tails trailing from the handlebars. Offers of help from us had been volunteered, but were politely refused. She'd done it so often she was an expert, Miss Stapleton affirmed.

But to get back to entrances—the interviewers arrived at Miss Stapleton's home, the two upper floors in a one-time private house not far from Central Park on New York's West Side. We waited a bit after pushing a doorbell, that soon turned out to be defunct, and were fortunately rescued by Danny, who heard our knocking.

Danny took us upstairs to the living room, where a small-fry picnic for his sister and a little friend was under way; Fritos and cupcakes were liberally scattered about on a cloth on the rug. In a few minutes Miss Stapleton arrived, somewhat breathless, and an already active situation became further activated. Full of an informal, if harried, graciousness she greeted her guests, suggested that the younger children go off to the park, picked up an incoming call, negotiated with Danny to run downstairs to get some cigarettes for her, and then suddenly looked up in some alarm, convinced she smelled something burning. A rush of all to the stairwell and a bit of inter-floor communication soon revealed, however, that no emergency existed. A tenant downstairs was using an electric hair curler. And at this point, there was that bicycle to take down.

Back to the living room. The room was comfortably chaotic: toys, a doll's house, stuffed animals; a television set prominently placed; one wall lined with books, a portrait in color of Miss Stapleton on another wall, and photographs at random on others—including several of the funny-pose type taken on a stage or movie set. At the end of the room is a dining alcove separated from a kitchen by a smart, modern wood-and-glass partition, which looks just a trifle formal and intrusive in the surroundings.

Finally, the interview seemed about to begin. But the tape recorder would not work. The agonized efforts of the interviewers were obviously unequal to this electronic revolt. Miss Stapleton, as concerned as ever she could have been over a curtain that might not have fallen on a last act, felt surely the difficulty must be the wiring in her house. She called the superintendent, the landlord, an electrician—all with a mounting sense of guilt despite our best efforts to reassure her. But it was all to no avail. She proposed the final solution—hold the interview sometime on the following Sunday; have the recorder looked at and perhaps choose a new place for the interview.

The following Sunday was decided on, and the interview would be in the library of a friend—with correct current guaranteed and the machine checked over. One of the interviewers called for Miss Stapleton shortly after two; on the way she suggested they stop in at a delicatessen and get some supplies, for it had been a late Saturday night—with her favorite game of poker—and a late Sunday rising with not much time to eat. Miss Stapleton chose some smoked whitefish, chicken liver pâté, cheese, pumpernickel and potato chips. They finally arrived at our destination. The tape recorder worked, and the interview was on—after the food, which Miss Stapleton ate with relish.

Miss Stapleton sat in a large armchair, alternating between a comfortable sprawl and a somewhat tense, elbows-on-knees, hands-clasped position when answering questions of particular concern to her. It seemed evident that the maribou-swathed glamour star of her youthful dreams no longer had much place in her heart. She was dressed comfortably in a simple dress. She wore two modest rings and a single-strand necklace of beads, which she soon removed and dropped to the floor. Her hair, dark with gray in it, was worn straight back in no special array, suiting well the informality and geniality which mark this quickly risen star.

Interview

INTERVIEWER   From what we have read, you came from Troy, New York, to Broadway to become an actress because you wanted to wear maribou, like actresses in the movies. In your case this proved a sufficient motivation. But I was wondering whether you consider this sound motivation in general for those seeking a career in the theatre?

STAPLETON   Well, no. I don't know what the initial lunge is into any profession—like, say, kids get a romantic notion of something, maybe to be a doctor, because it looks so nice—or a uniform—or the movies about doctors. And then, when you become a doctor, that's a different cup of tea altogether. But the initial desire may have come from a seemingly superficial reason. That's the only thing I can compare it to, because acting certainly didn't convert me, as you can see, into Jean Harlow, or a maribou-wearer, or anything. Statistically, it would be insanity to go into the theatre for money. According to the statistics, you should just stay home. The odds are just incredible. Oh, I suppose in the back of your mind you always hope that you'll get money. But, motivation? I don't really know. I was a poor kid. I had an unhappy home life. In the movies, it seemed, the actors all looked nice, made money and were loved. That seemed great to me, and so I wanted to act, I guess, be an actress.

INTERVIEWER   How did you start to act?

STAPLETON   I was in one play in grammer school and I remember I didn't know my lines too well. And I was in, I think, two plays in high school—very small parts. But nobody ever jumped up and down and said, "Gee, you gotta go to New York, honey!"

INTERVIEWER   How did you happen to go into the plays in high school?

STAPLETON   They needed somebody to play the older lady, and I was heavy. There were only two plays.

INTERVIEWER   Did they seek you out?

STAPLETON   Oh, no. In most high schools there's a drama group, society or club, or whatever.

INTERVIEWER   Did you join the drama society or club?

STAPLETON   To tell you the truth, I don't remember

whether I was officially in it or not. I was an extremely heavy-set girl—I'm still pretty heavy. So that I wasn't very active in any of the clubs and things like that, and I don't remember whether I was officially a member. I was in two of the plays they did in high school, but I did not set the world on fire, by any means.

INTERVIEWER But you had wanted to be an actress, hadn't you?

STAPLETON Oh, I had decided quite early, when I was about six or seven, that that's what I was going to do.

INTERVIEWER Did you do much play-acting as a child?

STAPLETON Oh, sure. You know, for my own amusement I would put on shows.

INTERVIEWER What got you interested in the theatre—touring companies of shows?

STAPLETON No, it was from going to the movies. That was the only so-called theatre that I saw. I guess I went to the movies just about every day of the week. I had no discretion or taste. I saw everything and I liked everything. I'd sit in the movies from as soon as I got out of school until the last show. I sure caught hell from my folks. And I kept a scrapbook and I fell in love with Robert Taylor.

INTERVIEWER Why do you act?

STAPLETON If I knew the answer to that! I really don't know, it's like something you want, and you plan on, and you save for, and you go to school, and knock around, and you eventually get a job, and you never ... I'm beginning to ask myself that now, and I'm thirty-four and gray-haired. It's a lot harder than I thought. I don't know why. Once you start, it's your craft, and you don't—there's nothing else. But, anyway, acting is what I know how to do. And I guess it doesn't really matter why, does it?

INTERVIEWER Do you get any special joy out of acting?

STAPLETON Very rarely. I must subconsciously get a great deal or I wouldn't be doing it. But on a conscious level, I don't.

INTERVIEWER Have you ever thought of chucking the whole business?

STAPLETON When I'm very tired, yes. Like writers on the road—when a writer's on the road, every once in a while something that happened during the day will appear in the rewrite. Last year, in *The Cold Wind and the Warm*, there was a lot of rewriting out of town, and Sam Behrman was so tired. So one day a speech came down for Eli—Eli Wallach, who played Willie Lavin—and I got hysterical, because it must have been just exactly how Sam felt. Eli had the new speech, and it said, "I think sometimes I'd like to go to work in a factory from nine to five, and know just what I have to do, and come home, and be so tired that I don't have to think about anything in the world, just listen to the radio . . ." And you knew that was exactly what Sam felt like doing that night. Well, that's how I feel lots of times.

INTERVIEWER What problem does a young woman of twenty-five face in playing a middle-aged role, as you did in *The Rose Tattoo*?

STAPLETON I was twenty-five then? Well, not too much if she's heavy, because weight, on the stage or in life, too—overweight, I mean—automatically you look older. So you don't have to go for any special make-up, like, if you have to play a part of sixty. To play the part of a sixty-year-old-woman would be quite a trick. But unless there's something vital to the play, or some point to be made about the age, you can be anywhere from twenty-five to forty-five and play that same part. No, it was no problem for me. Also, depending on the core—what they use in the Method, the term, "spine" of the play—the woman's problem from start to finish was simple and strong and clear. It was not like hard work to do it. I was younger; there was a great deal of physical stamina required, which I had then, which I don't think I have now. But there was no age problem—to play old was no problem.

INTERVIEWER You mention stamina—Brooks Atkinson commented about that. He said even a mediocre performance would have been remarkable in *The Rose Tattoo*, because the role of Serafina was so strenuous.

STAPLETON Physically, it was terribly hard—just to be out there that long, and talking that much.

INTERVIEWER Do you recall whether you were under any special pressure, knowing that you were being compared all the time to Anna Magnani, for whom the play was intended? What did you do? How did you combat this?

STAPLETON (laughing over the recollection): Well, I was aware of it, certainly. I mean, it was hard to avoid it, because two of the plays I've done were written for her originally. Well, it's like anything else—I cannot compete with anybody but myself, or I would have shot myself when Shirley Temple was, you know, the biggest thing in show business. I mean, where can you go from there? I guess I'm lucky, because if I'd thought in terms of competing with someone else, I'd go crazy. I can't do it that way. Anna Magnani is a great actress, and she's Anna Magnani. But I'm me, and I can only do the best I can. In the beginning, I suppose, it bothered me or worried me a little.

INTERVIEWER   Writers have that feeling too. But ultimately they must realize that they can only write the way they write.

STAPLETON   That's right. You can only compete with yourself, or else you'd go out of your mind. And it's tough enough, anyway. I don't think, myself, it's a good habit for an actor to worry about being like somebody else, or as good as somebody else. You just can't do it.

INTERVIEWER   That makes sense. By the way, you once said that you can only do a play if it has real beauty. What do you mean by beauty? Because, certainly, in a sense, *Toys in the Attic* is not a beautiful play.

STAPLETON   No—also, that was a kind of, well—what would you call it?—a cheeky thing to say. I must have said that when I was feeling terribly flush and well off, because if I needed a job, I'd do anything. You know there's no point kidding. Art goes out the window then.

INTERVIEWER   But still, your idea is to do beautiful plays?

STAPLETON   Well, again, the word beauty is a broad one. There were certain things in *The Cold Wind and the Warm* that were terribly moving and beautiful to *me*. The thing about *Toys in the Attic* is that, originally, I wanted to play Albertine. There were only two acts then, when I read it, and the thing that I loved was the relationship in this play of a woman and a man—one was white and the other Negro—and there was no fuss. That was it, and the world can go to hell and this is it. A marvelous man, a marvelous woman, and she doesn't explain him or carry on about it, it's there and you can take it or leave it. And I loved that. Anyway, so I read the play. I thought there was nothing for me in it, but that relationship kept coming back in my mind. I thought it was gorgeous to do it that way. So one night I called the author, Lillian Hellman, up and I said, "I read two acts of the play and like it very much, and I'd like to play Albertine." And there was a long pause, and she said, "I hadn't thought of you in a million light years." So I said, "I know." And she said, "Would you read for it?" And I said, "Certainly." So I read, and there was a long silence, and I could see I wasn't their Albertine at all.

INTERVIEWER Whom did you read for?

STAPLETON Oh, I read for Lillian and Kermit Bloomgarden, the producer, you know. So I said, "I get it—don't call me, I'll call you." So they said, "As long as you're here, would you read Carrie?" So I did, and I didn't read that too well either, but they had me read it a few more times. Well, anyway, like in all plays, there are certain things that you believe in or you like, and so you go with that and nothing else really matters. Then if it's a hit, that's fine. It's lovely for everybody, but if it isn't, you don't regret it, it's still beautiful to you. *Orpheus Descending,* even if it was a failure, is a beautiful play, I think. I also feel that way about *The Cold Wind and the Warm.* I know there was a lot of piecework done on it that maybe hurt, or helped, I don't know. But I don't regret it, I loved it.

INTERVIEWER When you say you would have liked to play Albertine because you liked the kind of person she was—does that indicate your prefer to appear in plays that have meaning to you and to the audience? Does it mean that you prefer to be in something that says something?

STAPLETON Oh, no! I hate agit-prop plays—hate all that jazz. Because I don't think they're a happy wedding. I mean, I think theatre's theatre, and if it happens to say something, fine. But I don't think—I can't get worked up about acting in a play if the acting of it isn't fun or interesting. Then, also, I don't care about sending my message. I can do that through Western Union. I really don't like those message plays.

INTERVIEWER You remarked that actors can't be choosy, unless they're flush. When you select a play, do you think of the commercial prospects only under certain conditions?

STAPLETON Well, if I read a script and like it, or am excited about something about it, or the playing of the part, that's *it*. The rest is not my problem. If I were a producer, I'd look at it differently.

INTERVIEWER But you said you'd do anything if you were broke.

STAPLETON Oh, absolutely. Certainly. Because that's my job.

INTERVIEWER What do you really look for in a role for yourself?

STAPLETON Oh, like George Kaufman said, "A drunken nun"—something flashy or interesting. Oh, I don't know how to describe it. I've been very lucky. I've liked the plays I've been in.

INTERVIEWER Is it wrong to think solely in terms of the commercial prospects of a play?

STAPLETON I don't think it would be wrong. Nobody sets out to be in a disaster, you know.

INTERVIEWER Don't many actors choose plays because of how the role will show them off, not worrying at all as to whether the play will be successful, or whether it's a good play or not?

STAPLETON By and large, I would think that's true.

INTERVIEWER Do you think that's good for actors?

STAPLETON I think so, because I think the other concerns belong in other departments. I mean, the director—it's his job to get the whole ship going, and it's the producer's job to make it a so-called success. So, naturally, the actor's function is to find the best part for him, or the part that he wants to do, let's say. Of course, in the beginning you don't have choices.

INTERVIEWER You mean, when you're a starting actress . . .

STAPLETON You take what you can get.

INTERVIEWER How do you study your lines? What is your trick of memorization?

STAPLETON Usually there's about three weeks' rehearsal. The only time I ever had any trouble was with this play. We all of us had trouble. But as a rule there's no problem. It goes with the craft—I mean, you train yourself, you memorize, like absorbing; you go through it with the book in your hand and gradually you just know it.

INTERVIEWER You read it over and over again?

STAPLETON You read the play a few times. I don't memorize before I go to rehearsal at all.

INTERVIEWER You don't do any preparation before rehearsals? Is there any special reason for that?

STAPLETON No, I just never have. You can usually learn your lines within two weeks. Certainly, if you work in stock, which I adore, you learn it in one week, and you just have to cram.

INTERVIEWER Do you do homework, once rehearsals start?

STAPLETON Oh, if you have to, yes. If it's not coming, after you've worked a couple of weeks, then you take your work home—you know, you have to learn it at night. That's all. So somebody will cue you, and you go over and over and over, till you get it.

INTERVIEWER It seems an amazing achievement, learning a role for a play.

STAPLETON I don't know how other people would do other things.

INTERVIEWER In other words, you were cut out to be an actress.

STAPLETON That's part of the craft. It goes with the territory. If you do it long enough, it's like—well, I don't know how a man would perform an appendectomy, but if he's learned to do enough of them, you have to assume he knows what to do.

INTERVIEWER Are you nervous on opening nights?

STAPLETON I think everybody is, of course. I black out. I get so nervous that I can't remember what happened.

INTERVIEWER What do you mean? You do go through the play.

STAPLETON I remember the opening night of this play, and I remember *Twenty-Seven Wagons Full of Cotton*, because Janice, my friend, was sitting in the front row and I could see her all the time. But I'm always like an automaton, opening night. The pressures are just too enormous. It's just too much.

INTERVIEWER There's nothing that you've discovered that can be done about this?

STAPLETON (sighing heavily): Nothing. Nothing.

INTERVIEWER How long does this nervousness continue?

STAPLETON I'm nervous every night, but opening night is more of a nightmare. So many things are dependent on that one time up to bat: the backers, the money, your reputation and everybody else's reputation. There's so much at stake that it just overpowers you.

INTERVIEWER It must be horrible.

STAPLETON Really, it's a nightmare, an absolute nightmare. And then there are those seven guys,* you know, that have to be pleased, and you can't be any better than you were two nights before, but you have to, somehow, get through it.

INTERVIEWER And, actually, this is the time you'd want to be most relaxed.

STAPLETON And it's the worst night of all. Technique alone carries you through. That's all that carries you through it.

* The reviewers for the seven New York daily newspapers.

INTERVIEWER Does it help to know that you are a good actress?

STAPLETON Not at all. Years ago, in the first show I was in, in *The Playboy of the Western World,* a marvelous actress, Mildred Natwick, was in it, a lovely woman, and I'd seen her in *Blithe Spirit,* and she was so great—and I thought, "Oh, God, it must be divine when you're an actress, and everybody knows you're good." So I said, out of my absolute ignorance, "Gee, Millie"—she was waiting for a train and I said, "Gee, Millie, it must be wonderful to know you're a good actress." And she looked at me like I was crazy. She said, "What do you mean?" I said, "Well, to be like you, you know. To know it." She said, "I don't know it." And I said, "You don't?" And she said, "No." I said, "But, but you are, everybody knows you are." And she said, "No," and I kept saying, "Yes," and she said, "No." She said, "You'll never know till the day you die." I should have left the theatre right then and there. I should have walked out and known it was not for me.

INTERVIEWER But don't you get some sense of confidence—don't you? After all, you have a reputation now, a formidable one.

STAPLETON You go along on the assumption that you must be all right, but you never know. And sometimes, walking along, just walking through a store, you get assailed by the thought, "But, my God, maybe I'm no good at all! Maybe I really can't do it at all!" No. You just have to hope each time that whatever it is, you get away with it again. That's why when you said about "the joys"—it's very rare that you feel that you've done it right on the button. Maybe two or three times in a decade.

INTERVIEWER In a decade?

STAPLETON Yes.

INTERVIEWER Do you think, perhaps, that this is a matter of what kind of a person you are. It is said that Ethel Merman . . .

STAPLETON It is said, yes, I've heard it—that Ethel is divine. Ethel has said, "Why should I worry? I know my part." Yes. That's great, that's healthy and marvelous. I suppose you should work, maybe, to develop that sort of self-protection.

INTERVIEWER Have you tried anything to overcome these nerves?

STAPLETON No. When I work, it starts about six-thirty at night. I start to burp. I belch—almost nonstop. I keep burping, all through the show, right up to the curtain, and right after, and then I'm all right. That's the only physical form it takes. You know, they can hear it on the other side of the stage—I mean, they call it the overture. They say, "Here comes the overture."

INTERVIEWER I've read that stage fright is a form of conceit.

STAPLETON Maybe, maybe.

INTERVIEWER A conceit of wanting to be perfect or terrific. This is what gives you the nervousness.

STAPLETON Oh, yes, because you want to be so perfect, of course.

INTERVIEWER But you always want to do a good job. The audience has paid for it.

STAPLETON Yes, but also there's something in it that's very egomaniacal, too, I used to be so self-critical—and in a way, it's a terrible kind of conceit. Once, years ago, I came out of the theatre, and a man, a director and his wife, whom I know, came up and stopped me to say they liked me, and I swung at them. And I thought about it after that, and I thought, "Now, that's going too far, I mean, really."

INTERVIEWER Why did you do that?

STAPLETON Because I felt I was terrible that night. I didn't like what I did. So now I smile, and I say thanks, but I can't really believe all that stuff. No, you can't be perfect every night, and you can't expect it of yourself, and you just have to learn to live with it.

INTERVIEWER You consider yourself a Method actress?

STAPLETON I suppose so.

INTERVIEWER Well, what do you think the Method has done for you, exactly?

STAPLETON Well, I made a lot of nice friends. Really, to tell you the truth, there's so much talk about the Method, I'm not sure what it is. I never did get around to reading those two books* that started all the trouble. It seems to me that the Method is more or less the same. Bobby Lewis once said, when the Actors Studio first started, "I teach the Bobby Lewis Method, Elia Kazan teaches the Elia Kazan Method, Lee Strasberg teaches the Lee Strasberg Method," and you find that the basic rules are the same, like in anything. It's just that the teachers are different, their personalities are different, or their stresses are different. It's

* *Actor Prepares* and *Building a Character*, by Constantin Stanislavsky.

just what works for you. In this play, for instance—in *Toys in the Attic*—you can't Method it up too much because, well—there's a certain scene in the first act which I didn't want to do. I don't think it's necessary. I think it's wrong. But I'm not the writer and I'm not the director, and they said, "Do it this way," so I have to do it that way.

INTERVIEWER What is that?

STAPLETON Oh, it's ghastly. In the middle of the first act, in order to set something up for the third act, so you'll know, you'll get a clue, that she's really a two-faced woman or whatever she is, I have to say—I've been talking for twenty-five minutes, yackety-yackety-yak, and so Albertine comes in and she says that she got a telephone call from her daughter and that they're* coming. And I get all excited, and I start singing dum, de, da, dum, and then she says, "The call did not come from Chicago, the call came from here." Then I have to stop and say angrily, "It could not have come from here!" Well, frankly, folks, I think that's phony and unnecessary, which I said. Now, there comes a point where you just do what you're told, and that's all. So whether I like it or not, that's what I'm supposed to do. I do not like it, and I don't agree with it, but my job is to do it. So I just forget the Method and talk up and hit the line the way it's supposed to be hit, that's all.

INTERVIEWER You say you can't "Method" up the play. What do you mean?

STAPLETON No, you can't "Method" it up, you see, because the Method is like all that inner working stuff, whatever they call it. How can I describe it? You see, I feel a lady who is maneuvering like that, who has all these obsessive things underneath, doesn't tip her mitt. She doesn't have to. She'll go right on being just as destructive as she was, in her own way, but it is a specific way. Now, in order to say all those other things the way I say them, I have to have certain little thoughts that lead into other thoughts, and so on underneath. But then at this point I have to stop still on a dime in the middle of the first act and belt out three lines so that they'll know she's really like that. Well, I can't find—the Method helps me not at all there, Charlie, just forget it.

INTERVIEWER But how should the Method help you?

STAPLETON I'll tell you how the Method helps you. According to the Method, you see, you have to give your-

---

* The reference is to Albertine's daughter and Carrie's brother, who are married and have been living in Chicago.

self. The Method is to be true, to be real, to be true to the part in the play, not for your own—as it's abused a great deal—your own self-indulgence; it's never meant for that, never has been. It's to be as true and real, and alive and fresh in the part each time. That's your job. And also part of your job, whether you like it or not, is that if that's the way the line has to be read, then you stop acting and thinking about yourself and do it the way it has to be done. And years ago, in *Rose Tattoo*, Tennessee had been away for two months. In his absence—well, there was one scene where I blew out a vigil light and then I'm supposed to run out on the porch. I'd added a little bit of business there—I'd found something, so-called, one day, that I thought was just peachy. And it didn't take very long, and I thought it was just elegant. I loved it. I just thought it was divine. I blew out the light, and then I had this one second of remorse, and that was my favorite time of the play. And a couple of other actors mentioned it, you know, and I just thought it was swell. So Tennessee comes back and sees the play. And he comes backstage that night and we were talking and he said, "What were you doing, slobbering all over the Virgin there?" I said, "Slobbering all over the Virgin?" I said, "Tennessee, I thought that was wonderful." He said, "Oh, that's terrible." He said, "She'd never do that." I said, "She wouldn't?" And he said, "Oh, no, that's awful!" I said, "It only takes a few seconds." And he said, "Cut it out." And there I had thought it was just divine.

INTERVIEWER You said that the Method teaches you to be truthful and real to the character, but doesn't any other method teach you to do that?

STAPLETON Yes. It doesn't differ from any other. There's no fight, there's no contest. There are other schools of acting, like the Delsarte system, which is now outmoded. That taught acting in a different way. Everything was divided. The whole body was divided into the mental, the emotional, the physical, including your eyeballs and your eyelids and your hands and your fingers, and there were certain positions for anger, rage, and all that stuff, you know. That was a way of teaching. Of course by the time you learned all those things, it's hard to open a door, you know. But the Method is, I guess, from watching many other actors act, a general sort of set of rules, that people who act do anyway!

INTERVIEWER One thing the Method would stress would be getting inside a character, getting to know this character—where he lives, for instance. Did you, for example, go to

New Orleans to see where Carrie might have lived? This would be sort of Method, wouldn't it?

STAPLETON   In a way, maybe. It depends on what you need. There's no point in making extra work for yourself. The essential core of Carrie is not that she comes from New Orleans—not to me, anyway—she could come from anywhere. Now, if I ever had to play a German or French—I don't have that accent, or that facility—I would have to do a lot of outside work before I started. But that's just common sense. You do what you need. And that's what the Method is for: to help you when you need it. If you don't need it, forget it. And it's also homework. You're not supposed to do it out on the stage, for God's sake. You know—wait till you feel true. You show up at eight-thirty and whether you feel true or not, Charlie, go.

INTERVIEWER   There's been a good deal of criticism of the, let us say, minor Method actors who use the Method to indulge themselves.

STAPLETON   It never was meant for that.

INTERVIEWER   And it brought out the worst in Olivier,* for instance, who yelped about how American actors constantly waste time in rehearsals theorizing over their roles, whereas what they should really do is work on a scene over and over and over.

STAPLETON   Of course, the Method doesn't disagree with that. Not at all.

INTERVIEWER   Well, then, there's a great deal of misinterpretation and . . .

STAPLETON   That's it.

INTERVIEWER   Helen Hayes was telling me once, before the opening of *Time Remembered*, that she was with some young Method actors, and she said the kind of language they were using—she felt she didn't belong, she didn't understand what was going on. And how they couldn't perform because they didn't "feel the part."

STAPLETON   Well, that's just a phase that individuals maybe go through. But it was never taught to me that way, never. It was made quite clear in one of the first productions at the Studio, years ago, when Bobby Lewis directed *The Sea Gull*—and I was away, and came back, and they'd been rehearsing quite a few weeks. The girl who played Masha got sick, or was going away, and I went in. So I remember one of his Method directions, toward the end,

* Laurence Olivier, who made these observations in a *New York Times* interview prior to the opening of *The Tumbler*.

was, "If she's not in the right place, push her there." It's just common sense. I went to Herbert Berghof, and he taught within that framework. The end result is the important thing.

INTERVIEWER   I imagine that one thing responsible for much of the controversy is that a lot of mannerisms became connected with the Method.

STAPLETON   Yes. That are not true.

INTERVIEWER   The Marlon Brando influence, the scratching and itching. In short, that to be realistic, you must also be somewhat . . .

STAPLETON   Yes, well, you see, that's not necessarily so.

INTERVIEWER   But I think that's the kind of thing that's been identified with the Method.

STAPLETON   But it's a wrong interpretation. Also, the Method . . . Like, when you do a play for quite a while, you get stale, so it gives you things—or tires to—you concentrate on different things, without throwing everything out of whack. There's a framework you have to adhere to and certain points that have to be made and beats that have to be accomplished in a scene. In the Method they tell you, "Look for things to freshen up." "Concentrate on a certain prop that you hadn't thought of before, a flower or something." It doesn't tell you to go off half-cocked or berserk or something. Just to recharge, to revitalize your work.

INTERVIEWER   How did you set out to construct the gestures for Carrie? You rub your hand down the side of your dress; or you touch your nose or twist your ear. How do you work out these gestures when you're designing the character?

STAPLETON   That's mostly all done in rehearsal.

INTERVIEWER   Where does the director leave off and you begin?

STAPLETON   It's all usually one. There may be certain areas of disagreement, but, like in that one point that I mentioned before, it was simply a case of too bad, I had to do it.

INTERVIEWER   At one point you sort of quickly touched your nose. Do you do that every night?

STAPLETON   I don't know where it was. Maybe it was itchy or something, or I thought something was there, I don't know. I don't know specifically.

INTERVIEWER   Carrie is the sort of person one doesn't often come across in real life.

STAPLETON   Now, you see, there I disagree. I come across Carrie and all sorts of people all the time. They're no strangers to me. Maybe I run around with the wrong crowd, or something. But when you read the *Daily News,* just one day, you go into shock at the different kinds of unusual people there are in this world.

INTERVIEWER For instance, when you come across a part like Carrie, and you read the part, do you bring to the part something beyond what the playwright has? I mean, your own experience, your own knowledge?

STAPLETON Everybody does—as much as you know about it.

INTERVIEWER Could you talk a little about this? It's interesting to us.

STAPLETON All I know is that for each part there is what they call a core or a spine, that is the main—like in everybody's life there is a core. I'm a mess in real life. I don't know what my core is, or my spine. But in the theatre I'm more disciplined than I am in life. In Carrie, as I see her, there's one thing—she's obsessive, or—oh, I don't know how to describe it, but I know a lot of people like that. Some quite close to home. I don't know all the analytical terms for it. All I know is that, in an active way, there are certain things she has to have, therefore has to do or be or get. And the line is there. The whole story is there, you know, in the play, so you know where you're going, and you know the main purpose of the part or the character, and everything else sort of comes out of that— all the other little things. This is a lady who *must,* who's going to, keep that family together; who wants her brother there and her sister there on any terms whatsoever at all. And so, therefore, that's what she does.

INTERVIEWER Stanislavsky advised his young actors to go out into life, to go to the park, anywhere, to watch people all the time, so that, presumably, when they came across a part, they would have a certain inner resource from which to play it.

STAPLETON Yes. Well, also, with writers. I've heard them say write about what you know. And to the actor— nothing in life, or in human behavior, can be alien to the actor. There is nothing that the human being can do that is a surprise, or a shock, or un-understandable. The actor is a mechanism, his own instrument. It's not necessary to go out and commit murder to play a murderer, but you must know that you are capable of it, as you are capable of doing anything. Therefore, depending on what the role is, or the part, you use whatever of yourself is part of that role, part of that character's makeup. And you extend that in yourself, because I'd hate to think that Carrie is the "real me."

INTERVIEWER   How do you achieve that breathless high-pressure plaintiveness in your voice?

STAPLETON   I think it comes from just having to talk so much. She never shuts up. And she talks about the most, to me, boring things. So I have to get all excited about things that really don't interest me at all. Everything's peachy for Carrie in the beginning of this play. Everything's going just fine. So that she's kind of pleasantly excited by everything, and that gives one a certain . . . Also, you get out of breath having to talk that much.

INTERVIEWER   What goes on in your mind to give you the idea of the heat of the day? You're constantly wiping your brow, you unbutton your blouse, you rub your hands on your dress—you're suggesting the heat. What do you summon in your mind to give you this feeling of heat that you convey across the stage?

STAPLETON   There again, that's done for you. If the curtain goes up and somebody's wiping his brow, you get the idea—it's a pretty old-fashioned way of doing it but we couldn't think of anything smarter. And, of course, the set helps that. It's terribly hot on that stage. It's hot as hell. The lights—everybody's bathed in perspiration.

INTERVIEWER   In other words, this is no trick of acting?

STAPLETON   Oh, no. You stand under those lights and you'd convey heat all right.

INTERVIEWER   How do you make yourself cry?

STAPLETON   I'll tell you something—if crying were acting, as Bobby Lewis said, "My Aunt Liz could be Duse." Some people cry easier than other people. I have what's known as leaky ducts. Crying is very easy for me. I can cry at red hats, card tricks, anything. Laughing on stage is much harder. But I can cry at anything.

INTERVIEWER   What do you do—do you say something to yourself?

STAPLETON   There are key words, or certainly you set up a pattern—now, I know that certain things that Rochelle's going to say to me in this play have to make me cry. So I have to not expect it, and when she says that my brother said something mean about me, that I never knew—it hurts my feelings. It's self-pity, and there's nothing easier in the world to feel than self-pity. So that sets you crying.

INTERVIEWER   Do you summon some image to suggest self-pity?

STAPLETON   No.

INTERVIEWER You just suddenly feel sorry for yourself?

STAPLETON No, no.

INTERVIEWER You are caught up in the play, aren't you?

STAPLETON Yes. You see, I have set up certain things. I have something that I use for crying that works all the time. There was someone, an uncle, whom I loved, who died. I just remember certain things he said, or did, and I miss him, and I can cry. For hours.

INTERVIEWER Do you use this prop all the time?

STAPLETON Yes, whenever I'm stuck I do that. I'm not usually stuck on crying, though, because almost anything can make me cry. Maybe I'm overly keyed up; that's part of my mechanism. Somebody else's is different. I used to do the scene where Carrie comes back from being fired after her boss has read that awful letter—I was thinking of the things he had said to me and crying. And our director, Arthur Penn, said, "You have to take all that emotionality out of it. You've got to play hard, cold anger." And so I did. I knew the attack on the scene with all the crying was not right.

INTERVIEWER Does part of what you feel and what you act come out of simply imagining that this is what is happening to Carrie? I mean, do you sort of lose yourself? Are you Carrie at that moment?

STAPLETON No, I don't start off that way, because I can't, because I wouldn't quite know what to do. So I start off by imagining that it's Vincent, my uncle, and that somebody has said something bad to me about him or something. Then you stop that, because if you do that too much, you can go crazy. So then it becomes my brother and my sister, and it's the play again.

INTERVIEWER This is a play that begins with an undefined tension. What do you do before you get on that stage to create that undercurrent? That curtain goes up, and you're sitting there and you're jabbering right away. Obviously you don't just go out there at eight-forty and sit down and start, do you? What do you do?

STAPLETON No—again that's technique. From the time you get to the theatre—let's say a quarter to eight, I like to be early—you sort of get ready to do your job. But you don't consciously, like, you know, make yourself prepare or anything. You put some make-up on, you talk, you sort of—and gradually, you're at work.

INTERVIEWER Can you have people in the dressing

room up to the moment before you go on, or do you need a period of quiet?

STAPLETON   I like a little quite, before.

INTERVIEWER   How long before the curtain goes up do you actually take your seat, sit in that chair?

STAPLETON   About a minute. If that long.

INTERVIEWER   Is that all?

STAPLETON   If that long.

INTERVIEWER   And you are in the mood of the play?

STAPLETON   Yes. It's not so much mood, or anything. It's a task, a job that you just sort of get ready for. You know, I was just thinking about laughing, what we were talking about before, and I was thinking about how it's easier to cry. But laughing, that is a terribly hard thing to do.

INTERVIEWER   Why?

STAPLETON   It's almost impossible, especially when you're supposed to laugh at a joke. If you've heard the joke once, it's pretty hard to laugh at it ten times.

INTERVIEWER   What trick do you use there?

STAPLETON   Fortunately, I don't have to laugh in this play. Years ago, Marlon Brando, to drop a name, told me that Oscar Homolka had taught him a thing—you have to practice it—of letting your breath out. I can't do it right now, but you physically pump the air out, and then you just start pumping it back in. It's an artificial way, but if you practice it long enough, then you'll be able to do it in an instant.

INTERVIEWER   That suggests an old debate—whether it's harder to play comedy than tragedy?

STAPLETON   They're both hard. That's like, is it harder to do an appendectomy or a spinal tap? I don't think there's a contest.

INTERVIEWER   Did you read what Jason Robards said in an interview? He said, "I am not anti-Method, but on the stage I have to know what I am going to do every minute; for that you need technique. You can't improvise a performance every night. By the time a play is ready to open, I'm so immersed in the character I am playing that I am confident the lines will come because they are the lines that the character would speak in that situation. But the framework of the performance has to be set. It can't depend on the way the actor feels that night."

STAPLETON   Absolutely. That's the Method. That's what the Method is supposed to equip you to do. Not just how *you* feel, but to perform that task, that way, each night.

The Method never was meant as a self-indulgent, sort of I-don't-feel-like-it thing.

INTERVIEWER   Have you had any classical training?

STAPLETON   No, I haven't had it. I do think you need a special training for that. Just breath control alone even, because that's hard.

INTERVIEWER   And the Method does not prepare you for that?

STAPLETON   No. You can see the Method up to a point, but again, you have to have something extra.

INTERVIEWER   There are some people who say that the Method has not yet proved itself for actors who wish to play Shakespeare.

STAPLETON   Well, if an actor works on the things that he needs to, to play Shakespeare, he can, sure. But the Method can't wash dishes, either, you know; it never said it could.

STAPLETON   Some foreign directors who have been here lately contend that American actors are afraid to "play out"—

STAPLETON   I disagree with that absolutely. I know one thing, Method or no Method—both Jason and myself, and Irene, they can hear us. They can hear us in the last balcony. One rule is "loud"—and Method, Schmethod, the audience has to hear you.

INTERVIEWER   Incidentally, wasn't Irene Worth trained in the British theatre?

STAPLETON   Yes.

INTERVIEWER   Does she ever have any comments on the Method people?

STAPLETON   No. Her acting's the same as ours.

INTERVIEWER   That goes back to what you said—if you are doing a good job, Method or anything else . . .

STAPLETON   That's right. That's right. You see, Irene has that same thing too—you can hear her in the back. She's absolutely real. She's a perfectionist. I'll tell you, I haven't been to the Studio in a couple of years, so I don't know much about what's going on now. But only a damn fool would—nobody would teach you to mumble. Your job is to be heard in the second balcony, and that's far away, and you have to be loud. You have to be heard. Anybody says anything else is a traitor to the Method.

INTERVIEWER   You're known to be a hard worker. Do you work on a role throughout the run of the performance, seeking perfection?

STAPLETON   Well, I don't know.

INTERVIEWER Don't some actors work on their roles right up to the final night?

STAPLETON I'm not a fanatic seeker—there's plenty of work just to do it straight, without finding too many things. Once it's set, if it starts to get attenuated, well, the stage manager checks usually, and gives you notes, you know, when you're getting slow or where you're losing something here or there. So a certain amount of work automatically always goes on. But it's best done either by the stage manager or the director, because you can't tell yourself where you're letting down or doing too much, or whatever it happens to be. So there's always something to work on, more or less.

INTERVIEWER We were very much interested in the remark you made—when you were getting ready to leave New York with the tryout of *Toys in the Attic*—that you and Jason Robards were just dead tired.

STAPLETON Oh, God, yes!

INTERVIEWER Why was that? Was that peculiar to *Toys in the Attic,* or do you find yourself terribly fatigued by rehearsals in general?

STAPLETON I think it's true for me, in general, yes. But in this one—it's hard to describe, but I was extremely fatigued. None of us could put our finger on it, quite. We all had great difficulty learning the lines, which was not usual for me or any of the others.

INTERVIEWER This fatiguing effect was particularly true of *Toys in the Attic,* and yet no one seemed to know exactly why?

STAPLETON No. Maybe it's one of those things you figure out, you know, a couple of years later.

INTERVIEWER Do you think this may have been because of the unusual amount of wordage?

STAPLETON No—because Tennessee Williams, God knows, can have whole long, long ... But there's something in this play—and as I say, I don't know what it is. Well, anyway, it's not very important, because we finally learned them, the lines.

INTERVIEWER We gather that you were also very grateful because Miss Hellman stood by her script during the New York rehearsals and refused to make wholesale changes. Is that true?

STAPLETON Yes. But I'm a little sorry I said that.

INTERVIEWER Why? She did make changes on the road?

STAPLETON She made some. But actually I felt, and still feel, that maybe the play could have been cut a bit.

But I'm not sure, I suppose Miss Hellman and Arthur Penn felt it was right this way.

INTERVIEWER But wasn't it a pleasure not to be constantly saddled with whole new speeches, as is so often the case on the road?

STAPLETON I don't know. That by itself isn't ever really terribly difficult.

INTERVIEWER Was there more—or less—changing in this play than most?

STAPLETON No, there was cutting, some cutting. There always is.

INTERVIEWER But there was little rewriting?

STAPLETON Yes, very little. Of course, I don't know what her habits were in the past.

INTERVIEWER What are the problems of an actor on the road, when plays are being rewritten?

STAPLETON (with a deep sigh as if even the memory tired her): Oh, exhaustion. The road is a strange time. It's hard to describe. Everybody's under terrible strain and pressure—mostly the writer, I guess. He's the most vulnerable. Everybody sort of knows it, and you try to protect him or be as helpful as you can, really. Because it's the worst time of all for him. Of course, the producer is the most worried—because, well, it may be all that money down the drain.

INTERVIEWER Did we understand an interview of yours correctly, in which you seemed to indicate that you are opposed to the actor's collaborating with the director and playwright in the writing or rewriting of speeches?

STAPLETON No, I'm not opposed to it. If an idea is good, I'm not opposed—but unless you all know each other very well, you can't presume on another craft. I mean, I'm not a writer. I'm not a director. They see it from, you know, another viewpoint.

INTERVIEWER Do you frequently find yourself saying about a line, "I can't say this line"?

STAPLETON Oh, no.

INTERVIEWER You don't say, "I need this line rewritten?"

STAPLETON No. Oh, of course, there may be some times when I might say something to be helpful, or . . . It depends on how good, or how close, your relationship is with the director or the writer. You know—you have to be terribly careful.

INTERVIEWER What secret of concentration do you have? What element of concentration do you depend upon, while you're performing? Do you hear other noises?

STAPLETON   Oh, boy. Yes. Well, that's a problem of mine. A lot of people don't have that.

INTERVIEWER   On the contrary, we find it's a problem for other people, too. Alfred Lunt was telling us that he could hear the radiators . . .

STAPLETON   (with sudden emphasis): Oh, that! That's notorious—when the radiator starts knocking!

INTERVIEWER   What do you do to combat the distraction?

STAPLETON   Well, nothing. With me it's special. If a truck backfires, I jump. I can hear everything. I get scared. I smell smoke—like I come off, with the goobers, and I say, "I smell smoke." But they know me now. And, a plane —those jets—all that noise. It terrifies me.

INTERVIEWER   In other words, you cannot obliterate the external world during the performance of a play?

STAPLETON   I can't. Other people can. Loud sounds just happen to bother me. They don't bother other people. But, me, I get terrified. I get scared that something is going to fall down, or there's going to be an explosion, or something. So, I hear everything.

INTERVIEWER   This must be a great problem for you— to keep in your role.

STAPLETON   It is. But that's *my* problem, you know. Everybody's got a problem and I'm stuck with this. The other night I was in the dressing room when a light bulb exploded. It sounded like a cannon. I don't know what happened, it popped or something. It was a terribly loud sound. Well, I leaped up, and some of the others in the company came running down. They knew that I might faint out of absolute terror. And I did almost faint.

INTERVIEWER   What happens with coughing?

STAPLETON   Oh, that doesn't bother me. All human sounds I don't mind at all. Coughing bothers Jason. He'll cough back. He does. He gets furious. I can see him—especially if there's a whole bunch of seals out there—he'll be saying, ". . . I made a little house up there . . ." and he'll go (imitation of coughs), but I just laugh. They can cough their heads off, as far as I'm concerned.

INTERVIEWER   How about chattering in the audience?

STAPLETON   That doesn't bother me.

INTERVIEWER   None of these things—only the noises from radiators and popping bulbs?

STAPLETON   That's right. Only those sounds terrify me, that's all. I know the sound of coughing, I know people talking, so it doesn't bother me at all.

INTERVIEWER   But you also know the sound of planes passing over.

STAPLETON   Yes, I know. But I can't get used to it. I have trouble in real life with it. Oh, yes. I don't drive by La Guardia Field any more. It takes pills to get me just to drive out there. I can exclude all the human sounds and noises. But anything that scares me, I—I . . . I've heard of actors, when there's a fire, they come on and they're very calm and entertain or something—not me, Charlie. I would be on the floor, or out. I couldn't move. I just can't move. Once, in *The Rose Tattoo*, in Philadelphia, I heard the fire trucks coming, and in the audience there was this rumbling. The fire, it turned out, was next door. But I didn't know that and I was on the stage. I just stood there and I turned absolutely white. I couldn't move, I couldn't even run, I couldn't do anything. It was a terrifying sound as they began to get up and start to panic, you know. But I just stood there absolutely numb. Then, fortunately, somebody in the audience was bright enough to avoid a panic. A man got up and said firmly, "Sit down." But me, I just stood there.

INTERVIEWER   What is your concept of technique in acting? You know, we sort of skirted that before. What importance do you give to it?

STAPLETON   Well, you see, it is a nebulous thing to talk about, anyway. At best it's hard to define the terms. That's what the Method tries to do, really. It's like in any craft, or art or skill—wherever there is a technique there are certain things you just have to learn.

INTERVIEWER   Have you spent much time in body training and body control, voice control?

STAPLETON   Yes, years ago I took some body classes —and voice class and speech work. All that depends on the school you go to, or if you can afford to go to these special classes. Some have a complete curriculum that way. It's all to the good. I don't do it much any more. I don't have time.

INTERVIEWER   I'd like to go back to the remark we made before about Olivier's article. That seemed to be quite a topic of conversation among theatre people for several days after its appearance.

STAPLETON   Well, I can't get too stirred up about those things, I really can't.

INTERVIEWER   Olivier complained that he found American actors were given to too much theorizing. He felt that in stead of talking, they should do a scene over and over again, rather than stand there for forty minutes debating about how the scene ought to be played.

STAPLETON   I don't know. I guess he went to the Studio on a bad day. That happens sometimes.

INTERVIEWER   He didn't say this about the Studio. He discussed it in terms of directing a television play. He said that he almost went crazy with the debates that went on.

STAPLETON   If he was the director, all he'd have to do is say "Shut up, and do it." Was he the actor? Or was he the director?

INTERVIEWER   He was the director.

STAPLETON   Then he could say, "Shut up. Shut up and do it."

INTERVIEWER   He did say that the actor must be disciplined and trained so that he automatically carries out the director's wishes.

STAPLETON   No one disagrees with that. The whole thing is over my head, really. I don't know what they're talking about. They get in these big, long discussions. I just think it's all talk. The Method is there. It's clear—what it is. If it's abused it's abused. But that's not the Method's fault. There are great actors that have never heard of it.

INTERVIEWER   That's true. Now, for instance, José Ferrer said that as far as Maureen Stapleton was concerned, she would have been a fine actress without the Method, regardless. Or, in other words, Method or no Method, you would have been a fine actress.

STAPLETON   Very nice.

INTERVIEWER   The point is, then, that, just like Helen Hayes, good or great actors don't need the Method, they will devise their own method.

STAPLETON   But everybody does more or less the same thing.

INTERVIEWER   Yes, I think José Ferrer said something to that effect, too.

STAPLETON   I can't get excited about the Method debate, I really can't. I don't take it seriously. I don't believe it, you know.

INTERVIEWER   It's quite possible that yours is the valid approach toward the subject.

STAPLETON   All the talking and carrying on.

INTERVIEWER   There certainly is a lot of talking and carrying on.

STAPLETON   I also know that there's a germ of truth in the carrying on, like there is in everything—because there are certain scenes . . . Well, when I go to the Studio, if I see a bed set up, I leave. Two years ago, or whenever it was, I was walking down the street and David Stewart stopped me and he was hysterical. He said, "You should have been at the Studio today." Because whenever there's a fancy guest there, it's the day that two people commit all the sins that the Studio is accused of, and like I say, when someone important is there, then it happens that day. And so David said, "You won't believe it! They did a scene from *Machinal*, and Helen Hayes had brought Ina Claire to the Studio that morning." Now, Ina Claire has forgotten more than most of us will learn in our lifetime. So, there's the bed set up ... And I said, "Boy, I'm glad I wasn't there for that." And he said, "First this girl comes out in a little shirt and panties, and a fellow comes out in shorts; then they proceed, and for twenty minutes they take turns pouring talcum powder on one another. Such self-indulgence and carrying on..." I said, "David, I don't believe it." He said, "It was excruciating. I don't know *what* she thought." If Ina Claire ever did a take-off on the Studio, that would close it for all time. Two weeks later I met Helen Hayes at a party and I said, "Helen, please tell me, what did Ina Claire say after her visit to the Studio?" And she said, "Don't. Don't. I didn't know what to do, or how to explain it." It's like, you know, you have somebody come in to visit your child and that's the day the kid does everything wrong. Well, that was the day Ina Claire came. And I've heard it on other occasions. There's been visiting royalty, and somebody will do one of those—well, it puts real devotees to the pit of the car, so that I can imagine what it does to somebody else.

INTERVIEWER Actors at the Studio get assignments, don't they?

STAPLETON They pick a scene. They're scheduled, and they do a scene; they work on it their way, or whatever, and then they stop and discuss. "What were you looking for? What were you trying to do?" All that is homework. But you don't do that on the stage, in a theatre. You don't prepare for twenty minutes, or make real coffee, that's pretty boring—or you don't wait for ten minutes until the spirit moves somebody. That's all done in school, that's classwork, that's not meant to be taken to work, you know. You don't do that. I know Noel Coward went to the Studio one day. Well, he was hilarious. He despised it. He said, "What is going on here?" I said, "Oh, Noel, it's fun—it's nice—it keeps me off the streets." He said, "You belong on the streets." And he said, "And the next time Lee Strasberg asks you what you were working for—say money." But really, it is a workshop, after all. And that is what it's for. Say you and I decide we want to do X scene from a certain play. We let the people know this is what we're going to do on a certain day, that is, our day to go before the class and perform. Lee may not know what you're going to perform. He just sits there and he watches, and then it becomes a matter of his criticizing, asking you what did you try for, what did you intend. Lee is like the rabbi, he has this long-range point of view, which is great—like we've all got forever to learn. But underneath it all, he's quite practical, too. I mean, he expects you to exert a certain amount of common sense in the usage of this thing, the Method. Now, we make jokes amongst ourselves at the Studio. There are certain things . . . I hate sitting and waiting fifteen minutes for the spirit to move somebody. It's just boring, that's all. And I *despise* all scenes on beds. I just *hate* that. I *hate* it. Can't stand to see people—it's obscene to me. I don't like it. Maybe I'm a prude. It's certainly vulgar in real life and I just don't like it on the stage.

INTERVIEWER Do they ever really wait fifteen minutes for the "spirit to move" someone? Do they wait for people to get in the mood, and so on?

STAPLETON Oh, yes. And, of course, that's the place to do it. But you're not supposed to do that outside, that is, when you're working in a play, where they're paying real money.

INTERVIEWER What's the practical application of learning to get in the mood?

STAPLETON Well, you find things, objects—how to use them, what will help you to respond more quickly. Each actor has a different set of problems. So what one person needs to stress, another one doesn't; and you work on what your own problems are.

INTERVIEWER I came across this recently. Sherman Ewing—who is a producer, or was—advanced the idea that the Method tends to produce actors with a creative and subjective approach to a part, whereas the training that devotes itself to strict training of voice and body instruction in stagecraft and the development of personality develops performers, which the public wants and does not have enough of.

STAPLETON There's a trick word in there, of course, which is "stagecraft." Now what the hell does he mean by that? What does he mean, stagecraft? That's what the Method is—*craft*.

INTERVIEWER He says the Method has a tendency to develop actors, rather than performers.

STAPLETON Again, what is his definition of an actor or a performer?

INTERVIEWER   I think what he means, when he says performer, is the star—like Ethel Barrymore, who could come out, capture an audience's imagination, and give a performance that was absolutely magnetic and all-powerful.

STAPLETON   Different individuals have that particular quality. That has nothing to do with the Method.

INTERVIEWER   Doesn't the Method have a tendency to level actors?

STAPLETON   No. No. The Method, as I said, is to help each—you use the part of the Method that you need.

INTERVIEWER   Marlon Brando would classify as a performer in the Ewing sense, wouldn't he?

STAPLETON   Right.

INTERVIEWER   Who else? Would Shelley Winters come into that category, having a magnetism that would make her a performer rather than an actress?

STAPLETON   (reflecting for a moment) I don't know. Now, certainly Julie Harris has it. Kim Stanley has it. And they're so-called Method actresses. But, you know, they don't scratch their behinds or mumble. And they have great magnetic charm, I think, or whatever it is. And certainly the Method hasn't leveled them off. No, it doesn't do that.

INTERVIEWER   Do you think that you would have become a first-rate actress, regardless of the Method?

STAPLETON   I don't know.

INTERVIEWER   Do you think you would have found your own method, or are you not prepared to say, since it may be said that in a sense you have no way of knowing?

STAPLETON   I don't know. I don't have any way of knowing. The training I had all came from people who teach one form or another of the Method, and as far as I can see, it hasn't hurt anybody. It just causes an awful lot of excessive talk about it.

INTERVIEWER   What do you think are the most important elements in your growth as an actress?

STAPLETON   Gee—that's hard.

INTERVIEWER   It's especially interesting, because I think you are the first actress we have spoken to who has achieved this distinction of being a very fine actress, who hasn't, like Lynn Fontanne, spent years touring, or in stock, the lack of which they, the Lunts, feel is a great disadvantage to modern actors.

STAPLETON   Yes, sure—experience, of course, for everybody, in anything, is the best. Well, I toured and I stocked, certainly not as much as they did.

INTERVIEWER Where do you get such opportunities now?

STAPLETON Now? There's stock. There's a lot of that —summer stock. There's television.

INTERVIEWER But with television, you don't have an audience.

STAPLETON That's true, but acting is acting. And, anyway, any place you can act . . .

INTERVIEWER The actors and actresses coming up now are going to have to depend on that, on television, because the stage has limited opportunities.

STAPLETON That's right. There isn't that much work, really. And, of course, the real old stock days were over long before my time, or when people could tour for years.

INTERVIEWER You said recently, "We actors are like dock rats. We have to survive. We are the deformed children of the world. The actor has to hang out his ego on a line for everyone to see, and weigh, and he'd better hang it on a good line." Now, what does that mean?

STAPLETON Well—what it says. It's always good to be in a good play. Look, in this country a kid says, "I want to be a dentist—a doctor—scientist," and everything is fine, okay. But if he says, "I want to be an actor," right away parents think they've got a nut in the house. Seemingly it's a very glamorous profession, but it isn't at all. There's quite a difference between crazy adulation—I mean, I'm always polite and nice to people, but I can't take it as a serious response to work. From what I understand, in England or abroad they're very calm about it. An actor walks down the street, and if they like your work, fine, if they don't, that's all right, too. But there's something else here, a fanatical quality, that actually people feel actors are childish or egomaniacal or babies, all that sort of condescending attitude that people really have underneath it all. I just don't think it's so. True, very often we have to play the part, because that's what people expect of us, you know. But it's not true . . . Oh, I suppose you have to be a little off base to want to act. But, about actors "being children"? Well, it's sort of an attitude I guess. But again, I don't get too excited about it, because I don't agree with it. I've seen actors under pressure, and I've seen the heads of state under pressure, and I know where the rocks are. We can't afford to have that kind of an ego. I don't know how to describe it. You paint a picture and if it's bad you paint another one. But in acting it's different. When an actor gets fired, it is the most devastating and annihilating experience. It isn't just your work that you feel is being rejected, it's your whole being.

INTERVIEWER You expose yourself so completely to other people's opinions.

STAPLETON Yes, exactly.

INTERVIEWER Which is an excruciating experience. And what you say is most poignant.

STAPLETON Oh, it's a devastating experience. I've been thinking about it a great deal lately. There are so many actors, you see, so that we are a very expendable, disposable commodity. The attitude on the part of those who hire us is, I guess, "I can go out and get somebody else." So, it's a very hard profession to have dignity about, because you're treated like—I don't know—like sheep.

INTERVIEWER That doesn't go for people of your status.

STAPLETON Not quite any more, but it did for a long time. I know what it is.

INTERVIEWER What do you resent most about the thing?

STAPLETON I didn't resent it at the time, because that's the way it is.

INTERVIEWER Where did you think it was most—the worst blow to human dignity?

STAPLETON The worst thing that happens is when an actor's fired. I've been thinking about it. Maybe we should do more. When this other problem* is settled we can come to that, I suppose. But it's just too heartbreaking.

INTERVIEWER People have to be fired sometimes.

STAPLETON Well, I suppose, I suppose—but it should be made harder, somehow, because it's too . . . The actor, when he is fired—I've seen what it does. It's an annihilating experience. And it may be at a whim or chance, or something—he cannot recover from it so easily. And I just feel that somehow, some way, it should be made harder to do it.

INTERVIEWER When a writer or actor gets fired, the whole person is being rejected.

STAPLETON Yes. It's the whole essence of your being that is devastated.

INTERVIEWER What is being said to the actor is, not just that you are no good, but that all of you is no good—that's the point.

STAPLETON "All of you is no good," that's right. It's incredible.

* The interview took place during the time of the crisis between the League of New York Theatres and Actors Equity, in the spring of 1960, that led to the Broadway blackout.

INTERVIEWER   Whenever you see in the paper, "There was a disagreement over the interpretation of the role"...

STAPLETON   That's a phrase meaning somebody got axed. And there's this general casting call. I know this is the way it has to be, but you can't think of it as such a gorgeous, glamorous life, if you're herded... Like once I went, years ago, with a whole bunch of actors to try out, and someone comes out and says, "You—you—you—you—All the rest of you can go." So you go.

INTERVIEWER   The longshoremen have something like that in the shape-up.

STAPLETON   Yes. That's exactly what it is, that's right. So you know, you can't get too hoity-toity with that kind of treatment. It kind of wears you down over the years.

INTERVIEWER   Would you say that analysis helps or hurts an actor?

STAPLETON   I truthfully don't know that much about it. I've been in analysis for five years. I should not think it would hurt. I don't... good analysis, no, it shouldn't hurt at all.

INTERVIEWER   What is your feeling about marriage and children for an actress?

STAPLETON   Oh, boy, that's the sixty-four-dollar question. Well... It's hard, I'll start with that. I haven't much frame of reference except myself. I have been married once and divorced once, and I found it a rather devastating experience. I mean, some people can do it easier than I. As far as the children are concerned, I realize that I should have spent more time with them in the beginning, when they were younger. And also, as I get older—now I look forward—I'd like to... I don't have to work, I don't have that—I'm just getting older and tireder, I guess. Maybe if I'd been unemployed a couple of years, I'd feel different. But right now, I sort of—I wouldn't mind knocking off for a couple of years and just functioning as a mother, because to try to do both is—something suffers, and it shouldn't be the children. I guess what I need is a rest, a chance to sort of recharge my batteries.

INTERVIEWER   Would you say this is peculiar to the actress? There are many women who teach and run a home. Do you think the problem of the actress is different?

STAPLETON   Not so much so, unless you have to go away a lot. That's the one thing that's very disturbing.

INTERVIEWER   Yes, that's it. I was thinking of Helen Hayes, who told me that there was a constant wrench, when her child was young—the whole business of not being able to be there when they wanted you.

STAPLETON Yes, that's right. I just—from now on I'd like to be there more.

INTERVIEWER Do you think then that actresses should not have children?

STAPLETON No, I don't say that. I say, if you're going to have them and want them, then you gradually discover you don't want to act as much as you did before you had them, but the wheels, then, of a career are already in motion.

INTERVIEWER This is where the grinding comes in.

STAPLETON Yes. Yes. It's not as much of a wrench on them, maybe, but I hate to go away, now. I just don't want to.

INTERVIEWER Will you tour with this show, or have you a choice?

STAPLETON I have a choice. I have a year's contract, I think—I forget what it is. But I don't have to go on tour.

INTERVIEWER How do you know when an audience "isn't with a play"?

STAPLETON Sometimes you get a feeling of coldness— that they're not responding to you.

INTERVIEWER What do you do to beat the audience, or win them back?

STAPLETON To win them? Well, you try everything.

INTERVIEWER Is it a matter of broadening gesture? What is it that you do?

STAPLETON No. As you gradually become aware of it, you just try to be more winning. Sometimes, when it's an audience of very rich people—a guy* coming home with one hundred and fifty thousand dollars doesn't even make much of an impression, you know. If my brother ever showed up with a hundred and fifty thousand, I'd faint. Then he takes out these clothes, you know—and finally, some nights, we know they're rich, because as Anne Revere says, they'd give that stuff to the maids, and a hundred and fifty thousand dollars to them is nothing. So they can't get terribly excited about our problems, you know. So then we have to try to reach them on another level.

INTERVIEWER There's no other level in that play.

STAPLETON Well, you know, anything. You try tears or you try laughing, or you try to emphasize something else.

INTERVIEWER Then you do deepen or broaden certain aspects?

STAPLETON I suppose. I suppose you do, yes. Or, if

---

* In the play, the brother returns home after a long absence with what is a great fortune for him and his sisters.

they're not going that way, then you try to get them on something else. It's like fishing, I guess. But you have to use the tools at hand, of course. You can't make up tools.

INTERVIEWER Does each one do it in his own way? You don't have any signals, do you?

STAPLETON No, but you sort of, you kind of ... Well, when you work together you know when you have a tough nut to crack, and you do with each other—you sort of sense it. You know.

INTERVIEWER One knows that the other is pushing a little harder, and plays in.

STAPLETON Yes. I don't know how to describe it. But Jason, for instance, will sense it, and then he'll give a certain speech another kind of zing, or do it high, or just try to be more heartbreaking—maybe get them that way.

INTERVIEWER Then you go along with him?

STAPLETON Oh, yes. Everybody does.

INTERVIEWER Do you have any idea why an audience is good or bad?

STAPLETON No. No, I don't.

INTERVIEWER You were rather brash, as a young actress. You called up Guthrie McClintic and asked for the role in a play he was doing. You practically challenged him to give you the part.

STAPLETON The only time I was ever brash in my life.

INTERVIEWER Do you recommend this sort of approach for young people?

STAPLETON Anything that works. About McClintic: somebody gave me a nickel. In those days, the phone was only a nickel. (I hate the telephone company—I'll go on record for that anywhere, any time.) I called him, and accidentally he got on the phone. I'd never gotten anybody in that office on the phone before. (It took me years to figure out where the different producers' offices were. I used to go to Max Gordon's old offices in the Lyceum—there was a big waiting room, and I went there for weeks and just sat. I didn't know whom you ask for, or anything. I sat there, because I felt like I was getting close to the theatre. Once I rode down on the elevator with him and George Kaufman, and I felt like I got a job.) But that whole phone call was an accident. It was an accident that I reached him. Ordinarily I am, or was, very bovine—like I don't get fidgety, you know, even with contracts. I just say, "Aw, the hell with it." But there was something in his tone—I don't know what it was—that made me angry. I rarely get angry. I said it before

I counted ten. I asked if Beatrice Straight was going to play Pegeen Mike, because she played it in stock that summer. He said very snippily—of course now I'm madly in love with him—he said that the information hadn't been given out of his office and "I don't see any reason why I should tell you." Then I said, "Well, I don't give a good God-damn who's going to play it," and a few other choice words. There was a pause, and then he said, "How'd you like to come and see me?" I said, "Fine, what time?" He said, "Three o'clock." I said, "All right, I'll be there."

INTERVIEWER   You don't recommend this as a general procedure?

STAPLETON   No, I wouldn't.

INTERVIEWER   What advice in general would you give young people, on the basis of your experience, for getting into the theatre?

STAPLETON   If you can do anything else, do it.

INTERVIEWER   Do you believe in the schools?

STAPLETON   I do in the sense that you would be with people who are interested in the same thing you are. You're not sort of floundering around not knowing where to go or who to see, or what jobs are available. Also, they talk a sort of common language and they're helpful to each other. So everything is sort of channeled and funneled through the same source. And it can't hurt you, God knows, if it's a good school.

INTERVIEWER   What kind of acting do you admire most?

STAPLETON   What I saw recently—a staggering performance—was Geraldine Page in *Sweet Bird of Youth*. It makes me cry even now, you can see. It was absolutely fantastic. Or Julie Harris in *The Lark*.

INTERVIEWER   Have you any dream parts?

STAPLETON   Never did. No, I figured I'd only work till I was about fifty, so it never occurred to me.

INTERVIEWER   What do you do in line with the general idea of improving your mind, your sensitivity?

STAPLETON   As I told you, I'm a great one for doing nothing. I go to an analyst. And the children, and the job, and that's about all I'm up to. I don't feel guilty about it, you know, and I'm not proud of it. It's like people say, "I don't understand music," like it was something to be proud of. I don't mean that. I just am very slow, and I don't have time. If my analysis finally takes, maybe then I'll have insights into things I should do, might do, could do. But until then I just believe in putting one foot in front of the other, keep on going.

Katharine Cornell

BIOGRAPHY

Katharine Cornell was born in 1898 in Berlin, where her father was studying medicine. Soon after her birth the family returned home to Buffalo, and some years later her father left the medical profession to become a theatre manager.

Miss Cornell's own entry into the theatre came after completing school and settling in New York City, where she got bit parts with the Washington Square Players. Subsequently, there were touring and stock companies and, when she was twenty-one, the part of Jo in a London production of *Little Women*.

Back in the United States, in September, 1921, Miss Cornell married actor-director Guthrie McClintic; a month later she gained Broadway attention in Clemence Dane's *A Bill of Divorcement*. A few years afterward—in the title role of Shaw's *Candida*—she played one of her most memorable roles in the play which she was to revive several times in later years. In 1925 came Michael Arlen's *The Green Hat*, in which she played for three seasons and which ultimately elevated her to stardom. *The Letter*, *The Age of Innocence* and *Dishonored Lady* followed.

In 1931 Miss Cornell and Mr. McClintic produced *The Barretts of Wimpole Street*, by Rudolf Besier. It was spectacularly successful, and Miss Cornell played Elizabeth Barrett on Broadway, on tour across the nation and, during World War II, for the Armed Forces in Europe. This play, too, marked her debut as an actress-manager.

In 1934 Miss Cornell appeared as Juliet. Then there followed such plays as Shaw's *Saint Joan; The Wingless Victory,* by Maxwell Anderson; and S. N. Behrman's *No Time for Comedy,* which she took on a coast-to-coast tour, traveling over fifteen thousand miles and playing fifty-six cities. Altogether, Miss Cornell has appeared in over fifty productions, the most recent of which was *Dear Liar,* by Jerome Kilty. Miss Cornell is one of the diminishing number of stars who consistently tour the country, and true to this tradition she toured in *Dear Liar.*

Her only movie work was the balcony scene from *Romeo and Juliet* in *Stage Door Canteen.* She has appeared in television in *The Barretts of Wimpole Street* and in Robert Sherwood's *There Shall Be No Night.*

SETTING

The main part of the house in which Katharine Cornell and her husband Guthrie McClintic live is a converted barn. But to describe it only as that is highly misleading. For it is probably the most elegant converted barn extant. Set commandingly over the Hudson River at Sneden's Landing, some ten miles from New York City, the barn's original lovely weathered shingles remain intact. But inside, while retaining its soaring height right to the ridge pole, the expanse of ceiling over the rough-hewn beams has been gold-papered to enhance the setting for the immense living room whose furnishings and style are Georgian in inspiration. It is a formal room, but it has an effect of inviting warmth and graciousness, partly because of the long glass doors that lead onto the terrace overlooking the Hudson.

On a level below this room, and again with a glorious view of the river, is Miss Cornell's suite: a bedroom and sitting room, in pale grays, predominantly French, the bedroom's decor accented by two four-foot wooden Chinese figures serenely gazing from shell-domed niches in the wall. In these two rooms particularly—but to some extent in other parts of the house—are pieces of furniture that could provide a biography of Miss Cornell's life on the stage: here something from *The Barretts of Wimpole Street,* there a chair, perhaps, from *The Constant Wife,* elsewhere a piece from another play.

It was in Mr. McClintic's library-study that the interview took place, with Mr. McClintic present and illuminating the conversation from his own vantage point as a participant in practically all of his wife's productions and as a leading American director and producer for many years.

The room itself, lined with books, has a somewhat Renaissance feeling, with its crimson accents, red damask furniture, marble fireplace, well-displayed *objets d'art*. Wherever space permitted, there are photographs: photographs of Miss Cornell at every phase of her career; photographs of their friends—the Lunts, Vivien Leigh, Laurette Taylor, Noel Coward, Ruth Gordon, Judith Anderson and many others—and a color candid group photograph with Helen Keller in it, Miss Keller being a close and an old friend of Miss Cornell's. A notable item in the gallery of memorabilia, in another room, is a newspaper photograph of a painting of a nude, the caption, in Spanish, noting that the painting is of Miss Cornell as Candida. This slight case of editorial mistaken identity arose during the South American tour of a collection of paintings from the Museum of Modern Art, which contained the nude picture *and* the Speicher painting of Miss Cornell as Candida.

Miss Cornell herself was back at her home relaxing after a long tour and a New York engagement in Jerome Kilty's *Dear Liar*, based on the correspondence between Bernard Shaw and Mrs. Patrick Campbell. Miss Cornell smiles easily and talks easily, interspersing only occasional gestures. Comfortably relaxed on a sofa, Miss Cornell quite effortlessly—or at least seemingly quite effortlessly—radiated that charm that has marked her in so many roles. Miss Cornell wore green slacks, green and chartreuse blouse and jacket, no jewelry, and her hair was informally brushed back.

The interview was interrupted midway for a delightful lunch in the main room in front of the high windows with a view out to the Hudson. Also present: four regular members of the household, dachshunds all in the same family, all Cornell-McClintic regulars at every meal, with their own chair nearby. And very properly trained.

Interview

INTERVIEWER Your father was interested in the theatre, I gather, and so was his father.

CORNELL That is absolutely true. I come from a theatrical family, but not a professional one, that is, not a professional theatre family. My father and my grandfather had a little theatre on the top of the house in Buffalo, and in the early days of Buffalo they put on theatricals, like a great many people do in smaller cities, and my grandfather was exceptionally good as a director, and my father, a very delightful actor, always, in anything he did.

INTERVIEWER Did your mother have any interest in the theatre?

CORNELL None at all. She had no interest. I'm just torn between my mother and father, because I'm as nervous as my mother was about speaking in public. This is hard to believe, I know.

INTERVIEWER Are you nervous when you get out on the stage?

CORNELL Always.

INTERVIEWER Every night?

CORNELL Every night. You learn to control it better all the time, but I assure you, the last night I played in Boston this year, in *Dear Liar*, I was as nervous as I've ever been in my life—not because it was the last night, but because it happens always, and I have to manage it. You learn to manage it better.

INTERVIEWER How do you learn that?

CORNELL Only by repetition of the feeling that you can't be sick on the stage!

INTERVIEWER Why should you be nervous? You've been trained, you've done it successfully umpty-umpth times?

CORNELL There's something very—how would you say? —frail within yourself, not a sense of security at all, in what the nerves, one's nerves, will do.

INTERVIEWER Would you say it was vanity?

CORNELL Yes, of course it's vanity. It's egotism. You want to be so darned good—and that, I think, makes people shy, and makes people self-conscious. It's not an attractive thing, I think, to be. You know, you see people and you think, "Oh, isn't that nice, they're so modest and it's so . . ." It's false, really. It's that they don't want to be silly or don't want to make a fool of themselves. It is conceit and it is vanity. I made up my mind quite a good many years ago that that's what it was. You just don't want to stub your toe, and you want to be at your very best, and how can one be sure that you're going to be at your very best every night in the week? You can't. So you're working with a medium within yourself that is very tenuous.

INTERVIEWER What do you mean when you say "at your very best"?

CORNELL   What you think is your very best. You're not always sure that the audience is going to feel that way.

INTERVIEWER   Now, is that something that you feel within you? It's not technique. I mean, you know you're going to come in the right door and sit down at the right chair; it's not that.

CORNELL   No, it's the plus. It's the plus in the actor— in good actors, shall I say, it's the plus. It's the thing that goes beyond just coming into a room and sitting down in a chair and picking up whatever you're going to do and saying, "How do you do?"

INTERVIEWER   Do you feel this within yourself, or must it come from the audience?

CORNELL   No, you feel it within yourself. But it is a communicative thing.

INTERVIEWER   You mean, when you know you're doing well, the audience realizes it?

CORNELL   Sometimes. Sometimes. Sometimes you can be very emotional with a thing, and you think, "I feel this so," yet as soon as you begin to feel it that way, the audience doesn't feel it that way. I think it comes between you and the audience—that they're conscious suddenly that you're feeling it, instead of feeling what you're trying to make them feel. They're suddenly aware of "Oh, she's crying," or, "How she feels this"—you know?—and that's wrong. You've got to be kind of aware of it and be able to do it over that thing.

INTERVIEWER   An interesting point.

CORNELL   It's such a confusing thing. We all arrive at a certain place, if we're good actors, of capturing an audience, or being good on the stage—but I don't think any one of the people you interview will respond the same way to the same questions you're asking. Just as, if you put them to Helen Hayes and Lynn Fontanne and Judith Anderson and Ruth Gordon and myself, or name whom you want— I'm not naming these wonderful young actors now, I'm just speaking of my age group—and if we were all sitting in a line, you could ask us the same questions—which I think would be a terribly amusing thing to do—and not one of us in that group would respond at all the same way. And yet, at the end, most of us come out pretty much the same. You know what I mean by that—we can please an audience, or disturb them, the same way.

INTERVIEWER   I imagine that *The Barretts of Wimpole Street* always moved the audience. But were there some nights when you felt it was quite different in quality?

CORNELL   Well, there were nights when it didn't go. It

didn't go. Yes, oh, quite. And often when I said to my back-stage visitors, "Oh, I wish you weren't there tonight"—that is one of the things most actors say, or, "You were out there, in front! Oh, God! How did you ...? Oh, this is too awful, I was terrible tonight!" or, "The play didn't go!"—they'd be absolutely amazed. It had gone wonderfully to them. Or some nights you'll say ... Often I've said to Guthrie, "It went awfully well tonight," and Guthrie'd say, "I didn't think it was so good. You overdid it." Or, "You were aware of things ..." Some nights, you know, it won't come alive at all. You can't make anything come out simply and naturally. You seem to be terribly aware of everything you do.

INTERVIEWER Does that have to do with your not being rested, for instance?

CORNELL Yes, it has a great deal to do with it. You must never be tired.

INTERVIEWER I was going to ask you about the form of discipline that you have applied to your vocation through your life. You are, by all the records, a most dedicated actress, and I found even as long as twenty or twenty-five years ago that you wouldn't smoke during the week, when you were acting.

CORNELL I don't. I finally gave it up entirely.

INTERVIEWER How do you pace yourself, actually?

CORNELL Well, I'm a pretty disciplined person. I mean, I was brought up—my father was a disciplinarian, in fact, he was a martinet. So was my grandfather. And I was an only child, and I was very sternly brought up, and especially on the point of time. My father often said, "You may never make a success of anything, but, at least, you can be on time," and I've spent my life being on time. I suppose I could count almost on my two hands the number of times I've been late for anything—anything. I would say almost anything, wouldn't you, Guthrie? (Mr. McClintic nodded agreement) I'm never, never late. I don't mind waiting for people but I simply cannot bear that they should wait for me.

INTERVIEWER What sort of regimen do you put yourself through? Well, let us say in *Dear Liar*, which I'm sure was a very taxing part.

CORNELL One of the most taxing ones I've ever done. You were listening, if you were not speaking. I would say that the person who does a solo performance, such as, perhaps, John Gielgud does in his *Ages of Man*, would be less tired than the person who did Brian's and mine—Brian

Aherne's and mine—because, if you're talking yourself, as I am talking at the present moment, I can make pauses. I can take my time. I can think it over. If I want to walk across the stage and back after a particular scene, I can do it. With dialogue, or two people, shall I say, on the stage—not a dialogue, but with two people working together—there wasn't a moment when I had not to listen to Brian, and vice versa, and always be aware that we must not respond before the audience responded. It's so easy for you to go off in your timing—for him to say something funny, and I would feel like smiling or laughing, and yet I knew that if I did smile or laugh, somehow the focus of the audience would move for a second past him to me and, consequently, I might break up a laugh that was coming. I had to wait till they began to respond, before I could. So it took constant effort. And if you were tired, you might naturally smile at something, or laugh at something, or take your handkerchief —I had to because I had a cold—but you knew all the time that you might do something that would distract just that second. And so you never could be at ease, at all.

INTERVIEWER How did you take care of yourself during the day?

CORNELL During the day I rested. I got up. I'd wake very early. I'm a farmer at heart—I mean, I'm up early, always have my breakfast by eight. And when I'm playing, between eight-thirty and nine at the latest ever. And I'd been awake a good deal of the time before that, before I had my breakfast. And then I would do whatever I had to do. If I had to be in town, if I had to have my hair washed —those things would be done in the morning. In the afternoon I never did anything. And I would have my dinner at five-thirty every afternoon. I'd lie down after lunch. I had a very light lunch. I would walk with the dogs—I have four —and I would have regular times for going out, about twice in the afternoon, after I'd been reading a certain amount of time, you know, and then come back, and I'd have my dinner at five-thirty. Then at six-thirty I would leave for the theatre. I was always in the theatre by seven-fifteen, anyway.

INTERVIEWER Did you allow yourself any social life?

CORNELL None at all. Never. Unless I had luncheon in town, and that never would be a matinée day. If I was going to see anybody I knew, I would have luncheon. That was the only thing I did. Of course, weekends I had people coming here. Weekends are marvelous. Sunday is a day of such joy when you're working. I feel so sorry for people who don't know what Sunday means! The people who don't work. It must be miserable, to have all the days practically the same—for Sunday is a God-given day, isn't it? You can do absolutely nothing. You don't do anything. You get into that old pair of blue jeans and you just don't do anything, but have somebody in to enjoy it, too, you hope.

INTERVIEWER   But during the week you allow yourself nothing in the way of social relations?

CORNELL   No. Once or twice, perhaps, in the whole season, I'll go out for supper afterward with somebody who's going away, or a party of some kind for some actor who is here.

INTERVIEWER   Do you receive people in your dressing room?

CORNELL   Love them.

INTERVIEWER   After they've gone, you immediately go home?

CORNELL   Right home and eat something—out of the icebox, or have something—a little soup on the stove.

INTERVIEWER   Has this been true throughout your career?

CORNELL   Yes. It's always been so. Hasn't it, Guthrie? Always. But I did find that certainly a play like *Dear Liar* took more energy. And of course I'm older, so that you have to husband everything much more, although it's the same pattern that I've always had.

INTERVIEWER   Well, now, when did you show the first signs of wishing to go into the theatre?

CORNELL   Right from the beginning, I think. Right from when I was a little girl at school.

INTERVIEWER   In what way did it manifest itself?

CORNELL   I was always making up plays, and I was always playing both the leading man and the villain—always. They must have hated me, all my friends, because I insisted on these things. I might just say in passing that from my early days I was very athletic. I was a very good athlete— tennis, a little golf, swimming—there was nothing in the way of ... I could even walk a slack wire.

INTERVIEWER   Really?

CORNELL   There was practically nothing in the way of athletics that I couldn't do. So my body was disciplined, that is what I was trying to say at the moment. My body was well disciplined always.

INTERVIEWER   In other words, it was your own environment. I mean, your father, the general feeling ...

CORNELL   That made me want to do that, to go into

theatre. And it came very naturally to me. I think it was that I was really out of a theatrical family, that they had it in them, and I had it in me, and I listened to them and heard them, and watched them do these little private amateur theatricals when I was a little girl.

INTERVIEWER Did you ever participate in those?

CORNELL No. No, never. Never. Nor did my father ever tell me anything, or show me anything to do. It was only after I went to boarding school that I became interested in putting on plays, and things like that, and I really went into the theatre to learn to be a director, till I married *him*—and he took it out of my hands, and I *had* to go on the stage.

INTERVIEWER I don't know whether this is sentimental or not, but there are stories in the newspapers that say that Robert Browning had some influence on your going into the theatre. Is this apocryphal?

CORNELL I don't know anything about it at all.

INTERVIEWER It turns up in several stories.

CORNELL I had no interest in either Robert Browning or Elizabeth Barrett before I played *The Barretts*. I was totally uninterested in poetry, and it's been one of the things that I'm hoping I'll be more interested in as I grow older.

INTERVIEWER What sort of early training did you get in the theatre?

CORNELL Well, my training in the theatre was, as I say—I just did, naturally, little plays, and then when I went away to boarding school I started a dramatic association there, because of my constant interest in it, and being a very bad student, it helped me out a bit. And then I was interested in writing plays at that time—putting on musical pantomimes and things like that. It was very easy for me to do it. Allegories and things. And I was quite good as a director, in these little things. And then, during my last years of boarding school, in doing these things, I met— Theresa Helburn,* I suppose, was the first person in the theatre I met. She'd just graduated a little while before from Bryn Mawr and she came out and coached us in the theatre, in our dramatic classes. And then we put on *Twelfth Night*, I remember, and I played Malvolio, and the girl who was going to play Sir Toby Belch sprained her ankle, and Terry played it. Perhaps that was about the only time Theresa Helburn ever acted. But I really don't know that. She may have acted often before that, I don't know. And then

* A co-founder of the Theatre Guild.

Edward Goodman, who was the head at that time of the Washington Square Players, came out and directed. He came out and directed a play that I wrote. I must tell you—the sad tragedy is that the play was called *Play*, which I think will give you a little idea of what I was going through at the time. And he said at that time to me, "If you ever want to go into the theatre, do let me know." And that constituted a real invitation to me. I thought I had a job.

INTERVIEWER   You never went to a dramatic school?

CORNELL   No. I thought of going into a dramatic school in New York once, and I went to a dramatic school and talked to the director. He said, "You must come and see one of our plays, we'd be delighted to have you." And I went to see a play and I didn't think it was very good. I thought I'd been doing just as well in my own theatricals at boarding school. So I decided to try to get the Washington Square Players to give me some directions. An awfully nice woman at the Washington Square Players was very kind to me and coached me a bit, and I got an understudy part with the Washington Square Players.

INTERVIEWER   Did you go into stock?

CORNELL   I played with the Washington Square Players two years, and in the middle of the second season—I mean, after my first season with them, in which I took any kind of a thing they'd let me do, you know, and of course you weren't paid anything in those days—I went out to stock and played for Miss Bonstelle,* to whom we owe a great deal in the theatre, I think. All the people of my generation—so many of us worked with her. She was the most amazing coach and actually worked us to death, didn't she, Guthrie? The last year I was there, Guthrie was directing.

INTERVIEWER   At each of these steps what do you consider was the most important thing you learned as part of your education as an actress?

CORNELL   Well, I don't know. You just learn so many things, with a person like Miss Bonstelle, in stock—playing nine performances a week every week for about sixteen to eighteen weeks, you know.

INTERVIEWER   You played a wide range of roles?

CORNELL   I played every kind of thing I could get. The second year, I played second parts. And the third year —that was the year Guthrie came out and directed, when we met and fell in love—I was playing alternate leads.

---

* Jessie Bonstelle, actress-manager-director, who encouraged many prominent actors in their early careers.

INTERVIEWER What was the value, did you find, later on in your career, of your training in stock?

CORNELL You hear the statement made, "Oh, it's a very stocky performance." You say you think that's a very stocky performance: it doesn't seem to be right; you don't feel it's—right. It isn't a compliment, I mean, you're giving them, when you say it's "stocky." But I think there is this thing about stock. You have to learn so quickly, so many things, that you grasp, very quickly, tricks. And you learn. This, I say, you have to do, in stock, if you're playing a play every night in the week, nine performances a week, every week. You get all that amazing quick training and work, because you have to study every night—and you have to throw that on the stage quickly. The thing that keeps you from not being a stocky actress—if you have this tremendous training—is the discrimination of what you carry with you, of the advantages you had from this playing so many parts; and allowing the things to slip away that you've done for emergency and exigence—I don't know whether that's the word or not, but, you know, the immediacy of having to do this thing now, this minute.

INTERVIEWER I assume then that when you began, you used tricks.

CORNELL Of course. You had to.

INTERVIEWER What are the tricks you used that you have since eliminated?

CORNELL I've tried to eliminate a good many of them, but I'm not aware now of what they were. But I only know that you quickly grasp any straw.

INTERVIEWER What do you really mean by the word trick?

CORNELL Well, Guthrie, what would you say? *I* think I mean that in stock it's a facility of mastering a thing. The only thing I can say is, it's what you see in an actor or an actress when you say, "It's a very stocky performance." What you really mean is it's a hammy performance. I don't quite know how to define it any other way.

MCCLINTIC One thing I think you gained in stock were those nine contacts a week with an audience. They tell you more than anybody. Laurette Taylor once said, in speaking of her days in stock, "Audience, audience, audience. That's the way to learn. They teach you."

CORNELL They do.

INTERVIEWER I would think they could tell you on the big things; that is, they may cry, or they may laugh, but in between, how do they teach you? Because they can't teach you whether your entrances are, for example, satisfactory, or whether you're getting to them all the time—or can they?

CORNELL   They can.

MCCLINTIC   I've lectured a good deal and I've found out. In the beginning I can tell if this is going to be a house that's going to laugh, or whether it's going to be a house I've got to be serious with. It comes over in the first two or three minutes.

INTERVIEWER   In other words, it's the whole experience of exposure that is the story of stock.

CORNELL   Yes. Yes, it is. Having to do it time after time with a different audience and the reception of different audiences to you. But the thing really comes down to what you have within yourself that's coming through. And when I said I eliminate, I meant you try to simplify acting always. That seems to be the thing that you do about writing and every other branch of art in any way—a simplification. It is a process of elimination—to do it simpler, to have a straighter line. Painting, writing, sculpture, anything.

INTERVIEWER   Where did you learn grace, body control?

CORNELL   Whatever I have, which I don't know is that, has come just naturally.

INTERVIEWER   How did you cultivate your voice?

CORNELL   I've never cultivated my voice. That's been just as natural to me. I have at times wanted my *r*'s not to come out quite so hard, because they were very much criticized and always have been, but I'm an upstate New Yorker and that's the way it's come.

INTERVIEWER   Is there anything you've done to develop breath control, for instance? Your breathing? Have you done anything in the way of breathing exercises?

CORNELL   No, no, no. I like to sing. I used to like to sing. I didn't take real lessons in singing, although I had a woman I used to sing with quite a lot because I just enjoyed it.

INTERVIEWER   Did you read a good deal about acting when you were younger? Do you read about acting? You have no use for theory, I would expect.

CORNELL   No. I don't know what I'd do with theory. I work terribly hard and I study terribly hard, and it takes me an awfully long time to get into a part—a terribly long time. It took me weeks after we played these parts in *Dear Liar*. It was like a jigsaw puzzle; it took all this last summer, having played it six weeks before, for us to get new things into the play, out of the letters. It was more like a jigsaw puzzle that had to . . . And suddenly it began to meld, as far as we were concerned. It suddenly fell into its place.

INTERVIEWER Could you elaborate a little bit more on what you mean by "work terribly hard"?

CORNELL Well, you think a good deal about the person you're playing, the woman you're playing. Nearly all actors bring a part around to their way of acting it. I learned very early the things I couldn't do, and didn't know much about the things I could do until I grew older, and still am learning, let's face it.

INTERVIEWER How did you prepare for the role of Candida? I mean, what was your method of approach to the role? The preliminary preparation?

CORNELL There, you see. This is hard for me to say, because you really do think about it, you work on it, you think what the woman—who your producer is, you try to find out what he wants of that part—and little by little, you evolve into the woman that Candida was. I'm saying it very badly, but...

INTERVIEWER Well, no. I'm only thinking now in terms of—for instance, do you take long walks, in this meditation?

CORNELL I suppose I do. I walked a good deal and thought about it. I don't get lost very often, you know, lost in my thoughts very much. And then, little by little you work on it and day by day you rehearse it. As Guthrie says, no one would ever give me a part from hearing me read. And it was lucky that I became a manager, because I never would have had a job. Just to hear me read . . . But let's see if I can make myself clear. I remember in Vienna once, I visited the grounds of the Schönbrunn Palace. It's, oh, so beautiful. And walking in the forest you couldn't see anything. But suddenly, with no path or anything, you *saw* through to the palace. There was no path, but it just seemed to me suddenly the trees didn't—it suddenly gave you a vista, and you saw it. And that is a little bit the way working on a part is: that you work, you feel around, you bring all these things to bear on it, these little things you feel. And of course you're helped by the director constantly, and you're working with the other people; and what they're doing brings more and more to it—how they approach it, how you work with them. And then, suddenly—clip—you're on the path, your foot's there and you can see through. It grows after that, too, but I mean, suddenly you know the kind of woman you want to be. There it is. And I've no other way of explaining it.

MCCLINTIC Very, very good.

CORNELL Thank you, sir.

INTERVIEWER   It's true of writing, too.

CORNELL   Yes, exactly.

INTERVIEWER   I mean, ideas. You're not aware, many times, that ideas are working in your mind, and then suddenly—well, for instance, one morning you're shaving and you suddenly think of how you could open a certain chapter.

CORNELL   And there it is.

INTERVIEWER   There it is. Apparently the subconscious is working, too.

CORNELL   Yes. And it's constantly working. (Pointing to her head) It's working back here at night; it's working constantly in your head, somewhere, and suddenly you say, "Well, that's the woman, there I am, on the path. I'm not good in the role yet and I won't be for a long time, but I've *got* her, I know what she is, for me, for me."

INTERVIEWER   How about gesture and movement? How do they develop?

CORNELL   It should come just normally right out of what you feel. You try to keep them as simple as possible. Sometimes when you see bad acting, you think, "If it's as hard as that to be good, I don't think I can be."

INTERVIEWER   To bear out what you say. I was sitting with one of the editors of *The New Yorker* recently, and he was telling me about his father, whom he regarded as a very astute man. He said, "My father said to me one day, after reading *The New Yorker*, 'This must be very hard work.' And the editor said, 'How did you know?' And the father said, 'Because it comes out so smooth.' "

CORNELL   Yes. Well, there it is. There it is. (Picking up an ashtray) Just moving to that thing and picking that up, quite simply, like that, has taken a long time to learn. Because it seems so simple. Because it's so right.

INTERVIEWER   When Mr. McClintic first saw you, he wrote a rather famous phrase: "Monotonous, interesting, watch." What was monotonous about you?

CORNELL   My voice.

INTERVIEWER   The voice?

MCCLINTIC   I might say the note started with "Interesting."

CORNELL   Oh, you didn't start with monotonous. Well, I'm glad to know that, too.

MCCLINTIC   I have the program somewhere. You see, in those days, when I was with Ames,* he would say, "When

---

* Winthrop Ames, a famous producer, known for his taste and fastidious productions.

you go to the theatre, keep the program and write about any new talent you see." I mean, not, shall we say, of the established people, because we knew them, but anyone that was fresh. His instructions were to write an opinion. Either you say bad or ... And so that was my training. And then he would take them—the programs, that is—and look at them, and he would make out a card.

INTERVIEWER   What was interesting about Miss Cornell?

MCCLINTIC   First, I was fascinated by a notice that Heywood Broun had written about her. That's why I went to see it. Mr. Broun said that at the Comedy Theatre, the Washington Square Players were doing something called *Plots and Playwrights*. There was a young actress, he said, a "dead white young American Duse." Now, as it turned out, Mr. Broun had never seen Duse and neither had I, but the phrase absolutely fascinated me. I wanted to see this dead white young American Duse—I knew her as a name, as a legend—and I went to see ...

CORNELL   Duse, not me!

MCCLINTIC   I thought she was charming to look at. I thought she was—she fascinated me. She was dark, she had an "over" quality, that's why I said interesting—I mean, a quality that arrested you, a quality you looked at. And I thought her voice was lovely but, I thought, I got awful tired of it; it stayed lovely all the time. It didn't seem to vary. That's why I said "monotonous." And I said "watch" because of the thing I said, that "over" quality. I thought there was an extra something.

INTERVIEWER   When you got to know Miss Cornell, had she improved on the monotony of her lovely voice, or were you the first to tell her that this was ... ?

MCCLINTIC   Oh, naturally. I mean, I sought her out. That was in, I think, in 1917 ...

CORNELL   Must we have dates?

MCCLINTIC   And then, next time I actually worked with you—I saw you once, but not on the stage—it was when you were in Detroit in 1920.

CORNELL   In the stock company.

MCCLINTIC   Meanwhile, you'd played Jo in *Little Women* with great success in London, and obviously, through those really hard-working years ...

CORNELL   It just came naturally. I didn't particularly think of monotony, but I was—my advice could follow my thought more, just as the movements follow your thought.

INTERVIEWER   In other words, you were never aware

that you were monotonous in your voice, but as you developed your thinking and acting, the voice changed.

CORNELL   Just as your movement follows the thought. If you're going to walk, you walk there, and you do it.

INTERVIEWER   That would come with greater confidence, I would say.

CORNELL   Greater confidence, and breaking up your speeches, you know, and thinking them more.

INTERVIEWER   What place does maturing have in acting? I think it is true to say that there are very immature people who act very well.

CORNELL   Yes, amazingly well.

INTERVIEWER   Well what is the difference?

CORNELL   Well, that's a God-given talent, I suppose. In some instances you have, with Duse, genius. It's a talent, but—what is it? I mean, you speak of a star, the star system. You can't describe it. There are many actors who are better than some of your stars, but they haven't got that peculiar thing that makes people identify themselves with you and want to come and see *you* play.

INTERVIEWER   There's been some feeling that the Method turns out actors but not performers, and that it's performers whom the public really wants to see. They want to see people who have the magnetism.

CORNELL   That's what you call the star. We have no better word for it. It's a good word, because it does mean that thing that is a plus thing. Let's say people can act circles around a lot of other people, but they haven't that quality. Of them you say, "That's magnificent, that's wonderful, but I don't terribly care." You don't identify yourself with that person on the stage. It's a magic. It happens; it doesn't happen. You see it in a few young actors now. I saw it in Anne Bancroft the other night. I haven't been to the theatre at all, so I mention that particularly because I've seen nothing else. But being very close to Miss Helen Keller, and knowing her very well, and having done the narration to her life, and knowing Annie Sullivan backwards, in every part of her, because I wanted to play her years ago . . . Well, what I started to say was that I felt that star quality so strongly in Miss Bancroft: the direct simplicity, some moving thing within her, although she was taut and could be extremely hard and strong in the part, yet in this you felt all these other things—it seemed to me the plus things I felt about her. I would hate to make too much of a statement on that because it seems you are eliminating so many other people. I only say it because I have just seen her.

INTERVIEWER   Do you feel that this is a combination of training and of natural talent, too?

CORNELL   I think it's a God-given thing, that's all. And she's had other things—she's worked very hard, she's done all sorts of things to add to that. But the thing in the end is —the ephemeral thing that we call God-given. It's something that is from the stars.

INTERVIEWER   When you started out, in your early years, did you study or imitate other actresses?

CORNELL   No. No, never.

INTERVIEWER   How did you avoid that? I mean, was this something you knew you should keep away from?

CORNELL   Yes. You just knew that you only had what you had.

INTERVIEWER   Have you ever believed that it was important to have a wide variety of experience in order to be an actor?

CORNELL   Experience? No. No, I have not felt it was necessary to have any experience whatsoever to be an actor. I don't think you have to go through any of the problems posed in a play, or anything else. It's a question of imagination entirely, I think.

INTERVIEWER   How do you develop that imagination?

CORNELL   That is, again, a matter of either you've got it or you have not got it.

INTERVIEWER   There's nothing you can do, reading, and so on?

CORNELL   No, I don't think you can.

INTERVIEWER   In other words, you don't feel that one has to go Greenwich Village to understand beatniks, or to live in poverty to comprehend poverty?

CORNELL   No, not at all, not a bit—not a bit. None of it. No. No, I don't think so at all. I think it's just a question of limitations of imagination. I think the actor must have an imagination. I've never learned enough about Method acting to understand why you've got to feel these things so much. I should think you waste all your time . . .

INTERVIEWER   What would Lee Strasberg—the Method man—think of that?

CORNELL   He might say that's why I'm not a very good actress. I don't know what he thinks about me as an actress, but I mean, he might say, "Well, if she did all those things, she might be better." I don't know. I can feel a physical thing that one can do—I have done this many times. By breathing, you can raise the tension and excitement in you so that you can come in on top of a scene, where you've got to come in high. The old actors used to call it "shaking the ladder." They used to have the old string ladders, rope ladders, that came down from the flies. And the old actors, for the big, big scenes, you know—the tremendous scenes—they'd go and take this ladder and shake it. And they'd shake it so hard. And I can do it in a minute; you can do it in a minute. You can get your circulation up in one second. Then you get so you don't have to shake that ladder, you can do it by breathing. And often I do it with my breathing. That's nothing I've learned from anybody outside. And I've often done it with my hands on my knees. And I did it when I came in in *The Green Hat,* at the end, where—no, I didn't do it, Leslie Howard did it—when after I killed myself . . . I showed Leslie how to put his hands on his knees, and he'd come in like that. Because your whole flow of blood is very high. It's just a mechanical thing, to get your circulation up. I don't have to live through anything in a cellar; I don't have to see somebody dead down there. I can do it myself, mechanically, and with the help of my imagination.

MCCLINTIC   I can only say that once, during the thirties, I went to the Group Theatre with Laurette Taylor, and I won't say what the play was, but at the end of the second act, she said, "You must take me out of here." And when we got out on the street, I thought she was going to be ill. She said, "Why must they make acting a malady?"

INTERVIEWER   A malady! That's a reaction, isn't it? I was going to ask you, how does one stretch one's imagination? Imagination, presumably, can be stretched, like muscle, can't it?

CORNELL   Well, it's a question of elimination. Your first reaction to something may be very limited; and then you begin to—well, all I can say is, to think through.

INTERVIEWER   I was very interested in coming across the statement that you were offered a role with William Faversham, and you turned it down because you felt that you weren't ready for it.

CORNELL   Decidedly. That was when I was with the Washington Square Players.

INTERVIEWER   How did you know that you weren't ready?

CORNELL   Well, I suppose it's that innate good sense of mine.

INTERVIEWER   I was just wondering whether you had good advice, or whether it was just natural, good sense.

CORNELL   No, I had no advice at all. I knew it by

myself. It just seemed to me that it was a terrible risk. And I'll tell you frankly, I'm rather lazy. When I do a thing, I work terribly hard at it, but if I can get out of it, I will. And I think that I was afraid of it. And I weighed the risk, the odds—the one chance in, what?—that I might be good. As a matter of fact, I don't even remember the name of the play now. I've forgotten who played it.

INTERVIEWER How did you plot your career? Did you consciously plot your career, or was there an instinctive guidance?

CORNELL Instinctive, I think. I think it was instinctive guidance. And then a little later, after I married, I had Guthrie's guidance. But in the beginning, it was just an instinctive protection, self-defense.

INTERVIEWER How, Mr. McClintic, do you look at guiding a career? I mean, do you see a pattern—a progress from role to role, or a period of similar roles? Please relate it to Miss Cornell.

MCCLINTIC Well, with Kit I felt, when she'd made her first success, that it was wise for her to play as many parts, as many different parts, as she could, as they came to her. She had many, many offers. For instance, Mr. Woods*, when she played *A Bill of Divorcement*, felt she should be starred immediately. Well, we both felt that would be a great mistake, because she would take on the onus of being responsible for a play, and if the play failed, that was that; whereas if she remained a leading woman and the play failed . . .

CORNELL That was *The Green Hat*, darling.

MCCLINTIC No, I'm talking about before that. After *A Bill of Divorcement*, Woods wanted to star her.

CORNELL That's right, darling. Absolutely right.

MCCLINTIC And so for some time when he was saying, "Why, you're wasting your time, you're star material," it meant nothing. We wanted to play as many parts as was feasible for her to do.

INTERVIEWER It was said about your Candida that it was a model of tenderness, poetry and supreme womanliness.

CORNELL I didn't even know it was said. But I do like it.

INTERVIEWER How did you work for this tenderness and poetry and womanliness?

CORNELL Well, I felt that not only was Marchbanks, who was in love with her, her child, but her husband also

* A. H. Woods, author-producer.

was her child, and I felt they both were children, and I was very motherly. I was a woman—they both were my children. And no matter who played it, I always felt that, you see. I played it with Marlon Brando. Marlon played a beautiful performance of Marchbanks. I played with Orson Welles, with Burgess Meredith. I played with Ricky Bird from England, and Robert Harris—I played with five Marchbanks.

INTERVIEWER   Did you modify or change your interpretation with each new production?

CORNELL   No. I never changed my interpretation. It grew. The difference, you see, between growing and interpretation—well, there it's like imagination; it expands, it grows and it expands. Mind you, I think people sometimes go too far on a thing. You can think you're doing very much better on a thing, when you really aren't.

INTERVIEWER   Does that mean you get new or different insights into a character?

CORNELL   Deeper insights.

MCCLINTIC   She had greater wisdom, wisdom and humor—much more, in the end.

CORNELL   I think I had much more humor, too, in it. Worldly humor—you know what I mean—warmth of humor. Which is a wisdom, isn't it?

MCCLINTIC   You had more wisdom.

CORNELL   I must tell you something funny about that last production of *Candida* that we did for the Army and Navy, during the war. We had an all-star cast, Burgess Meredith and Dudley Digges and Raymond Massey, and Mildred Natwick, Brenda Forbes played it sometimes. And it was done wonderfully well, I thought, and it had been tremendously received by the critics.

MCCLINTIC   Can you wait one moment? Can I just say one thing? This was the only performance that I know of . . . We were doing it for five performances only, that was the original scheme—and we were sold out almost before the announcement came out, you know, with this cast. All the New York press asked if they could come. And we said, "This is a benefit. It's been reviewed before. We're not doing it for notices or for anything else." And it's the only time that I know that every leading critic in New York *bought* his tickets for the opening performance of *Candida*.

CORNELL   As I was saying, after the third performance, we decided that it was so good, we could go on, and we talked it over and the actors said that they all would like to go on. But I was feeling quite miserable. I was living up here and I felt quite miserable, and I went to the doctor's in the morning, this was on a Friday, I think. At any rate, I was feeling wretched. I went to the doctor and I explained my dear symptoms—because I'm a complete hypochondriac anyway—and he said, "Let me see your eyes." He looked at my eyes and he looked at my neck and he said, "You have German measles." I said, "I can't have German measles!" He said, "You have." I said, "What can I do?" He said, "Well . . ." I said, "I can't stop this allstar cast now. It's the beginning of a tremendous thing for the Army and Navy. I can't stop, I can't get these people again." He said, "Well, how do you feel?" I said, "I don't feel awfully well, but I think I can play. But," I said, "won't I give the measles to everybody?" And he said, "Well, you've come out with it now." I must add that it didn't show much on my face, only in my eyes; and it was on my body. And he said, "You've given it to them by now." And he said, "If you feel you can play, you play." And I played right through and never told one single solitary soul till toward the end. I played with German measles, and I wanted to say that you can see how susceptible I am, because in the first scene of *Candida,* just before Candida comes on, the husband says, "My wife's coming home today," and the curate says, "Oh, do you think that's wise? Haven't the children got scarlatina?" My husband says, "Scarlatina nothing—German measles." So, you see, all you have to do is talk to me about it and I get it.

INTERVIEWER You really felt your part! Now, I'd like to bring up something you have discussed in the past, and that is, the proportion of intellect that goes into acting. I gather that you feel that there is danger in too much intellect.

CORNELL Yes, I think there is. No danger, of course, with me. But there is a danger. I mean, you can emasculate a part. You can just think too much about it and tear it all to shreds, like talking about something you're writing before you've finished it. You know, you can pull it all apart and analyze it and analyze it and analyze it until there's nothing left to it. I've known two or three people who are wonderful critics, you know, perfectly wonderfully helpful people, who analyze so much about themselves that they just don't act well.

INTERVIEWER How do you strike a balance between the intellect and your feelings?

CORNELL I don't think you have to. I just think that happens without you. You don't know where your intellect stops or starts even. I don't think so. You can delight in talking about a role till you can wreck the thing, I think.

INTERVIEWER   It's like leaving the fight in the dressing room?

CORNELL   Yes. Yes, it is.

INTERVIEWER   That's interesting, because you are again substantiating what the old pros have been telling us, and that is that if you talk a thing out too much, you destroy the little mystery that's your own.

CORNELL   Yes, it is a mystery. It is a mysterious thing we're talking about—this strange thing that you can't quite put your finger on—and you do destroy it by overtalking, because in going through all of that you lose something of the mystery of it.

INTERVIEWER   Have you seen actors destroy their roles by too much analysis?

CORNELL   I have felt that they did.

INTERVIEWER   Would this be a matter of overintellectualization?

CORNELL   It's more, I think, a matter of the great pleasure one has in talking about oneself, and thinking about one's own problems, and talking about one's own problems till you bore everybody else to death.

INTERVIEWER   Could it be the reverse, an insufficient intellectual or intuitive grasp of a role, and the making an attempt to get it through repeated analysis?

CORNELL   It could be that.

INTERVIEWER   I would like to ask a question that turned up at the lunch table before, and I would like to ask it before we forget it. You said something about not reading the reviews, or Mr. McClintic not showing you the reviews if they're not good.

CORNELL   I scarcely have read any reviews at all for years. That sounds kind of affected, but it isn't meant to be affected.

INTERVIEWER   No, there's a reason for that, and I think that there must be—there's a validity to that, and I'd like to have you tell me about it.

CORNELL   Well, the validity with me is that after you get to a certain place in acting a part, when you finally produce it and you do it ... I mean, there you are, the morning after—you have to do it, you have to do it again tonight—one is not—no, I don't know anybody who is immune to bad criticism of themselves. As I said a little while ago, if somebody wants to criticize something helpfully and help me in what I'm doing, Guthrie's the one who can do that, and there are one or two friends of mine who can help a little. But he's the main one who can do it. But if somebody, say a critic, doesn't get what you're trying to do, it's awfully discouraging to have them wham at you. And I'd much rather be able to go in and face the cast who knows you haven't read the bad notice you got that morning.

MCCLINTIC I can give you an example of what Kit means, I think. I remember when I was at the final lighting rehearsal of *Romeo and Juliet*—in New York we had an entirely new balcony, we'd never been on it, never acted on it before.

CORNELL The balcony scene.

MCCLINTIC Yes. And we had never had the balcony. Anyway, the night before, at the Martin Beck Theatre ... You see, we closed on a Tuesday afternoon in Toronto, and the Century was specially held and we had a private train coming from Toronto to Buffalo to pick us up and take us to New York to open on a Thursday night. On the Wednesday night, we couldn't have the entire production—it was rather big—so we had the balcony, so they could play on it. We had no lights, but they played—she did, to be familiar with the balcony, and Basil Rathbone, where he stood, down below. The next day—in that day it was permitted—I was lighting the balcony, and I think we had a stand-in. And suddenly who should appear—she had an opening night that night—but Kit, on the balcony, and she said, "I am going to stand in," and did. It was a fairly important night, because she'd never played Shakespeare before, and we had had some unfortunate notices out in Milwaukee, from Chicago critics. And, you know, you felt them sharpening their knives to come in. I'll never forget this—Kit said to me, "You know, I'm not really very nervous tonight." And this to me was utterly amazing. I said, "You aren't?" She said, "I think I know more about Juliet than anybody who's watching it tonight, and if they don't like me, that's their privilege, but I know what I'm doing."

CORNELL I don't think I've ever been so right about it—but there it is.

MCCLINTIC But she did.

CORNELL Well, we'd worked on it a whole year—I did probably know more than most people in front.

INTERVIEWER Then you would say that it is better for actors and actresses not to read the reviews of a play until some time after the show has opened?

CORNELL I think so. After we opened in this,* Guthrie said, "Well, the morning papers don't like it." And I said, "Well, I'm just not going to read them, then. Because I've worked a year on this and I've got better all the time working on it, and I know my way through it. There's nothing more I can do. I would be delighted if they had liked it." I remember that even when you said the afternoon papers raved, I said I don't want to read them any more, because I like them when they're good for me, I've got to believe they know what they're talking about when they're not good. So I'd rather not.

MCCLINTIC Let me tell you an amusing story about criticism. Laurette Taylor told me once, when she was playing in a play written by Philip Barry, called *In a Garden,* which, by the way, was written for Kit—Laurette played it for Arthur Hopkins and it wasn't a success. And there was a great deal of dissatisfaction. Philip wasn't pleased with her performance, and she wasn't pleased with Philip, and she'd been used to playing for Hartley Manners* with whom she could do any damned thing she pleased and it was all right. And on the last night, Hopkins had said, "Please, Philip, try to remember that this is an extraordinary actress, and if she wasn't right in this part it was my fault, not hers." So Philip was very contrite, and went off—and he told me this story and she told me this story—he went off and bought a beautiful bouquet of flowers to give to her at the end and to make up. And he came into the theatre, and she was making a speech. Laurette would make a speech quicker than anyone in the whole world, and they were frightening. And she was saying that the young author hadn't learned his trade, and started in criticizing the play. Well, Philip was so—I mean, he thought, "How dare she start telling the audience what I didn't do in the play! What *she* didn't do!" And he picked the flowers up and shoved them into a garbage can and walked out of the theatre. Hopkins was so mad that he never allowed a picture of Laurette to be put in the Plymouth Theatre during his tenancy. He went back to her and said, "You never apologize for what you've done. You've done it. You believed in it to the extent that you took it. And you cannot say anybody else is to blame." And she said to me, "He was absolutely right." And I believe that.

* *Dear Liar.*
* Hartley Manners, Miss Taylor's husband, who wrote *Peg o'My Heart* for her.

CORNELL   Yes. That's true. You just have to take it both ways, you just have to go ahead.

INTERVIEWER   And now for a subject that is very dear to you, and to Mr. McClintic, and well it might be. How did you come upon *The Barretts of Wimpole Street?*

CORNELL   I had a very nice woman who was a very good actress, Katharine Stewart, an elderly woman who had very few parts—she was a very large woman and she couldn't get many parts—and she needed help, one way or another, and especially the help of doing something. So she became our play reader. And during a season—I was playing *Dishonored Lady,* I think—she sent two plays back to the office and said, "These plays I think you should really read." Guthrie was in California, doing a picture, and when I finished my run I was going to go out through Panama to get there. And I did. And I took these two plays—I can't remember what the other one was—and I read *The Barretts of Wimpole Street.* Gertrude Macy* was with me, and I said, "Gert, you've got to read this tonight. No, you've got to read it right away." We were lying on the deck. I gave it to her to read, and I read it again, sitting beside her—I couldn't let one word go. I read it twice. I said, "That play I want to buy. How do I buy it?" And she said, "Well, the agent is so and so." When we hit Panama I sent a cable to the agent and I said, "I want to buy—if the rights are free —I want to buy *The Barretts of Wimpole Street* for America." When we got to San Pedro, just before coming to Los Angeles, I got a cable saying, "Am able to buy the play." I was able to buy the play. So I got off the boat and I said to Guthrie, "I bought you a play this morning. I got the cable saying I could buy it." He looked rather startled. He couldn't be sure of my genius at buying plays. I said, "You've got to read it right away." And he took it up to his house and I said, "It is not for me. This play is one I want you to produce." So he read the first act aloud to us. We were all sitting there, about four of us. And after the first act he said, "What do you mean, you don't want to play the part?" I said, "No, I don't see myself as Elizabeth Barrett, at all." I said, "She rather bores me." He said, "This play is for you." And, by Jove, it was. But isn't this an interesting thing? Here I bought a play because I liked it, a play I thought was so extraordinary I wanted Guthrie to have it. And he read it and said, "You've got to play it."

INTERVIEWER   Which throws off the next question, of

---

* Miss Cornell's long-time friend and business associate.

course, because I was going to say, "What was it in the play that persuaded you that you ought to do it?" Anyway, why did the role bore you and yet the play was so interesting?

CORNELL Well, you know, she was nothing but a "feeder." And the play, well, it's magnificently written. I mean, it's one of the best-written plays I've ever read in my life.

INTERVIEWER Why was it turned down so many times?

CORNELL Goodness, many people lost their jobs over that play.

INTERVIEWER I understand it was turned down by over two dozen producers.

MCCLINTIC Twenty-eight. Gilbert Miller, for whom she was working at that time—it had been sent to him for Kit, and he had turned it down.

CORNELL Ethel Barrymore turned it down. Any number did.

MCCLINTIC Al Woods said, "My God, Kitty, they don't want to see you, sitting on a sofa, sick!"

CORNELL That's what I thought. You see, she was a complete "feeder." She was there all the time on that couch. I like to have some scenes, you know—I mean, I want to have some scenes. But she fed everybody in that play. She fed Mr. Browning. She fed everybody in that play from beginning to end. And it was a tiring process.

MCCLINTIC I must tell you this, though. We opened in Cleveland—four performances only. And this is rather startling. At that time there was a critic in Cleveland named Archie Bell, very well known, who's now dead. Of the three critics in Cleveland, one of them being our friend the late William McDermott, only Archie Bell liked it. He liked it enormously. But McDermott felt it was too bad that Kit couldn't find a play good enough for her. He didn't think this was. And the other critic, whose name I've forgotten, said, "The only reason she could have chosen this play was because she was on the stage all the time," which shows how much *he knew*. Now, this is very interesting. The reception on opening night was unbelievable. We couldn't quit, the way that audience was carrying on. It was fabulous. I mean, the people went crazy.

INTERVIEWER Was this in Cleveland?

MCCLINTIC Yes, Cleveland. And on the second day, you couldn't possibly get a seat for any performance. They were just standing...

CORNELL One of these electric things.

MCCLINTIC Then we go to Buffalo. Now, Buffalo is where Miss Cornell's family, friends, and everyone else lives. We went to a big party at a charming house there afterward. I remember an old beau of Kit's came up to me and said —and he looked at me rather censoriously—and said, "You're not bringing this into New York, are you?" We were opening in New York the next week, and I said, "Yes." And he said, "Well, this is like the stuff in Hoboken, where they sell beer between the acts. They're going to laugh it off the stage." I said, "Laugh what?" He said, "The father—I never saw anything more ridiculous than that . . ." I said, "It's a legitimate laugh." He said, "Legitimate? What does that mean?" So you see, if you went by what your dear friends told you, you should never have come in. We opened in New York the following Monday, and there was a big opening at the Metropolitan. We were playing at the Empire Theatre, and you came through West 39th Street to come by the entrance. It was a stormy, terrible rainy night. The play at that time was three hours long. We hadn't made some cuts that we later made, particularly when we went to the Army. And the curtain went up, with Miss Cornell on the stage, with exactly fifty-two people on the lower floor of the Empire Theatre.

INTERVIEWER How did you prepare for Elizabeth? What did you do? Did you read about her?

CORNELL No, I didn't. I didn't—I hadn't read any of the poems, even.

INTERVIEWER Did you go to England?

CORNELL No, I didn't.

INTERVIEWER You did nothing at all to get any external aid?

CORNELL No, nothing at all other than, as I say, to work on the part itself. But I had no—I never read any of the things that she wrote except the *Sonnets from the Portuguese,* that's all.

INTERVIEWER You and Mr. McClintic mentioned the fact that this was a play in which you sat on a sofa all night long. What is the problem for an actress who has to sit in one place all evening?

CORNELL Well, it's physical, mostly. I tell you, I had the most awful time. In my second year of playing it I thought I was going out of my mind, because of the position of my body, in which I had to project over here, and had to lie this way—because if I didn't, everybody had to play upstage to me, you see. So Guthrie had to direct it so it was on a line. Mr. Browning sat here, and I'd get out like this for scenes—you see, on the couch. But my neck—I used to call it a sofa neck, like Weaver's bottom, you know—I had a sofa neck. And they found that out in Baltimore. I mean I really did go down when I was playing there, I went every day and was under observation for days there—the orthopedic people. And they finally came to the conclusion that it was exhaustion and the fact that I was lying with the lights in a certain position; that I needed glasses—stronger glasses, which I didn't know about—and that this terrible pain of the big muscle was from holding my head, constantly. So they made me change my position. Now you put your feet up—you put your feet up, like that—I had to have my feet up. And you can see how cramped you are. You're absolutely lost. You can't move, you have no ease of body. Finally I got so that I lay this way, you see. But I didn't know that in the beginning, because people came on this side of me and people came on that side of me, to play these different scenes, so that the person had the opportunity—when it was their scene—for me to play to them, without changing my position. Some of them—Guthrie saw this play played all over the country—some of them played it with the couch going up and down so you were facing the audience all the time, with the other people coming and playing to you in all the scenes.

MCCLINTIC   I saw it in Budapest once, with the woman who played it playing straight to the audience, and the other actors had their backs to the audience. And there were a couple of other things that were wonderful, very interesting—she was a very charming woman, by the way—but when Mr. Browning first comes in, she says, "Those great and glorious poems of yours," and she took his hand and put it right inside of her bosom, which was a rather extraordinary Victorian gesture for this period. Later, he has to say to her, "Miss Barrett, give me your hand," which made him seem like a sissy. So I said to her later, "Why, why did you do that?" So she says, "No one in Hungary knows who she is. I must make her interesting."

INTERVIEWER   What made you want to take *The Barretts* overseas, to our Armed Forces, and what was so rewarding? And why do you think it went over the way it did?

CORNELL   There again, when they approached me to go overseas, my natural reaction was fright. I didn't think I was right. I mean, I didn't think I was a comedienne, I didn't think that I'd have the right kind of stuff to take overseas. Then

I remembered *The Barretts*. Remembered? I mean, I was scarcely away from it. *The Barretts* had played in seventy-two cities in the United States, to standing room. That meant that human beings all over the country got it, were thrilled by it, and that it caught them. And to feel that the G.I. was anything but a wonderful human being was ridiculous; to feel that he had to have nothing but comedy or leg shows or guitars, was absolutely wrong. I mean, it was untrue and it was demeaning, to think they couldn't take anything in their stride, *if* it was done well. *If* it was done well. So I said that I would go if I could take *The Barretts of Wimpole Street*. And it was a terrible strain, for there were seventeen people, about five thousand pounds of displaced weight—and they sent word to Washington that that's what I wanted to do. Well, the U.S.O. and the powers that be, I don't know who all they were, thought it was ridiculous. Well, at that time I knew Frank Mc-Carthy. He was a press agent before he was with General Marshall, and he was his press aide, you see—Colonel Mc-Carthy, he's now in Hollywood. And he was a great friend of Francis Robinson,* who was with me so long. So I got in touch, or rather Francis got in touch, with Frank and had him come to my hotel—I was playing at Baltimore—and I said how I felt about this, that there was no question about it, that it was large but I knew we could do it, and I knew that it would be a success. I said, "It's about the home life of a family. I know it's not exactly theirs, but it's got a lot of excitement in it, with the father this megalomaniac. It's got all the elements in it of excitement." Finally, General Marshall sent word to me that I should do it. General Marshall's wife was an actress, and she liked *The Barretts of Wimpole Street*. This is the way things come around. We rehearsed it. We took all our shots during the hottest summer you can imagine, in '44. And we had the whole cast, got everyone we wanted, and they were all passed, but it was awfully slow work, and we felt, "When will we ever get briefed somewhere?" I can remember one young director came—who is a very, very successful director now in television—and he said, "They won't take it, Miss Cornell, they won't take it for twenty minutes." I said, "Well, we've been doing it for a long time, and I don't think they'll take anything for ten minutes if they don't like it. And I believe we can make them like this play." So they

* Former press representative for Miss Cornell, and now assistant to Rudolf Bing, director of the Metropolitan Opera House.

had to go ahead. They had to go on with it—we had our
sets made. And we were sent, finally—at last, we were sent
out to Mitchel Field, which, of course, was the base of
"the spoiled babies." They were the wonderful Air Forces
who could go anywhere in the city, they could go to any
theatre at any time they wanted. So they gave us the hardest
place to go and be tested. And, I tell you, that play went
as if a storm of the sea waves—I've never heard such applause, or such excitement in my life. We stood there and
heard this noise and we couldn't believe it. We didn't
know—perhaps they're throwing things, we didn't know. And
suddenly we just burst into tears, it was so wonderful. And
those majors and colonels who had been a little bit that
way, were completely bowled over. And they came back
on the stage and said, "We just can't believe it, you're all
right." It was the same thing right from the start over there.
We played our opening in Bizerte. General Larkin was our
marvelous general there in Naples—outside of Naples. He
said, "You're ammunition, we'll keep you going up," which
was one of the greatest compliments we could have had, I
think. "You're ammunition, we'll keep you going up." And
he kept us going, up to the Fifth Army, then up to France,
to Holland. Well, nothing's been like it. I tell you, nothing.

INTERVIEWER   This has been your greatest experience?

CORNELL   That is, to us—to all of us, everybody who
was in it.

INTERVIEWER   Do you think actors have an obligation
to tour?

CORNELL   No, I don't think so, necessarily, but I think
they lose an awful lot if they don't. I mean, I think they
lose a lot of the—the covered-wagon feeling about the theatre. It gets to be so stale, just playing in New York. I feel
sorry for these young people. Some of these young actors
wouldn't think of going out of town. Wouldn't think of it.

INTERVIEWER   Why shouldn't actors feel an obligation
to tour? Why should actors just skim the cream in New
York?

CORNELL   I don't know. But this I do know, and
that is, there is no such thing as a New York audience. I
won't say that I've always been successful by any manner
of means in New York, but I've had a percentage, I would
say on the right side, of successes in New York, as against
failures. And I believe a great deal of that is due to the
fact that I have played the road. The people who have
seen you on the road, do want to see you again in New
York. They saw you in such and such a place. It happened

this season with *Dear Liar*. It was wonderful, the response we had on the road with this thing. We had to play the same theatres that every other company's been playing lately and said such terrible things about. You know, about the theatres not being clean. But how can you afford to have a theatre kept clean all the time, in good condition, when you have three plays a year? You can't. You have to take it and scrub it up as you go. But it would not be that way if more of our profession would return to the old practice of touring.

INTERVIEWER Do you enjoy touring?

CORNELL I suppose I do, although I must confess that I find I have great difficulty in eating on the road. That's why I enjoyed my land-cruiser,* because things could be cooked for me, and I can eat only what you might call a doll's dinner. I have no tummy at all for it when I'm acting—for eating—and yet you've got to eat. That I find is, perhaps, the hardest thing you have to take on the road; the hours that I have to eat, and rest afterward before I go to the theatre. And it is a lonely existence. But you do see some nice museums.

MCCLINTIC A number of years ago Mrs. Fiske said to me, when Kit had just played in *Bill of Divorcement*—Mrs. Fiske wanted me to do a revival. I had just done *The Dover Road*, and she wanted to present to me the idea of doing a revival of *Becky Sharp*, which was one of her great successes in other years. She said in this curious staccato way she had of speaking, "I want to do it while I still keep," and she also said, "I hope Miss Cornell will not neglect the road." She said, "Too many of our young players feel it's beneath them to go on the road." She said, "New York, to me, is just a stem."

CORNELL That was the way she was. And a few of us feel that way about it, but I think you're right when you say we feel a responsibility to do it. And to an author.

MCCLINTIC In the old days, of course, before the days of television, before all of this, Mr. Frohman's stars— Maude Adams, Ethel Barrymore, John Drew, Otis Skinner—all of them went on the road every year. John Drew played three months in New York and then toured the entire country with a success, so the whole country knew him.

* A specially designed truck in which Miss Cornell toured in *Dear Liar*.

CORNELL In Seattle, Guthrie as a youngster saw Sarah Bernhardt; he saw all those people.

MCCLINTIC Laurette Taylor paid for her neglect of the road. For years only New York had seen her. She played *Peg o' My Heart* for six hundred and four performances, at that time the longest run New York had ever known. She spurned the road. She played only for New York. She played in New York continuously from 1909 until 1924, and then when she went to Chicago she was absolutely amazed that nobody gave a damn whether she was in Chicago or not. They didn't know her.

CORNELL I think they miss something in every way. I think that young actors miss the kind of excitement of it. I don't know, it's a very . . .

INTERVIEWER The old vagabond days of the trouper, I suppose.

CORNELL I think that you have to have a bit of that in you. Not that I feel such a trouper still, but I've enjoyed it and I've loved it and the road's been wonderful to me.

INTERVIEWER How do you keep your interest in a long run?

CORNELL Well, there again is what I said at the table a little while ago, that every night is an opening night.

INTERVIEWER You don't feel the way so many actors feel, that after six months they're operating in a vacuum?

CORNELL I think it's hard, often, if you're not doing business, but then you don't play any more if you're not doing business. But if you're doing business, I don't quite see that. I think you should be carried along by the feeling of "it's an opening night every night, you've got to be fresh, you've got to be rested, you've got to give them the best you've got." You know what I mean—they deserve the best you've got, they've paid a tremendous amount to come to see you that night. I know it sounds grandiloquent, or grand-elegant, the way I say it. But that is how I feel.

INTERVIEWER Why have you avoided Hollywood and television?

CORNELL When I was in—modestly speaking—most demand in Hollywood, was when I was doing *The Barretts,* when I started myself out as a manager. And I felt that you couldn't do both. You just couldn't serve both masters. And then, as it went on, and time went on, and I was better known as an actress, then it became harder to feel that you could just say, "Oh, I'll go and do a part in Hollywood," because I don't think you can do that. I think

Hollywood is a very important—movies are a very important medium, and that just because you are good on the stage is no reason to think you can be good in a picture. But you can't just go back to the beginning and play an early picture. I mean, you can't go back and play a small part in pictures if you're a well-known actress, because they say, "What's wrong? What's wrong?" And the managers wouldn't let you. The producers out there wouldn't let you. And, perhaps, again, it is self-protection on my part. I didn't want to be a failure, and I did also feel that you had to learn a lot about it, and to put you into a good part when you might not be able to carry that good part would be a stupid thing to do.

INTERVIEWER Does this apply to television, too?

CORNELL I did *The Barretts* on television, and I played *There Shall Be No Night* on television. I enjoyed doing *The Barretts*. That was a play I knew very well, and knew the woman inside out, and though I was very nervous, I think it went well. In fact, I know it went well. The other one didn't go so well because I didn't know it so well, and I was unhappy. I think probably I'd be happier on tape-recording things now, and yet I think they lose something on that, too. And since that time, since my unhappiness in that, I have just said no.

INTERVIEWER How long do you think you're going to continue acting?

CORNELL That I would never know. I've often said —I've said it several times this year, "This is the last one I'll ever do." I suppose if something very right for me came along, I think I'd like to do it, but not next year. I'd like to do it the year after.

INTERVIEWER What is your problem of getting plays now?

CORNELL Well, it's age, to a certain extent, isn't it? To get them that suit you, at a particular age—I don't even necessarily feel I want to play a principal part.

INTERVIEWER What do you think have been the advantages or disadvantages of being directed by—

CORNELL By my husband? Well, I can say that there have only been advantages, as far as I'm concerned, and I think he feels pretty much the same way. Because all my successes have been with him, under his direction, all of them. We've had some failures, too, but my successes have all been with him.

INTERVIEWER Do you rehearse at home?

CORNELL No.

INTERVIEWER   You don't work on—

CORNELL   He may work at home, but not me. He might talk to me—coming home in the car, he might say, "I think you overdo that scene," or something like that, but that's all.

INTERVIEWER   Do you ever argue with him?

CORNELL   Oh, yes. We argue. For instance, he didn't want to do *The Green Hat,* the one we spoke of a little while ago. He thought it was a terrible play. Well, I knew I had something I could do in that play, and it might be a bad play, but I knew I could do it, and so I fought him on it, and I was right in it.

INTERVIEWER   That's in the choice of a role, let us say. He was right about *The Barretts,* definitely.

CORNELL   Absolutely.

INTERVIEWER   He gave you your supreme role.

CORNELL   Yes.

INTERVIEWER   I mean, there's always a danger in a marriage . . .

CORNELL   Well, that doesn't, hasn't come into it. We may argue off the stage a good deal. But, well, we're here together, still.

* Mr. McClintic died on October 29, 1961.

Paul Muni

BIOGRAPHY

Paul Muni was born Muni Weisenfreund in Lemberg, Austria, September, 1895. His parents performed in vaudeville-type shows and circuses, and when he was a youngster the family emigrated to the United States, settling for a time in Chicago, where he was educated. His first stage appearance was in 1918 with the Yiddish Theatre stock company in New York City, and subsequently he became a member of the Yiddish Art Theatre company, working in New York and on tour across the country. He appeared in 1924 in London in *Sabbethai Zvi*, with Maurice Schwartz.

He remained on the Jewish Stage until 1926, when he made his first appearance in an English-speaking part in *We Americans* in New York. He went on to do a number of other plays, and in 1931 soared to his great success as George Simon in *Counsellor-at-Law*. There followed many other outstanding stage roles, including those in *Key Largo*, *Death of a Salesman* in London, and most recently, in 1955, in *Inherit the Wind* in New York.

Much of Mr. Muni's activities have centered in Hollywood (his first movie was made in 1929), where he has had a spectacularly successful film career. Among his best-known films are *I Am a Fugitive from a Chain Gang, The Good Earth, The Story of Louis Pasteur*—for which he received an Oscar—and *The Life of Emile Zola*. He is married to Bella Finkel, once an important actress on the Jewish stage.

SETTING

Mr. and Mrs. Paul Muni live in an apartment in a fashionable section of New York's East Side. It is a spacious and pleasant home. We interviewed Mr. Muni in his study; with us was Mrs. Muni, who has worked closely with him throughout his career, often acting as a buffer between him and producers, agents and others.

Mr. Muni's comfortable study is not very large and it gives an initial impression of having come right out of *Better Homes*—the furniture is on the modern side without being extreme. Books line one entire side of the room and the other walls are covered with brown-grass cloth on which there are the right number of prints for balance; a television set occupies one corner. A meticulous orderliness marks the room. Next to the telephone, on a little table beside a sofa, there is one of those gadgets Mr. Muni is so fond of, a device for finding telephone numbers quickly. There is a clock on the bookcase, and on the desk more gadgets and another clock.

On a hanging shelf, interspersed among the books, stand some of Mr. Muni's prize trophies, dominant among them the Oscar he received for his portrayal of Louis Pasteur; the gold-colored spiral Volpi Cup awarded by Italy, also for Pasteur; and a smaller statue awarded by Argentina for his performance in *The Last Angry Man*. The books on the shelf range from plays to histories; from biographies and reference books to *Auntie Mame*.

The interviewers were seated on a sofa, and Mrs. Muni in an easy chair, but Mr. Muni sat in a straight-back chair pulled up beside the desk, on which he would occasionally rest an elbow, his head on his hand. He has gray hair, but an extraordinarily young-looking face; his amiable manner and bright and ready smile quite belied his admission that he is a "pretty difficult customer." Mr. Muni talked with interest about the theatre, the movie, his years of work. His voice is on the quiet side but is invested with a compelling quality. He sat quite still. He wore a white shirt, a tie, brown sports coat and gray slacks. He had on tinted glasses.

Mrs. Muni matched perfectly her husband's easy, down-to-earth manner. Despite their long-term residence in the film capital, there is nothing "Hollywood" about these people. Mrs. Muni wore a simple black dress with some touches of white, a wrist watch, no other jewelry. She calls her husband "Muni"—once his first name.

Interview

INTERVIEWER As you see, we weren't discouraged by your warnings on the telephone, and so here we are!

MUNI Well, I have never allowed myself to become a spokesman or an expert in the field of the theatre, the movies, or acting, or anything of that sort, and I say this not with any false modesty or any humility or humbug. I say this because as a matter of truth in my very many years—and I say many years with considerable justification, because I've been acting for fifty-three years, not good but acting, especially in the early days when I was just knocking around in what we called nickel shows—I've never permitted myself to give out on acting. Because, frankly—and I hope you believe me—I know nothing about acting that I myself can say, "This is a theory about which I have found out and I've pinned it down and I'll sign my name to it." I wouldn't sign my name to anything that has to do with acting, because it's such a volatile thing—call it an art or a business or whatever you want to choose. I don't even know what to call it.

INTERVIEWER I don't think it's going to be as painful as you are trying to make it sound. Now, let's start off with a warm-up question. How did you come to go into the theatre?

MUNI My parents were in the theatre, in the old country. They were in what was known as the cheapest form of variety, Yiddish vaudeville, as it was once called. My father, originally—as it was told to me, I wasn't witness to it—had been what was known in those days in Austria as a tingle tangle schauspieler.

INTERVIEWER A tingle tangle schauspieler? It sounds like a carnival player.

MUNI Some sort, something of that sort. He was in vaudeville. He'd knock around in places; sometimes he may have been with a little circus. I'm not too clear on it. I recall my father and mother—he took her into the profession—talking occasionally among themselves and sort of putting things together. He was not a good boy when he was a youngster. He ran away from home when he was about twelve years old. He belonged to a Hasidic family somewhere in a Galician town. The Jewish people were very much persecuted at that time, but the vaudevillians and the circus people, for them there was no such thing as persecution. They just traveled around all over. They were like gypsies, you might say, and that was—that started the ball rolling. We were left alone a great deal. My parents were traveling about, knocking about, and we were left in other people's homes. I have a rather vague recollection of my background and I've never attempted—for some reason which I can't even understand myself—I've never tried to go into the business of checking up on all of these things. I never cared very much who I was, where I came from, what my parents were doing. But we came to London, I think, at the turn of the century, and my parents played there; first in a legitimate theatre, and then my father leased a theatre for himself and became the sketch artist and the boss. And at the turn of the century, 1900 or 1901, we came here. There was a group of variety theatres down the East Side on Clinton Street and on Suffolk Street, and then in Brooklyn, near the bridge, there was a Yiddish—there were about thirteen or fourteen little vaudeville houses. When I say vaudeville, I mean Yiddish, Yiddish vaudeville, where they would do sketches, and they were what they would have called in the jargon, they used to call, "single turns," where a single would go out and sing songs. At that time there was Belle Baker and Sophie Tucker, and all these people were part and parcel of that group, you see. And there were a group of others. There were some who later on became quite well-known actors. Some went to England, and some of them later went on to—it wasn't Broadway then, because Fourteenth Street was the theatrical neighborhood, I think, at that time. We lived downtown, way down on Clinton Street or Suffolk Street, I don't remember. We moved around from one place to another in these coldwater flats on the fifth or sixth floor, or somewhere. But we still moved around—Cleveland, Chicago—and I actually started in Cleveland in 1908.

INTERVIEWER   I'm interested particularly in asking you about your association with the Yiddish theatre. Did the Yiddish theatre foster its own kind of acting style?

MUNI   Well, now, when you're talking about the Yiddish theatre, you're talking about a facet of the Yiddish theatre, because the Yiddish theatre—I didn't belong nor did my family belong to the Yiddish theatre. That was the theatre of my wife's family. She's one of the Thomashefskys. Her mother was the sister of Boris Thomashefsky. They were the legitimate theatre. They were the high class. They were the big time. And I was what was known as the nickel-show actor. We used to play for a nickel, for a dime.

INTERVIEWER But you did work, subsequently, in what is the Yiddish legitimate theatre.

MUNI I'll tell you how I got into that, and that was a rather interesting experience. At the time we used to have touring companies coming from New York to Chicago. Among them were Adler, Kessler, Thomashefsky. There was an actress, a very famous actress, called Bertha Kalich. They were then the equivalent of the Barrymores. In the Yiddish theatre they were the tops, the very tops. Well, in the summertime they used to tour the so-called provincial towns, and among them was Chicago. There was Philadelphia, Boston, and so on, then Chicago. And invariably they needed an "extra," you know, they wouldn't take the whole company. They'd do a repertory.

INTERVIEWER Like our summer theatre packages.

MUNI That's right. They'd do about eight or nine plays and they'd just take principals along with them, the so-called well-known New York actors, and for the rest they'd get local talent. I was one of the local talents among maybe twenty or thirty others who were what they called the Chicago boys, Chicago talent. And I had the opportunity at that time to be drawn from the group with a few others to play certain roles with the big companies that came from New York. Therefore, I became fairly well known among the first-class actors, I mean the top actors. Ultimately my name was sufficiently well known that a chap named Jacob Kalich, who was the husband of Molly Picon—he was a manager in a Boston opera house—heard about me and he sent me a letter. I don't think he wired me, they wouldn't spend that kind of money. And he hired me to come to Boston to be one of the company. Well, anyway, when I came to Boston in 1917, I was there about four or five weeks working with top actors, I mean top road actors, not New York actors, because they were sectionalized. In other words, there was a terrific aristocracy among the Yiddish actors, much more than among the American actors that I know now. Because today you can get a night-club performer to go into a Broadway show and be a big hit all of a sudden. That couldn't happen in our day. There were three actors' unions. There was Section One and Section Two and Section Three. Section Three was the variety actors, the vaudeville actors, where my father and mother belonged. Section Two was the road legitimate actors. Section One were the New York actors that played in New York. They had thirteen or fourteen theatres in and around New York, and then they would tour. They were the tops, you see. Now, I didn't belong to any union. I wasn't good enough to belong to any, and that's true. But being a local boy in Chicago, whenever they were in need of an extra hand, they'd call on me and one or two others.

MRS. MUNI   Now get back to Boston.

MUNI   Well, we closed because of the flu, and then I went from Boston to Philadelphia and played in the vaudeville house. I had to live, you know, I had to eat. My salary was all of—I started with about twenty-five dollars a week, or twenty-two dollars a week, and built it up to about thirty-five dollars a week. I was about to sign a contract to go to a legitimate theatre when Maurice Schwartz, for some reason which I can never understand, sent a chap to Philadelphia, and all of a sudden they signed me up to do the Irving Place Theatre, which was at that time the Yiddish Art Theatre.

INTERVIEWER   And this was the top?

MUNI   The Yiddish Art Theatre was *the* theatre.

INTERVIEWER   To get back to that question about acting in the Yiddish theatre, was there a warmer style of acting than in the American theatre? Is that true?

MUNI   I don't quite know what you mean by warmer theatre.

INTERVIEWER   More emotion.

MUNI   I would call it a broader type of acting. In other words, the broad gesture and the melodramatic pose was more in line. But then when Schwartz came along, he created the so-called literary, arty theatre. That was the first type, where he first had Ben Ami with him; he had Ludwig Satz, he had Celia Adler, he had all the very finest talent of that day. And he brought us a wonderful character actress called Abramowitz; a miraculously wonderful actress, she was occasionally called the Yiddish Duse, but she was a character actress, an elderly woman who had the most natural quality on the stage.

MRS. MUNI   That was a turning point in the Yiddish theatre.

MUNI   And the naturalistic theatre came in. We were doing a Yiddish Stanislavsky kind of theatre. As a matter of truth, we did do numerous Russian plays by Chekhov and Andreyev and Gorki. We did *Lower Depths;* we did *The Seven Who Were Hanged,* by Andreyev; *Anathema*. We did some very excellent . . .

MRS. MUNI   And also that was the period where Sholom Aleichem came in.

MUNI   That's right. And we did a great many Sholom Aleichem plays and David Pinsky plays, if those names ring a bell.

INTERVIEWER   Yes.

MUNI   So we did the better type of plays, and I was with this company from 1918 to 1921.

MRS. MUNI   You only worked for Schwartz a few years, and I think spoke to him for a few months during the entire time.

MUNI   We used to converse through a third person. He'd say tell him that so-and-so, and I'd say tell him so-and-so. We got into a hassle the very first season that I got in there because—not for myself, this sounds a little bit doctored up and I'm sure it's hard to believe, but it's true—because he insulted an actress, a colleague, and an actress that I disliked heartily, but he was so crude and so brutal in his method of . . . He didn't like her, he wanted to get rid of her, and I knew her very well for many years. In fact, she and her husband worked for us in Chicago many years before that. And I, for reasons that I don't understand, managed to be very independent, keep myself very independent, never cared whatever happened. I mean, I would have my say, and I was always the first one to speak up. I was sort of a *chutzpanik*—a wise guy.

MRS. MUNI   He was always quitting.

MUNI   I was always—I always said, "Nuts to you," and I would quit, that's it. That's stayed with me ever since.

MRS. MUNI   And it still pertains, too.

MUNI   That has been a characteristic which I'm not happy about, but nevertheless there it was. Whether it was caused by an inferiority complex or whether it's because I felt I could get along without the other guy or something, whatever it was, I don't know. It needs a psychologist for this. At any rate, I worked for Schwartz from 1918 to 1921, and in those years I don't think I spoke to the man more than about perhaps two or three times.

MRS. MUNI   He directed you.

MUNI   He directed, yes. And then later on, when he left for Broadway—he did *Anathema* on Broadway—he left me there to carry on for him. In other words, I played the roles that he would have played.

INTERVIEWER   In combining the old bombastic Yiddish acting school with the more naturalistic acting of Stanislavsky, what is it you think came out of this? What kind of style?

MUNI   Frankly speaking, my own personal style, and the style that I could not change—and the people that I worked with were of that style—was the naturalistic style. We never allowed ourselves the type of—you know, this musical comedy or the musical show-type of acting, with the broad gestures.

MRS. MUNI   Even in the dramatic theatre downtown, even during that period, there were two styles of acting. There was my Uncle Thomashefsky, who was a hamfaddo, and then there was Adler, who was also hamfaddo, regardless of what anybody else says.

MUNI   They had all perfected methods.

MRS. MUNI   But then there was the man called David Kessler, who was the greatest of them all.

MUNI   He was the naturalistic actor. Then Rudolph Schildkraut came along, and he was a German actor, of course; and then everybody sort of moved their allegiance or their affection to Rudolph Schildkraut because he became the epitome of great acting. And he was, of course, one of the greatest, since he knew his acting from the real school. But the Yiddish theatre—what you are trying to find out is the transition.

INTERVIEWER   What I'm interested in is—George Abbott, for instance, is supposed to have said that you combined a naturalistic or realistic style with emotion, yet without the bombast. That was peculiar to you and very effective.

MUNI   Well, that is the style that we had in the naturalistic theatre.

MRS. MUNI   No, Ben Ami had the same thing.

MUNI   There were two types of non-Yiddish theatre. There was the type of non-Yiddish theatre where they did the melodramatic play. Everything was very broad. And then they did the type of play that—they were naturalistic. I can't recall now the various plays that I had seen at the time.

INTERVIEWER   The big American revolution came after the visit here of the Moscow Art Theatre in the twenties.

MRS. MUNI   We went to see all of the Moscow plays. And then later on Reinhardt came. He came with his German—and this too helped change the whole tenor of acting.

MUNI   At the time I was doing *Four Walls*, Reinhardt and Kenneth Macgowan came backstage one day, and of course she ... This is a cute story—Mrs. Muni can tell it better than I can. In *Four Walls* I got to the point where I got bored with the thing and I started clowning a little bit, you see. She was in the play with me, and she always objected to any kind of clowning, you know, she was very rigid about those things. So as I was coming through the door and I was doing some sort of a stupid thing there, she said, "Stop that, Reinhardt's in the theatre." So I said, "All right, go on, you're kiddin' me, ha, Reinhardt's in the theatre." I had a habit occasionally, all of a sudden, when I felt in the mood, a little nutsy, to speak whatever I had on my mind. So I gave voice to it. I said, "Aha! She wants me to stop kidding." And sure enough after the second act was . . .

MRS. MUNI   After the show they all came back.

INTERVIEWER   How did the Yiddish theatre happen to pioneer in this naturalistic movement?

MRS. MUNI   Well, I think that one of the people who was very, very responsible was first of all Uncle Boris, my uncle, who brought over this writer called Ossip Dymov, and he was from the Russian theatre style.

MUNI   Yes, he had written in Russia.

MRS. MUNI   And he had an influence.

INTERVIEWER   Now, obviously you never went to dramatic school or . . .

MUNI   Oh, God forbid!

INTERVIEWER   You never had a dramatic coach. You don't miss it at all?

MUNI   I don't know, I personally don't miss it, maybe the audience misses it. I don't miss it. I couldn't tolerate that. I wouldn't have any patience with . . . I went through a rigorous workout. I lived in the theatre ever since I was conscious of the fact that I had to go on the boards and appear before an audience. I lived there from ten in the morning till twelve at night every single day. When everybody else was gone, I was acting. I was on the stage doing something, making believe, doing all sorts of things. I was a very ardent theatregoer at that time. Whenever anything happened, whenever anything new came along, whether it was American or foreign or whatever, I went to see it. I was addicted to the theatre at that time.

INTERVIEWER   Since you're the first person we've spoken to who was with the Yiddish theatre, could you tell us a little about what was unique in the training you got there.

MUNI   I wouldn't know. As far as I am concerned, there was nothing unique about it—it was just working. I mean, it appears to me that this business, these so-called

theatre schools ... I was prone in a way, and still am prone,
to be a little skeptical and perhaps ...

INTERVIEWER   Iconoclastic?

MUNI   Well, that's a very high-class word. I consider it
somewhat absurd to try to mold talent. That can't be done.
I realize that there's such a thing as form and style and
format and plan, and so forth, which has to do with pure
technique. Now, practice makes to me—practice makes
technique. Acting is to me an unorthodox business. It has
no ritual to it, it has no style. it has no method that can
be, that you can say, well ...

MRS. MUNI   That's heresy.

MUNI   What?

MRS. MUNI   That's heresy.

INTERVIEWER   Well, let him say it, it is important.

MUNI   No, no, it isn't important. Look, I assure you
I'm not sitting here like a Buddha giving off with wisdom.
I'm just telling you how I feel, and I'm prejudiced. I tell you
that right off the reel. I'm prejudiced, and therefore I can
only see what I can see. Perhaps I have blinders on and
I can't see wider than the horizon of the eye or on the
sides, but to me there is no such thing as restricting—I can't
conceive of restricting a volatile force such as talent in any
form. You are within a certain area, whether it is on a
canvas or on a platform or whatever. It's not music, it's not
painting, it's not things that you put down and you say that
you have to follow the scale, you have to follow this note,
you have to follow this, this particular composition, or the
rhythm or whatever. Each person creates his own format,
you might say, and therefore I'm always interested in seeing
something new. I mean, I always admire something new,
even though it may not appeal to the majority of people,
but I admire the adventure. I admire somebody stepping
out and being an innovator in a new field and trying something new, using that volatility that is in the human kind,
because otherwise you restrict and limit the creativity of
the human being, of anyone who can create.

INTERVIEWER   Then what of the Stanislavsky Method?

MUNI   I wouldn't dare—I consider it ridiculous for me
to name methods, to say Stanislavsky, or Tairov,* or other
such things. I've read and I have in my library here and
in my closets all sorts of books on various styles of acting,
and I find that they confuse me. I don't agree with them.

---

* A Soviet producer who in 1914 founded the Kamerny Theatre and a
system that reduced his actors to the status of puppets.

I don't disagree because I don't know. I don't pretend to stand in judgment on people who have made a study and have gone thoroughly into the thing, which I have never done. And it would be highly intolerant and stupid of me.

INTERVIEWER In other words, you have relied primarily on your technique to start, and on your instincts and on your intuition?

MUNI Well, I can tell you a little story. It's my wife's story, she can always tell it better. She had a grandmother, and they used to ask her how do you make a . . .

MRS. MUNI Are you spoiling my story?

MUNI All right, you tell it.

MRS. MUNI My grandmother was a very, very good cook, and people always wanted her recipes, and one of the things she made very well was apple pie, and one woman approached her and asked, "Mrs. Thomashefsky, how do you make your famous apple pie?" And she waited a minute and she said, "Well, I wash my hands, comb my hair, and I put on a clean apron and I make apple pie."

INTERVIEWER And that's your way.

MUNI I go to the theatre, I put on the make-up, I go on the stage and I act!

MRS. MUNI It's not quite that simple.

MUNI No, I work on things very diligently.

MRS. MUNI The interesting work is before he ever goes into rehearsal.

INTERVIEWER I was coming to his methods of procedure, but I wanted to know, just in passing, why you remained separate from the Hollywood crowd and the Broadway crowd, as you mentioned to me over the telephone.

MUNI I'm an introvert.

INTERVIEWER Just as simple as that?

MUNI Just as simple as that. I can't find any other logical answer, and this is to me the simplest and the most logical answer. And if any one wants to refute it, they'll have to give me the reason.

MRS. MUNI Don't look at me, I won't refute it.

MUNI That, of course, is a paradox, because an actor presumably must, in order to act, be an extrovert, in order to be able to exhibit himself. And this is a rather complex question, which I, myself, have never found an answer to, because when I get into a role, that is, when I used to get into a role, something that I felt warmed me a little bit, I had no inhibitions. I had no feeling that anything was either pushing me or holding me back to do anything. It was just a natural manifestation of something that had to exist, had to be, had to be done. I never gave it any thought. In other words, I never tried to analyze it.

INTERVIEWER Well, I was going to ask you—in line with this introversion and this sort of retreat, do you feel then that the artist has no particular obligation to society as a citizen?

MUNI None whatsoever. None whatsoever. The type of actor or the type of artist, for that matter, the type of creator—I'll put it that way—who carries that kind of a— what should I say?—a kind of emblem or that kind of a label, if you want to call it that, he says he has a mission in life, he has something to perform, he wants to do good for the world, or he wants to help the world or something. It somehow creates a cynical something in me that just doesn't sit well with me.

INTERVIEWER When we interviewed the Lunts, they didn't say that they had this mission at all. On the other hand, they said that when they played in Robert Sherwood's *There Shall Be No Night,* it was a high point of their career, not only because it was a very good and successful play, but also because it had . . .

MUNI Something to say.

INTERVIEWER Yes.

MUNI Well, that can be perfectly true, but that comes after. In other words, it seems . . . I'm not speaking as an authority on anything here and I'm not trying to be modest about it. I'm telling you what I feel is the absolute truth— what can happen is this: An actor primarily wants to act, he's *got* to act! One, to make a living. Two, because he knows of no other way of—of taking up his time. He's got to do something. If he has nothing else to do and his business is acting, he's got to act. Well, when you get a play, or you get something to do which has something to say, which is purposeful, has depth, and something with which you are compatible, that it sort of strikes a note . . . Each of us, it would seem to me, has, whether consciously or unconsciously, a kind of inner protest about something—desire, wishes, mostly protest. You feel that certain things need to be said. Now, if you find a play that in some way or other articulates very eloquently those things which you, yourself, have inwardly, instinctively, or in some manner or other it responds to the very feelings that you have, you see, then you say it with greater conviction and you enjoy the saying of it. Now, let me . . .

MRS. MUNI I have to argue with you there, because, just to take a case in point, you were determined in 1955 and a few years before that, that you'd had it; you didn't want to work, you didn't want to do anything. And we came to New York just on a vacation, and Herman Shumlin submitted the play *Inherit the Wind*.

MUNI   Yes, well, that was McCarthy.

MRS. MUNI   And this was a thing that had been bothering him, the McCarthy thing, and he said something which I remember, he said, "I felt a shrieking silence."

MUNI   That was McCarthy, that's quite true.

MRS. MUNI   "A shrieking silence" he said, "sitting in my den, and not being able to do anything," and he did not want to go into the theatre, he did not want to do a play, but yet when Herman sent the script over and he read it—now this was his chance to make his protest.

MUNI   That's true.

MRS. MUNI   And he did that. And the same thing was with Zola, that he felt that this was something that had to be said.

MUNI   It was during the Hitler period, it was during the anti-Semitic period. Surely we have our emotions, our feelings, our reasons.

MRS. MUNI   No, as against what you said that that comes later and very many . . .

MUNI   I'm talking about the average play that has nothing, that doesn't have to deal with any political matter, with any matter of, of personal prejudice or bias. I mean, if you're going to do a play about a family or something—it doesn't involve politics, it doesn't involve religion, it doesn't involve anything. It's just a—it's a play. I mean, you can't be for it or against it. You're either for it because it's beautifully written, because the characters are solid, because you believe in them, because you see them, the images are good, and you feel you can—somehow or other you feel that you may be able to—get under one of these images and convince an audience that you are XYZ or whatever the name of the character is.

MRS. MUNI   Yes, well, I'm arguing with him, you know, because I always argue with him.

MUNI   Please do, I love to be argued with.

MRS. MUNI   I mean, for instance, after you had made *Scarface*, and then you were on tour with *Counsellor-at-Law* and you got a wire from DeMille—we were in Detroit at the time—you got a wire from DeMille: "I have a wonderful part for you, just like *Scarface*. Will you do it?" Muni sent him back a wire: "I've already done *Scarface*. Not interested."

MUNI But that's another thing. That's got nothing to do . . .

MRS. MUNI No, but I mean you had said what you wanted to say in *Scarface*.

MUNI I didn't want to repeat. I've always tried to avoid—I don't know how well I've succeeded, I may not have succeeded at all, but at least it was my intent, my desire—to avoid repetition as much as possible. Therefore, if one goes back and tries to—if he feels it's important enough—to check back on the various roles that I've played, he will find a variation there, rather different from the average American performer. I've played so many different parts. We go back to the very first play, *We Americans*, and to the next play . . .

MRS. MUNI *Four Walls*.

MUNI *Four Walls*. And so you find a variation of roles, a variation of . . .

MRS. MUNI They must know that story with George Abbott and Sam Harris, when Max Siegel brought Muni up for the part . . .

INTERVIEWER No, I don't.

MRS MUNI For the part in *We Americans*, which was an old man of sixty or something and Muni at the time was about twenty-eight, I think.

MUNI I did *We Americans* in about 1926.

MRS. MUNI And Max Siegel brought Muni to Sam Harris, and Sam Harris looked at him and he said, "Could he play a man of sixty? He's just a young kid."

MUNI I said it so happened that I looked younger than my years.

MRS. MUNI And Muni was on his way out of the office—he got very angry—and Max called him back, and he finally did this man of sixty in *We Americans*. Then the following year, after Muni was through with *We Americans*, George Abbott—John Golden and George Abbott were going to do *Four Walls*, and again I think it was Max or somebody that said how about Weisenfreund, you know—George Abbott called Sam Harris and he said what do you think of—I've got this play with this young gangster, and so forth—and he said what do you think about this fella you have, Muni Weisenfreund, and Sam Harris said, "Oh, no, he only plays old men."

MUNI That's true, that's a fact, because they typed me.

INTERVIEWER I want to say one more thing about this McCarthy business. Without making it sound too hifalutin, in a certain sense, you, as an artist, could not have taken a duty of citizenship more seriously or eloquently than by doing this play.

MUNI That, perhaps, may be true, but it was my inner hatred of the man and what he stood for and that whole period. It was a Hitlerian period, when everything was boiling inside of us and when Mr. McCarthy came along with his methods, and I—it so happens I've got recordings that I made in California of most of his, of his . . .

MRS. MUNI The trials.

MUNI The trials, and his arrogance, and the method of his, of the carryings on.

MRS. MUNI In other words, he saw it happening here.

INTERVIEWER Did you hope to do something at that time?

MUNI No, no. I never anticipated—it isn't in my nature to think of what's likely to happen, or what I would or might want to do tomorrow. Another one of my idiosyncrasies, among the many, is that each day works itself out, you know, as it does. I don't plan what I am likely to do unless it's something already in the mold.

INTERVIEWER But when *Inherit the Wind* came along you, nevertheless, felt some special . . .

MRS. MUNI Oh, this touched the person.

MUNI I felt that there was bigotry involved, and where there was bigotry—and this was anti-bigotry—I felt that it was something that I could be sympathetic to. As a matter of truth, it seems to me—maybe I'm wrong, I'm inclined to think I'm wrong—it seems to me that the so-called, I don't want to use the word artist . . .

MRS. MUNI Say artist. It's not a dirty word.

MUNI To me, it's a dirty word. It's not his business to set forth a plan wherein he says, "I'm going to devote my life to do . . ." I mean, if he were going into religious work or anything like that, it's one thing, but he's an actor, and as such, it isn't his responsibility. I don't think it's his responsibility. I don't think it should enter his mind that he's going to crusade for anything. What he's primarily looking for is a good part in a good play.

INTERVIEWER In other words, you don't like the word artist, you don't like all this . . .

MUNI I don't like all these trimmings, these extras.

INTERVIEWER You regard yourself as a craftsman with a job to do and you do it as well as you can.

MUNI That's right, a journeyman actor.

MRS. MUNI No, he just happens to be fortunate and

have a taste that goes in the direction—that comes out in the right direction.

MUNI Anything one is likely to say about himself— my feeling is that anything I'm likely to say about myself might either be misconstrued or even I may say it and not really, truthfully feel it. I may say it and I mean it when I'm saying it, it's true, but if I was to dig deep, or if someone was to dig deep, if a psychoanalyst were to try to analyze me and say, "Wait a minute. You think that's what you are, but it ain't so." And I'd have to believe it wasn't so. It's a very difficult business to be able to speak about yourself, and why you do XYZ, and why you do this and don't do that.

MRS. MUNI Well, the answer is this. During the years even when he was very young, and at the time that he made this hit, his first real hit in *Four Walls*, there came along this fellow who was Mae West's manager. What was his name? Linder, Jack Linder. And at the time, he came along with a play, you know, one of those cheap melodramas, and offered him a thousand dollars a week, which was unheard-of money for him at the time and he, he turned it down.

MUNI One of the things I will—if it applies here—one of the things I think I could say for myself, and I don't deserve any particular credit for it, is that the matter of good taste, I think, is uppermost in my mind. I wouldn't undertake to do anything that I—whatever my conception of good taste is—feel that it's in bad taste. If it's in bad taste, I'll leave it alone, whatever the rewards may be from a money standpoint, or from the standpoint of creating a furor, or some other standpoint.

INTERVIEWER What do you think are the prerequisites for an actor who embarks upon playing historical characters like Zola, Darrow, Juarez?

MUNI What are the prerequisites? Well, I've found, since I've had no education to speak of, since I didn't—I had no fundamental ...

MRS. MUNI Formal education.

MUNI Today every boy of thirteen or fourteen has at least gone to a two-year high school. When I was in the primary school, the fourth grade, that was the end of my schooling. The prerequisite to working on anything is making a thorough study, devoting as much time as one can, and one's energy will allow, to delving, probing, doing research. And there are other rather tenuous things involved here which are difficult to describe, because I, myself, don't attempt to analyze them for myself. I'd be afraid to. I'd be afraid because of the self-consciousness that might—that might enter in, and a self-consciousness per se would destroy the imagery, the business of letting yourself go—you know what I mean?—of not looking into yourself, of not watching yourself. Now, it's hard to make a parallel or to give a comparison, but if any of you are acquainted with—well, you drive cars, don't you?"

INTERVIEWER Yes.

MUNI Now, maybe as a youngster you've ridden a bicycle. If you look at your wheel, you'll lose your balance.

INTERVIEWER That's right. Ice skating is another example. If you try to look down at the ice you lose your balance and fall.

MUNI That's right, you'd fall. Well, similarly, if I can make that parallel, in acting if you start looking at yourself closely, you're going to lose your balance. You've got to look out. You've got to look at a distance. You have to think in a distance. You have to think of other things. As a matter of fact, if this would have any cogency to this particular discussion that we're having, when I go into a play, one of my methods—if I may call it a method, I hate using words like that—at any rate, one of my tricks is to examine the fellow that I'm talking to, try to analyze him on the stage. Who is he? What is he? Where does he come from? Why is he here? Or anything like that so that I divert my mind from myself and throw it out into the distance, very much like this bicycle business. I don't look at my wheel. I look at the other fellow and I listen to him. I'm an exceptionally good listener, which is a rare thing in the theatre. Actors as a rule don't listen to other actors. Good actors do, but the average run-of-the-mill actor doesn't.

MRS. MUNI You were saying, darling, that you listen to other actors and that you see them in a better . . .

MUNI That's right. Here is a case in point, in *Inherit the Wind*, that carries the point, I think, and it explains my feeling about those things. In *Inherit the Wind* there was the actress, Bethel Leslie, who had a scene with me. And one night the stage manager came into the dressing room and said to me, "Mr. Muni, I want you to know that Bethel is not wearing the same blouse that she's been wearing." That shocked me terribly, and I said. "Well, why are you telling me that?" He said, "Well, I didn't want you to be upset when you see a different blouse." I said, "I never saw her blouse. I didn't know that she wears a blouse." And I said,

"Now that you're talking about it, what it's going to do is it's going to kill the scene that I had with her because now you've made me conscious that she's wearing a blouse." I was real mad at that time. One is inclined to think, "Well, now, don't put on an act like that—that you're so thoroughly immersed in your work that you don't even know she wears a blouse." I do know, but those are the things that are in a number of layers below. But what primarily is pertinent to the work is to react to what she does, how she does it— she or he—what she's saying, what it refers to. It's a combination of many things.

MRS. MUNI   And also, you said as far as you were concerned it was the first time you were seeing Bethel.

MUNI   That's right. And in talking about Bethel Leslie, I said, "To me, she's not Bethel Leslie." Of course, as I say, those things I don't like, as a rule, to go into, because it puts a kind of—it sounds a little bit far-fetched, like affectation. I know myself to be a one-track person. I cannot absorb too many things. I very frequently meet up with people who are doing a number of things at the same time and I'm always amazed and envious of that. I'm not able to do that. If I read a newspaper in my den and somebody steps around out there, I don't know what I'm reading. Well, on the stage, unless I'm thoroughly absorbed and concentrated and immersed in what I'm doing, I'm out of it, and when I'm out of it, it seems to me that there's no amateur in the world who is as ungainly. Even hands begin to bother me. Now, an actor's first business—it's been my experience, and also what little I've heard—the actor's first problem is his hands. When he starts acting—what to do with the hands? You follow? You frequently see young actors putting their hands in their pockets, because they don't know what to do.

MRS. MUNI   They're moving the furniture.

MUNI   Or they'll stand and hold onto something, and do that, you know, because they're not yet experienced and they're conscious of themselves. In other words, instead of this working—that is, the thought and the projection and the looking ahead, not in the front, of the bicycle—they're looking at themselves and there are those hands, and what to do with them. And then they put them in their pockets. Then again you have the hand actor, what we called the *Spiegelschauspieler*.

MRS. MUNI   The looking glass actor.

MUNI   The mirror actor, the fella who's at home and plays his parts before a mirror, and he's not thinking of what he's doing, but he's doing this (making gestures), and he's doing all that, you know, these acrobatics. That is even worse. It's better if he keeps his hands in his pockets. The prime thing, it seems to me ... Now again, I don't—for heaven's sake, I'm not speaking as an authority about acting. I'm only talking about the way I feel and what I've experienced. Now I know what I'm doing with my hands because I'm talking about it, I'm conscious of it, but every now and then I'll move my hands. Well, the same thing applies on the stage. Why? Because what I'm interested in—I'm looking at you, I'm listening to you, and everything else is involuntary. Everything works by itself.

MRS. MUNI Now, for instance—may I interrupt here? —for instance, when Muni was doing movies and he'd finished a scene and the director would say, "Cut," and he'd say, "Oh, it's too bad. The scene was very well done, Muni, but you muffed a few words." And he used to get very angry and say, "So what? When I speak to you in life, don't I muff words every once in a while? What's wrong with muffing a few words?"

MUNI I recall, apropos of that, I recall that I did a film and I wasn't acquainted—I didn't now anything about pictures, you know, the technical process.

MRS. MUNI Still doesn't.

MUNI And invariably I used to tell the director, I said —because they used to say, "Now look, we're coming with a smacking close-up"—I said, "For heaven's sake, don't tell me and make me conscious of the camera." At first I pleaded with them, and then I got very angry, and once I walked off. I said if you're going to tell me ... They thought by telling me it would help me, that my facial expression wouldn't be too ...

MRS. MUNI He wouldn't mug.

MUNI I wouldn't mug or anything like that.

INTERVIEWER Did you study this matter in looking at your own films?

MUNI I haven't seen my own pictures. I had made about eleven or twelve of them, and at first I hadn't seen one single inch after making them. I never went into a projection room and never went into a theatre to see them. I made the last one ...

MRS. MUNI *The Last Angry Man.*

MUNI *The Last Angry Man* I haven't seen. I haven't seen an inch of that film. Not in the studio, I mean, while I was taking it. They all went into the projection room to see what they called the trailers.

MRS. MUNI   The dailies.

MUNI   The dailies.

INTERVIEWER   Or rushes.

MUNI   The rushes. I never went in to see rushes. It scared the hell out of me. It made me self-conscious, because once I'd see myself up there, I wouldn't be able to work the next day.

INTERVIEWER   But how do you teach yourself to get over possible weaknesses?

MUNI   I have weaknesses, but I don't teach myself.

INTERVIEWER   Or, how do you improve?

MUNI   I put on the make-up and I get in front of the camera and I open my mouth and I try to remember the words, and if I don't remember them, we go over it again.

MRS. MUNI   Try to think what he's doing. That's really what it is.

INTERVIEWER   I'd like to come back to the historical characters. You were saying that you do a lot of reading about them.

MUNI   Yes.

MRS. MUNI   That's the part of it he enjoys most. He has done a terrific amount of research, an awful lot of it.

MUNI   Yes, the most interesting part to me is the research. I enjoy that because I find out things that otherwise I would not have known.

INTERVIEWER   Could you give us a sort of count-down on how you did the research for one particular role?

MUNI   I couldn't give you a count-down in order of the way it was, but I know . . . For instance, when I was working on *The Story of Louis Pasteur*, I read most everything that was in the library—in the studio, where they have their own library—and most everything I could lay my hands on that had to do with Pasteur, with Lister, with his contemporaries.

MRS. MUNI   All his contemporaries.

MUNI   I immediately brought up or had someone lend me books, and I would for months on end continue to read.

MRS. MUNI   That was one of the reasons he always insisted upon having the script so early.

MUNI   I read everything. I mean, characters that had nothing—I mean, a fellow like Ehrlich, who had no connection with Pasteur, actually any contact with him, but he also dealt in the same field. I read up everything I could on Ehrlich and others like that.

MRS. MUNI   There's a wonderful collection of Beethoven

books in our library because at one time he was going to
do Beethoven.

INTERVIEWER   Do you study photographs, too?

MUNI   I study photographs, but not so much.

INTERVIEWER   What does all this do for you?

MUNI   I don't know. I don't pretend to—I don't want to
know.

MRS. MUNI   He absorbs it.

MUNI   It's one of those things. You become saturated
with some kind of psychological images, if you can use that
term at all. It's one of those things that you do not—you do
not methodically work out. It's one of those things that you
throw yourself into, a kind of, if you can call it that, miasmic
thing that is just a conglomerate business, and you just pick
out whatever instinctively seems to fit into the pattern of what
you—what you're looking for.

INTERVIEWER   Did you ever go to the Pasteur Institute,
for instance, outside of Paris?

MUNI   I went there. And when I did a film—which was
not a successful film, it was an unfortunate affair—on the
life of Juarez, I went to Mexico, traveled around various
cities there, wherever Juarez was known to have had any
influence of one sort or another, where other characters were
in some way or another connected with Juarez. And I made
every possible exploration and investigation that I could at
the time, as the time allowed.

MRS. MUNI   Before he did *Bordertown*, in which he
also played a Mexican, all of a sudden, out of a clear sky,
Muni came home with a Mexican flower boy that he had
found down in Los Angeles. And he brought him home and
he put him to work in the garden.

MUNI   He became a gardener and I worked with him.

MRS. MUNI   And then he spoke to him and got his
rhythm.

MUNI   I got his—the feeling of his character, of his
accent and his general moods. It wasn't any... In other
words, what I'm trying to get over is that there wasn't any
specific method. There wasn't any arithmetic arrangement
there. It was a catch-as-catch-can business, you know what
I mean?

MRS. MUNI   All done by ear.

MUNI   That's right. Whatever I could derive, whatever
advantage could accrue to me, whatever happened, I tried to
go to that particular thing to help me out in the role that I
was about to play. That was about it.

MRS. MUNI   You would even... For instance, with me

—I mean, before he got married to all the dictaphones and things, I used to cue him on all of his roles and then, every once in a while, this was my job, to tell him what I didn't like. I was never allowed to tell him what I did like because that made him self-conscious; but I would say, for instance, "No, I don't think you're doing this scene right or reading it right." And then all of a sudden he'd say, "All right, you do it. Let me see how you do it." And I'd have to do it my own backward way.

MUNI And now this I will say, I have no pride in the sense of being a creative artist. I'll take and steal from anyone that I can in order to develop whatever it is I—wherever I can get an advantage, wherever I think I can be helped, I'll resort to whatever I can without committing mayhem.

INTERVIEWER Where beyond books is that?

MUNI Well, it's going to localities where certain peoples live. It is talking to certain people. It is working on yourself. It is relying considerably on your imagination also. I mean, it's not a thing that you have, because in the final analysis there's nothing—what should I call it?—there's no geography, there's no mathematics that two and two has got to make four. You do whatever you can to acquire whatever knowledge, whatever information you can. You contact whatever people you are able to contact in order to absorb whatever you're able to absorb, and whatever there is within you, the capacity, to acquire and then make use of it.

INTERVIEWER Who were some of the interesting people you contacted besides the Mexican?

MUNI Oh, so many. I wouldn't attempt now to...

MRS. MUNI During *The Good Earth* he brought home a Chinese fellow from San Francisco.

MUNI Yes, yes. I had a Chinese person with me for quite a long time. I talked to him, I listened to him.

MRS. MUNI Just listened to him, got the rhythms.

INTERVIEWER You have been known to be extremely meticulous in make-up. Does this also help you in terms of your imagery?

MUNI Make-up with me was very much like playing bridge is to somebody. It was a game. When I started in the profession, when I was all of maybe eleven or twelve years old, I used to go into the dressing room, in the theatre that my father ran, at twelve-o'clock noon, or ten o'clock in the morning, buy a pound of grapes or something like that, and some bread, and I'd stay there until the performance, and put it on and take it off, and put it on and just smear my face. And put wigs on, because my father had a lot of wigs, you know, which were changed—we'd put crepe hair on in certain places; we took one wig and made four or five different character wigs out of it, and I played around with it and it was a hobby. I enjoyed it, you see, and that ultimately developed. Then I used to buy a lot of grease paint and I'd fool around with it.

MRS. MUNI I remember one of the things, when we went into *Four Walls,* that was so difficult for him. Because, you recall, when he did *We Americans,* he had a beard on and the wig and everything. And when he started doing *Four Walls,* he said, "I feel naked." Because he went right on the stage as himself. He had nothing, just color on his face.

MUNI It's ture. I'd swear to heaven that it's as true as we're sitting here. I opened that door and I was as embarrassed as if I lost my clothes. All of a sudden I was naked, because there wasn't some sort of a smear or anything. I didn't have any beard or wigs.

INTERVIEWER How did you prepare for Darrow? I mean, how did you study for Darrow's appearance, his Midwestern speech, the paunch, the shuffling walk?

MUNI The same way that I prepared for any other role. I just read up on Darrow as much as I could. I asked people who had any acquaintanceship with Darrow. I have a very good friend, a judge in Pittsburgh, who...

MRS. MUNI A Supreme Court justice.

MUNI He's a Supreme Court justice of the State of Pennsylvania, and he knew that I was working on Darrow, and he'd had personal contact with him and he gave me some information. I have long letters from him.

MRS. MUNI And then also you have—what was it, the Irving Stone...

MUNI The Irving Stone book.

MRS. MUNI And he played—he'll kill me for this—but he played that part for two years practically, on and off, and until the last performance, before the show started, half hour before, he read at least one chapter of the book again.

MUNI The reason for that is to sort of whip up a kind of mood.

MRS. MUNI Get into the thought. One very cute thing that has nothing to do with Muni, on this Darrow business. Joseph Welch, you know, who recently died, saw the performance of *Inherit the Wind,* and then he came backstage to see Muni. Then he told a friend of mine, whom he didn't know that we had any connection with—they talked about Muni at a party that they were at—he said, "I saw the play and I was fascinated with the performance and everything and then I went back to see Mr. Muni," he said, "and I walked into his dressing room and right above his mirror was a big picture of Darrow," he said, "and then I was really fascinated."

MUNI   Now there's a strange thing that I myself am not able to explain. I had this picture that . . .

MRS. MUNI   It was sent to you.

MUNI   It was sent to me, that's right. I had it over my mirror there, my make-up mirror, and invariably—and this is like a superstition, you know, like somebody knocks wood— I, invariably before I went on-stage, I took about five minutes' time, shut the door, nobody was allowed to come in, and I just looked at the picture.

INTERVIEWER   Quite understandable.

MUNI   But I mean it, it sounds like a moronic thing to do.

INTERVIEWER   No, no.

MRS. MUNI   He made contact.

MUNI   I mean, these are things that people will do. It's the first time I ever mentioned it, how important it was. I never mentioned it to my wife.

INTERVIEWER   How about the Midwestern speech? How did you learn that?

MUNI   I didn't learn anything. If it was Midwestern, it was an accident. I don't know what my speech is. I don't know whether I speak Midwestern now or not. I've played Englishmen. I've had a play, *Yesterday's Magic,* didn't run very long, with Jessica Tandy and Alfred Drake, and I played an Englishman in it and I spoke with an English accent.

MRS. MUNI   And you were bad.

INTERVIEWER   Why do you, or did you, use the tape recorder and the dictaphone as much as you have?

MUNI   To help memorize, because the ritual of constantly reading the part or the script or whatever it was, was a tedious business, and occasionally when I memorized I would get sort of pictures, I mean images, that would appear. I would see certain things while I was listening. Well, I used to do that. In fact, I used to write out my part many, many times, but that was before the recording business came in. Now I listen, actually, not only to memorize—it's more than that. You go beneath the thing. The words begin to mean nothing any more. As I understand it, some actors, perhaps most actors, work on the theme first, on the idea first, on what they are. I work on something else. I work on words, nothing but words. I don't even try to analyze what the words mean, and keep on it, and this goes on and on and on. I keep going over it, just . . .

MRS. MUNI No intonations, no . . .

MUNI With no inflection, no intonation, no trying to analyze anything. Just words, words, words, words.

INTERVIEWER In other words, you set up a tape recorder much as we have here.

MUNI That's right, and keep the bloody thing going day and night. Even when I go to bed at night. I very frequently used to go to bed and have my tape recorder near by, and then in the morning when I got up, the thing was spinning around and I realized that I fell asleep.

MRS. MUNI Even while in the car.

MUNI And even while we were driving in the car I had the tape recorder. It ultimately came, like a child who learns a language without knowing what—it just repeats words. Then when that was over with, when the words were sufficiently acquired, in other words, sufficiently imprinted . . .

MRS. MUNI Registered.

MUNI Registered. Then I would begin to get underneath the words. What's it all about. And then I would sit down and start writing my own thesis about the thing, what logic it has, when I consider it right or wrong, what the character motivation is, et cetera. In other words, I would then try to analyze what the thing was about, but the words already would be in my pocket more or less.

INTERVIEWER When do you learn the business?

MUNI Well, the business I don't worry about at all. I never prepared business. When you say business, you mean mechanics of the theatre?

INTERVIEWER I mean the gestures, the facial expressions.

MUNI That I never do. I never have prearranged mannerisms or gestures. I have mannerisms which are mine, which unconsciously—people tell me that I do certain things and I'm not even aware of it, and undoubtedly I do them always on the stage.

MRS. MUNI I had this with Herman Shumlin, you know. I'm always around when Muni's rehearsing in the theatre or on the screen, and there were certain things that happened during rehearsals, that he would do, that would bother Herman. And Herman would never tell him, he would tell me. And I'd say don't talk to him about it, leave him alone and he'll throw it away if it's not right. There was one instance where Muni had a scene, when we were in Philadelphia, and at one point, all of a sudden, a new thing came because he was, you know . . .

MUNI   Groping.

MRS. MUNI   Groping and trying different things, and I know that's how he works. So came the scene—I don't remember exactly, but at one point—this was on a Friday night, I remember that—all of a sudden out of a clear blue sky, Ed Begley said something to him, and Muni said, "Oh," and it got a terrific laugh. And Herman and I were in the back, what I called maternity row because we used to walk up and down with labor pains, and Herman ran over to me. "I don't like that, Bella," he said. "Will you talk to Muni about it?" I said, "Not tonight, I won't." I said, "Let's see tomorrow's matinée and evening." I said, "He may throw it away, don't worry about it." He said, "Well, do you like it?" I said, "I'm not sure. I'll want to live with it until tomorrow night." And I didn't say anything to Muni, and I determined if it still bothered Herman and myself by Saturday night, Sunday I would talk to him about it. Saturday night Herman came over to me and he says, "Don't say a word to him. It's right."

MUNI   At the moment my feeling—generally I say my feeling, as if I'd thought it out; I hadn't—but my feeling is that the entire business, any creative business, has to do with constant experimentation, without your knowing that you're experimenting. In other words, if you become rigid—but I would never permit myself, at least to my knowledge, to rigidly fall into a format, into a framework, into a kind of thing that you say, "This is it. It's all set." I am sure that if that were the case I'd get so weary of the thing, I would run away from that theatre right away.

INTERVIEWER   In a long run such as *Inherit the Wind*, how did you manage to keep your interest and freshness in that role every night?

MUNI   Because if there was that freshness there, then it was because I was not thinking of myself, but always listening to the other fellow. And I always found something interesting in the other fellow. And mine was a reaction—not an action, but a reaction.

INTERVIEWER   I shall never forget you when Begley was sitting in that chair, in the courtroom, and you were going after him like a tiger.

MRS. MUNI   You know, this is very funny. On many occasions . . .

MUNI   Well, it never was the same play.

MRS. MUNI   It just happened that he and Begley were

on wonderful terms right throughout the play—the whole company was wonderful—but sometimes when he felt that he was low, he himself was low, he'd set out to get Begley angry.

INTERVIEWER How?

MRS. MUNI The tempo, picking it up.

MUNI Certain things that I did to get him mad.

INTERVIEWER In other words, surprising him.

MUNI I mean, the business of preparing anything and putting it into a frame and staying within that would kill me. If I had to do that, I just never would be in the theatre.

INTERVIEWER How do you change your performance from night to night?

MUNI Whether I change my performance or not is for someone else to say.

MRS. MUNI Yes, yes, he does.

MUNI But I do know that I never hold rigidly to the mechanics of a performance. I'll sometimes choose to stand in a certain position. Sometimes I'll stand at my desk and sometimes I'll sit, and sometimes I'll go over to the judge's desk and I'll move to the witness chair and get behind the witness, or do something like that as long as I don't disturb the other actor. And very frequently I would tell the other actor, and I would ask him first, I'd say, "Will it disturb you if I don't stay within the mechanics, constantly the same way?" And usually a good actor will say, "That's all right as long as it's not going to change anything in regard to the scene." So they're very nice about that. But you get very weary, you know, of being a robot, a puppet, and just doing the same thing all the time.

INTERVIEWER I hear directors today say this is something they often have trouble with—getting the young actors to move about, or even not to stand with their back to the audience.

MRS. MUNI I heard at a dress rehearsal, I heard Muni say something to a young actress whom we both liked very much, who has the habit of so many of the younger actors now of thinking it's very artistic to turn your back on an audience. This is all right in small doses, you know, but this particular actress had a big scene and she was playing most of it upstage; and he finally stopped and he said so, and he took her shoulder and he said, "This is your scene. The audience is out there. Face up to it. Play the scene."

MUNI But I don't believe in standing right smack in front of an audience.

MRS. MUNI No, but I mean they do.

MUNI But even so . . . I mean, for instance, when I played—we did a little thing for a month, a Ben Hecht thing, for nothing, when Marlon Brando . . .

INTERVIEWER *A Flag Is Born?*

MUNI *A Flag Is Born.* And Marlon Brando had this scene where he's talking out to the audience. That was all right because that was purposely arranged that way and, of course, the way Marlon Brando played it—with his great gift that he has, it was magnificent. I was enthralled with it, just listening to him. But when an actor, who is just, you know, the average actor, starts playing a scene and he stands there in front of the audience like that, it's no good either.

INTERVIEWER Have you done anything in particular to develop your own voice?

MUNI What do you mean, develop your own voice?

INTERVIEWER Well, it has been said that a Muni whisper can be heard in the second balcony of any theatre.

MUNI That is a resonance that I evidently have had. I don't know whether I still have it, but it's a resonance that I have, a God-given something that has happened to me for which I'm very grateful.

INTERVIEWER You have been concerned with concentration on the stage. Do you think this is one of the most important requirements?

MUNI The most important, not one of the most. I would put it in the first place.

MRS. MUNI The only time he gets ornery with a cast or with a stage manager or anything is if somebody stands off-scene, behind the scenes, watching him, and he's turning to an actor and he sees that somebody standing backstage.

MUNI It's very difficult.

MRS. MUNI You'd better run!

MUNI It's very difficult. I will admit very frankly that I am . . . When she says ornery, she used the right word, because at times when I do get into that kind of a tantrum I realize that it's not natural. It's a kind of ailment of some sort. I just cannot tolerate anybody off-scene. Once I turn around and I see a face that distracts me from whatever . . . Because it takes a devil of a long time for me, and especially the older I get, to throw myself into something where I can try to partially believe that it's true. And when suddenly I turn around and I see a face—whether it's the stage manager or whoever it is; some actor standing there and looking out, and they think it's perfectly all right because the average actor doesn't worry about those things—I immediately will get off and I'll ask them at first, once or twice, please not to do it. But if they do it again, I get very mad.

INTERVIEWER Where do you rate imagination or intelligence in an actor's equipment?

MUNI Imagination, I think, is the better word, because intelligence . . . You know, in the Gorki play there was one line there—I'm not going to quote it verbatim, I don't recall it verbatim—but there was one line where an actor in *Lower Depths,* I think he says, "I knew an actor," he says, "that couldn't sign his name, but how he could play Hamlet."

MRS. MUNI One of the greatest actors that I've ever known—Kessler, David Kessler—was a boor, a completely uneducated boor, but a great genius.

MUNI I'm inclined to think there are different types, and one would say that here intelligence is needed and here pure emotion or instinct is most important. Now, there are actors who have an instinctive quality. There was a great Italian actor, a Sicilian actor, Giovanni Grasso—they called him Commendatore, an address of honor—and that man . . . If ever you saw a boor in your life, he was the prototype and the representative, and he could have been everything that measured up to the word. I mean that you say, "This is a boor."

MRS. MUNI A complete primitive.

MUNI In the fullest sense of the word. Just by looking at him. And he did these primitive Sicilian plays, remember, but he could—and I say this whenever I mention it on rather infrequent occasions, I always get a little emotional about it because he had that wonderful quality about him— he could, like turning on a faucet and turning it off, he could make people cry or laugh like this.

MRS. MUNI Remember how he used to bring that actress out to bow? He'd bring her out by the top of the hair on her head.

MUNI He had the face of a hog. No personality whatsoever. But when he played a scene, all of a sudden there were hysterics in a theatre. I mean, either they were weeping like mad or they were laughing like mad.

INTERVIEWER What was the essence of this?

MUNI It was an inner talent, an inner quality of being

able to transfer some hypnotic quality—if you want to choose to call it that—to transfer whatever he felt, and he had a terrific capacity for feeling. I am sure that there was very little up here. There wasn't any mental acting at all. It was pure emotion.

INTERVIEWER   You have said that an actor must also have a sturdy physique.

MUNI   Did I say that?

INTERVIEWER   You can disown it. This is only part of our research.

MUNI   I don't recall saying a sturdy physique. Well, I should think it would be very accommodating if he did have one. But there was an actor, as I recall, I didn't see him personally—he was a cousin to the great writer in Russia, Chekhov—who I understand was a consumptive, a very fragile person. He was one of the greatest actors in the Russian theatre.

INTERVIEWER   Did you do anything to keep in physical condition?

MUNI   Not a thing.

INTERVIEWER   You have no particular regimen when you are working?

MUNI   No.

MRS. MUNI   All he does is worry.

INTERVIEWER   Worry?

MRS. MUNI   I call him the worrier's husband.

INTERVIEWER   Do you ever succeed in achieving relaxation on the stage?

MUNI   Ever?

INTERVIEWER   Well, how do you achieve relaxation?

MUNI   Relaxation on the stage I have never achieved, except at certain periods in certain plays when I was on the stage but not active. When I was an actor, let's say, for instance, in a courtroom scene, when I was sitting, whether I was a lawyer or whatever, at a table with my back to the audience, and somebody else was playing the scene out there, I would actually, in order to build up a little more energy, I would deliberately let go to relax.

MRS. MUNI   A second breath.

MUNI   Yes, to relax in order to accumulate sufficient energy to go on with the rest of the play. There's a time when I deliberately stop the clock, if I can use that term, and stop thinking. I deliberately sort of let go when I know that nobody is watching me. It's rare but it has happened.

INTERVIEWER   Have you preferred Hollywood to the theatre?

MUNI   No, I haven't preferred either to either.

INTERVIEWER   You did so much work out in Hollywood, I was wondering whether you had any preference for Hollywood.

MUNI   Well, if I were to be honest with myself and if I were to try to analyze this situation, which I never have —as I say, the last thing that I do is examine my own reaction to things—I would certainly say that the theatre is a much better medium for the actor than the film, if for no other reason than that he goes through at one fell swoop with the whole plot, so that he doesn't have to chop things up into little things. And there are other reasons. The mechanical business of sticking a camera into your face, if they're going into a close-up, and you have to concentrate on the scene, and it's devilish and difficult to try to make yourself believe that there isn't a camera in your face. And you're talking into a lens and you're supposed to be talking to another human being and you know bloody damn well you're talking to a lens. And to be able to so metamorphose yourself into the sense of making yourself believe that it's not so, is a tough job. You try to do it, but you succeed only partially.

INTERVIEWER   What is your feeling toward acting on television?

MUNI   I've done so little on television.

INTERVIEWER   Why is that?

MUNI   Nobody's asked me, and I don't think I would care for it very much. I certainly wouldn't want to be doing a series on television, or be doing a regular program on television. I would only possibly be interested if some special thing were done that I could become interested in, but other than that television is a variegated medium. In other words, they can do television so many different ways. They can do it piecemeal and they can do it all at once. They can surround you with a lot of cameras from all different angles and take it all in one fell swoop, you see.

MRS. MUNI   Which you did in Playhouse 90.

MUNI   That's right. Where in an hour and a half—however long it took . . .

MRS. MUNI   An hour.

MUNI   An hour? They had cameras all over the place and they had all kinds of angles and . . .

MRS. MUNI   You never saw an unhappier man in your life.

MUNI   The way I feel about television is, it is essentially a director's, a mechanical, medium. I wouldn't say that I would dislike doing certain things in television, because first of all you have terrific exposure, which is important. In other words, without an audience you're not an actor. If you don't have one person watching you, you can't act. If you have fifty thousand or fifty million watching you, it's terrific. And if you have something that you want to do that appeals to you, and you know that you're doing it before an audience, even if you're not even fully conscious of it, but subconsciously you realize that this is being seen by millions and millions of people, and you have something worthwhile doing, why, naturally it makes a lot of difference.

INTERVIEWER I suppose television would be rather difficult for you in terms of the kind of preparation that you seem to do.

MRS. MUNI Yes, that's one of the very important considerations.

MUNI It is. Invariably, whenever they offer me something, and they're still occasionally coming across—of course, I'm a pretty difficult customer generally speaking—I invariably say to them that I have to have the script at least four weeks ahead of time, which is not cricket in the television business. There they give it to you a week or ten days at most, and that for me is not good enough.

INTERVIEWER Which of the roles that you've played has given you the greatest satisfaction?

MUNI In films or in the theatre?

INTERVIEWER Well, maybe we ought to categorize that.

MUNI It's a little difficult for me to say, because I have been in so many different areas of the theatre. I've been in the Yiddish theatre. I've been in vaudeville.

MRS. MUNI Don't forget we were in vaudeville in the Yiddish theatre.

MUNI And I've been in films and I've been on Broadway. I'd say that on Broadway the most gratifying would be *Inherit the Wind,* and in films it would be a tossup between Zola and Pasteur. I might add that *The Good Earth,* while I considered myself very, very badly chosen for that role—I didn't do a good job in it—the film itself was very worthwhile. Now, there may have been a number of other films that I could also say that I preferred.

MRS. MUNI My favorite—nobody asked, but I'll tell you my favorite—was *We Are Not Alone,* by James Hilton. The whole picture was a gem. Ed Goulding directed it and Flora Robson was in it.

MUNI I didn't see it. You see, the thing is I haven't

seen these films. I can only speak of those things that I enjoyed most while I was working on them.

INTERVIEWER Did your satisfaction in *Inherit the Wind* come from the feeling of your answering McCarthy?

MUNI No. It was a satisfactory engagement. Originally I disliked Shumlin. Our personalities didn't jell.

MRS. MUNI Too much alike.

MUNI He's an angry man and I'm an angry man, you see, and we're both very rigid in our positions. At the rehearsals we weren't getting along. He avoided me, I avoided him. I'm a nice guy really. I get into trouble with everybody. But finally it turned out; it got to be a very successful play.

MRS. MUNI They had a mutual respect for . . .

MUNI I had a great respect for him. Inwardly he's a really nice fella and a very gifted man, Shumlin, and I had a high respect for his talents, for his knowledgeability. The truth is that if I didn't have this eye situation* come up, I would have stayed with it as long as the play ran—I mean within reason, of course—but after the operation . . .

MRS. MUNI You still went back after the operation.

MUNI I went back but I couldn't—I couldn't take it any more. I went back and I said I'll fill out the season, I'll stay until the end. As a matter of fact, my season ended May first and I stayed until . . .

MRS. MUNI It ended May thirtieth and you stayed until the end of June.

MUNI That's right. I stayed a month longer, because when I went out of the play they still had standing room then.

INTERVIEWER What was the satisfaction from *Pasteur* and from *Zola*?

MUNI They were just well written, but we actually had quite a hassle with this fellow—what was the name of the producer, the main producer?

MRS. MUNI Wallis.

MUNI Hal Wallis.

MRS. MUNI And Jack Warner.

MUNI Hal Wallis and Jack Warner. They said, "What kind of a picture is that?" They didn't want to do it. We sneaked in *The Story of Louis Pasteur* on them.

MRS. MUNI Making a picture about bugs. Who'll know what you're talking about?

MUNI No, no. At first—*The Pasture* they called it . . .

MRS. MUNI No, no, no. What's his name, Wallis, came

* Mr. Muni had to undergo an operation for the removal of his left eye.

up with an idea. He sent a note which Bill Dieterle still has. After the picture was finished, he said nobody's going to understand what you're talking about, and he said at least if you'd finish it up by saying, "And since then, all the mothers are grateful to him because they now have pasteurized milk."

MUNI   That was Wallis. Actually, they fought us on it and it so happened that I was fortunate. I held the thing up at that time because of a contract that I'd made. Again it's the rigidity about that contract that they couldn't make me do any picture unless I okayed it, and when I okayed it, it had to be substantially as it was written. They had to do it. They sent me script after script which were so terrible that I just couldn't accept them. They were supposed to send me three scripts, and if I didn't like theirs, I was to send them three scripts.

MRS. MUNI   Then you ganged up on them. Dieterle, the director, the producer and Muni ganged up on them with *The Story of Louis Pasteur*.

MUNI   And the other arrangement was that if I didn't accept their three scripts and they didn't accept my three scripts, they'd have to pay me a half-salary and I wouldn't have to do anything. That was the time that I was, you know . . .

MRS. MUNI   The white-haired boy.

MUNI   I had made one picture after another that was considered very arty. I don't know how much money they made. Like *The Good Earth, Pasteur,* and the chain gang picture, *I Am a Fugitive from a Chain Gang,* and *Scarface*. They knew that so many studios were out to get me to sign, and all that, so they wanted to keep me there and they gave me leeway, a lot of things that normally an actor wouldn't be able to get. So, therefore, we practically pushed it down their throats. They just didn't want to do *Pasteur*.

MRS. MUNI   They made it under terrific protest.

MUNI   Under terrific protest.

INTERVIEWER   And that's the one that won the Oscar!

MUNI   That's right.

MRS. MUNI   And for which Harry Warner later got the red ribbon from France.

MUNI   The strange part of it, the ironic and comical, I would say, is that most of those things that were forced down their throats were the things that they got the most credit for.

MRS. MUNI   A strange story, and Muni remembers this, too—a strange story. He had all this experience with *Pasteur,* which he made under complete negative feeling from the studio. They fought, the three of them . . .

MUNI   You know what they spent for *Pasteur* to make it? Give a guess. Two hundred and sixty thousand dollars!

MRS. MUNI   Five weeks. In five weeks they made it. Anyway, with this protest from Wallis and Warner, and all of that, well, finally, they sold it at a smaller percentage to the exhibitors because they didn't think they had a picture. And it opened in a second-run theatre in Chicago, and then all of a sudden this thing went, you know, and with the Academy Award, and so forth. Then later that year, the following year, they submitted some story to Muni, and I don't remember what it was, he did not want to do it. And Jack Warner called him up to the office to try and persuade him, and he said, "Muni, for God's sake, why don't you listen to me? After all, I gave you *Pasteur*."

MUNI   And then he said, "This has got social consciousness in it."

INTERVIEWER   In preparing before we came up here, I came across a story that said you never wanted to be a star in the theatre, and that you said you never have enjoyed the success that you've had the way other people have enjoyed their success. Now, why is that?

MUNI   That's right. I don't know. I don't know because I've never—perhaps it's because I'm a coward and the responsibility was too much for me. I don't know why. That's again, as I say, self-analysis. I don't want to go into it. The truth of the matter is that I've always shied away from—I never sought for the top spot anywhere and I was willy-nilly pushed into it, in the theatre and in pictures.

MRS. MUNI   He's the only man I know in this profession that became a star despite himself.

MUNI   That's the truth. That is one of the real truths that I can swear to. That I had no desire to be a leading man or a star or to have my name . . . As a matter of fact, to give you as a last commentary on that—when I came down and saw my name up in lights in this last play, *Inherit the Wind*, I got bilious. I got sick.

INTERVIEWER   No fooling?

MRS. MUNI   He was scared to death.

MUNI   I was walking up Sixth Avenue toward Broadway. After all the pictures that I've made, after so many years in the theatre, after never having played a subordinate role either on Broadway or in films—and if you check back you'll find out that I never was anything but the leading man and the so-called star. And yet when I walked up from

Sixth Avenue to Broadway and I saw Paul Muni in *Inherit the Wind,* I got sick to my stomach. And I got nervous and unhappy and I thought—I don't know what I thought at the time, but I was sick. I was unhappy about the whole thing.

MRS. MUNI   The night that he signed with Herman to do *Inherit the Wind,* and I think it was my birthday and I had a few people for dinner, and he sat there, he was the most miserable man in the world.

MUNI   Well, it's because . . .

MRS. MUNI   There's no other name for it. It's running scared.

MUNI   No. It's a desire. There's a desire for . . . First of all, if one wants to make a kind of an analysis, a self-analysis, you say for one thing you have a self-respect for yourself. You're afraid to fail.

INTERVIEWER   Maybe it's conceit.

MUNI   I'm conceited but in an oblique sort of way.

MRS. MUNI   In a modest way. In other words, he's *mesh-ugeh*—crazy.

MUNI   I think conceit is necessary. I think one should have what we call conceit, or vanity, or whatever you choose to call it. It's allied to self-respect. It's allied to believing in your own worth.

INTERVIEWER   You must be a very nervous man on an opening night.

MRS. MUNI   What do you mean, opening night? He's a nervous man, period.

MUNI   I'm nervous every single night before I go on, up to the last performance.

MRS. MUNI   You should go up to him and touch his hands before he goes on the stage. Anyway, let me tell you a story which has nothing to do with your tape. We were married almost forty years ago. Schwartz hired me because I was marrying Muni and they were going on tour. So he hired me—engaged is nicer, huh?—engaged me to play all the leading lady roles, which meant that I went into a whole repertoire, you know, and all leading parts. And we were married all of two or three weeks at the time. We went on and we played a Peretz Hirschbein play and Muni played my grandfather. And I had to finish a curtain by walking from the back of the stage to a table at the front of the stage with a plate of soup. This was a slow curtain, a very tense moment and I'd had very little rehearsal—there were so many details, you know, I'd had to learn several parts. Well, comes the night—and, as I say, we were married two or three weeks at the time—and comes this part and

I'm not quite sure of the cue. I turn around to him, my grandfather, standing next to me, and I say, "Muni, when do I start?" And all I get from him is "Ha!" I freeze inside of myself and I walk. The curtain goes down. As soon as the curtain goes down he gives me what-for. "Don't you ever dare to do that to me on the stage. Don't you ever dare to talk to me." I went into the dressing room and I cried.

INTERVIEWER Is that why you left the stage?

MRS. MUNI No. But I cried my eyes out and I said what kind of a man did I marry?

MUNI A nut.

MRS. MUNI Well, I learned quick.

INTERVIEWER Are we going to see you on Broadway, Mr. Muni?

MUNI I don't know.

MRS. MUNI You'll be more likely to see us in Timbuktu.

MUNI No, my desire is to be on a wonderful fishing boat somewhere.

MRS. MUNI You know, apropos of their never seeing you on Broadway again, it's like with Sam Harris. You must know that story. During the actors' strike he had a character actor that used to work for him for years, you know, and then he went on strike, and Sam said, "Don't ever hire that son of a so-and-so until we need him!"

INTERVIEWER That's right. In other words, what you are saying is, if Herman Shumlin comes along with an *Inherit the Wind,* he's liable to take it.

MRS. MUNI That's the answer.

MUNI I wouldn't be surprised!

Anne Bancroft

BIOGRAPHY

Anne Bancroft was born Anna Maria Italiano in September, 1931, in the Bronx, New York. She attended Christopher Columbus High School, where she was an Arista student, and went on to study acting at the American Academy of Dramatic Arts. From there she got a start in television with a part in *Torrents of Spring,* for which Worthington Miner chose her. Following this, under the name of Anne Marno, she appeared in a number of television shows, including "Suspense," "Danger" and "The Kraft Theatre." After doing television work for about a year, she took a screen test, as a result of which she received a contract and went to Hollywood. Miss Bancroft appeared in some fifteen films, including *New York Confidential, Naked Street,* with Anthony Quinn, and *Don't Bother to Knock,* in which she played Richard Widmark's girl friend, a role that brought her attention. After some years on the Coast, Miss Bancroft returned to New York to continue her acting studies, and in 1958 she got her first Broadway role, as Gittel Mosca opposite Henry Fonda in the two-character play, *Two for the Seesaw.* Overnight she became a star and the sensation of the season. Her role won her an Antionette Perry Award. This play was fol-

lowed by *The Miracle Worker,* in which she played the part
of Annie Sullivan, teacher of Helen Keller, once again scoring
a personal triumph in a leading hit of the season. Both of
her Broadway plays were written by William Gibson, directed by Arthur Penn and produced by Fred Coe. Miss
Bancroft has been married, but is now divorced.

SETTING

Although neither of us had met Anne Bancroft before this
interview, she is the sort of person we were inclined to call
Annie very soon after meeting. This was not because it is
traditional in the world of the theatre to call nearly everyone
either by first name or "darling" at first meeting, but rather
because Anne Bancroft has that rare natural and informal
quality that makes it easy and appropriate. Natural and informal may in fact be a bit on the stiff side, although Miss
Bancroft has considerable dignity. Warm and exuberant might
be closer to the mark. In any event, she seems to have that
rather rare quality of being "down to earth" despite a meteoric rise which should have made her head spin. It is true,
of course, that interviewers have only a relatively brief time—
although sometimes an unusually revealing opportunity—to
know their subject, and while it can be imagined that the
spirited Miss Bancroft could dip on occasion to moodiness or
even anger, it would be difficult indeed to envision her as being anything other than herself.

We met Miss Bancroft at the theatre following an evening
performance of *The Miracle Worker,* and went with her to
her apartment in a remodeled brownstone house in New York's
Greenwich Village. The apartment occupies the first floor—
bedroom at the front, living room in the middle, and at the
rear a combination kitchen and dining room. We settled in
the room at the rear, with a few minutes taken out before
the start of the interview for some mint tea with a dash of
cognac, which Miss Bancroft quickly and easily prepared.
This room has been redone to accommodate a kitchen and
a dining area, the two sections of the room separated by a
counter. The kitchen is thoroughly workmanlike, with some
of the utensils making an attractive wall display, particularly
a handsome set of shiny copper pots. The kitchen has olive
walls contrasting with the light blue ones of the dining area—
a white ceiling over both. In the dining area itself, which appeared to serve equally as an informal living room, there is a

two-sided sofa in a corner, before which is a round dining table and a few wooden armchairs pulled up to it. The furnishings are simple—rather on the Early American side—with decorative jars and jugs, a series of iron trivets on a wall, light fixtures cased in lattice work, some green glass bottles with candles, a small bookshelf with several dozen books. All in all, a decor hardly alien to Greenwich Village but with a somewhat Fifth Avenue lift to it. On one wall there is a large oil painting of city back yards—the buildings an impressionistic green, with lines of washing hung out between them, the whole scene suffused with a brightish light which somehow gives it a certain melancholy.

Miss Bancroft was dressed entirely in black—in what we gathered was a preferred outfit of hers: black dress, black sweater, black stockings, black shoes. A small gold watch on a gold bracelet comprised her only jewelry. But black outfit or not, Miss Bancroft is by no means a muted personality. She has a natural gaiety, which, however, can be quickly transformed into a deep thoughtfulness when she is talking about certain aspects of her life or the theatre. She obviously involves herself intensely in what she is doing. At times she spoke with immense animation and excitement; occasionally a flicker of impatience appeared when a question seemed to bore her. Her hands were nearly continously and expressively in motion, and it was not until after two A.M. that Miss Bancroft's dynamism became blunted by fatigue.

Interview

INTERVIEWER You are one of the unusual young women, according to what I've read, whose parents actually favored their child's going into the theatre. Is that true?

BANCROFT Yes.

INTERVIEWER Why, I wonder, did they want you to go into the theatre?

BANCROFT Oh, well, I don't really know why, except that I think my mother always had kind of fantasies, you know, of herself going into the theatre, and then along came this daughter who would have done anything to please her mother, and therefore the mother saw a fulfillment of her own dreams in her child.

INTERVIEWER Did she act or sing?

BANCROFT She didn't, but I did, so that when I came

along and started to express things that she had felt all her life—and I started to express them in songs and dancing, and through what I did as a child—it was then I could express the things that she always wanted to express.

INTERVIEWER   This is almost a direct parallel to Helen Hayes' experience.

BANCROFT   Really?

INTERVIEWER   Her mother had wanted to go into the theatre and wasn't allowed to, as I recall, and when Helen came along and she saw that her child had talent, she did everything in her power to develop it.

BANCROFT   Well, it wasn't that my mother wanted to go into the theatre—that would never have entered her mind, really—but it was that she wanted to express herself, I think, and she never really could, never really found her own talent.

INTERVIEWER   What did you do in terms of singing and dancing and entertaining that gave them this feeling?

BANCROFT   Ever since I was old enough to open my mouth, I was singing and dancing—and I'd rather do that than anything else in this world. I'd rather do that than eat or sleep, and I often did. You know, I'd be singing and my mother would be looking for me and I'd be on the street corner singing for somebody. Or else when she'd come in my room late at night, when I was supposed to be asleep, I'd be singing, or making up stories.

INTERVIEWER   Where did you learn these songs?

BANCROFT   Oh, I picked them up, like off the radio.

INTERVIEWER   Why is it then that, as I gather also from what I've read, you began to think in terms of becoming a laboratory technician?

BANCROFT   Because I just never in my wildest dreams ever thought that I ever would be an actress.

INTERVIEWER   But you had been in the dramatic society at Christopher Columbus High School.

BANCROFT   Yes, but not in my wildest dreams did I ever really think that—I mean, I thought it was like a fantasy, you know, like kids have fantasies, and I thought that's what it would remain all my life.

INTERVIEWER   In other words, you yourself did not have a driving determination to go into the theatre.

BANCROFT   Absolutely not.

INTERVIEWER   At what point did your mother step in and say, "Look, Annie"—your name wasn't Annie, but let us say . . .

BANCROFT   Marie.

INTERVIEWER   Marie. When did she say that you were going into the theatre?

BANCROFT   She never said that I was going to go into the theatre. She just said she'd looked into a number of schools and asked the teacher about me, and the teacher said that this is a good school, you know.

INTERVIEWER   Was this more or less without your knowledge?

BANCROFT   It was without much thought on my part. I mean, I really didn't particularly care. Whatever my mother said went. My mother said this and it was this, and if she said that, it was that. There never was any kind of a conflict.

INTERVIEWER   So you went to the American Academy of Dramatic Arts. And this was the first professional training of any kind that you ever had?

BANCROFT   That's right.

INTERVIEWER   In retrospect, what do you think of drama schools for training?

BANCROFT   Well, I'll tell you. I think they're of absolutely very little value when you're a young person, because I don't really think that you know, that you understand. I mean, I, myself, my mind had to mature so much before I was able to understand what I'm doing. I was twenty-five before I really understood what the whole creative process of acting was. And I think that everything I learned at the American Academy that was on a creative level, was of no value to me. But the good thing about that school is that it doesn't teach those things. It doesn't teach theories, it just teaches voice and speech and fencing and dancing, and those kinds of things, which are good. They're the only things you could learn at eighteen. I wasn't even eighteen when I went there, I was sixteen and a half. Now, really, would I possibly understand anything about motivation and justification, and things like that, and character motivation? Never—at sixteen and a half. All I cared about were boys, anyway, at sixteen and a half.

INTERVIEWER   I gather also that you moved from the Academy directly into television. How did that happen?

BANCROFT   Worthington Miner's wife—he was the producer of "Studio One"—his wife was teaching at the school and saw me during a lunch break rehearsing a scene by myself.

INTERVIEWER   What scene was that?

BANCROFT   It was a scene from a play called *Fly Away Home*. I was playing this Mexican girl, or something like that. Then I was—if I never knew anything about acting, one thing

I always had was this great vitality, whatever that means. But, anyway, she saw me and told me to go up and see about this program that he was going to produce, so I did. I went up and I read among a number of other people and for Robert Fryer—he's now a producer; he was then the casting agent—and I read for him and he loved it. He loved my work. I could tell he did. And he sent me in to read for Worthington Miner, and I did, and then, you know, they picked me.

INTERVIEWER Do you think it was good for you to go into television that way? As an actress, did it do you any harm? Or did it do you any good?

BANCROFT Who knows, who knows. I don't know.

INTERVIEWER How long did you stay in television then?

BANCROFT I stayed in television about a year and a half.

INTERVIEWER And from television you went directly to Hollywood?

BANCROFT Yes.

INTERVIEWER How did that come about?

BANCROFT I was helping somebody with a test. And I did a part in *The Girl on the Via Flaminia* and Twentieth Century Fox on this side, on the East Coast, thought it was so good that they should make the test for really both of us. So they gave us equal footage, you know, and equal close-ups, and things like that. And it went to the West Coast and the West Coast said, "Well, we'd like to sign up that girl," so they did, and then I went out to the West Coast.

INTERVIEWER You made about fifteen films before you were in *Two for the Seesaw*.

BANCROFT Yes.

INTERVIEWER What turned you toward the stage at this time?

BANCROFT Well, I'd reached a certain point . . . Now, everything that happened to me, you know, in my career or artistically, the same thing was happening parallel in my life. I had reached a point in my life and in my career where everything seemed to be going downhill. I just kept getting worse and worse and worse. Every picture I did was worse than the last one, and every man that I was in love with was worse than the last one. It was just—everything was just seeming to be going downhill, until finally I was really in such a stew that I didn't know if I had any talent. I was really lost. By this time I had gone into analysis, you see, and through analysis I—you really have to stop and look at yourself, and in looking at myself I realized that I was lost and I had to do something quick. And I am, I don't know—somebody must have hollered at me too loud one day, and I just went home, packed my bag, told them to call my mother and tell her I was coming back East and that I was going to study to find out if I had any talent. And I was going to get another doctor on the East Coast, and—and I just was very tired with what I was doing at that time. It was like I had to challenge myself, because all my life, you see, I'd told myself that I was the greatest thing that had ever lived, and all my life I believed it, and it was obvious that the outside world was telling me at this point that it wasn't so, like, "It's not so, because look at this what you just did and look at that and they are pretty rotten." So I realized that I had to do something to really let myself know "Are you what you think you are or are you not?" It was kind of like I had to face myself.

INTERVIEWER   Did this come through analysis on the Coast, or did this come just before you went into analysis?

BANCROFT   No, this came after analysis. I knew something was wrong, that the picture I had of myself and the picture of what I saw of myself on the outside—the reality of it on the outside—well, they were different.

INTERVIEWER   These were B pictures you were making, I gather.

BANCROFT   Yeah, like D and E.

INTERVIEWER   Then how did you come upon *Two for the Seesaw?*

BANCROFT   I was coming back here to New York for my sister's wedding, and somebody had the script and said, "When you're in New York look up this guy, Fred Coe,* because I think you'd be wonderful for this part." So I went to see Fred Coe, put on this great big act that I was Gittel, in the flesh—and I didn't bother to tell him that I was somebody else in real life but that I could act Gittel. See, I just made him think I was Gittel, and he liked me very much. Then I met Bill Gibson, the author of the play, and he liked me very much—he thought I was just perfect for it.

INTERVIEWER   I'm curious about this business of Gittel. I have seen different versions of how you made Coe think you were Gittel. What is really the true story?

BANCROFT   Well, I'll tell you exactly what happened. I was waiting in his outer door, in the outside lobby, and he was inside in his office, and I took off my shoe and was scratching my foot and making sure that when he'd open that

* Television and Broadway producer.

door that's the way he would see me—with my shoe off, scratching my foot, talking, you know, to this girl very directly, very openly to his secretary, just like I was Gittel. And then when he called me I went inside—I picked up my shoe, naïvely, as Gittel would do, and I went inside, and before he could even say a word, I completely dominated the whole scene. I said, "Do you have a john?" And he said, "Yeah," and I said, "Oh, I have to go so bad." And I went into the john—I didn't really have to go, you know, but I saw I had to go through the whole thing so that he wouldn't think that I was lying, putting on an act. And then I came out and I said, "Thanks," and that's how it was, like that. That's how I remember it.

INTERVIEWER   You once said in describing your work —it was when you were interviewed in connection with *Seesaw*—you said that in the movies all you did was "feel," you never did any thinking.

BANCROFT   I depended so much on my other actors, you see, that whatever the other actors made me feel, is what I played. It never occurred to me whether the character was different from me or what the language of the character was, or how that character would express it. If an actor made me feel anger, I would get angry. It wouldn't be that maybe this character cannot expose anger and therefore, instead of showing anger, would withdraw. It never occurred to me that people would do anything other than exactly what they feel—you see?

INTERVIEWER   The directors in Hollywood never gave you any guidance in this direction?

BANCROFT   Absolutely none. I'll never forget . . . Once I did a scene in a picture and I didn't know how to play that scene, I really didn't, because I'd never experienced it. When I was in pictures I could never play anything that I had never experienced, and I couldn't experience it in the picture. It was a girl who was going to go out and commit suicide in the very next scene. I had never experienced anything like this in my life, so therefore I couldn't play it. And the director never, never could help me. All he did was just take the scene, thirty-three takes, and each time he was like expecting God somehow to come down and strike me with the right meaning to the scene. Today I could do that scene in two minutes, not that I have experienced it, but I have experienced similar things to it that I could use now to play the scene.

INTERVIEWER   At one time you said that you hated all the years that you were in Hollywood.

BANCROFT   I never said that.

INTERVIEWER   And other times you said you weren't sorry for being out in Hollywood, because you learned a great deal in Hollywood.

BANCROFT   For one thing, nobody ever ... One good thing about a director never telling me anything was that I was never told the wrong thing either, so I never learned any wrong things, you know. I was really just a bunch of raw feelings that nobody ever bothered to direct or misdirect, so that when I came here to study I was still just a bunch of raw feelings, and thank God, you know, I was put into the hands of a great director who knew exactly what to do with those things, and a writer who had written a part that was so perfect for me at that stage of my life, so that I could just take everything that I was, which was quite pure, because it had never been misguided, and just let it go.

INTERVIEWER   When you had to prepare a role in television or in movies—before you came into the theatre proper and under the guidance of, as you say, a great director—and before you became involved with Method, how did you prepare for a role?

BANCROFT   I didn't. I didn't. I learned my lines. Then they said move here and move there, and I did. And they said bark, and I barked, or, you know, whatever they'd tell me, I'd do.

INTERVIEWER   You obviously were a very good natural actress in order to be able to carry on as long as you did in Hollywood.

BANCROFT   Oh, I'm sure I was. I'm sure that it was always there.

INTERVIEWER   The transition from the movies to *Two for the Seesaw* was a matter of a couple of months, is that right?

BANCROFT   From the movies to *Two for the Seesaw* was February, March, April, May, June, July, August, September ... We went into rehearsal in October, didn't we? Yes, October.

INTERVIEWER   The thing that interests me is your feeling that you'd grown so much in that period. Was it the director who enabled you to bring across your greater powers?

BANCROFT   It was—it was the right moment for me because I was at a point in analysis, too, you see, where I was beginning to see what I was as a person, was beginning to catch my own identity as a person, which had a great deal to do with it.

INTERVIEWER   I don't mean to get too personal. Please don't answer anything you feel you don't want to.

BANCROFT   I won't.

INTERVIEWER   But could you tell us a little bit more about what powers were released in you by the time you got to *Two for the Seesaw*, which had not been released before?

BANCROFT   Well, it was the simple power, I think, of knowing a brilliant man. When I saw it—what was in Arthur*—and I could recognize it and I could trust it, I put myself in his hands. You see, I was always able to do that, I was always able to put myself in people's hands and say, "Okay, here I am, mold me." But my mistake in the past was that I could do it with anybody, good or bad. What had happened was that I had the ability then, at that point, to recognize something brilliant in the man as a director.

INTERVIEWER   But where in your own experience, through analysis or whatever it was, were you able to call the best from yourself? Because that had to happen. Not even the best director in the world could do that if you weren't able to pull it out of yourself.

BANCROFT   Yes, too true, but I don't know, I can't tell you that. I do think that because the role was Gittel, the success was easier to achieve.

INTERVIEWER   Perhaps because that was closer to home in your own background.

BANCROFT   Not only in my own background, because I don't believe that accents or background or that I come from the Bronx has anything to do with it. I think it was because emotionally I was built a great deal like the girl, and that emotionally I knew people who were built a great deal like the girl. It was the emotional life of the girl that I felt similar to, and it had nothing to do with her being Jewish, or from the Bronx, or that she was twenty-eight, or she was a failure at dancing. All those were extra added things which were wonderful to have in common, but that wasn't the thing that was really the core, the spark between the character and the actress. It was the emotional life of Gittel and myself that was so close.

INTERVIEWER   You once said you did a lot of research on Gittel, but nobody ever asked you about it.

BANCROFT   Right.

INTERVIEWER   Well, we're going to ask you.

* Arthur Penn, director of *Two for the Seesaw*.

BANCROFT All right, fine.

INTERVIEWER How did you prepare for Gittel? I'd like you to try to reconstruct as much as you can, step by step, what you did first, what did you do second, what did you do about learning Gittel's background.

BANCROFT The first thing I did for Gittel was to be with my sister. I have an older sister who I believe is constructed exactly like Gittel emotionally. You know, underneath this very hard, funny, flippant, coarse exterior is a soul that is so sweet and so lovely and so really willing. So it was kind of like studying my sister. It was also a study of myself, and a real close study of myself, because I sensed that areas in Gittel and myself were the same—the failure in marriage and the failure with men all the time. And then also I went to dancing classes and studied dancers. I went to dancing class for three weeks before we started rehearsal. Gittel was studying dancing, you know. That's it. And many people think that when I say that she was studying with José—everybody thinks it's José Greco. But it's not, It's José Limon, the great modern dancer. And so I went to José Limon's classes and studied in those classes and met people who were not talented dancers, who I thought Gittel was much more like—the non-talented ones. And also I watched Greenwich Village people, because I was at that time with Herbert Berghof's classes for a while. I didn't even know what a loft was when I studied the script or when I first got the script, and she talks about a loft all the time. But then I found out what a loft was because that's where Herbert Berghof's classes were—they were in a loft, you know. And even before I knew I had the part, it was on my mind. It's like once you read something that really, you know, inspires you, you never forget it. It's like if I bought a newspaper, I would buy it as Gittel. I wouldn't buy it as me, I'd buy it as Gittel. No matter what I did, I would do it as Gittel would do it.

INTERVIEWER In terms of speech and mannerisms—did you really have to go back and study the speech and mannerisms?

BANCROFT No, that sort of just came. All I had to do was just be around my sister for a while and it just automatically came.

INTERVIEWER After you watched your sister and you studied the background and analyzed yourself, what would be the next step? What did you do after that?

BANCROFT That was about it. That was about as much

as I had to do, I thought, and then I sort of figured I was ready.

INTERVIEWER   And what about Annie Sullivan? How did you proceed there? I know that you went to the Institute for Physical Medicine and Rehabilitation, and you went on a roller coaster blindfolded.

BANCROFT   Yes, I was blindfolded. I had a tape over my eyes when I went on the roller coaster.

INTERVIEWER   Whose idea was it to put the adhesive on?

BANCROFT   Mine.

INTERVIEWER   In order to see how it felt to be blind?

BANCROFT   Yes. Actually, I wanted to see how it felt to feel so dependent, really dependent on other people, *really*.

INTERVIEWER   What did you do about learning about Annie Sullivan?

BANCROFT   I read everything there was to read about her; every book that was ever written about her, I read.

INTERVIEWER   And did you go where she came from, to her home?

BANCROFT   We went up to Boston. We went up to the Perkins Institution, too, while we were there giving the show. We were up there, and I saw her letters, her handwriting, walked through the places she walked through. But, of course, it's not the same. And besides, I didn't find that very helpful anyway. I don't find those things helpful, you know, these exterior things, I just don't find them helpful. The only thing I really find helpful—I found the books very helpful, and, of course, most of all I find the script the most helpful thing. You see, I've only worked with one author whom I trust to put down the truth, and there is not, in *Miracle Worker*, there is not one ounce of untruth in it. What he has done, then, is taken the truth and put a theatrical life to it. And even in *Seesaw*, you know—if you study *Seesaw*, the character of that girl is so exquisitely written, there just isn't anything he doesn't tell you right there in the script. It's all right there. If there's anything you want to know, you just look through the script and there it is, one place or another.

INTERVIEWER   Nevertheless, you seem to do a lot of this external research.

BANCROFT   Well, I do all those things, but I find that they give me the least amount of help. Most I discard. The most amount of help comes from my author's concept, and then my director's image, and, then, my own, which I get from the things that I read in the script and these internal things that I do with myself—you know, where am I the same as Annie and where am I different from Annie?

INTERVIEWER   When you first read *The Miracle Worker,*
did the character assume proportions immediately, or is this
something you think about for a long time?

BANCROFT   Oh, no, I have to think about it.

INTERVIEWER   Then it comes over a period of time?

BANCROFT   Yes. Every once in a while it'll hit you and
there it is. It's like . . . You look at the script of *The Miracle
Worker.* Now, what is the script, what is the whole thing
about? It's about a woman who if she does not teach this
child, both she and the child will perish. Of course, I have
nothing like that in my own life, so I have to take something
else in my life about which I have to say, "If I don't do a
certain thing, I will perish." So, well, it's kind of like a parallel
to her struggle.

INTERVIEWER   Did you have an actual parallel?

BANCROFT   Yes.

INTERVIEWER   That you could tell us about?

BANCROFT   No, I can't tell you what it is, but it's an
actual parallel—that if I don't do this and if I don't go
through the entire struggle with it, no matter what it entails,
I will perish as a human being.

INTERVIEWER   You said that when you were sixteen and
went to drama school, you didn't get anything out of it. Was
it because you didn't have the emotional resources?

BANCROFT   It's not the emotional resources—I didn't
have the brains. It's the brains. I find it's the brains that are
the most important thing, I really do.

INTERVIEWER   But by the time you got to *The Miracle
Worker,* you had this equipment?

BANCROFT   Yes, and much more.

INTERVIEWER   Was this a matter of living, of reading,
of feeling?

BANCROFT   It's a matter of thinking. Really, it's a matter
of learning a thinking process. It's a matter of becoming aware
of what it is you're doing, of what it is you're feeling, and
then it's a matter of controlling it any way you want with
your brain. See, that's the difference between what I did in
Hollywood and what I'm doing here. It's that in Hollywood
all I did was just from feeling. I didn't control it or manipulate it with my brain. It just flowed, you know, as a river
flows. But along comes a thing called a human being and
takes that river and he floats logs down it or he builds a dam,
and out of that comes electricity, you know, and greater
things come from a natural resource. My natural resource is
my marvelous energy and my marvelous emotions, which

flow very easily. But I never bothered to ever control them or manipulate them or really use them. You know, that's really the greatest joy in acting—getting those feelings, which always come spontaneously. But to take them and just give as much as you want, to just say to yourself, "I want to give this much," and just that much comes; or "I want to give that much," and that much comes out of all those feelings. Or you say, "Now I'm feeling this amount of hostility. Okay, now I have to pull it in because I can't show all that for such-and-such reasons. Because he is the girl's father, and I can't show too much because he might throw me out on my ear." So I control it, you know, and that's the wonderful thing, the controlling and the shaping of it, as a sculptor does with a lump of clay when he sculpts it to make whatever he wants from it. It's what you do, really. You do whatever *you* want, which I never did in pictures. I just did whatever came.

INTERVIEWER   In what way did Arthur Penn stimulate you to think and to gain this control? How did he reach you?

BANCROFT   Well, it was such a slow gradual thing. Do you know about the initial episode with him?

INTERVIEWER   No.

BANCROFT   That first really opened up, I think, a great many things to me. We were doing a scene in *Seesaw*, and it was written in the script that she says to him, "Come to me, come to where I am." You never heard this story?

INTERVIEWER   No.

BANCROFT   So in the script the man is supposed to be over there, and I'm here. I'm supposed to be soothing him in a way, and I'm supposed to say, "Come to me, come to where I am," and he's over there. But Arthur's directing, he doesn't go by the script, you know, the movements in the script. We just moved around. We were moving around, and when I came to that line the man was sitting right beside me, and I said, "Arthur, we'll have to cut that line because he's sitting here," and Arthur said, "No, say it anyway." I said, "Arthur, how can I say that line? He's sitting right here." And he said, "Well, think up another meaning for it." I didn't know what he meant at first, but then it was like, I can't tell you, it was like getting one of those great insights you get when you're on the couch in analysis. It just came to me like that, and I said, "Holy mackerel!" And then I could say that line meaning five hundred things. Well, not five hundred but so many things. It could mean like come into my heart because my heart is still, I'm at peace, so come in there. It could just mean, you know, a simple thing.

INTERVIEWER You could give it a poetic implication.

BANCROFT Anything that I wanted, anything I wanted. It could also mean just come into my arms, come here to these arms. It could mean that, too, you know, just anything.

INTERVIEWER And this grew out of your growing intellectual powers.

BANCROFT That's right, that's right—my beginning to use my intellectual powers through analysis was where it all started, you see.

INTERVIEWER In having to think about yourself? In having to think there are many more meanings in life?

BANCROFT That's right. That's exactly right.

INTERVIEWER At what point, then, did you become involved with the Method, and go to the Actors Studio?

BANCROFT I went to the Studio after I opened in *Seesaw*. Arthur thought—because I couldn't, of course, stay under Arthur's wing all the time because he had other things to do—that I needed some place to go and develop my new authority over myself.

INTERVIEWER Is Arthur a Method director?

BANCROFT First of all, let's clear up right away about the Method. All right?

INTERVIEWER Right, let's go.

BANCROFT First of all, I have never read Stanislavsky. Second of all, every actor has a method. When you say the Method, you mean Stanislavsky's Method.

INTERVIEWER Right.

BANCROFT I don't think . . . I think there are about three people in the whole world that really understand Stanislavsky's Method, really. You know, like Lee Strasberg understands it, and Stanislavsky understands it, and maybe one or two other people. But nobody really understands Stanislavsky's Method that much. And the thing is that if Stanislavsky's Method doesn't work for you, if it doesn't free you, if it doesn't allow you to do your best work, then you don't use it. And that doesn't mean that you're not a good actor or a great actor, you know. It doesn't mean anything. It just means that this is the only man that has ever put his method down in such detail that if anybody who had talent and didn't know how to free it or didn't know how to work with it, that if they wanted to, there it was, written in detail. You do step one, step two. There it is. It's all in detail, and in an inspiringly written way, I hear. And if you want it and you need it, you take it; and if you don't, then you don't.

INTERVIEWER Why haven't you read Stanislavsky?

BANCROFT Well, first of all, I don't read very much. Second of all, even if I read it, unless I could do it, I wouldn't know what he was talking about. I really don't know what he's talking about when I read it. See, when I hear Lee Strasberg—when I'm looking at a scene, and then at the end Lee Strasberg explains it, and the student says, "Ah, yes, I see what you mean," and I can experience it as they're talking about it, and it's happening dynamically in front of me—then I can understand.

INTERVIEWER Apparently a lot of people misinterpret it.

BANCROFT Absolutely. Misinterpret it, misuse it terribly.

INTERVIEWER But as far as you are concerned, what you needed most was someone to uncork your thinking powers, whether it be Stanislavsky or Delsarte or . . .

BANCROFT Or Dr. Fisher, to help me control it.

INTERVIEWER The thing that helped you uncork your thoughts more was analysis?

BANCROFT Yes.

INTERVIEWER So it isn't really Lee Strasberg who does that.

BANCROFT No, no, it's not that he actually does it, absolutely not. Actually, no one thing has done anything for me in my life. It has always been a combination of things. I can't say it was Arthur Penn, I can't say it was analysis. It was a combination of those things and my own self in a certain period, a certain readiness to understand. And it was always a combination of things. And it's a combination of my present analysis and my present awareness, because of analysis, that makes me able to understand Lee Strasberg, and by understanding Lee Strasberg I am able, then, to put it into practice in the theatre at night, and reassure myself that what Strasberg said was right, and that it works for me. Not everything he says works for me, but whatever does work for me, I have a chance to go every night and try it.

INTERVIEWER Can you give us an example?

BANCROFT Well, I'm trying to think. Yes. We were talking about preparation work once, I remember; once it helped me very much. Sometimes, you know, you're preparing for a scene, and you have to come on cold to a scene if there is no scene previously leading to that scene, so that you have to come on with only what you imagined comes before it. And the director asks a certain result from you, or needs a certain result because of what the scene has to do for the play; so he wants a certain thing and you can't get it, either with the other actor or from the script. Well, Lee was talking about preparing in a way so that you picture yourself in an atmosphere that will, when you walk into the next scene, produce that result. Now, this first scene in *Miracle Worker* is sometimes very, very difficult, because it's supposed to really combine two very, very strong things —a dichotomy, really, in Annie. She's supposed to want desperately to go and see that kid and start living and start working, and really put everything she's learned into practice. She's dying to go, and yet there's got to be that kind of fear of "if I leave, I'm leaving the only thing I know, the only thing I've ever known." So it's really supposed to tell a great deal, and yet it's got to tell it in a way, you know, where she's kind of saucy and clippy and fights back with the authority figure in the scene. And I remember Lee talking about preparing in this way, of preparing to be in an atmosphere that would then, when you walk into the next scene, produce the things that you wanted, the two feelings that I needed. So I went to the theatre that night, and I knew very, very well that I had the sauciness and I had the ego, the real ego thing. It was all there and it was ready to go. But I have to have the other thing *you see,* there, too, which is working for me, that must come out later on in the scene. I've gotta have that—the fear. Therefore, I have to figure out what kind of atmosphere, or what kind of situation, Annie is in before she goes to this scene, that will give me, the actress, that fear. So my preparation that night was thinking of Annie's room, of every familiar thing that she would have to leave. And that was how, when I went on stage, I had all the ego thing—it was all there, and it was fine, and then when he brought out the ring, suddenly the ring reminded me of every familiar thing that I was leaving behind. And it was there—all of the fullness, all of the fear and the love, and everything for this man and this place, was there—and it worked. It was great, it was terrific.

INTERVIEWER A criticism of American actors that has been voiced by directors from abroad—for instance, Willi Schmidt from Germany and Jean Meyer from the Comédie Française—is that our actors do not have a classic background, that they don't have the tradition of acting in terms of the classics. For instance, they might ask how a Method actor would do Molière.

BANCROFT Well, now, I don't really understand that. Maybe it's because I'm too young in my development, but I don't understand. If you get a character in Molière—why is Molière different from Arthur Miller?

INTERVIEWER Molière belongs to a tradition that no longer exists.

BANCROFT So you find out what that tradition was. You look it up and you find it out—what they did—and then you do it. That's the behavior of your character; that's the external behavior of your character. As for what you're going to feel inside—you'll work the same way, I'm sure, for Arthur Miller as you will with Molière. How it comes out— you do with every character, with every different character you play. Annie Sullivan and Gittel Mosca feel many things exactly the same way. The only difference is, that Annie— when it comes out—her behavior is different from Gittel's. Therefore, when it comes out, it's in Annie's behavior or it's in Gittel's behavior. So, if you're going to do Molière . . .

INTERVIEWER Where does technique come in here?

BANCROFT I don't know. I mean, what technique do you mean? An internal technique or an external technique?

INTERVIEWER The manner in which you lift a cup would be technique, wouldn't it?

BANCROFT I would lift the cup in the manner of the character.

INTERVIEWER You mentioned before, purely spontaneously, this business of parallel experience. Now, you're a young actress and—well, to be a bit extreme, you don't have to kill a person in order to play the part of a killer. How do you re-create this parallel experience? It is not very clear to me. Could you explain that a little?

BANCROFT You mean, how do I find it?

INTERVIEWER Yes.

BANCROFT Let me think for a minute. It's so hard to answer just like that without thinking for a minute. Well, if you study the script . . . For instance, I know what Annie will go through in order to achieve what she wants. I know what is at stake. In thinking of those things, I get an emotional response. In getting that emotional response, automatically something comes, you know, the reason why I'm having that response. And I'm having that response because something in my life must mean the same thing to me as what teaching that child means to Annie.

INTERVIEWER On that line—do you consciously try to enrich your experience in life? Is that important? Are there any ways in which you feel an actor should enrich his experience, or do you feel that experience can only be ingested simply as it comes?

BANCROFT   Obviously I do feel that certain things have to be sharpened. I know that I have great feelings about being helpless, a hatred for being helpless. I can't stand it, simply because I know the ability that I have to be helpless. This is very personal, but I must say it to make my point. Love, because it has such strong feelings inside of me. And, of course, you know what Annie is working for— that the child must not be helpless, she must not be dependent on *anyone* for *anything,* she must learn to be a human being independent and depending on herself. This is Annie's fight. I know I have those same feelings that Annie has, and now I feel I must heighten them. So I heighten them by blindfolding myself, because then I'm helpless and I must depend. That's why I had to commit myself to that blindness for the amount of time that I did. It heightened in me. I also realized so many things happened to me, in my personality, because I was dependent on, you know, a certain friend of mine. So many things happened. How much sweeter I was, and how much less I exposed my real feelings to him, and to, oh, feel so many things happening to me—the heightening of all of these inner things. I got all those things sealed in this bag, and then I say, "Well, now, this is good for Annie and that's very good for Annie. No, that won't work. Well, maybe it'll work in that scene. We'll see, we'll keep it out there." See what I mean? It just brings everything up to the top so you can pick them more easily. That's the reason, sometimes, to enter into an experience that will bring these things up.

INTERVIEWER   Under what circumstances, when you're working on a role, do you find that you do your thinking best?

BANCROFT   In rehearsal. That's where it happens; the best of it happens there.

INTERVIEWER   You don't go for a walk in the park to try to figure this out?

BANCROFT   If I'm having a particularly difficult problem, yes, I certainly do. I'll do anything I can in order to solve it, but my best thinking is done in rehearsal.

INTERVIEWER   What procedure have you found best for learning lines?

BANCROFT   I have to be cued. I have to get somebody to cue me, and go through it, go through it, go through it.

INTERVIEWER   Do you learn your lines first before you begin working on the business of the character, or do you take it the other way around?

BANCROFT Really, I have no set style about that—whatever is best.

INTERVIEWER Both Gittel and Annie are taxing roles, especially Annie because of the physical battle with the child. What do you do for relaxation? How do you keep in shape in terms of disciplining your body? Do you have any regimen?

BANCROFT I just don't worry about it. I found at the beginning of this play that I would worry so. I had to eat the right food, and I had to do this and I mustn't do that. I must do this, I must do that, I must do—till, finally, I was going out of my mind. And I just said one day, you know, the hell with it, and I just don't worry about it. I just go on. It's acting. That scene that we do—the fight scene—is acting, and if I'm ready to act, then I'm ready to do that scene. If I'm not ready to act, then I'm not ready to do that scene.

INTERVIEWER What do you do when, as you say, you're not ready to act and it's curtain time?

BANCROFT Of course, most nights I'm fully aware of what my parallel to Annie is. I'm fully aware of that most nights. But if I ever feel that, "Jeezus, I'm not in the mood, I really just don't feel like acting," then I have to just sort of concentrate on things that will inspire me. Sometimes it may be words of Helen Keller, maybe words of Annie Sullivan's. It may be just Bill Gibson's work or it may just be the very heart of acting, you know. It's just something that will make me think that it's worthwhile, that there's a reason for it all.

INTERVIEWER During the run of a play do you feel it important to lead a quiet life, perhaps cutting down on your social activity?

BANCROFT I have a very active life. I find that the more I am with—of course, it may be just the role that I'm in—but the more I have to do with people, the more eager I am that night to give what I got that day on the stage.

INTERVIEWER From what then, do you draw the most stimulation?

BANCROFT One of the most inspiring things for me is the Actors Studio—to see actors working at their craft and talking about it and listening to Lee Strasberg.

INTERVIEWER How many times a week do you go there?

BANCROFT Twice.

INTERVIEWER Have you been doing that all the way through both plays?—*Seesaw* and *Miracle Worker*?

BANCROFT Yes, yes.

INTERVIEWER   In what ways are you working to improve as an actress?

BANCROFT   Well, to be able to free more and more and more of myself, to be able to reveal and expose and give more and more of myself. Because I really feel (a modest giggle) that there isn't anything that's been written—because if it existed in some man's mind and he put it on paper, then it must be actable, you know.

INTERVIEWER   To follow that, how do you see yourself achieving this goal?

BANCROFT   By just every day, you know, you ... You see, there's one rule I have on stage, and that is that I will never let myself get away with the phony. I have to cry, I mean I *have* to cry, really have to cry twice in my play, because there are lines that cannot be said unless I do, or there is a next beat that cannot be done unless I do. So I have to cry twice in my play. Both times I can get away with it, because once I'm in the dark, in a corner, and nobody sees me; and the other time I have my glasses on, you know, the dark glasses, and nobody knows if I do or I don't. You see, I realized this very early. Immediately I thought, oh boy, I can cheat here, wowee. But I cannot let myself. I mean, if I let myself go one night and I get away with it, I will just keep letting myself get away with it, and so I just work with myself so that I never let those moments go by. I work and work as hard as I can to achieve those moments, and not just slide by them.

INTERVIEWER   I don't know if I completely understand you. Do you actually mean real tears?

BANCROFT   I mean really cry. When I'm really crying the result is, of course, real tears. It's tears, you know. But that's not so difficult. You can do that a number of ways. You can sniff ammonia—I guess there are lots of ways to do that. No, by crying I mean to actually stimulate the emotion of something that will produce real tears.

INTERVIEWER   What do you do? Ferrer has told us, for instance, that when he was in *The Shrike,* he killed his mother and he killed his father and he killed his aunt and he killed his uncle; and all these things in order to bring out that emotional reaction. At least, on the bad nights that was so. On the good nights, the power of the play did it.

BANCROFT   The very play does it—exactly, the very play.

INTERVIEWER   In other words, if you are riding with the play and if you are completely lost in your character, then the crying comes.

BANCROFT   Not lost, I don't like that word, lost.

INTERVIEWER   What should we use?

BANCROFT   Found. It's not really lost, because lost has the connotation of, you know, like you don't know where you are. I know where I am precisely at every moment. It's not lost—if I'm really doing my best work.

INTERVIEWER   Then you will cry naturally out of the course of the action in the play?

BANCROFT   Yes, that's right. If I'm really in my character, really in it.

INTERVIEWER   When you're not completely in it, what do you do?

BANCROFT   What do I do? Well, I use anything. I'll use any thought, *any* thought. Well, for instance, if the tears don't come in *The Miracle Worker* in one of the scenes where I must cry, then I have to go back, then I have to re-create a scene where the same thing happened, you see, which is a scene of rejection, a scene of helplessness, of wanting to give, wanting to help, and the person won't take it, a feeling of being mistrusted. Any one of these things, any one of those feelings. I have to think of a lot of scenes in my lifetime that caused that feeling.

INTERVIEWER   What are you doing to develop your voice?

BANCROFT   I take voice lessons three times a week.

INTERVIEWER   Are the lessons designed to improve your vocal projection on stage?

BANCROFT   They're designed just to improve my speech, because my voice—not necessarily for the stage, but just for my own body—because I obviously have a very unhealthy placement of my voice, or I did have.

INTERVIEWER   What do you mean by an unhealthy placement of your voice?

BANCROFT   When I went into *Seesaw*, my voice was placed so unhealthily that if I'd project it, I'd bang my vocal cords together so that I developed nodes on my larynx. So I had to learn how to re-place my voice so when I projected I didn't have to bang them together like that.

INTERVIEWER   What do you do about further developing the grace of movement of your body?

BANCROFT   I move pretty well. I don't think that there is really anything that I couldn't do in movement if I studied, so there isn't any specific thing that I'm doing because there is no need for it. If I knew that I was going into a musical or going into something where I had to have, you know, ballet-like movement, I would do something about it. But there isn't a dance I can't learn in three minutes. I can just do that sort of thing.

INTERVIEWER Do you have any special séance that you go into before the curtain goes up? Do you have to lock yourself in the dressing room, without seeing anybody for a minimum of time, or anything like that?

BANCROFT No, no, no. You see, I have not pinned myself down and I don't think I really want to do that, to pin myself down. See, I allow myself freedom, so that whatever it is I feel like giving that night, or whatever kind of mood I'm in, I'll use that night in the show—do you know what I mean? It's like, for instance, I was telling you about for the first scene I had all the ego that night, all that ego was right there, but I knew that I needed other things and I wasn't quite sure that they were there for me to give. It's kind of like I have to evaluate myself for a few minutes before I go on stage to see what it is I haven't got, what I have to work for, what is not free, you know, what isn't open enough to work. And yet that's not sure-fire either, because some nights I can go on laughing ha-ha-ha with the boys, you know, having a great time laughing with the kids, and I'll go on and everything works for me like that, like a dream. So I really don't know. And sometimes I can sit and ponder and work and all, and I'll go on and nothing works—I just don't have it.

INTERVIEWER There was some hint not too long ago that you were thinking in terms of doing a musical.

BANCROFT If I find . . . Look, I don't care what my next show is as long as the script is terrific. I just haven't read any good script, musical or non-musical yet.

INTERVIEWER What are you looking for, or what kind of play do you want to do? What does the theatre mean to you?

BANCROFT This is what it means to me. I was hoping you'd ask that question. I think my job as an actress—the job of my talent or what I want to do with my talent—is to give to the people what I believe are certain realities of life, certain truths. Because I know one of the hardest things in life is to not only see a truth but to accept it. It's a very hard thing, reality—to see and accept and to realize it as a reality and a truth. I could get up and I could lecture and just lecture and lecture and lecture that this is a reality, that anything that puts the spirit in a dungeon is a sin, and that the greatest joy in the world is liberating that. And so I could get up and make a speech, but I don't think an audience would be quite so willing to accept it as they would be when it is embellished within an entertainment form, you see. If you put it in an entertaining form and then say what you want to say to the world—and you put it within the theatrical form—I think it gets to them easier, more easily. They don't feel that it's being thrust on them. They're not only getting a truth, but they're getting it done in this way, in this charming way or in this theatrical way or in this dynamic way—and it's easier, I think.

INTERVIEWER How do you relate this to the plays you've been in?

BANCROFT In *Two for the Seesaw,* one of the themes— one of the things that it says—is that you must face the truth about yourself and you must be honest about yourself before you can ever really give on any mature level. A script, before I really want to do it, has to say in it some of the things that I have come to believe in—you know, to point out what we must do in order to be better human beings. It has to give human beings something that will make them better. That's what a script has to do.

INTERVIEWER But you're not limiting yourself to serious drama.

BANCROFT Oh, no. I think a musical can say some wonderful things. I think certainly *Gypsy* said some marvelous things. It was just they get kind of buried underneath all the gay songs and all that singin' and dancin', but nevertheless that's the reason for doing it.

INTERVIEWER Comedy also?

BANCROFT Certainly. You can say truths in many ways. You can say things that will better humans in many ways. It doesn't all have to be, you know, atomic bombs.

INTERVIEWER To shift around a bit here, it has been said that imagination is of the utmost importance to an actor. Do you think it is possible to develop one's imagination?

BANCROFT I don't think my imagination ever needed developing. I think that was one of the problems that made my life so hard—my imagination was too great. I spent probably much more than half my life imagining the world as I wanted it to be. My imagination was out of my control then, but it, nevertheless, was greatly developed. What I have to do is control it and mold it more.

INTERVIEWER Do you think that there is any way to develop imagination if it is lacking?

BANCROFT I really think that if you're an actor, your imagination is really developed. I just feel that anybody who ever dreams or wants to be an actor must have an enormous imagination. I think the two of them are so much together.

INTERVIEWER   How vital is the theatre in your life? Do you love to act?

BANCROFT   Sometimes.

INTERVIEWER   Only sometimes? Explain that a little bit.

BANCROFT   Well, some nights I'll go out on-stage and I can't think of anything I'd rather not do than act. I just don't have the energy. I don't have the desire. I don't feel the inspiration.

INTERVIEWER   Do you encounter that often?

BANCROFT   I encounter it whenever my life is not in good working order. Sometimes that's often and sometimes it's not.

INTERVIEWER   Have you tried in any way to live defensively, so that your life will be in good order all the time?

BANCROFT   No, because I'd rather learn how to live great than not great. That's much more important. If the two of them go together, if living great means then that I will act great, that's terrific; but if living great means that then I won't be able to act great, well, then I'll just have to not act great.

INTERVIEWER   But until we learn a certain discipline or a philosophy or something, we can't be at our fullest powers.

BANCROFT   Yes, but I don't do it because it will make me happy. I do it because it will make me live better.

INTERVIEWER   So it's the same feeling.

BANCROFT   Yes, absolutely. Look, here's a perfect, perfect example. Last night was the first night this new little girl* went in, and I knew within the first ten minutes that she was not Patty Duke and I got so angry—I went out on that stage and I was so angry. But unless I would have allowed myself to get angry and to do the things that I did, I don't think I would have been able to come to what I came to tonight. In getting angry and in riding with that anger and letting it come out and being almost to a point of being cruel—somehow it just set me to thinking today. First, of course, with my analyst, and then talking with myself and other people, because it was on my mind. And I really came to a realization of why I was wrong. Everything was, you know, on the side of the child. She's five years younger than Patty Duke. She never had Arthur Penn to direct her. She never had eight weeks of rehearsal, eight weeks on the road. And I was demanding of this child that she should be Patty Duke, with whom I had played for over a year, and from whom I knew what to expect, to sense when she would do something. And

* The child actress who substituted for Patty Duke.

I was expecting this same kind of thing to happen between this kid and me, when, you know, it was impossible. But I had to let it happen, because obviously that's the way I learn things. I gotta have my head banged against the wall for me to learn those kind of things.

INTERVIEWER   You said, when we met you at the theatre, that the child had said to you, "You're so nice to me tonight."

BANCROFT   Yes, but, you see, it really worked. Isn't it strange? Because the kid last night, by my cruelty... See, she was the kind of a kid who could make you angry at her, because she was saying—she was there three days in rehearsal, and she says, "When do I get star billing?" Nine years old! Now, isn't this enough to get you started right off? So I was ready to get angry with her. It was as if I said to myself, "If she is the kind of kid who has that kind of ego, she is gonna have to deliver." But then when she didn't deliver, and had that ego, then I really got mad.

INTERVIEWER   The problem of working with a child actor is sometimes...

BANCROFT   It's a problem.

INTERVIEWER   Many experienced actors avoid being left on the stage alone with a child for too long a time, because invariably the child draws the most attention.

BANCROFT   Steals the scene—absolutely.

INTERVIEWER   And you succeed in *Miracle Worker* in not letting that happen. You take that risk.

BANCROFT   It never even entered my mind that anybody (laughing) could take the stage away from me. However, when we were on the road and Patty was sitting there playing with the dog and pulling its ears, and, you know, doing all these things with the dog—well, a three-ring circus couldn't compete with that. And I realized I had a problem, and then I had to cope with it when I realized it. If it had been right, if it had been right for the scene, I would have allowed it to go on, but it was not right for the scene.

INTERVIEWER   When you say you suddenly realized you had a problem, what do you mean?

BANCROFT   Because the audience was looking at this girl playing with the ear.

INTERVIEWER   Then what did you do?

BANCROFT   Well, the first thing I did was to then develop my side of the stage. That's the first thing that I did. I poured on a great deal more meaning, much more power. I really went in and studied what I was doing on that side and, you know, poured energy and everything I could. I tried everything on my side of the stage. When that didn't work, then I just went over and on-stage I slapped Patty's hands and told her—it fit perfectly into the character—that her playing with the dog was embarrassing Annie Sullivan, because she was talking to the dog, which is a shameful thing to Annie. So it worked right in. I could use it as the character as well as the actress—getting so angry because of that shame that I slapped her hands.

INTERVIEWER   What are the problems that you have found as a young artist, as a young star? I mean, you come East and you fall into the role of Gittel, which catapults you to the front ranks of the theatre. Then you come back with Annie Sullivan. Which says, "This proves that I merit my place"—I'm not trying to flatter you, you know what's been said. This was a great challenge—Annie Sullivan—because coming up the second time is the important time.

BANCROFT   Yes.

INTERVIEWER   Being raised to a very important position, your name is important, your name has become Box Office. People know Anne Bancroft as a young star. This must have created problems for you. What are the problems that stardom creates for a young artist? Or aren't you aware that this had created problems for you?

BANCROFT   I don't think I'm quite aware, because I don't think I can really separate what has brought me problems because I'm a star, or what has brought me problems because I am what I am, you know, who I am. I really can't separate the two. But then, of course, I suppose I am a star because I am what I am, huh?

INTERVIEWER   Say, a college student may be reading this interview some day. What can you offer by way of example to this student to help him avoid the traps that exist all along Broadway for the young star. How have you managed to maintain your two feet on the ground? That's what I'm getting at.

BANCROFT   How have I managed? Well, first of all, do I have my two feet on the ground?

INTERVIEWER   You could tell me.

BANCROFT   I don't even know if I do or not. No, I don't know. I think maybe because things don't appear in the paper about me doesn't necessarily mean I . . .

INTERVIEWER   Now you're being mysterious.

BANCROFT   Well, I hate to appear dull, you know. I'd much rather be mysterious than dull. It's just—if there are traps along Broadway, they have not been traps for me. Because I do what I want to do and, therefore, it's not a trap, is it? You know, if I prefer to fall into something, it isn't a trap.

INTERVIEWER I should think it's very hard, when one achieves this kind of success, not to be overwhelmed by the flattery that must inevitably flow, and to maintain the values by which one has lived and not to throw them overboard.

BANCROFT Oh, you talk of those things. Yes, those are traps.

INTERVIEWER And you've had more money than you've ever had before, let's say.

BANCROFT I do not. I had much more money in Hollywood. They paid very good in Hollywood. Are you kidding? I had much more money in Hollywood than I have here, and I worked less, less weeks out of the year.

INTERVIEWER You have more praise, though.

BANCROFT Yes, that I've had.

INTERVIEWER Which can make it hard to keep one's head.

BANCROFT Absolutely. Yes, that can be a trap. You just cannot believe everybody. You have to pick the people that you're gonna believe. But, you know, in the beginning of Seesaw, when I didn't know what the hell I was doing really —I mean I knew, but I didn't really have that much control, it's like it grew and grew and grew and grew—but in the beginning of Seesaw I never knew when I had a good night or a bad night, so if somebody came in and said you were marvelous on a bad night, I would have thought I was terrific. But now when I have a bad night, I know it. I know when I'm at my best. I try to do my best every night, but I know when my best was not my greatest. And when people come back and say, "You were great," I know that I was not. And I almost say, "What'd you know, you dope, you don't know nothin'." I really get so hostile toward them, you know.

INTERVIEWER If I had seen your play and I was taken backstage, I'd say to you that you were great whether or not I thought you were great.

BANCROFT You would?

INTERVIEWER Sure I would.

BANCROFT Well, there you see what the problem is.

INTERVIEWER Yes, but I can't put myself in the position of a critic. In the first place, it would be very unkind for me to say anything else.

BANCROFT True.

INTERVIEWER If I thought you gave a shoddy performance and were gypping me, then I would say nothing. But you expect a lot from people, perhaps.

BANCROFT   I certainly do. Oh, I certainly do. Absolutely. Like I expect this kid to be Patty Duke, you know. Oh, I do. I make terrific demands.

INTERVIEWER   Now, a few random questions we've wanted to cover before stopping. Did you consider the problem at all, when you were going into *The Miracle Worker*, of the success you'd had in *Seesaw*—that you had to equal or surpass it? Was this a bugaboo of any kind?

BANCROFT   No, it never entered my mind. I went into *Miracle Worker* because *Miracle Worker* said something that I wanted to say. It never entered my mind, those things. I just don't think in those terms of I gotta equal it. I'd be in a panic. I wouldn't be able to do a thing if I thought in those terms. Thank God I don't. But it never entered my mind.

INTERVIEWER   You have spoken about analysis, and you have found that it has helped free you as an artist.

BANCROFT   It's helped free me as a human being.

INTERVIEWER   As a human being. But there are some people who fear analysis as being a flattening influence.

BANCROFT   Well, I think they fear that their whole artistry is based on their neurosis. I feel that if my artistry is based on my neurosis, well then, my artistry will just have to go out the window. Because I think a human being is the finest thing that's ever been put on this earth, and it's bigger and better than anything else it can produce.

INTERVIEWER   In other words, if you found that your artistry depended upon a neurosis, you would rather be a happy human being than an artist.

BANCROFT   Not necessarily a happy human being, but a non-destructive human being. I would rather be a healthy human being.

INTERVIEWER   You would give up acting in order to be the kind of human being you have a picture of.

BANCROFT   The kind of human being that I think I am, or that I'm becoming aware of—yes.

INTERVIEWER   If you had it to do over again, what advice would you give to an actor or an actress in terms of avoiding mistakes that you've made, or what would you say to a young actor or actress who is setting out on the road?

BANCROFT   First of all, I don't think that anybody should avoid mistakes. If it is within their nature to make certain mistakes, I think they should make them, make the mistakes and find out what the cost of the mistake is, rather than to constantly keep avoiding it, and never really knowing

exactly what the experience of it is, what the cost of it is,
you know, and all the other facets of the mistake. I don't
think that mistakes are that bad. I think that they should
try and not do destructive things, but I don't think that a
mistake is that serious a thing that one should be told what
to do to avoid it.

 **BARD BOOKS**

distinguished modern fiction

A SELECTION OF RECENT TITLES

FICTION

AMERICAN VOICES, AMERICAN WOMEN Lee R. Edwards and Arlyn Diamond (editors)	17871	1.95
BETRAYED BY RITA HAYWORTH Manuel Puig	15206	1.65
THE CASE HISTORY OF COMRADE V. James Park Sloan	15362	1.65
A COOL MILLION & THE DREAM LIFE OF BALSO SNELL Nathanael West	15115	1.65
A GENEROUS MAN Reynolds Price	15123	1.65
GOING NOWHERE Alvin Greenberg	15081	1.65
THE GREEN HOUSE Mario Vargas Llosa	15099	1.65
THE LANGUAGE OF CATS, And Other Stories Spencer Holst	14381	1.65
LEAF STORM, And Other Stories Gabriel Garcia Marquez	17566	1.65
LES GUERILLERES Monique Wittig	14373	1.65
A LONG AND HAPPY LIFE Reynolds Price	17053	1.65
NABOKOV'S DOZEN Vladimir Nabokov	15354	1.65
PNIN Vladimir Nabokov	15800	1.65
RITES OF PASSAGE Joanne Greenberg	15933	1.25
62: A MODEL KIT Julio Cortazar	17558	1.65
WHAT HAPPENS NEXT? Gilbert Rogin	17806	1.65

Wherever better paperbacks are sold, or directly from the publisher. Include 15¢ per copy for mailing; allow three weeks for delivery.

Avon Books, Mail Order Dept.
250 West 55th Street, New York, N.Y. 10019

DISCUS BOOKS

DISTINGUISHED NON-FICTION

A SELECTION OF RECENT TITLES

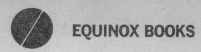 **EQUINOX BOOKS**

Large format theater and cinema

THE BEST SHORT PLAYS OF 1970
  Stanley Richards (editor)   13144   3.95
THE BEST SHORT PLAYS OF 1971
  Stanley Richards (editor)   13243   3.95
THE BEST SHORT PLAYS OF 1972
  Stanley Richards (editor)   17186   3.95
CINEMA BOREALIS: Ingmar Bergman and
  the Swedish Ethos   Vernon Young   13292   3.95
THE COMEDY OF NEIL SIMON   Neil Simon 15370   3.95
CONTEMPORARY FRENCH THEATRE
  Bettina L. Knapp (editor)   16840   4.95
CONTEMPORARY GERMAN THEATER
  Michael Roloff   13664   4.95
THE FILMGOER'S COMPANION, Third Edition
  Leslie Halliwell   13151   3.95